SHRINK

by Dr. Martin Obler
with Jed Golden

Andrew Benzie Books
Pleasant Hill, California

Published by Andrew Benzie Books
www.andrewbenziebooks.com

Printed in the United States of America

First Edition: January 2016

10 9 8 7 6 5 4 3 2 1

www.shrinkautobio.com

ISBN 978-1-941713-10-5

Cover painting by Evan G. Silberman
Cover and book design by Andrew Benzie

*To my sister Rachel, who was taken away to
a mental health hospital when I was four.*

—Dr. Martin Obler

*In memory of my first wife, Peni Cenedella Golden;
and my sorely missed friend, Ry Greene.*

—Jed Golden

TABLE OF CONTENTS

Introduction

BOOK I

BOOK II

REQUISITE ANNOUNCEMENT

This book, my story, contains sensitive material involving my family of origin and others, and most importantly, my patients, since I am a psychotherapist. In order to meet the rigorous standards of my profession regarding issues of confidentiality and privacy, I have seen fit to use made-up names for just about everyone, other than myself, who appears in the book. I have also drawn various people as composites and altered their profession and neighborhood, etc. In short, I have gone to great lengths, including fictionalizing dialogue and personal history, to protect patient privacy. Without such subterfuges, this book would have not been acceptable.

That said, I want to be explicit that what follows is my story and I have tried to tell it as honestly and down-to-earth as I could, within the confines outlined above.

Into each life some rain must fall.

from the poem *The Rainy Day* (1841)
by Henry Wadsworth Longfellow

INTRODUCTION

Somewhere inside myself, I felt I had turned the tables on life. My greatest fears that my life would be snuffed out, one way or the other, had not come true. I had made it through the craziness of my family, the poverty of my Brownsville, Brooklyn, childhood, and had defied the odds of life in the ghetto by graduating college, getting my Ph.D. and becoming a successful psychotherapist. I never could stop talking about how far I had come and how good I was at operating in the world. I could be a pretty obnoxious person. On the more attractive side, I could be entertaining, funny, unique (with my bundle of insecurities, my heavy-duty Brooklyn speech, my endless self-promotion and self-inflation, and my walking the NYC streets, greeting strangers by saying "Hi *shagitz*" or "What's up, *faygalla*?")... as seemingly at ease in the outer world as a human being could be.

Try as I might to ride over my insecurities, they were out there in plain sight for everyone to see and often cringe at. As I got older, past middle age, I began facing the permanent effects on me of the direness of my childhood.

The tables turned another turn. I was definitely not so pronouncedly the person who defied the consequences of his upbringing and was in charge and in control of everything. Although I kept up my bravado and my confident front out of force of habit, I was more than a bit humbled by my medical problems, problems with my kids, my second wife... and the ubiquitous evidence of my aging; all of this led to my being prone to the myriad self-doubts that festered beneath my exterior personality. Was I really so different than my patients?

Thoughts of this kind are not welcome by me, though I appreciated some of the philosophical implications—i.e., I was not so superior to everyone else.

This comedown in life has made me a more sympathetic human being and someone who did not have to prop himself up all the time—to keep up the self-inflated image.

This takes me to the book itself.

I chose to not strictly follow a chronological approach to my story, preferring to interpose in CHAPTER TWO and CHAPTER SEVEN demonstrations of Marty Obler at work as a shrink early on in his professional career. I think this serves the purposes of conveying an important part of his future development and evolution as a person and therapist and is germane to a central consideration of the book—how his early life affected his professional life... and putting those two strands together to bring in a third strand, his self-inquiry and self-analysis that takes up the last chapters of the book in which the reader has to do the final weaving of the three together.

But with no further ado, let me begin with my future mom's arrival in the U.S.A., in circumstances that are hard to place in the mind...

BOOK I

CHAPTER ONE:
CHILDHOOD

S ometime in the year 1911, my mother, Sadie, came to the United States from Poland. She arrived at nine years of age to Ellis Island after having traveled unaccompanied for weeks on an ocean liner. When an entry official asked her where she came from, she replied in Yiddish but mentioned the word Bialystok. She placed the immigration papers her family had given her on departure into the man's hand, and he looked at her, puzzled as to who she was. He must have wondered how it happened that a nine-year-old girl came to America by herself. Since she did not speak a word of English and was illiterate and seemed to have no sense of what she was doing here, he came to the conclusion that she was mentally defective and he had better push her through the immigration process. So he gave her a simple intelligence test as verification; naturally, given her inability with English, she could not decode the questions, and failed with flying colors. He pointed to an assistant with a yarmulke on his head, and told him to take care of this little girl. The man spoke to her in Yiddish, which made her feel better. He took her hand and went with her on a small boat that left from Ellis Island.

After she got off the boat, she somehow made her way by herself to one of the Jewish enclaves on the Lower East Side, near Delancey Street. She was just standing in the street crying. A woman walked up to her and in Yiddish asked, "What are you doing here?" My mother responded in Yiddish, "I'm trying to find my brother."

"Where does he live?"

"In America."

"Where in America?"

"I don't know. His name is Samuel Lynchevsky."

"Can you spell that?"

"I can't. I don't know how to read or write."

"Where did you come from?"

"From Bialystok."

"Where are your mother, father, and sisters and brothers?"

"They're running away from the Polish soldiers."

The woman understood the gravity of the girl's situation and said, "Come with me." The woman took her in to her own family, and told her: "You'll work for us; we will feed and house you, and we'll help you find your brother." So my mother lived with them, cleaning, cooking, and caring for the children, never learning how to read or write, never attending school, never setting foot in a playground where she could be with kids her own age and never making contact with her brother. She had been rescued from the streets by a charitable act of the woman (my mother who had difficulty with names, called her 'the redhead'), but had been saved to become an all-purpose maid for her family. Yet my mother, upon being asked by me, whether the woman had been kind to her, responded with strong affection: "The redhead took care of me when I was sick," and tears welled up in her eyes as she spoke. She was grateful that they took care of her when she couldn't work— they didn't throw her out to fend for herself. She had little awareness of how circumscribed her life with the family had been, or that she had lost what was left of her childhood in being saved by the redhead.

As an adolescent, in addition to her full time household responsibilities, she found some low-level part-time job in the neighborhood to earn a few dollars spending money. She needed this because the redhead did not pay her a salary. Existence for her amounted to work and more work. She had no friends, no social life, and whether this was the result of personal deficiency or the result of the peculiar circumstances of her servitude in which she had almost no contact with her peers and almost no chance to evolve the necessary social skills, I am unable to say. I would guess it was a combination of both personal and environmental factors.

She was a strange figure in the household, not officially designated a live-in maid but not integrated as part of the family. From what I could piece together, she was not thought of as an adopted daughter, and even friends and neighbors of the family wondered what her place was in the home. Based on stories she told me in my childhood, people liked her but would make fun of her since for a number of years she could only speak Yiddish mixed in with some English phrases; she rarely ventured out of the apartment, except to her unskilled jobs; and she did not know how to make her way around the city at large. Even as a kid, I had to accompany her to any doctor or dentist's appointment if the office was located outside the neighborhood. When my mother reached the age of about nineteen or twenty, the redhead and her family came to realize they would have to do something with her, so they took her to a *shadchan*, an arranger of marriages. He set up a marriage for her with my father Saul, who was working as a steam fitter for a shipbuilding company subcontracted to the U.S. Navy. His job only paid a subsistence salary. His mother was desperate to get him married, and even though he was fifteen years older than his prospective bride, she pressured him into the marriage. He was reluctant to marry my mother from the very beginning; I guess his hesitation was well-founded since over the years he came to feel it was the worst decision he had ever made. The marriage took place, and the dismal economics of their life together kicked in right away. My father and mother were so poor that they couldn't even get an apartment on the Lower East Side and wound up in Brownsville, Brooklyn, where the poorest of the poor Jews lived. Sadie proceeded to get pregnant with my oldest sister, Rachel, and then in quick order had two more daughters, Debbie and Phyllis, and, finally, me, Muttla, as I was frequently called in the family.

I was born during the depression, on December 31, 1936. I'm not exactly sure when, but sometime in this period of economic hardship, my father lost his job; he had gotten lead poisoning while welding the steam fitting pieces. The government paid him a small pension, but it was far from enough to live on. This forced my mother, who was taking care of the children, to work in low-paying part-time jobs, once again, so we could minimally survive with the additional assistance of Jewish philanthropic agencies. The drudgery of working, cooking, taking care of the house and her children began to wear her down. She hated her life, and blamed her husband for taking her away from the home she had known on the Lower East Side.

My father went out every day looking for work; whatever small sums he earned as a deliveryman or pushcart peddler, he spent drinking at the local pub. We survived on the food given to us by the Jewish Center; the few dollars my father received in his pension check; and the wages my mother earned. Most of our meals consisted of some preparation involving the Jewish agency's allotment of butter, eggs, bread, jam, American cheese, and powdered milk. But on Fridays, for the Sabbath meal, my mother, who was a terrible cook, would prepare the treat of the week, a dish called 'chulin,' made up of chunks of chuck meat, potatoes, and vegetables cooked for twenty-four hours straight until it became an unsightly blob of brown gravy with a lot of stringy meat.

One morning when I was about four years old, I awoke very hungry and wanted breakfast. I sat at the table waiting for anyone to feed me. Eventually my father got up and joined me. We both sat there waiting for the women to serve us breakfast. Shortly, my sister Debbie, who was thirteen, came into the kitchen; I could see in her eyes the hatred of my father, not only because she was expected to make him breakfast, but because of the scornful attitude towards him she picked up from my mother. She wasted no time in starting to verbally abuse him.

"You drunken bastard. You *alter kocker*. You're like a *shvartze*. You just sit there and do nothing. Do you ever bring a quarter into the family? Every night you come home drunk, puke your guts, and then you wake us all up, force yourself on momma, and stink of booze; then you get up in the morning and expect to be served like a prince."

My father's face reddened; I knew from the time I was a toddler that he hated my sister. He got up from the chair and grabbed her by the collar of her shirt and pulled her towards him. When she tried to resist, he whacked her across the face. Somehow she pulled away from him, grabbed her schoolbooks and ran out of the apartment, turning to me as she left to say, "Get yourself something to eat." My father and I looked at each other and realized we weren't getting anything to eat. He shrugged his shoulders in commiseration and said, "Muttla, what can you do?"

He may have been an enemy of my mother and my sister Debbie in our household, but I always loved my father and I knew he loved me. I could always make him laugh. Later in life, making him laugh to ease the pain of how he was treated in the family became a self-imposed responsibility of mine. So, there we were sitting at the kitchen table waiting to be fed. I wasn't sure just how the process worked... why the waiting was supposed to lead to the desired result. After a spell of sitting, I tried to speed things up.

"Papa, make me some eggs," I pleaded.

He opened up the icebox door and saw there were eggs but no butter. At that point my mother came in through the door, carrying the wash she had taken down from the backyard clotheslines strung across tenement buildings.

My father accusingly declared, "The kid wants breakfast and there's not a damn thing to eat." He glanced at me, then added, his voice picking up in volume, "Look at us, we're just waiting here. You *kurveh*." I could see the mounting anger in both of them. I should add that by this time my mother spoke marginally passable immigrant English, but the way I have her speaking here, to my father, is the way I remember it, which is a major upgrade of her English.

"You *alter kocker*. You come home drunk and *shtup* me. You bring in no money. You do nothing in this house, and you're a crazy bastard like your witch mother." (My mother relished reminding him that his mom had gone mad; about two years prior to the scene described, she was taken away by ambulance to be institutionalized.) "The kids need clothes, and you come home without a cent in your pocket. Who else would put up with you? And you sit here waiting for me to feed you, as if I'm supposed to supply the food, make breakfast, and clean up too. What are you good for?"

"I'm gonna get out of this miserable house," my father said and jumped up.

"*Gai gezunterhait!*, with my blessings. I'm sick of your face."

My father raised his fist to hit her, and I quickly started crying. I had detected early on that if I cried and seemed upset, they would stop fighting... at least in the daytime. Their fights in the daytime were mostly verbal, whereas at night when my father came home drunk, the encounters were vicious and brutal, and they terrified me. I would watch them fighting and feel helpless.

On this morning they calmed down because I was upset and crying, and my mother grudgingly said to my father, "Take Muttla, go to the Center, get some butter and I'll make breakfast." She was telling him, in effect, 'do something, you useless man.'

Walking with my father hand in hand, in the streets, was a lovely thing for me. I felt secure being with my father outside of the chaotic household and away from the insults and battles.

As we headed to the Jewish Center, I saw an old man with payess, a Hasid, holding a little boy's hand, just as my father held mine. We were walking towards each other, and a delightful, peaceful feeling came over me. However, once they got close to us, I realized that their relationship was different than ours. An altercation was taking place. The little kid looked up at the Hasid. He said, "Fuck you, you old bastard.

"You say fuck you to your *zadeh,*" and then he walloped the boy hard on the side of the head, and added, "Drop dead, you little *putz.*"

Seeing the old man hit the boy made a huge impression on me. I felt terrible for the kid, who was on the ground crying and screaming and hitting the pavement with his fists. But I also felt relieved that violence was part of other families besides mine.

My father went over to talk to the man because my father was against hitting male children. While he talked to the man, who I found out was the boy's grandfather, I went over to the boy, and tried to comfort him. I saw he was grateful, and I realized I was able to make him feel better. The Hasid was also grateful: When he finished talking to my father, he reached into the deep pocket of his black robe and pulled out a shining quarter, which he gave me.

In that moment, I had a flash of having breakfast at the corner candy store. Right then and there, I got the idea that I could make kids feel better and make money.

We proceeded towards the Center as I looked admiringly at the shiny quarter. The attendants at the Center were always friendly with me and sometimes would hand me a lollipop when I got to the front of the line. They gave us the parcels of food we were entitled to with the coupons we got from the Jewish agencies. Outside, back on the street (and lollipop-less), we walked for a while, until we came to a store where they sold ice for the icebox, and after buying ice, we headed for home. But as we were passing the candy store I asked my father to take me inside and let me buy breakfast with my quarter. He took me in, got the owner, who was behind the counter, to put the block of ice in his icebox and we sat down on the counter stools and asked for breakfast. I held up the quarter for the owner to see it. He knew how poor I was because he used to see me looking in from the doorway, enviously watching people eat. I can remember standing in the doorway and thinking that people in the booths might offer me some of their food out of pity. I could see that the owner was happy that I had a quarter. After a bit, he brought out a big tray of eggs, hash browns, toast and jam, and, best of all, salami... which my father and I set to work on.

*   *   *

One day, late in the afternoon, Carly's and Moishe's mother said to me, even though I was only five, "Muttla, you are good with the kids. Maybe you want to make a little money and watch my baby." She pointed to the baby, Moishe.

"Yeh, Carly and Moishe are my friends. I like the little baby. How much are you payin' me?"

"I'll give you a nickel."

"How much is a nickel an hour?"

She reached into her dress pocket and pulled out some coins, showing me with the finger of her opposite hand, the nickel. "I'll take the smaller one," I said as I pointed to the dime, pretending that I didn't know it was worth more.

She handed me the dime, and I began to push the carriage. That was the beginning of my career as a baby sitter on Herzl Street.

The baby started to cry, and I instinctively knew what to do. I picked up the formula bottle, stuck it in the kid's mouth, and proudly strolled down the street. In the warm weather, the block teemed with people—mothers on the stoop, minding their babies; kids playing stickball in the street; half-dressed, squealing boys and girls of mixed ages dashing in and out of the manipulated spray from an open fire hydrant. As I walked down the street pushing the carriage, I felt so proud and important that I had a job. Everybody turned and looked at me, a little boy taking care of a baby. Suddenly I heard a shout from the top of the roof. I turned towards the sound, and saw my mother's head peering through a windowless kind of porthole in the wall enclosing the roof. "What are ya doin', Muttla, with the *kleina kind*? *Du bis a meshugeneh*? Whose kid is it?"

"Mrs. Abrams, the mommy of Carly and Moishe. She gave me this" (I held up the coin) "to watch the baby." Her worried look vanished, and I could see that she was proud that I had earned the money. I loved my job. I didn't even think of it as a job. I would hold the baby and rock him, and other mothers sitting on the stoop began to trust me to take care of their kids. I got a reputation in the neighborhood as being 'good with *kinder*.' I loved making money, too. It could make the difference between going hungry and being content with food in your stomach.

"Muttla, *du bist a gooten kind*, making the money," my mom said, before withdrawing her face from the circular hole.

My father too was proud of me, but wanted to know, "Is it hard to take care of the babies? And what do you get out of it?" I wasn't sure how to explain to him that I enjoyed taking care of the babies, enjoyed the contact with the outside world. Some evenings I would sit in the house of the baby's parents and listen to the radio with them. They would invite me to dinner, which was an unbelievable treat for me—an opportunity to eat food that was not prepared by my mother and not consisting of rations for poor people. I was struck at how warmly and affectionately the family members spoke to each other as they ate. Reflecting back on it, I must have felt the way my mother did when she lived in the redhead's apartment on the Lower East Side.

On these evenings, I was a content little tyke, sitting in a quiet apartment, tucked away from my screaming, fighting family. But the time would come when I would hear a knock on the door, and I knew it was my sister. I felt like crying because she was coming to take me home. On any given evening, something like the following would ensue: My sister Debbie came in and grabbed my hand and pulled me out of the house. While walking down to our apartment, she would start belittling me: "You stupid, *pisher*. You let that rotten whore [the baby's mother] take advantage of you. What did she give you, a penny?"

I vowed that one day when I was strong enough I was going to punch my angry sister in the mouth.

I can remember in one instance, I didn't seem sufficiently upset by her tirade, so she added a more hurtful remark: "You're just as stupid as your sister Rachel." I cringed at the mention of my sister Rachel's name. She, like my grandmother, had been carted off to a mental institution. I hated Debbie for reminding me of my sister Rachel and the terror I felt at how that might happen to me. They could take me away from my family. But then and there, I didn't dare say anything to Debbie; I knew, if I did, she would say more cruel things to me, and, very likely, smack me to boot.

However on this evening, something occurred with my father and me that led to a whole new story, one that had a lasting effect on me.

As soon as we entered the apartment, I started to cry loudly and my father questioned me, "What's wrong with you?"

"Debbie called me 'stupid' like Rachel. Are they gonna send me away like her? *Tateh,* I'm scared. Please don't send me away."

My father's fists tightened and I was hoping he'd belt my sister. Debbie wisely hurried out of the room. My father took me to the bedroom I shared with him, intent on comforting me and putting me to sleep. Before I fell asleep I asked him if we could go to see Rachel in the place that she lived. My dad promised me that we would go on Sunday, just a few days away.

That Sunday, we got off the Long Island Railroad and proceeded by foot to the King's Park Mental Hospital in Long Island. This was my first visit to see Rachel. As to why I asked to see her, I can only conjecture that it was a way of alleviating the terror of abandonment that Debbie's remark had sparked in me. If I could know where she was and see her then it wouldn't be so terrifying... the thought of my being completely lost and abandoned.

On nearing the hospital, I was quite taken with how big the buildings were. They were made of red brick, and had smokestacks on top from which filthy smoke poured forth. We entered the building where Rachel was housed and my father spoke to the proper authority about getting to see his daughter. After a short wait in the visitor's room, an attendant brought Rachel out to us, leading her by the arm. She was dressed in a drab, green smock; she seemed very old, although in actuality she was only in her twenties. It was as if she had transformed into an older looking woman from the pretty girl I had remembered before she was taken away. A memory came to me of how tenderly she had taken care of me as a baby.

Her face had little expression until she saw me. Her focus was suddenly intense and her whole body seemed to tighten. She pushed the attendant's hand away from her arm, rushed at me, and began to claw my face with her nails. My father and the attendant grabbed her and pulled her away. She shrieked, "Why did you bring the little one here?"

The attendant got her in an arm lock and pushed her out of the room, while another attendant closed the door behind them. I was petrified by what had happened, beyond my capacity to think. The tears rolled down my face and tingled as they ran into the scraped flesh. My father tried to calm me. Soon a nurse came and administered to me, cleaning my face with antiseptic and putting gauze pads on my wounds. On the way out, carried in my father's arms, I was collected enough to have a quick mental picture of Rachel being bodily forced out of the room by the attendant. In the safety of the reaches beyond the hospital, I thought to myself that my sister would live where she was for the rest of her life. They would feed her every day, because she could not survive on her own. And she would never earn any money. I wanted to know more about Rachel. I looked up into my father's eyes, and asked him, "Why is Rachel here?" He replied, "You can't understand."

Having advanced about fifty feet from the building we left, I peeked around my father's shoulder and glanced at the smoke coming out of the chimney of the brick building. I noticed that there were bars on the windows. I never saw my sister Rachel again.

*   *   *

During the depression, Pitkin Avenue, in Brownsville, was the equivalent of the modern day shopping mall. The stores were lined up one after the other, with lavish displays of fancy clothing, shoes, every imaginable kind of food, household goods; and there was the well-known movie palace, the Loews Pitkin, where Saturday night, lines would extend around the block.

I would go shopping with mothers of the babies I was taking care of, pushing the carriage along the streets and hoping the mothers would buy me a treat. I knew if I put on a sad-but-hopeful face as I stared at the toys or the candy and cakes, they would feel sorry for me and buy me something. I was successful much of the time playing the role of the deprived child. As I pushed the carriage along, looking at all the wonderful things in the windows of the shops, I marveled at the world where people could afford to buy what they wanted.

Some of my happiest moments were walking down Pitkin Avenue. Sometimes on weekends, in the late afternoon or early evening, the wealthier, non-welfare mothers I worked for would take me in to the Loews Pitkin to care for the baby while they watched the movie. I would stand at the back of the theater, not far from the mother on an aisle seat, and look at the movie while rocking the carriage. Two movies I saw in this off-and-on way were lavish musicals made in the depression era. On screen were people who luxurious apartments with servants to wait on them, people who were wearing beautiful gowns and impeccable tuxedos... and young, good-looking people who danced and sang on stage and looked as if they never had a worry or sad moment. I did not know about the make-believe world of Hollywood at that age, but certainly I knew that what I was seeing was not the world of Herzl Street in Brownsville.

One day I was walking along Pitkin Avenue wheeling a carriage with the baby in it of one of the loveliest and kindest women in the neighborhood; she was what I would describe now as fair-skinned, dark-haired, Eastern European with a delicate, beautiful face. In passing the Woolworth's 5 & 10, my favorite store, I stopped to gaze at the charlotte russes in the front of the store, where the tempting, aromatic baked goods were on display. The russes cost five cents a piece. My mouth watered for the yellow sponge cake with the mound of whip cream topped by a maraschino cherry. I had watched jealously other kids eating them, but I could only surmise the joys of biting into one.

The lovely mother saw me staring at the charlotte russes, saw me inching in closer to get a better look. She knew how hungry I was for that pastry and took us inside. I didn't see myself as a little child but as the caretaker of babies; however I could tell she saw me as a five year old and she dug into her bag, found a dime and bought me the desired object. The taste of it was indescribably delicious as I licked the whip cream and then bit into the sponge cake. I had never tasted anything like it. I looked at my benefactress, and her face appeared to me to take on an angelic look. It was the face of the lovely, nurturing mother I wanted, the face of the dark-haired, fair-skinned European beauty, which would romantically haunt me for the rest of my life.

I suppose the angel of the charlotte russes was so appealing to me because she was beautiful while my mother was plain, her looks worn down by her hard life; she had some sophistication while my mother had none; she was warm and generous, my mother was angry and preoccupied with economic survival; she seemed to adore her baby and couldn't hug and pamper her enough, my mother was too bitter about life to give me the attention I longed for. Her bitterness was probably a just reaction to the impossibility of her life, but sociology was not a substitute for a small boy's need to be held and hugged and kissed and made much of. My mother's bitterness seeped into the family and corroded the lives of her husband and children. She was bitter even towards the adopted child, Billy, who lived on the floor above us. Her real anger was directed towards Billy's mother because she would take up too much of the space on the shared clothesline. But my mother had no problem saying the thing that would be most hurtful to the offending party. And having found the most effective dart, she saw no reason not to throw it on any occasion that called forth ill will towards a neighbor. So that when the neighbors would holler at my parents for disturbing the peace at night with their loud fights, she would not hesitate to bring up Billy's parental history.

"Shut the fuck up you crazy bastard lunatic," someone would yell out after a particularly loud fusillade on the part of my mother.

Someone else would echo the sentiment and maybe offer a further assessment of my mother's least attractive qualities. This would send my mother running to the window to shout back: "You dummies, what about the family up there with the adopted kid?" I always pondered what Billy had to do with the neighbors' objections to the fighting in the middle of the night, but it did not seem to give my mother pause. Fighting, screaming, and yelling in the back alleyways of the tenements occurred every night, and my mother and father were among the worst offenders. My father would come home drunk from the local pub, and Sadie would start screaming at him and putting him down. Eventually Debbie would join in, pouring her own molten fury at him: "You *plosher*, you stink of piss and shit. Where is the money for the family? All you're good for is to stick that big shlong of yours into momma. You're a pig"

If he were too much in his cups to defend himself, Debbie and my mom would start to hit him. As I listened to the three of them fighting and screaming, I shook with fear and humiliation. I dreaded facing the neighbors in the morning, but worse than that, was my anxiety at the helplessness of my father; and it was during these devastating fight scenes that I built up an unshakable resolve to never be vulnerable like my father. I would have a respectable job, make enough money to support the family and would never get drunk.

It is not a fortuitous circumstance for a little boy to be exposed to the helplessness of his father. I experienced this at home, and sometimes in the streets. I can remember my father and me walking down Strauss Street toward Pitkin Avenue. While walking, we passed the little stand, which sold great blended drinks, including my favorite, coconut milk with Hershey syrup. On top of the stand was a large picture of an attractive blond Wac drinking a papaya-mango shake. I asked my father to buy me my favorite drink, but he was short a penny. The drink cost six cents but he only had a nickel in his pocket. He wanted to satisfy my craving and I could see his concern at not being able to provide me with the little delights that fathers get for their children.

The stand owner, seeing the distress of my father and not wanting to be part of the solution, asserted, "Don't ask me for anything. I know you want to get something for nothing. You either got the money or don't got it."

Despite the harsh words, my father had the nickel exposed in one hand while continuing to probe his pockets with the other hand to see if he couldn't come up with the missing penny; in doing this, he was hoping that the man would see my pleading eyes and give me the drink for five cents.

"You rag picker, if I give you the drink, then you'll keep coming back again and again. You'll squeeze the blood out of me. If I give it to you, everyone will ask me to do it for them."

My father's ploy didn't work, and he was humiliated in front of me. He bent his head down in embarrassment and shame. I felt guilty and sorry for him, even though I wanted the drink.

This reminds me of another incident involving the stand owner, who by the way was tall, thin and had a mean look about him. Towards the end of the summer, my parents announced to me that I had to go to school (kindergarten). The next day I went out by myself to test the verbal directions my mother had given me on how to get to the school. I went out, even though she had said she would take me the first day of school. My mother couldn't read or write and had memorized the streets I needed to walk; I wanted to make sure of her directions and to see whether I could get to school by myself. I ended up walking in the opposite direction of the school to where the fruit-drink stand was located. I veered off Pitkin Avenue and placed myself near the stand. I can still remember standing there, on the street, lost in thought about what it was going to be like at school, and that I would have to give up baby-watching. I was upset at losing the opportunity to be with the mothers and babies to make a few cents, and to get out of the house. Who was going to buy me treats like the charlotte russe? I was immobilized. I didn't know what to do or where to go. I kept thinking I had to go to school and I didn't move. It was then that a little black kid about my age tried to cop an orange off the stand. And the owner saw him, grabbed him and said, "You *schvartze kholyereah*, I'm gonna teach you a lesson," and he hit him with an open hand in the head.

The boy tried in vain to hold back his tears, but started to cry. He looked at me, and I looked at him (while the stand owner was looking at us both), and it clicked in me, at that moment, that the little boy was pleading for me to help him. Propelled by some inner force, I went over to him and whispered a few words of reassurance. Then, without hesitation, I took his hand in mine, glanced defiantly at the owner, and walked him away. I can't remember what I did with the boy, but I'm sure he calmed down and got home.

For reasons unknown to me at the time, I was not scared of going to school the next day. Probably, the incident reassured me that I could befriend kids at school, and that I would find a way that they needed me and that I would protect them. And if I could do that, I'd be all right.

My mother took me to school the following morning. As soon as I entered the building, I was fine. In fact, I loved school. I felt at ease and relieved that I could spend a good portion of the day away from home. It was easy for me to make friends, even with the tougher street kids, and, as gifted as I already was at manipulating adults to get what I wanted, I had no trouble getting the teachers to like me.

Once in school my life began to change. I spent time with kids my own age. After the three o'clock dismissal bell rang, we'd get together in the school yard and play games like marbles, Chinese handball or punchball, or we'd have running races; sometimes we'd meet at another kid's apartment house and play indoor games, or go out to the street and play ring-a-levio or walk around. This was all hugely welcome to me. Not only did I make a few special friends, but my world began to expand as I talked to other kids and visited their homes, much like the way it expanded when I did the baby sitting. And what was nice was that it turned out that I didn't have to give up my babysitting entirely; I still did it now and then in the evening or on weekends.

When I got to be a few years older, my friends and I would congregate in the streets and in the park. Sports became a big part of our lives: we would spend hours playing basketball and handball in the park, stickball in the street, and go swimming at the Betsy Head Community Pool down the block from where I lived. I was strong and fairly athletic, so I could hold my own in competition with the other boys. Babysitting had helped me to get a modicum of independence and a toe in the outside world; now I was out in the world much of the time and I began to feel less closeted, less dependent on my mother, and less stuck in the family sinkhole—from which there was no escape as long as there was no alternative to the quarrels and misery poisoning the atmosphere at home. I also found strength in an odd part of a child's world—the use of magical thinking to counter the helplessness of being a child. While I can't be sure that as a baby I shook the beads and rattles strung across my crib compulsively to relieve tension, or, similarly, touched the bars of the crib, for that purpose, I do have a sense that I was compulsive as well as curious. I can recall at around three years old touching the walls above my bed for security when my grandmother used to shriek and pull out her hair in her hysterical fits.

I was perpetually anxious and frightened, and often urinated in my bed. I slept with a rubber sheet under my bed sheet and was terribly embarrassed that my sisters would find out in the morning that I had again made in my bed. Sometimes I felt I couldn't cope... that there were too many things threatening my well-being. I created a belief system whereby if I did certain things in a certain way ritualistically, I would gain magical power. I remember when I was five or so touching the walls near my bed a certain number of times and if I did it correctly, before the advertisements came on in the radio programs, then I would not make that night in bed. If I said enough times to myself, mommy and daddy will not die, they'd be okay, the fighting would stop and in the morning they'd still be around to take care of me. Or if I repeated over and over again the words, "My mother is okay, my mother is okay," then that would guarantee that she would be home safe on the days she worked... and I was taken care of by a member of the family. By the time I was in third grade, I avoided certain words, such as "sickness," "polio," and other words referring to grave situations and death. By not saying these words or looking at them in print, then terrible things wouldn't happen to my family or me.

As I got older, I transferred a lot of my magical thinking to competitive sports. On the basketball court I would make sure to bounce the ball a certain number of times before the game began, and if I did this, not only would my team win, but everything else in my life would be okay. And during the game, if I were on the line for a foul shot, I would bounce the ball something like eleven times before shooting. My friends would holler, "Take the fucking shot already." And I did the same type of thing in handball. Before the game started, I would have to hit the ball eight times against the wall; if I mishit the ball I would start over again. I came to feel I could manipulate the outcome of the games I participated in; all I had to do was follow the correct designated ritual to the letter… and if things didn't work out, it was because I was somehow imperfect in following the system. So the system was not at fault.

Magical thinking entered my world even in the worst circumstances. At twelve years old, I was walking my close friend, Dom, home, when we saw his mother lying dead on the street pavement before his apartment house. We saw an ice pick in her back, and we both realized that his father had killed her with the ice pick, which he used on his job as a delivery iceman. The horror in Dom's face panicked me, but I knew I had to do something to help him and myself. We both were in shock, and he began to sob. I said to myself that if I could count to twenty-four before one minute was up, then not only would this help Dom recover, but this kind of sickening occurrence would never happen again in my life. I made the count within the time span.

At the end of that, I said, "Let's get outta here."

"Yeah," was all he could say.

I took his hand the way I did with the black kid at the fruit-drink stand, and brought him home with me.

On reaching the apartment, I was so happy to see my mother. Quickly, I got her alone, to tell her what had happened. I told her, and asked her if Dom could stay with us. To my relief, she said yes. She then said, "Sit down at the table and I'll fix you something to eat."

We sat down, "What does the guinea want to eat?" she blurted out in front of him.

I had to laugh, even though I was ashamed at her stupidity and insensitivity; but it did relieve the tension in my mom and me… even Dominick found it funny. We all laughed, and I turned to my mother and said, "Ma, what do guineas eat? Ravioli, spaghetti, lasagna, everything you can't make. Bring out the usual shit," which meant, in these better days after the war, overcooked meat and potatoes. But what was served didn't matter, just being there and eating together brought a relief to him.

After a week at my house, Dom moved into the basement in a building where an Irish friend of ours, Donnegan, lived. Donnegan was a powerful weightlifter whom most everybody was scared of. I too was scared of him, but I understood him: I knew he was a fearful kid who had been sexually molested and physically beaten by his father, and his only protection was to use his strength to intimidate the people around him. But he was a good friend, and at various times he had put up kids who had to leave their homes, letting them stay in the basement of the apartment house where he lived. His buddy, Jimmy, was living in the basement when Dom moved in. The basement housed the boiler and various machines and tools and stored stuff and had a cement floor… it wasn't much to look at, but, as I said to him on his arrival, "It's not great, but its home," which was my way of communicating, "What the fuck, it's the best we can do." He himself summed it up in his reply, "It's better than nothing, I guess."

Dom didn't stay in the basement for more than a couple of months; he moved in to an apartment in which a few of his relatives were living, and supported himself by working on the docks in Brooklyn. Donnegan, sadly, was one of those ghetto kids who never really had much of a life. While staggeringly drunk, he crashed a wooden milk crate over a Puerto Rican man's head and killed him. He did a long stint in prison for manslaughter, and came out a disheartened, lonely man.

At this time of my life, I started to grow up quickly: I was about to enter junior high school; I was out in the streets a lot; I was becoming fairly competent and self-reliant; even the magical rituals lessened, because I was not so fearful; it helped that I put on weight and had a pretty muscular build—it was not for nothing that around the age of twelve I had been graced with the nickname 'Moose.' In the last two years of elementary school, I had to grow up quickly because life on the streets began to get rough. The need to be able to handle myself in the streets of Brownsville started to change the way I saw myself. An ugly encounter took place when I was about eleven that I would never forget and never forgive myself for. I was leaving school to run an errand for my mother on Belmont Avenue, where numbers of pushcarts were lined up one after the other, selling food, clothes, kitchen-stuff, as in a flea market. Normally, I would meet my friends after school and we would head to the park to play ball; however on this day I was walking through another section of the neighborhood near where my mother worked. As I turned on the corner of Hopkinson to Livonia Avenue, I heard my father's voice yelling, "Rags, *alte zachen.*" My face turned red. There he was in broad daylight, collecting old rags and brownish yellow potato sacks, as he had done for years after he lost his job. I could tell he was drunk, and it was the first time I had seen him on the streets with his pushcart since the days I was a little kid and would walk alongside of him as he collected his goods. Unexpectedly, a group of tough kids who were friends of mine were walking towards him and, fortunately for me, did not see me. These were the same kids, years before, who would protect me from bullies in the neighborhood trying to get a few cents from me that I had earned by my babysitting.

My friends walked right up to my father and, without provocation, began hitting and kicking him. Howie yelled at him, "You old fucking, smelly drunk."

My body tensed and I could feel the sweat on my face while I watched my friends beat him and knock him down. I wanted to go to his aid, but I didn't want to expose to my friends that I was the rag picker's son. So I didn't do anything but cringe and watch. A few years later, when I evolved into a gang leader in junior high school, I would never allow myself to become as vulnerable and fearful as I had been on that day.

I can't bring up some of the painful incidents in my childhood without going back in time and including the scene of my grandmother being taken away to the mental institution. I was only two years old, and I was home when they came for her. In terms of the impact on a small child, things don't get much worse. When I think of it, I still shudder and feel doubts and anxiety that turn my stomach to jello. Seeing her fear and being taken away, to some mysterious place for some mysterious reason, posed a threat to my existence of no small proportions. It is the raw fear of terrifying disappearance, what tots have been known to feel when their product is flushed into the lower regions. For all intents and purposes, to my mind grandma could just as well have been flushed down the toilet as taken away.

As a two year old, I can't rely on what I remember took place, but this is the way I have it in my mind. My father and mother were in the kitchen shouting at each other about my grandmother, who was in the adjacent living room with me. She was mumbling incoherently in Yiddish as she tore out little chunks of her hair. Whatever she was trying to say, I intuitively understood that she was cursing my mother. My mother hated her and would yell at my father to get her out of the house for good. As the shouting escalated in the kitchen, my grandmother herself started screaming... and the effect was so frightening that I lay face down on the couch and put my hands over my ears. I nevertheless heard a door slam and it was my mother running out the front door and I saw my father chasing after her. After a long time in which my grandmother was sitting in a chair, whimpering and rocking her body up and down as she held her head between her hands, my parents came back followed by two men. The men were wearing some kind of uniform. My parents led the two men, one white and one black, from the kitchen into the living room. The men approached my grandmother and gently helped her stand up. I was surprised that she didn't offer any resistance. They walked her out of the apartment and the last I ever saw of my grandmother was the image I had of the two men guiding her out the door. If this whole depressing, frightening, glimpse of family life that has been etched in my conscious and subconscious mind wasn't bad enough, a couple of years later Rachel too was packed off to a mental institution—though I was fortunate in that I wasn't home for that one… though having a vital sister one day and then coming home and to learn, in a murky way, that she is not coming back for a long time (actually ever), is not too fabulous for the mind to grasp… anyway, if all this were not upsetting enough, any reference to either of them was a rarity in the family, so it was as if they ceased to exist within the family structure—except by their disappearance.

A conversation between Phyllis and me took place when we were young adults. It concludes the chapter, on a slightly, but not altogether, lighter note. It started by my asking her how she could have left me in the movie theater at the age of seven… for the whole afternoon, when she was supposed to be looking after me. [My mother had left me in her care, and she dumped me in the Albemarle Theater on Saratoga Avenue while she went gallivanting around with her friends.]

"But Marty, you could take care of yourself. And you enjoyed the movies, you told me."

"I did, Phyllis. The movies were great. But what was I gonna do when you didn't come to pick me up at 6:30? I didn't know how to get home by myself from the theater."

"I always eventually showed up and you were waiting for me."

"But I was still a small kid and it was dark by that time. You think I didn't understand that you were screwing around with the boys? It's the same bullshit you gave me when I was nine years old. I knew you were pregnant and momma took you to the hospital for an abortion."

"No, Marty, that didn't happen. I was a good girl. Anyway, what did you know about sex when you were nine?"

"I can't take it. You gonna deny the reality for the rest of your life? What do you think I was doing when I was nine and rubbing against you and squeezing your tits?"

"Please, Marty, don't talk like that."

"And momma was just like you. Remember when you went to her and you said, 'Marty is doing those things again, touching me and rubbing against me.' Remember, Phyllis? And momma said, 'Marty would never do those things, he's a good boy.' Now tell me, Phyllis, that that never happened."

CHAPTER TWO:
A CRICK IN THE NECK

One of the first patients who powerfully brought out in me the exasperation I felt in the craziness of my primary family was Warren. I have worked with Warren for many, many years and he still is my patient... and will always need to be. When Warren walked into my office at his initial consultation with me, I was confronted with my first private patient who was up there with my sister Debbie in her denial and misrepresentation of reality. Technically he would be classified as a bipolar with psychotic features. It was not hard for me to see that therapy with him was not going to be the same as the therapy I had been doing with my other patients, whose illnesses were less extreme. Warren had been living on the fringe for over twenty years, had been in and out of mental institutions over that time, and was on a regimen of anti-psychotic medications. The last therapist who had seen him, and had referred him to me, indicated that he had reached an impasse with him after nine years of treatment. He concluded, regretfully, that the best he could do with Warren was maintenance therapy work to keep him from cracking up, but even that scaled-down goal of treatment was becoming tenuous. This therapist had heard about my work with patients with mood disorders of a milder nature than Warren's and had a feeling that my strong personality and unorthodox approach might be applicable to treating Warren's condition. I believe he was right.

By our fifth consultation-session, I still hadn't made up my mind whether I was going to work with Warren, since I was not convinced that his kind of mental problems were amenable to therapeutic treatment. I did think long and hard about why his previous therapist had resigned himself to doing only maintenance work with him. Usually I ascertained after a meeting or two whether I wanted to take on a patient.

The session turned out to be as much a regular therapy session as a consultation. I wanted to explore more directly how he might respond to a more probing inquiry into his personal distortions and projections. And I got my fill of his psychosis.

His description of interactions with people, both at work and in his neighborhood, was similar to my mother's paranoid accounts of our neighbors and the hostility they harbored towards our family. Warren kept repeating that the people in his office, especially the women, were out to get him and he could tell by their constant staring at him what they really wanted from him. When I asked him what that might be, he responded by telling me to use my imagination and figure out what most women would like to have happen on meeting an attractive guy.

"Are you suggesting that Jane and some of your other co-workers are staring at you because they got the hots for you?"

"Yes, but I couldn't flirt with them… and now it's obvious, they're pissed."

"Did you do anything that provoked them?"

"It's not what I did, it's what I didn't do."

"How so?"

"I ignored them, not intentionally to hurt them, as they think, but because I'm shy and don't know what to do around women. I've been like this all my life. I'm not going out of my way, purposely, to ignore their sexual overtures—I was just trying to hide my embarrassment."

"Then, their rejection of you is prompted by what they perceive of as your disinterest in them, right?"

"I can't be a hundred percent sure, but at least four or five of them hang around with Jane and talk about me."

"Well, maybe that's what you want to believe."

"What else should I believe? They're pissed at me because I ignore them. I can't help the way I come off."

"Is it possible that you come off much differently than you imagine?"

"I don't know what to say, you're losing me."

"Listen, Warren, I see here in your previous therapist's summary that it is pretty commonplace for you to imagine that people are talking about you and making fun of you because you're so unresponsive to them. He mentions as an example your feeling that your super's two attractive daughters, who live across the street from your apartment, have also turned against you because you ignored them and hurt their feelings."

"I would say so. I don't react like other guys and this gets to them. They think I'm peculiar. However, I would think all of this makes me an interesting patient for you to have, am I right?"

"Did that just pop up in your mind? I'm not sure how you arrived at that conclusion?"

"I've always had an uncanny ability to read other people's mind; I can see it in their nonverbal clues. It's easy for me to tell what they're thinking and feeling."

"So let me get this straight. All these women send out nonverbal signals to you and you can tell what they're thinking and feeling?"

"I'm not bragging, but that's the way it is. And I do the same thing with you… that's why I had the feeling that you think I'm an interesting patient."

"Listen Warren, you're driving me batty. I feel like I'm in my old apartment in Brownsville with my sister Debbie and she is insisting that all the men in the building want her. Now, you have to understand, Warren, that was a gigantic distortion."

"You mean these men had no interest in her?"

"I wish they did; but the truth is that Debbie was lonely and hungry for a relationship with any man, anywhere, any place she could possibly find one. After getting the picture, even as a young kid, that no one was showing up at our doorstep, I realized that she was changing everything around to make her feel better: she was not particularly good-looking… and with her personality she turned off most men, yet she continued to believe that men were chasing her."

"And I'm just like Debbie?"

"You create your own reality, like her."

"I am not too pleased that you think I'm like this sister of yours."

"You don't think that you distort reality?"

"I don't think you understand."

"Can you tell me what it is that I don't understand?"

"... all the nonverbal difficulties I've had with people over the years. You may not want to hear it, but I can pick up on things people are thinking by just looking at them."

"If your problems are not tied up with the way you misrepresent to yourself the interchanges that occur in your office, then I'm at sea as to what kind of therapy we need to do here. Maybe you should be doing therapy on me."

"Doctor Obler, I'm letting you know of any nonverbal exchanges I have with people... but you get annoyed with me when I'm talking about the things that go on in the office."

"Is there something else that you want to tell me about?"

"Yesterday I was approaching my apartment in Park Slope, and a neighbor of mine was coming directly towards me with his dog. When he saw me, he jerked his head up in the air so he wouldn't have to look at me. Clearly something about me was bothering him."

"How do you know that his jerking his head had anything to do with you? Maybe he had a crick in the neck."

"I have a whole history with this guy... we never say hello to each other when we pass in the street. Obviously, he thinks I don't want to have anything to do with him... and this upsets him."

"... like the women in your office."

"See, you don't understand."

"Maybe. But the way I see it is that you turn everything around. It's called projection. You're angry at the guy with the dog because you believe he rejected you, but you reconstruct it so that his reaction is a result of your rejection of him; at the office, the girls think you're strange and weird, but you can't face that, so you reconstruct it so the reason that they are disgusted with you is because you're rejecting them... not to mention that you really want to fuck them."

"No, you don't get it. They want me to find them attractive and sexy."

"Warren, face it, you're a lonely, frightened, isolated man who feels all alone in the world. And that is the one thing that is real."

"Well, there is something to what you're saying."

"I'm glad you see that. And I've been thinking about how it would be helpful if you could get feedback from other people beside me."

*   *   *

At our last consultation session, I let Warren know that I thought I could help him, and would be willing to work with him, if that's what he wanted. I also mentioned to him that the work we would be doing would be quite different than what he was used to with his previous therapists. Then I added that, as a condition of my working with him, I wanted him to enter group therapy.

I have to say that it was more than a bit manipulative of me to hinge my taking him on as a patient with his going into group. I knew he really had no choice. He was desperate and on the verge of cracking up, and his maintenance therapy, with its dependence on pharmacology, was becoming less and less effective. I knew that he would resist going into group, simply because his whole syndrome was based on his lifelong fear of people. I also knew that I was taking a big chance by putting him in group, considering that he was a person with bipolar psychotic features and that obviously this could undermine the group. But being as brash and arrogant as I was, I assumed that

I could control everything and make it work for Warren and the other group members. The risks didn't stop me.

But looking back in hindsight, I can see that it was pretty astounding that I could act with such confidence. If he went bonkers, all hell could break loose.

Predictably, when I brought up his going into group at the session, he balked. He said that he didn't need to work with other people to get better... but, to give his exact words, "I just need to become less rejecting." However I had no trouble bullying him to enter group therapy. And I also had no trouble telling him, "You're a crazy motherfucker and you have to admit to your self-delusions if you're going to avoid another hospitalization." It didn't escape me for a minute, the power I felt at saying this to him and controlling everything, in a way that I couldn't in my own family. Warren caved-in to my pressuring him, and agreed to my terms.

Warren's immediate effect on the group was not auspicious. He did not, like most new group members, initially take a back seat and get a feeling of how group worked; instead he jumped right in, often inappropriately taking up a large portion of the group's allotted time with his paranoid projections that women were overreacting negatively toward him and rejecting him because he ignored their seductive glances. Respectfully, in the first couple of sessions, the members of the group let him hold forth, but after that some of the group members became exasperated with his taking up such a large part of the sessions; also, they began to detect that there was something off about Warren and that his account of his problems with women appeared distorted.

Over time, the group got to know Warren a lot better, and got used to his personal strangeness and the tension and intensity that was a staple of his personality. Some of the group members were sympathetic with his problems, some were a little confused as to why he was in group. And, one member—

Edith—was overtly hostile towards him and actively campaigned to oust him from the group.

Her hostility peaked in a session some seven months later. Warren, near the end of the session, in his self-centered manner, was holding forth obsessively about himself. She interrupted him:

"Look Warren, I'm tired of spending session after session listening to your problems with women. Let's face the truth. We just support you because we feel sorry for you. The fact is that it would take a miracle for you to find any woman to go out with you more than once. You may not want to believe it, but there must be something more to why women are rejecting you than that they're so attracted to you."

Maynard, who often sided with Warren because he felt sorry for him, asked, "What are you trying to say, Edith?"

"That he's hopeless. Even a woman who's desperate would be disgusted with Warren once she finds out how cheap he is. How would you feel, Maynard, if you were a woman and the first thing the guy says to you when you meet at the restaurant is, 'Let's be clear, we're going to split the bill'? Maybe if he didn't look the way he does and seemed to have more personality…"

"Obler, you've got to stop her. I don't know how much more of this I can take. It's insult after insult."

"He does have a point," Mark asserted. He clearly was not feeling comfortable at Edith's vitriolic attack on Warren.

"Say what you will, I can't believe that women wouldn't just walk away when they first look at him. I know I would."

"Obler, if she doesn't stop ridiculing me, I'm going to shut her up."

"See, Obler, I warned you about him. You heard what he said. I'm not going to stay in a group with a nutcase who threatens me."

"Take it easy, Edith," Maynard said in a calming tone. "I've been in group therapy for twenty-three years… people get angry at each other and make idle threats."

Beatrice, a young woman who was quite fond of Edith, also tried to downplay the altercation: "Edith, I think you're overreacting. Maynard is right—people in group get angry, but it doesn't mean much."

"I don't think I'm overreacting and I'm curious to see if anyone else takes Warren's threats as seriously as I do."

"I'm scared of him, too. Even though I feel somewhat better about him now than I used to. I still am scared of him, especially when he becomes so hostile," Antonia admitted. While generally, she was one of the more level-headed of the group members, it was necessary to keep in mind that she had also had a number of violent episodes with her husband.

Mark told Edith: "I think you're being a little too hard on Warren. The guy is having a difficult time with women, and I don't feel that you have any empathy for him at all."

"Don't you think he's got to start facing some reality?"

Maynard spoke to Edith's question: "I don't think, Edith, you can understand Warren's problem with women. You're a beautiful woman, and a lot of people turn on to you, including the men in the group. Have some sympathy. Try to imagine what it is like to not have anyone interested in you for years."

"I don't feel sorry for him. Not only is he cheap and ugly, he's crazy, too, and doesn't—and I mean this—*doesn't* belong in the group."

I asked, "Edith, who does belong in the group?"

She responded by asking a question of her own: "So what are you saying, Obler… that I'm as screwed up as Warren?"

"… that's not a discussion I want to get into; however, I will say his egocentricity is not so different than yours."

"Don't put me in the same class as that misfit. I've never been in a mental hospital. I make a good salary. I've got plenty of friends, and loads of men who want me. I don't flip out every six months."

Antonia remonstrated with Edith: "Look, Edith, I've got misgivings about Warren too. But there is room for all kinds of people in group, including someone who has had nervous breakdowns. So I don't see the point you're making."

"I've got no problem with different kinds of people working together in group; my problem is with someone who is so far off the scale that he doesn't belong here."

"Obler, she has no right to tell me that I don't belong here. You put me in this group."

"I think we're upsetting Warren, and it's unfair," Beatrice said.

"I agree," said Antonia.

"Maybe we should look at why Edith needs to go after Warren so relentlessly and why she reacts so strongly to his being in group," Mark said.

I tried to bring some conclusion to the session: "I think it's a good point, Mark. Edith, you've been uncomfortable with Warren since he entered group, and perhaps that has a lot to do with Warren taking up so much space in the sessions. You might try to answer why it is that you seem to be so much more upset by Warren's presence than the others. And Warren, perhaps you ought to look at your impact on the people around you."

Antonia said, "That sounds like a good way to begin next session."

It turned out that Warren did not show up for the next three group meetings and what worried me more than that was that he cancelled for the first time his private sessions with me. He explained in a telephone message that he needed some time on his own to put into perspective his relationship to the group and to me. He went on to say that he was becoming increasingly clear about the larger perspective of his role in the world and would return to therapy when he reached his ultimate clarity. By his message, I could comprehend where he was heading. He had gotten so upset by what had happened in group that the manic phase of the bipolar condition was kicking in, which is not unusual in bipolars... for them to use mania as a way of defending against the blight of anxiety and depression. I tried to

35

contact him a number of times, but he did not return my calls. Finally, he phoned and let me know that he would be attending the next group session. I didn't push any questions on him, but simply suggested that when he comes to group, that he make some attempt to explain why he had missed the meetings. However, I encouraged him to first come in to see me in private session; but he declined. I sensed that he was in a full-blown state of manic grandiosity, and did not want me to interfere with his feelings of powerfulness.

Warren came into group excited and agitated. His clothing was rumpled; he was unshaven, and it was evident that he hadn't been looking after himself. I realized that when I had spoken to him on the phone, I had forgotten to ask him whether he had been going to work; but I could tell by the way he looked, he hadn't. On seeing Warren, Mark got up from his seat and hugged him. "I'm glad that you made it."

Alex told Warren: "I called you a couple of times and left messages. We worried about you."

I motioned for Warren to sit in an empty chair, but he shook his head in refusal. He started speaking to the group while standing up: "I've got a lot to say and I intend to say it, even though most of you are not going to appreciate what I've been through. I also don't think you're going to comprehend some of the concepts that I'm going to present but I'll try to simplify it as much as possible. Let me open with what happened to me right after I left the last session."

I interrupted him: "Warren, why don't you grab a seat and instead of your delivering a monologue, let's just talk."

"I have very little interest in what you have to say, Obler, and certainly no interest in what that bitch Edith has to say. But I have no problem talking to the rest of you. What I'd like to do is first explain what I've been through and the revelations that have come to me." He remained standing.

"Oh, so you've had revelations…"

Maynard testily replied to Edith: "Give him a chance…"

"Don't worry I can handle this…" Warren assured.

"Go ahead with what you wanted to tell us," Antonia prompted.

"The last time I was here I felt very bad as I was leaving and I could see in the faces of the people opposite me on the train how uncomfortable I was making them."

"How could you tell this?" Mark asked.

"I know most of you have had trouble fathoming the sensitivity that allows me to pick up on the slightest nuances in other people's response to me; in truth, I don't need someone to tell me about how he feels about me... my spiritual antenna enables me to read his mind and know what he's thinking. I'm on the same wavelength as God. By the time I got out of the subway and started walking home, the bad feeling I had when I left group dropped away."

"Warren, what's this about your being on the same wavelength as God? Does that mean you're like God?" Samuel wanted to know.

"God has imparted his knowledge to me."

I couldn't stop myself from asking, "Is this an Old Testament God or a new Testament God?"

Warren replied, "That's old-fashioned thinking. You have to look at things in terms of cosmic awareness, without the biases of individual religion. I had a dream in which I was speaking to God."

Beatrice addressed me: "Why are you poking fun at him? I'm very upset."

Mark said, "Obler's been through this messianism with Warren before."

Maynard tried to get through to Warren: "Warren, it's really hard for me to follow you and your pipeline to God, but as a friend I advise you to not turn your back on Obler and the group. You need all the help you can get."

"Maynard, I appreciate your concern, but I'm way beyond the group. I just came to tell everyone that I don't need therapy anymore and to say goodbye." Antonia said, "Warren, listen to what Maynard is trying to tell you."

I asked Warren, "Have you been taking your medication?"

"Are you getting my message, Obler? I'm talking about clarity, that stuff fogs my brain."

"Yeah, it's fine to say that, but can't you recognize that you're back in your exalted view of yourself? And now suddenly you don't need help from anyone, including the group and me; naturally, you don't need your medicine either. By listening to what I and the others are saying, you can save yourself a lot of pain and misery. You're going to end up regressing, all too predictably, into a delusional state where you won't be able to take care of yourself and will have to be hospitalized. Does that sound familiar?"

"Familiar, in my past history. But I'm not the same person I was then."

"Warren! think about what Marty is saying. He's trying to stop you before it's too late," Alex told him.

Edith reiterated what she had been contending all along: "I've been trying to get everyone here to recognize that he needs a lot more help than we can give him. I don't think he belongs in the group." Then, in an unusual moment of concern for Warren, she added: "But Warren, don't ignore what Marty and everyone else is telling you. You can't afford to screw up again."

Edith's comments were more than Warren could take. Here she was showing some feeling for him, and yet saying he didn't belong in group. All this while he was feeling at the pinnacle of his powers, feeling superior to everyone around him.

Warren blurted out, "I told you, Obler, that it would be pointless to explain why I made the choice to leave group." His agitation grew more pronounced; then, without saying a further word, he turned and walked out of the office.

Antonia suggested that someone go after Warren and try to get him to come back.

I felt the same impulse, but I took a different position: "I don't think it would do any good, Antonia. When a bipolar, like Warren, gets into a full-blown manic state they don't listen to anybody. They think they have complete control of their life and live in a grand delusion that they can do almost anything they want."

"... so then what happens to them?" Samuel asked.

I answered, "For people like Warren, it's only a matter of time before they crash and wind up in a hospital."

Edith, again showing her sympathetic side, questioned, "... and we should just wait for that to happen?"

I told her what I thought and probably what most of the others thought as well: "Either he gets back on his medication and resumes therapy, or he may well be institutionalized for a spell."

CHAPTER THREE:
JUNIOR HIGH SCHOOL

By the time I had finished elementary school, World War II had ended and life in Brownsville was slowly but noticeably changing. The soldiers came home from the war and the economy was booming. Many of my neighbors stopped depending on philanthropic handouts and were able to get jobs. My family did not do as well as many of the families around me had because my father had respiratory problems that kept him from obtaining a regular job. But my two sisters were close to completing high school and were able to get jobs and bring money into the family. We now had better clothes, a refrigerator instead of an icebox, a toaster, more furniture and could afford to shop in the food markets for most of our food as opposed to the peanut butter sandwiches we relied on from the Jewish agencies. The big family purchase was a 12-inch black and white TV, bought in 1948, and now I could watch in my home the Brooklyn Dodger baseball games. Strangely, my family was one of the first families in the neighborhood to have a TV, which resulted in my new junior high school friends hanging out with me after school to watch the Dodger games. I was no longer as embarrassed by my family as I used to be; I realized that my friends too came from immigrant families of whom they were embarrassed. We shared a common identification as being American kids and we looked at our parents as foreigners who didn't even speak English well and referred to them as "mockeys" (foreigners).

My junior high school was located much further away from my home than my elementary school had been, and was near to the dilapidated neighborhood of East New York, which was the last bastion of Jews to emigrate from Eastern Europe to New York City. Junior High School 66 was an immense building with iron gates on the windows and looked like a prison. And it might as well have been a prison, considering the atmosphere and discipline of the institution. It was an all-male school and every morning the boys would line up at eight o'clock in the courtyard in front of the school where attendance was taken and one by one we would holler out "present" when our name was called, class by class, by the home room teacher. In reality, it didn't matter much whether attendance was taken, since even if someone were absent, somebody else would yell present for him and the faculty didn't seem to care, preferring to have a good attendance record.

Compared to J.H.S. 66, the elementary school I went to, was like a private school. At least in the elementary school there was a pretense of an educational institution and the principal and teachers took their jobs seriously, so we had a feeling that this was a real school and run the way a school should be. The junior high school reflected the crazy life in East New York and the worst of Brownsville, and I saw that the teachers and administrators running things were just as looney as the people in the streets.

I was placed in what was labeled the One Class, which was made up of capable students who were underachieving. There was a small group of students who were placed in the SP classes, which meant that they were the brightest and the best-functioning students in the school. Only one kid from the Herzl Street area, where I lived, made it into an SP class, and this pissed off my friends and me, since it was not exactly a vote of confidence of our standing in the world. The other classes in the seventh grade were designated as numbers two, three, four, five and six and students were placed in them according to their I.Q. scores on the Stanford Binet Intelligence Test, with the higher scores in the lower-numbered classes. We knew this because the individual school records were available for students to scrutinize, since most of the time no one was even in the records office to stop kids from looking at official documents.

The curriculum that all seventh grade students shared consisted of six subjects, each one taught by a separate teacher who was also a homeroom teacher. The number One Class homeroom teacher was a lonely, sweet, ineffectual young Italian woman named Louisa. She taught all six classes of English. She adored all her students in the class and could never accept that we did some of the antics we were accused of doing by the other teachers. The second subject was taught by Miss Rosa, a math teacher, who happened to be totally inarticulate. The third subject, some type of practical economics course, was taught by Miss Hofstra. She was a two hundred and fifty pound black woman, who carried around with her a light club, which the students knew she would use on them if they acted out in her class. The teacher of the fourth subject was a woman who the kids believed was deaf and dumb, Miss Taistra. She was the Poetry, Music, and Art instructor. All communication between her and the students took place on big signs posted on the wall. The teacher of the fifth subject was an old maid, drunken alcoholic who felt little compunction to be sober in class. She taught American History, and found occasion to refer to every famous person in history as a "fucking son of a bitch." The male teacher in the other subject, Woodworking, was pretty ordinary and undistinguished.

In the seventh grade some of my old friends and I formed a gang. We had been playing basketball and stickball together for years. Because the school was located in such a run-down neighborhood, away from the streets we had grown up on, we all became increasingly turf conscious. After a number of incidents in which the kids from our little group got mugged and beaten up, we started to talk about the idea of forming a gang for mutual protection. Breaking up into a gang was not a new idea in Brownsville and East New York, since there was a long history of street gangs, starting during the depression years and continuing through World War II. Most of them were

DR. MARTIN OBLER / JED GOLDEN

formed along lines of ethnic background and usually covered about a ten-block radius. There were Irish, Italian and Jewish gangs. The gang my friends and I had started, in junior high school, was mostly Jewish, but there were a few Irish and Italians; we even included two black kids, which was unheard of at that time.

Joining forces in a gang wasn't only for the purpose of greater individual safety. It also had to do with finance. Most of us came from poor families and the only way we could get spending money was to take local jobs in the fruit and grocery stores on Sutter and Pitkin Avenue. But we began to see that in Junior High School there were opportunities to make some money by exploiting the other students. Lots of kids needed protection, and were willing to pay us a small amount of money to provide this service. We provided another service as well, two or three kids from the gang had gotten hold of some illicit pornographic picture sex-stories, which were called Hot Books, and we began to sell them to the kids at school.

However, it wasn't long before we ran into trouble. A bunch of us were sitting in the library reading the Hot Books.

Timmy exclaimed, "Look at these tits. I can't believe it."

Renaldo added, "Boy would I like to suck on them."

"Listen to this," Erwin said, as he began reading from one of the books:

" 'So you little guys like my big black pussy, huh? It's big enough for all you guys to fit in at the same time.'

'Listen momma, my wong is so big there won't be enough room for anyone else if I come in you.'

'Oh, you think so. Give it to me big boy.' "

We were rolling with laughter at this dialogue, in which this big fat woman with an enormous cunt and tits was asking the students to fuck her all at the same time. But, obviously, part of what made us laugh so hard was the tension we felt having to do with the sexual excitement that we were feeling from reading the books.

"You gotta hear this," Renaldo said. " 'The fly on the rear of the elephant was readying himself to insert his pecker, and as he did so, he shouted to the elephant, Am I hurting you big boy?' "

We started to crackup when into the library waddled heavy Miss Hofstra, with club in hand.

"What is going on here, you little rodents? Let me see the crap you're reading."

We all froze, and as she moved to take the book out of Renaldo's hand, I said, "Hold it."

"What's the *hold it*, Obler?"

"We were given an assignment by the librarian to catalogue the new books by the Dewey Decimal system. We found these books hidden in a pile in the back of the room and we're trying to give them the right numbers."

Miss Hofstra grabbed the book from Renaldo and quickly thumbed through it. Her facial expression changed immediately. I got the feeling she was getting excited.

Big Bubba, the biggest and dumbest kid in the gang, asked her, "Pretty hot stuff, huh?"

She wasted no time in whacking him with her weapon.

"We've got to figure out who put these books here. This stuff shouldn't be in a library, for kids to see. It's against the law."

"What should we do Miss Hofstra?" I inquired.

"Give them to me. I'll take care of them."

Ollie said, "Can I keep the one I'm reading? I've already borrowed it from the library."

"Where did you get this stuff, Ollie, and how much did you pay for it?"

"From the fag."

"Which fag?"

"The one who is coming onto us all the time, offering us money and candy."

"You mean that fag who is a flunky for the mob?"

I was pretty surprised that Miss Hofstra knew as much as she did about what was happening in the neighborhood; I wasn't, however, surprised at the way we talked to her and the way she talked to us.

Ollie couldn't help from saying, "That son of a bitch gets the stuff from the Italian geeks, and he gets it for next-to-nothing."

I said, "Listen Ollie, did he suck you off? Is that how you got the books?"

"Are you crazy, Moose? I paid him for the stuff."

This was some of the background of how the gang got into the business of selling Hot Books. As for Miss Hofstra, she confiscated the books to protect us from their pernicious influence; but that did not stop business from going on as usual.

In the middle of the seventh grade our gang, The Trojans, started to get a reputation in the neighborhood as a force to be reckoned with. We gave the appearance of being a tough gang, but most of it was just bravado. The world of Brownsville was continually getting more dangerous; there were stories circulating in the neighborhood that were pretty scary.

Some kids from Sutter Avenue had made it known that they had wandered into the Italian enclave near East New York and had been attacked by the controlling gang of that section. There was also a rash of robberies in which various gang members from other neighborhoods were holding up storeowners in our area. I found out from my sister Debbie's new boyfriend, Sid, who was a local *runner* for the mob, that some mob members were concerned that these activities were drawing unwanted attention to violence in their territory.

By virtue of sticking together the gang members felt greater security and were less likely to become victims of outside aggression. On a social plane, we were in a stage of transition to middle adolescence, and were trying to get away from our families. Hanging out together gave us a new family and a new identity. In addition, we were having a lot of fun, part of which involved creating a different way of life than that lived by our parents, who were relatively isolated and whose central focus was on survival economically. Whatever social life existed for most of our parents, it had to do with their extended family. But what my friends and I were discovering was that we could have a lot more fun and more satisfying experiences outside of family ties.

Being a part of the Trojans became a whole way of life for me and my friends. From 8 A.M to 3 P.M. we were in JHS 66 and looked forward to being in school, not because of any academic interest, but because of the fun we could have in basically antisocial behavior within the school system. Moreover, we found ways of making money by various means—as mentioned, selling Hot Books, and providing protection for the weaker kids; also setting up betting pools in baseball and football, and on occasion, recruiting some disturbed, or retarded girls to offer sexual favors for money.

Although rumors floated throughout the school about our money-making activities, there was no crackdown to eliminate our business ventures.

After school, the gang members would play sports against other loosely-knit groups in the neighborhood. And when we weren't playing sports, we would hang out together in a basement room, which we rented from one of the gang member's parents. We spent less and less of our time in our own apartments and began to use the gang as a surrogate family. We would cook in our basement room, invite girls to join us, have parties and spend a lot of time—often until the late hours of the night—just fooling around.

Most of our energies went into having fun, and we made it a point to do as little schoolwork as possible; a few of us paid some of the willing, better students to do our homework for us. Things went pretty smoothly for a long time, but during the eighth grade, incidents in school occurred that caused us to have to put a damper on our money-making endeavors; also there were turf-related fights with other gangs, sometimes leading to police involvement.

And things were happening in my own life that caused problems for me. Sid had moved into my family's apartment and was starting to overstep himself. The following exchange took place:

"Sid, you son of a bitch, I told you once and I'm gonna tell you again, if you don't keep your fucking hands off Debbie or you threaten Sadie and Saul another time, we'll break your goddamn fingers."

I said this to my brother-in-law with twelve members of the gang standing behind me. Sid and Debbie had just come out of the apartment building at Herzl Street, and we were waiting for him. Some of the kids carried weapons, like bats and chains, and were prepared to use them. When Sid married my sister and moved into my family's apartment, eight months earlier, I had been intimidated by him. He had a reputation for being a lower-rung member of the syndicate and he never let you forget this. He even boasted to me once that one of his relatives had been in Murder Inc. I had played this card to elevate my position within the gang. But, then, he started to become abusive to my family and attempted to take control. He began telling us what to do and ordering my sisters and mother to serve him and clean up his room, and once in a while even tried, unsuccessfully, to order me to go out and get him sandwiches and cigarettes. I could tell that he was a little unsure of himself with me because he was uncertain about how powerful the gang was in the neighborhood. He crossed the line with me when he would smack Debbie, and even began to demand that my father give him money from his rag-picking pushcart business.

"I never touched your friggin' sister, ya little prick," he yelled at me while grabbing Debbie by the upper arm. "Tell him, Debbie, did I ever touch ya?"

"Lemme kill the motherfucker," Joey threatened, pushing me aside. He was holding a plank of wood with large nails sticking out of it. He was only twelve years old, but was over six feet tall and weighed close to two hundred pounds and had the build of a gorilla.

"Listen, Marty, or Moose, whatever they call ya, do dees guys know who I am?"

"Who are you?" Benny asked Sid.

"If any of ya little motherfuckers put a hand on me, ya ain't gonna be long for this world, put it that way."

"Marty, don't touch him, he's my husband."

"Debbie, you stupid bitch, I don't give a shit that he whacks you around every day or that you have to suck the bastard's dick, what I don't want is for him to threaten papa for the few bucks he makes every day. If he ain't making enough money running numbers, let him go to work. For that matter, the two of you have been sponging off Sadie and Saul for too long. I want you both out of the house in two weeks."

"It's as much your sister's apartment as yours. Ya only got bar mitzvahed a year ago."

"You suddenly turn Jewish?" one of the gang asked him. "Let me see your dick... that'll prove it."

"That's a good idea, I want to see the big shot's wong. I'll bet it's a quarter of an inch," Mario added.

"Solly, where is that magnifying glass of yours," someone else chimed in. Debbie jumped in front of Sid to protect him, and pleaded: "Please Marty, don't let them take his dick, he's my husband."

All of us broke up with this remark of Debbie's.

"All right," I said, "we'll give the little shit one more chance. And for our trouble, he'll have to cough up twenty-five bucks a month."

I hardly went home anymore to sleep. In addition to Sid, Phyllis brought in a boyfriend to live with us, who was AWOL from the peacetime army and was in hiding. There was hardly any room for everyone to have a bed. I moved into my father's room because Phyllis and Eddie took over the living room. Being at home was getting intolerable for me. My sisters were continually fighting with their spouses over the fact that they were the only ones working full-time. When I pointed out to Debbie that Sid seemed to be making good money with the syndicate, she let me know that she hadn't seen a penny of it. I let her know that I had no trouble getting the twenty-five dollars out of him.

My father was wearing down, physically and emotionally; he spent much of the day drinking in the local bars and when he did come home he would sit on the radiator and rock back and forth, as if he were an old man. I knew that Debbie and Sid cursed at him when he was drunk and I suspected that sometimes they hit him. But more and more I grew weary with the whole situation at home and absented myself as much as I could.

The Trojans' operation at JHS 66 ran as smoothly as ever until Moscowitz, who had become a flunkey for the gang, running errands for us, got into trouble with Miss Hofstra. An altercation occurred between them one day, resulting in his transfer to her class:

"Erase the board, Moscowitz, like a good boy."

"How come, Miss Hofstra, you're always asking me to do the dirty work in this class? What about Obler and Johnson and Leibowitz? They never do anything."

"Listen, you little runt, when I give you a command, you do it."

"Tell him, Miss Hofstra," someone encouraged.

"Now clean the board, like I told you to," and, as she yelled this at him, she ripped off the bow tie that he came to school with every day.

"Don't touch me you fat *schvartze*, and give me back my bow tie," he screamed, crying at the same time.

Spontaneously the class began shouting in unison, "Bow tie, bow tie, bow tie."

Miss Hofstra grabbed Moscowitz by the hair and pulled him out of his seat, while holding up the bow tie before him with her other hand. She said, "You want your bow tie, you little midget, well here it is," and she forced him to the front of the room and pressured him down underneath her desk, throwing the bow tie at him. "This is where you're going to spend the rest of the school year, under my desk."

"Miss Hofstra," I remarked, "is that a punishment or a reward?"

"Butt out of this, Obler. We don't need to hear from you."

Moscowitz did end up spending two weeks under Miss Hofstra's desk, inches away from her skirt, before she relented and let him return to his seat. The bargain that he had struck up with her to get out from under, and also away from her not infrequent passing of gas (he confided to us) was that he would reveal to her some of the secret operations of the Trojans in school in return for his change of location. After that, the administration started to investigate into the covert activities of the gang.

"It's come to our attention that you guys have been running some kind of business out of our library here," the principal of JHS 66 said, with obvious displeasure, to me and four other members of the Trojans.

"Is that an accusation or a question?" I countered, acting as if I were more annoyed than I really was.

"We've got reports here from some of your classmates and teachers accusing the Trojans—I believe that is the name of your gang—of running a protection service and selling pornographic books for profit."

"Would it be better if we gave them away for free?" Pauly asked.

"I'm glad you think it's funny. Do you think it's funny, too, Obler?"

"I don't think it's funny, Principal Haines, but this is a dangerous neighborhood and the students don't get any protection from the school... just last week Hermanski got his ass kicked right outside the entrance to the school during the assembly period. What about that?"

"I've been informed that some kids from an outside gang came into the school looking to settle a score with your gang, and when they couldn't find any of you, they left and beat up Hermanski, who happened to be coming up the front stairs as they were departing."

"That's what I was saying, Principal, no student is safe here… you should be protecting them."

"How was it in your day, Principal Haines? Were things as rough as they are today?" Mario asked him.

"In my day, we didn't have these kinds of problems; everybody knew their place. No one would dare to come into the school that didn't belong there."

"Why was that?" Mario asked him.

"Well, we had one gang that ran all of Brownsville and East New York and they controlled everything."

"Was that Murder Inc.?" Willie questioned.

"It sure was fellow. You can't imagine how bad it was, the kind of poverty that existed. People had to eke out a living anyway they could."

"… that's exactly what we're trying to do. That's why we're selling the Hot Books."

"So you're admitting, Obler, that you broke school rules and that you engaged in illegal activity. You understand that means suspension?"

"Is there anything we could do to avoid getting suspended?"

"That would have to be worked out with your parents."

"What do you suggest we do?" Mario entreated.

"Bring your parents in, we'll have a meeting and see what can be worked out."

The meeting was held in Principal Haines' office early in the morning and went about as I expected it to. A small group of parents showed up. For the most part, they sat meekly and in fear, trying to comprehend why their kids were in trouble. I can't remember most of what took place in the meeting, but two exchanges stood out in my mind, because they reflected the futility of the principal's attempt to engage the parents in a dialogue. One of the exchanges involved my parents.

At some point in the discussion, Principal Haines turned to my parents and confronted them with what he saw as my leading role in conducting an illegal business at the school. He spoke to them harshly and gravely about the seriousness of what I had done.

"Do you realize Mr. and Mrs. Obler that your son is the head of a gang called the Trojans, and he apparently set up a business selling dirty books in school? He and his friends found a contact in the local syndicate [the principal didn't know that my brother-in-law was one of our contacts and lived in our apartment] who has been supplying them with this illicit material and they used the school library as the center of their business activities."

"How do you know my son is the one responsible for all of this?" Saul asked.

"We've heard it from some of our reliable students, one or two of whom bought these books."

My mother inquired, "My Marty did this?"

"Not only did he do it, but you have to understand, Mrs. Obler, that he took advantage of these kids and has been making a lot of money off of them."

"He is? How much is he making?"

And then she questioned me, obviously impressed, "Muttla, how much are you making?"

Later in the discussion the principal turned to Leibowitz's father, who was not among the meek and fearful parents, and confronted him about his son's brutality connected to the protection service the gang supplied.

Leibowitz's father had a reputation locally for being the strongest man on the East Coast of America; it was rumored even that he had tried out for the 1936 Olympics. He made his living since the beginning of World War II as a showman, demonstrating his strength in street shows. He pulled cars attached to chains up slight inclines with his teeth; he also lifted up with his hands big trucks while someone changed the tire. Everyone in the neighborhood feared and admired him.

"Your son Leibowitz is the enforcer behind the Trojan's protection business."

"… what does he do?"

"The gang provides, for money, protection to the kids in school, and if the students refuse their offer, your son beats them up."

Leibowitz's dad's face flushed, and you could see his fury. Right then and there he grabbed his son and lifted him off the ground with one hand and slapped him in the face with the other.

"Is that the example I gave you of how to act?"

The principal ended up suspending us for two weeks, during which time the other gang members, who were not accused of any wrongdoing, continued the operation.

The gang's profile was less pronounced after the parent-teacher conference. The illegal activities continued in somewhat abated form, but we paid more attention to operating discreetly. In ninth grade things were relatively peaceful since we were not intentionally provoking the school administration and they were leaving us alone. There was, however, a change taking place in Brownsville that went beyond the localized activities of gang life. After World War II, the Jewish population in Brownsville began to make some economic inroads. Jews got jobs in the garment industry, the meat industry; jobs managing small businesses; jobs as accountants and bookkeepers, and were hired as money managers in banks and financial institutions that were sprouting up throughout the city. The Jews in Brownsville were able to take advantage of the prospering economy, while the Italians and Irish from the surrounding neighborhoods were not as poised to do this. The Jewish emphasis, even in poor neighborhoods like Brownsville, on the value of education stood them in good stead, as well as their resourcefulness in both saving money and spending it wisely. There was strong resentment of the economic progress Jews were making, and this hostility filtered down from parents to their children.

About this time I began hearing a lot of Irish, Italian, and black kids in and around Brownsville referring to Jews as *Kikes, Yids, Heebs,* and cheap bastards. The Trojans became a prime target of gang anger because we were largely Jewish and because we were rumored to be so successful in making money at JHS 66. Things got pretty bizarre when one of the rival Italian gangs from Brownsville decided to come after the Trojans with the intent of ripping off our Hot Book proceeds. They came into JHS 66 because they thought we'd be taken by surprise and wouldn't be able to put up much resistance.

A group of some ten kids entered the school and forced a few of the students to tell them where they could find 'Obler and his gang.' They were taken, on the threat of violence, to our Art teacher's class, Miss Taistra. They came into the class, and unexpectedly confronted the total silence, typical of her non-speaking approach to education. She taught her classes by pointing with a pointer to signs all around the room, which she changed daily; it was our job as students to read the signs and pick up from them the class work that we would be doing. We had always assumed that our teacher was language-impaired and everybody understood that nobody could speak in class, even to ask a question about the classroom work. All questions had to be handed in to her in writing. Everyone knew that our concerns would be met by the signs on the wall, and, if not, she would construct new ones on the spot.

She was a short woman of slight build, in her early fifties, who always wore sunglasses even in the classroom; she usually dressed in old-fashioned, flowing black dresses and would wear a scarf around her neck or would wear pants and a jacket, which women didn't wear in those days. On her head, she wore large-brimmed hats, often with plastic fruit pinned to the top. She was a strange woman and looked as though she were still clinging to an older time. When the Italian gang came into the room, the first thing they saw was Leibowitz and Eli looking at a sentence on a sign that was asking us to identify some painter by his work. Nobody was talking or even looking as if they were about to talk. For a moment time had stopped as the kids from the intruding gang (who had never seen a class with signs instead of talking) fell silent; and the students (who were stunned at the sight of strange kids bursting into their classroom) were also rendered speechless. This freeze ended abruptly when chairs started flying and the kids from the two gangs began fist-fighting. The other students formed a circle around the combatants to watch the fight. Miss Taistra, who was shorter than the spectators, became increasingly exasperated at not being able to see what was happening. Her face became inflamed with rage and she pounded on the back of the kids who were blocking her view. Suddenly we heard a piercing scream that stopped everyone in their tracks. This was followed by the first words we had ever heard her utter: "Get the fuck out of the way. I want to see this." All of her students were flabbergasted. After a few seconds, the combat in the room was replaced with hysterical laughter by the students; and the Italian intruders were again miffed and mute. Miss Taistra made a path by pushing her students aside, and walked right up to the Italians, stuck her pointer into the face of one of them and began yelling, "What are you guineas doing here, uninvited in my class?" The question was reiterated by a couple of her students: "Yeah, Miss Taistra, What are the guineas doing here?" When one of the transgressors started apologizing to her, seemingly out of fear, some of us found it hugely funny. There was no way that we could resume battling each other in this looney-tunes environment.

By the time graduation rolled around I had a fondness for the school and knew that I would miss its unchecked wackiness... as I saw it, the spirit of the place evoked the spirit of The Three Stooges.

At the thought of graduation, I wondered whether the freewheeling, irresponsible times with my buddies were coming to an end. Our neighborhood was changing and even though we had gone through a lot of hardship and suffering together, going back to the early years in elementary school, the fun and camaraderie we had together outweighed the hard times. Underneath the toughness and brutality there had always been a feeling of communality—we belonged somewhere. Now the personal bonds that had evolved over the years would be dissolving as we broke up and went to different schools... but, perhaps, even more importantly the world around us was changing. Some of the families who were prospering would leave the ghetto and move out to the newly-developing, lower-class suburbia, like Levittown; those remaining were confronted with random violence, gang wars, and a lack of community. By the beginning of the 1950's when I started high school, the favorite saying of the kids was "It's time to get out, the *schvartzes* are moving in." As familiar as I was with the abusive way people treated each other in my neighborhood, nothing prepared me for the following situation.

Eli Hermanski got a blow job from Solly in the summer of 1950 during a heat wave. They had been playing monopoly with me and a few other friends. In the middle of the game, someone, out of heat frustration, flipped the board over, sending the money, cards, houses, and board pieces flying. Spontaneously most of the group hurtled out of Solly's home screeching and yelling on the way to find relief from the sweltering day under an open hydrant. As Eli reported it later to some of us in the gang, Solly and he had stayed behind, and without any forewarning, Solly unzipped Eli's fly and commenced to suck him off. Eli was thirteen years old—a year younger than me—when this took place. In his account of what happened, he claimed he was too shocked to stop Solly. I couldn't let that go, and suggested to Eli that he was full of it. I let him know that he must have enjoyed what happened to him and that Solly must have picked up clues that he was not opposed to what took place. Eli ignored what I said, not wanting to draw attention to himself by arguing with me.

Eli's story got out to the gang at large and many of the guys started lining up in our makeshift clubhouse to get a blow job from Solly. Interestingly, he was never ostracized by the gang for being queer. They seemed not to have a big problem with it. There were a couple of adult queers in the neighborhood, who, not infrequently propositioned kids to have sex with them for money. This too was not considered a big deal. The problem in the Eli-Solly situation arose a number of days later when some parents of gang members got wind of what had gone down and decided to handle the problem themselves.

Amazingly, they formed a vigilante group of about fifteen people and marched around the corner from Herzl Street to Solly's apartment building on Blake Avenue. Some of the gang members were yelling to the marching parents "Kill the motherfucking faggot, kill the motherfucking faggot." It didn't take a course in psychology to figure out that the gang members who had turned against Solly did so to relieve their own homosexual fears. As long as Solly was dismissed as a pervert, then he was different than they were.

When Solly came out of his building to see what the commotion was all about the vigilantes grabbed him and threw an actual rope with a noose around his neck and dragged him to a nearby lamppost, adjacent to my favorite candy store. Solly was so weak, so the story went, that he could hardly stand up. They flung the rope, after a number of unsuccessful attempts, over the top of the lamppost and, only then, confronted him with the charges against him. One of the parents shouted, "You lousy homo, sucking off young kids. We don't want creeps like you in the neighborhood."

At the time this took place I was a block away playing stickball. One of the gang members came running up to us in the middle of the game, shouting, "They're lynching Solly, they're lynching Solly." I turned to him and said, "What in hell are you talking about?"

"I'm not shitting. Murray's parents are leading a mob in front of the candy store and they're going to string up Solly."

Everyone tore down the street to see what was happening. Just as I arrived they were beginning to pull on the rope to lift Solly up. When they saw me, and the others, they held up. They knew that I was one of Solly's friends.

"What-the-fucks-going-on-here?" I demanded.

Yankila, a neighborhood kid and a peripheral gang member, shouted, "We're gonna kill the queer bastard for what he's done."

"What did he do to you, Yankila?"

"You know what he did."

"Yankila, you cross-eyed, stupid son of a bitch. He's one of the gang. You think you're less of a fag because you got the blow job instead of giving it?"

I could see Yankila backing down as I confronted him. The parents saw the situation turning around and wavered. They were afraid of my power; they also knew that gang members had a code of loyalty to one another and that I was clearly claiming Solly as one of the gang. I, with a couple of friends, went over, pushed Murray's father aside, removing the noose from poor Solly's neck. Another kid twisted Yankila's arm behind his back and walked him off to get a beating. The lynching incident was over.

In front of the lynching crowd, I had to act the role of the big man, but the incident shook me up. Despite the fear that entered me when I first saw Solly about to be strung up, I had been able to act. It was not the same immobilizing fear that had paralyzed me while watching my friends beat up my father some years ago. I never really knew whether the people in the neighborhood would actually have followed through and killed Solly, but nevertheless I had no choice but to act.

By the time of the Solly episode, I had attained a great deal of power and control over what happened in the neighborhood. What had shaken me up was the insight I had, in spite of my successful efforts on Solly's behalf, that the world, where such an incredible episode could take place, was crazy. By the time I had entered junior high school, I still deluded myself into believing that there were only a few families like mine that did not have all their marbles. I mistakenly assumed that most of my neighbors lived a somewhat normal life. Yet here were these pathetic vigilantes, who had to be as crazy or crazier than my family.

I knew after the Solly incident that I had to get the fuck out of Brownsville. Some of the brighter and more sensitive gang members and I began to open up about our inner doubts involving the life we were leading. The Solly incident made us look differently at our world. We started to become aware that most of the neighborhood adults were beyond the pale. We all knew that things were a lot calmer and saner in the adjacent, more prosperous neighborhood of East Flatbush. Even though times were hard economically for the East Flatbush families, it was inconceivable that things could ever get to such a point where they could actually form a lynch mob, and attempt to hang a fourteen-year-old kid for giving a blow job to a willing participant. For the first time a few of us gang members admitted to each other that there was a lot of violence and strange behavior on the part of adults in our families. The one occurrence that we all had referred to was Dominick's father killing his mother with an ice pick, but now we heard that Philly's dad regularly chained his two daughters up and beat them in order to make sure that they wouldn't be promiscuous; that the two sides of Leo's family engaged in physical and verbal fights at family gatherings over a possibly nonexistent inheritance that one side had supposedly cheated the other side out of; and that Erwin confessed to the following secret about his father, who was one of the few people in the neighborhood to have somehow managed to accumulate enough money to open his own business on Rockaway Avenue:

Erwin explained, "I want to make it clear to you guys that what I'm gonna tell you about my father… if he finds out that I told anyone about this stuff my ass ain't worth a plug nickel."

We all assured him we wouldn't say a word, despite our knowledge that whatever Erwin told us would be spread far and wide by the next morning. That was just the way of life in Brownsville.

Philly said, "Okay, get on with it already."

"Don't rush me." It was not easy for Erwin to tell his story, because he knew all too well how the gang could make a person pay for revealing any kind of personal weakness.

"You know the two fat Aunt Jemima ladies that work in my father's store? The ones he pays sixty-five cents an hour?"

"I could use that money," Philly interjected. Erwin turned bright red as he continued the story. "He paid them that much because he's been fingerfucking them regularly in the back room for the last two years. And when I was about thirteen he started teaching me the ropes. So sometimes when Ethel or Hanna tried to say no, he would order me to hold her and he would fingerfuck her and then he'd hold her and I'd finger her."

When this story of what went on in the backroom came out, I and some of the others cracked up. Here was one of the few people in the community that had made money and become respected for his achievement, so that to think of him as a crazy motherfucker forcing those fat colored ladies to provide sex for him and his son was too funny for words. Our ranking of Erwin started at that moment, and we couldn't stop our laughter.

I spontaneously burst out singing the Aunt Jemima advertisement, "Mammy's little baby loves shortening, shortening. Mammy's little baby loves shortening bread."

Erwin's best friend, Leo, got infuriated with me and said, "What the fuck you makin' fun of Erwin for, Moose? What about your mother?"

"What about my mother?"

"How come she's always chasing Ollie?"

"Maybe she wants her money back."

"It's been six months and it's only a quarter, Moose."

"So what? You putting that in the same category as Irwin's father fingering those women in the back room?"

"I hate to break the news to you, Moose, but we saw your mother hiding behind the entranceway to the grocery store, waiting for Ollie to make an appearance on the street. And when he turned on Amboy, she darted out and started screaming, 'Gimmee the quarter you little *schvance*.' I myself saw

Ollie take off heading for the Saratoga Avenue station. Your mother was running behind him with two bags of food. And when he got to the station, he had to jump the turnstile and head to the other end of the station to get away from her."

Erwin added, "I gotta hand it to you, Moose, your mom's a really dignified lady."

I felt so ridiculed in front of my friends, at my mother's queer behavior, that I diverted the attention away from her by telling the story of my sister Debbie hitting my father with a broomstick while he sat on the radiator in the winter trying to stay warm.

It was hard for the group to control their laughter at picturing my mother and sister beating on my helpless, drunken father, but after they had gotten their laughs at my expense, we split up. The conversation we had had that day ended pretty ugly. It reflected how hard it was for us to sustain a serious conversation about our lives. Still, among us, there were glimmerings that we were increasingly aware that life in the neighborhood and in our homes was disturbing and inhospitable. Somewhere inside of us, I suspect, we understood that the people we were growing up with were tearing apart the very fabric of their lives.

In the pool hall on Saratoga Avenue, which bordered East Flatbush, I started to meet a bunch of kids whom I could see lived differently than my friends and me. They befriended me because I was a good pool player and had a reputation as a tough and savvy gang leader. Bernard, one of the kids I got friendly with at the pool hall, invited me to his house on Avenue H in East Flatbush. I spent a couple of weekends at his home, motivated in part by my interest in a young girl who lived in a two-family dwelling on his block. I didn't do very well with her, but staying in Bernard's home was quite an experience.

His house was full of musical instruments and books and his refrigerator was stacked with fancy foods. More importantly, I could see that the people in his family related to each other in a more sensitive, humane, and communicative way compared to what I was used to in my family. I felt safe with them… I began to have an inkling that the damage that had been done to me psychologically might be extensive and if I didn't begin to do something about it, and start living more in keeping with the way these people lived, my problems would only get worse. On a more positive note, however, I could see that I was able to fit into this more caring and cosmopolitan world… that I had developed strengths and a confidence that Bernard and his family admired. I was tough, I caught on quickly to what was going on around me, I knew how to listen, and I was bright. I impressed them, even though my manners were only slightly more advanced than a primate's and my Brooklyn speech thick as it could be, when I wasn't consciously trying to sound more civilized.

CHAPTER FOUR:
HIGH SCHOOL

The thought of spending another summer hanging around Herzl Street with my gang of friends did not seem like a good idea, especially after having gotten a glimpse of a different life in East Flatbush. Their way of life didn't include the violence that the gang and I had gotten used to accepting. When the gang lieutenant, Warner, who was a close friend, forced himself on a girl on a rooftop, which I personally witnessed, I realized I couldn't take any more of the cruelty and senseless brutality that surrounded me.

However, not long before summer began, I and some other gang members were involved in a lurid sexual scene where we took advantage of a girl who had run away from her home in Canarsie. One of the social misfits in the neighborhood, and not a member of our gang, had been thrown out of his house, so he brought her to live with him at his makeshift home in an abandoned store. Word got out that Steven was having sex with her, and the idea that she might be available for our (the gang's) sexual needs excited us. A guy in the gang—who happened to know her slightly—convinced her to put out for some of us, and, then, one night Ollie kept Steven busy while five of us lined up outside the store. Even though she was a banker's daughter from a middle class family, she was out of it and may have been slightly retarded. She was nineteen but looked younger and rather sexy. I went first. Sex with her was brusque and impersonal, and I remember that I was struck by her making sure that I used a rubber. On leaving I told Renaldo that it was his turn, while the other guys wanted to know how it went. I told them it was great. I left and walked down the street.

Two kids from a rival Italian-Irish gang in Canarsie came up to me and asked me, "Where is the girl?" I realized word had gotten out about what we were going to do. It turned out that they were pissed because we were having sex with a girl from their territory. I knew I was in trouble. After a short verbal confrontation, they started to hit me and one of them kicked me in the nuts. Fortunately, Warner—who was last in line—saw what was taking place and hustled to my rescue. He faced the two toughs down, which was not hard for him since he had a reputation throughout the neighborhood of being a powerful and vicious fighter. The two guys took off, threatening that they would get back at us. I put my arm around Warner's shoulder and we walked down the street laughing at their idle threat. After walking about two blocks, we heard police sirens screeching, and when we turned back towards the store, we could see that the police car had stopped in front of it. The dickheads had ratted on us.

Four of the gang members were arrested and the story made the headlines of the local newspaper. Because of community pressure the police had to hold them on trumped up charges. There was not much to legally hold them on a felony charge since the girl was not under age or forced to have sex; and the gang members themselves were under sixteen and, in actuality, I was the only one that had sex with her. They tried to bargain with the four kids arrested, telling them that they would drop the charges against them if they informed on the ringleader of the gang. The gang members did not cooperate, knowing that they were under age and couldn't be prosecuted. But one of the rival gang members from Canarsie, who only knew me as the Moose, told the police that that was my nickname and, I might be the head of the gang (which I unofficially was). Word got out that the cops were looking for me. It was, however, very clear in the neighborhood that it would go badly for anyone who squealed.

The cops arrested the social misfit who had taken the girl in, so as to relieve the pressure on them, but they couldn't make the charges stick against him either. The girl's prominent father insisted that the Moose be caught and brought to trial for having coercive sex with his daughter. It became apparent that I had to flee Brownsville.

My friend Bert, who was a member of the gang, spoke to his brother Kurt about giving me a job at a summer camp in the Catskills. Kurt was an Israeli leader of a Zionist, leftist political movement recruiting young American Jews into the movement by offering them jobs at the camp. He offered me a job as a waiter and I took it. It would be my way out of Brownsville, both to escape the police and to begin a new life, hopefully along different lines than the life I was currently leading.

The six-week summer camp was a mindblower for me. Most of the campers and staff came from lower and middle-income Jewish families and had a refinement and sophistication that was absent in me. I do remember, however, having for years secretly yearned to have a girlfriend who came from this kind of background. What initially surprised me most was how many of these girls, whom I believed were unattainable, were attracted to me, a poor kid from the streets. But then that could have been part of the attraction. Before long I was in love for the first time in my life. The recipient of my affections was Alice Stern, an intelligent, pretty girl from a good family, the kind of girl who before this time I could only fantasize about. My gut feeling had always been that this sort of classy, desirable female would never show any interest in me. My gut however was not being fed the right information. It seemed that my domineering personality worked for me in this new environment, just as it had worked in my neighborhood. Alice, lo and behold, responded positively to my overtures. We did, though, have a problem: she was cautious sexually, and I was forward and impatient, used to the brusque sexual contacts with the girls from the neighborhood. She kept insisting that girls from her background didn't go further than kissing and petting. I tried to force myself on her, but she didn't give in. I knew I had to change my approach; my plan was to make Alice jealous. To do this, I made a conspicuous show of enthusiasm for a girl named Sherry. I thought it would be easy to fool around with her and relieve my frustration. But that wasn't the case. I had been badgering her to go beyond just kissing and restrained petting. One early evening, I made my move:

"C'mon, Sherry, give me a break. Can't we do more than kissing?"

"What if I have sex with you and word gets out?"

"Don't worry about it. Nobody is going to find out what we're doing. Everyone is at the campfire, and those that aren't down on the sports field are doing exactly what we'll be doing in the bunk."

"Doing what?"

"Look Sherry, what do you think the moans and groans you sometimes hear behind the bunk are about? Everyone is making out. Do you want to be left out?"

"So what are they doing?"

"You're a good-looking girl, Sherry, and I'm attracted to you."

"What about my freckles?"

"I know the kids tease you about your freckles, but I like them."

"Don't do that, Marty."

"You have a great pair of tits. I would love to see them. Didn't you ever make out with guys before? Most of the girls in camp have."

"But I don't want to get pregnant. Everyone says I should be careful."

"I don't know what your mother told you, but I'm certainly not going to take advantage of you and screw you in the bunk. I am, however, really attracted to you..."

"Do the other girls let you touch them?"

"Of course they do."

At that moment, I reached over and again put my hand on her clothed breast. This time she didn't take my hand off, but then after fondling her, I started to get really horny. I couldn't help myself: I unbuttoned my fly, hoping that I could get her to touch me, or better yet, to go down on me.

That's all it took. Sherry ran out of the bunk screaming and crying. I ran after her to try to keep her quiet, but it was too late. The other girls from her cabin were returning from the campfire, and they quickly surmised that I had done something sexual to make her near hysterical. They scowled at me. In the aftermath of the Sherry histrionics, I was not too popular for a couple of weeks with various older campers, waiters and counselors. Everyone knew about what I had done, and some kids were even talking about going to the director to get me thrown out of camp. I didn't worry about them, however—after all, I wasn't the only guy in the place trying to make out with a girl and I was right, they didn't follow through.

I was distressed still, by the harsh judgment of me by some of the girls who had previously admired me and shown a passing interest in me. It would take a few weeks before I could recoup some of my diminished status with them. But in spite of all my troubles, it was not long before I set in motion my next move with Alice.

Pretending that I was deeply affected by the fallout from the Sherry debacle, I slid into this pre-manufactured speech to Alice:

"Alice, I fell in love with you the moment I saw you. Remember the scene when Ezio Pinza sings 'Some Enchanted Evening' and falls deeply in love with the stranger across the room. That's how I felt with you these last few weeks. I never believed that a girl like you would even notice a guy like me, much less fall in love with him. You don't know what it's like for someone whose family is poor, and who has no hope of making a better life for himself. Out on the street, I used to fantasize about the pretty girls who were riding in the big cars with their father. I always felt that these girls were out of reach and that the only girls I would have were sluts. I only went to Sherry because I was desperate and lonely. I have been trying to tell your friends for weeks how sorry I am about what happened with Sherry. But I didn't know any better. I hope you can forgive me and we can continue to see each other even after the summer is over." All I wanted was to make sex a part of our relationship, and with that inglorious speech I was able to take Alice at least to a further level of petting. After the flap over my conduct with Sherry, I was a bit more subdued.

Even though I wasn't ready to fully fall in line with Alice's sexual restraints, I could appreciate, in theory, the idea of having healthier, less sexually-driven relationships with girls; I could see that I had changed a fraction for the better and was beginning to realize that women could play a meaningful part in my life, aside from providing blow jobs. For the last two weeks of camp, life for me was relatively uneventful. On the last day of camp, when my new friends and I exchanged telephone numbers, we hugged and kissed (the males and females) each other on the cheek, and this was new to me: I had never before seen friends displaying affection for each other in this open way.

Back in Brownsville, much to my relief, the police had left off searching for the Moose. It seemed, as the prior sexual activity of the girl in question became known, interest in pursuing the case dwindled. Soon after getting home, I took a stroll over to our gang clubhouse. On greeting my old pals, I couldn't help but be aware of the difference in demonstrativeness between them and my friends at camp. No hugging for gang members. I loved the feeling I had had when embracing my camp compatriots, and part of that had to do with the sharing of feelings and emotions openly without having to worry about whether that made me less of a male.

On coming home from camp, I spent most of the time at Alice's house in the best section of Bensonhurst. I would eat with the family, and even though I was a poor kid, her parents were beginning to see me as a boyfriend prospect for their daughter. I became part of the whole *mishpocha* (family thing). I tried, as best I could, to spend a little time with the gang, but it was apparent that my interests were elsewhere. I felt their disappointment, and it hurt me. However, my estrangement did not abate. I did not feel comfortable anymore with the infantile jokes and putdowns that were the mainstay of gang humor. As for the violence and illegal activities, I wanted no part of it. For a while, I remained a member of the gang, but in a peripheral way.

In September I received a letter from my junior high school informing me I had been turned down by Thomas Jefferson and Tilden High School; I had expected to go to one of these neighborhood high schools. The letter was a big blow to my ego, for the only members of our gang who did not get into a local high school were Abe Horowitz and myself. Abe was somewhat slow socially, so it sort of made sense to me that he would be shipped off to a trade school in another borough. Even though I had graduated junior high school with only a sixty-five average, I always assumed that my IQ test scores would be enough to carry me into Jefferson or Tilden, which were not very impressive academic institutions to begin with and almost every asshole who got through junior high in Brownsville could gain admission to one of those schools. The letter indicated that I had been assigned to Straubenmueller Textile High School. What the fuck was going on? Straubenmueller was considered to be one of the worst trade schools in the city. It dawned on me that the sneaky bastards were shipping me off to a trade school in order to break up the gang. The administration in the junior high school and the high schools must have gotten together and decided that it was in the best interest of all of them to exile me to the foreign land of Manhattan and limit my contact with the gang. They must have figured that I would be a troublemaker in a regular academic high school, what with my reputation as a gang leader.

On the first day of school I was floored by the look and condition of the building itself. It was a huge, factory-like building made of gray stone, with metal grates on the windows; inside, the paint was peeling on the walls and the halls smelled rank; outside, garbage was strewn on the sidewalk. Then and there I decided to head right for the Dean of Students' office and negotiate a deal with him that would be advantageous to both of us. On entering the Dean's office I was surprised to find that he was expecting me. He was a stocky Irishman of medium height, already starting to show the signs of being a middle age drinker. Before I could open my mouth, he handed me a copy of my counseling record from junior high school. It was his way of letting me know he was aware of my past history.

After I indicated I had checked out my counseling record, and nothing in it surprised me, the Dean let me know right off he was not going to pussyfoot around with me:

"Let's be clear with each other, Obler; I don't want any bloody trouble from you here."

"What makes you think I'm going to cause you any trouble, sir?"

"Stop the crap, Obler. We know all about you and I'm telling you, you fuck around here, and we'll make your life miserable."

"I think, sir, you're jumping to conclusions. I intend to be a model student. If we can come to an understanding with each other, you won't have any trouble from me. I don't have any idea why a guy with my brains was sent to a trade school but I know this much: The less time I spend here, the better. So why don't you show me around and let me get a feel for the place and the students. Then let's see what kind of an understanding we can come to."

The Dean began showing me the school. While walking past the enormous weaving rooms, full of antiquated looms (brought in, I later found out, from manufacturing plants in Worcester, Mass.), I couldn't help laughing to myself. I, as street smart as I was, couldn't have imagined that the NYC Board of Education planned on preparing me for a career as a weaver. I guess the Dean caught a smirk on my face and responded with these words, accompanied by a malicious grin: "Now would you like to see the lunchroom, Obler?"

Without saying a word, I turned and headed back to his office. Before we had a chance to sit down I confronted him with my proposal.

"Here is my suggestion. I attend classes, even the weaving class for about six weeks, just to establish my presence here. Once the teachers get to know me and I get to know them, they keep marking me present, and at the end of the marking period, you fill in the grade card with a C for me. For my part, I'll keep gang activities out of the school."

"Obler, this isn't Brownsville. This is my turf. Don't make proposals to me, I'll tell you what to do."

"Is that a challenge, sir?"

"Take it any way you want."

"Look, sir, you know the game. Because I'm a student under eighteen, and this school is the lowest of the low, if I cut up what are they going to do? There is no other place to send me to. I know they got to keep me here. There are no gangs in Straubenmueller, and I'm sure you want to keep it that way. All I ask for is that we have nothing to do with each other. You leave me alone and I won't bother you. At the end of 1954, you give me a weaving diploma and I'll find a job. In the meantime, I'll go to a trade related field in the garment center."

"You can go now, Obler. You think you're pretty smart, don't you?"

I got to him, but I could tell he would go along with my proposal. He was afraid I would make waves, and upset his little fiefdom at Straubenmueller.

For the allotted six weeks, I went to school and after school I worked a part-time job in the garment center pushing clothing racks. The Jewish owner of the business liked me and let me work off the payroll. I worked hard and got along with everybody, so at the end of the six weeks I was hired full time. I would go every morning to Bickford's on Thirty-first Street and Seventh Avenue for breakfast. Bickford's was a coffee shop that had a similar spirit to the Automat cafeterias, a people's place in which bums, vagrants, alcoholics, unskilled workers and businessmen sat side by side and talked comfortably with each other. The special was four eggs, hash brown potatoes, toast and coffee, all for twenty-nine cents; sometimes I would gulp down more than one breakfast. Then I would go to work pushing the racks and emptying or filling the trucks in the loading bay.

Once every few weeks I would check in with Dean (O'Rourke) at the trade school to make sure that he was meeting his end of the agreement. By the what-are-you-doing-here look on his face I could tell he was unhappy to see me. I didn't trust him or the school, so I wanted to be sure that they weren't crossing me. I checked the truancy reports in the main office to be sure I was not on their list. I also checked the grade rosters to see whether I was getting my agreed-upon C grades. The Dean was keeping his half of the bargain. And I was keeping mine.

At the end of the day's work, I would ride the subway to spend the evening with Alice at her house. During our time together, I pretended to Alice's family that I was in school all day, plugging away at my academic and vocational interests. It was not long before Alice and I began going on weekends to a Zionist youth center in Boro Park; this center was set up by the youth organization connected to our summer camp. We attended lectures on socialism, introduction to Marx and Engels, and "aliyah" (emigration to Kibbutzim in Israel). We were getting interested in living a different way of life in Israel, as our relationship got more serious. I was falling in love with Alice, and she seemed to feel the same way toward me. Eventually we began to think of the possibility, after graduation, of settling on a kibbutz. But that was not the way it worked out. Once again, my sexual appetite created problems in my life.

Over a year into my relationship with Alice, I couldn't resist having intercourse with Mindy, whom I met at the youth center. She was a friend of Alice and the girlfriend of Bert, whose brother got me the summer camp job. Mindy was a voluptuous but depressed girl whose reputation was that she was an easy make. She interested me, beyond her sexuality, because rumor had it that her father was a mathematical genius who, for a time before alcoholism interfered with his life, had made some contribution to Einstein's theory of relativity. Once Alice, Bert, and I trudged up to the Bronx to visit Mindy, and the four of us spent the afternoon with her father discussing the virtues of socialism over capitalism. The Third Avenue El rumbled overhead throughout our time there, while her father talked and drank scotch; he drank until he slurred his words and I could hardly decipher what he was saying. As I was leaving, Mindy pulled me aside and told me how impressed her father was with me. At that moment, I knew I would have sex with her.

One afternoon I was hanging around the youth center, knowing I had a few hours to waste before Alice would meet me. I said hello to Mindy, who was heading up to the top floor. I waited a few minutes before following her up. When I entered the room, she was lying on a couch pretending she was half-asleep. I went up to her and began unbuttoning her blouse. She opened her eyes as I was unhooking her bra. She never said a word to stop me.

Later, Alice arrived. I was so excited by my conquest that I tried for the first time to have intercourse with her on the same couch I had been with Mindy. I soon found myself telling Alice, "I don't know how much longer I can hold out. I love you."

"You know my feelings about not having intercourse before marriage. That's what my parents expect from me. It's also what most of my friends feel is right."

"Well, your friends are full of shit. I know for a fact that one of your friends has been fucked right here in the youth center."

"Who?"

"I can't tell."

"None of my friends would do that. You're just trying to convince me to sleep with you."

"I learned my lesson at camp with Sherry. Can't you see that this is true love? I'm wild about you and I can't wait any longer."

Alice never gave in to my attempt to coerce her, but one day we were heavily petting on her living-room couch, and in a bit of disarray clothingwise, when we heard the key turn in the lock of the front door. As we were hastily reassembling our clothes her mother and father walked into the room and saw us. The relationship was over. They threw me out of the house, and I struggled home doubled up with the worst stomach pain I had ever experienced. I knew in spite of Alice's love for me, she could never stand up to her parents and would have to bow to their demand that she not have anything to do with me.

On my way home the pain didn't let up, so I called Solly and asked him to meet me in the lobby of my family's apartment house on Herzl Street. Solly had become more pronouncedly queer—more flighty—since the lynching days. I always liked him although I had treated him poorly in front of the gang members in order to avoid being too closely identified with him. But when I was alone with him, I found him to be a sensitive, intelligent, caring person. And that is why I called him.

On walking into the lobby, I saw Solly and burst out crying.

"What happened, Moose?"

"She's going to drop me. I don't want to lose her."

"Why will she drop you?"

"Her parents came in while we were in a bit of an awkward position with our clothing."

"Is that a reason for her to stop seeing you?"

"She's too much the good Jewish daughter to stand up to her parents. On my way out of the house I pleaded with her to come with me, but she couldn't do it."

"I understand why you feel the way you do. And I know it won't mean much to you now while you're in such pain, but there'll be plenty of other girls to fall in love with. You're special. You're a bright guy who feels for people and someone I can talk to."

"You're not going to like what I did with Bert's girlfriend."

"You got to be kidding. With Mindy? What happened?"

"I fucked her at the youth center on 50th Street."

"Holy crap. Does Bert know?"

"I hope not. I've already got a rep as a scum bag with the women."

"No kidding."

"Do me a favor, Solly. Don't tell anyone about any of this. I know you're still buddies with Bert."

"Bert is going to go bananas if he finds out. Did you force Mindy to do it?"

"She didn't stop me."

"Was she good?"

"She had big tits."

Six days later Bert woke me up with a telephone call at two A.M. Solly swears he never said a word to anyone about Mindy and me, but keeping a secret was never a strongpoint of his. It was my fault for telling him. I was only half-awake, but I heard Bert yelling and screaming into the phone.

"How the fuck could you do this to me? The girls at camp were right about you. You're a fucking low life. You use everyone. I don't know why I introduced you to my brother, and got you into the movement. I thought you had more to you than the other fuckheads in the gang. I see I was wrong. How could you hurt such a sweet, weak girl like Mindy?"

"Hey, I didn't force her. Why ya blaming me? She's your girlfriend."

"I'm glad Alice dumped you, you prick. You better watch your ass, man. I'm not gonna forget this."

"Don't threaten me, ya little *mockey*. You know better than to do that." In the days following Bert's angry call, I started to think about what I had done, and how I deceived him and exploited Mindy. And, for that matter, my behavior with Alice wasn't so hot either. I began to get a deepening sense that my life was going nowhere.

Some months before Alice and I broke up, I started to pal around with some new friends, marginally connected to the Zionist-Socialist youth movement, who hung out in Washington Square Park and other areas of Greenwich Village. They were a little older than me and came from educated middle class families. They looked upon me as a bright, raw, tough, lower class kid who had considerable potential to pull himself out of poverty. In some ways I became a reclamation project for them. We would spend long night's way into the morning discussing socialism and capitalism, the working class… and a more humanitarian world.

My friend, Jeffrey, the most intellectual of the group, told me to see a foreign film, *La Strada*, directed by Frederico Fellini. This was only the second foreign movie I had ever seen. I was quite taken with it. I found myself identifying—at least a small part of me—with the Anthony Quinn character, a strong silent, brutal, manipulative man who misused the woman in his life (played by Giuletta Masina). I had told Jeffrey that I wanted to change and become more like the good-natured, kind-hearted, philosophical clown in the movie, who tried unsuccessfully to help the victimized woman leave the abusive Quinn character. We both laughed at the mutual recognition of my likeness to the brutish, selfish male character.

The old strategies of manipulation and conning were wearing thin. My friends in the Village were sharp enough to catch on to the self-serving and controlling way I was used to operating. They liked to think that in their world people treated each other caringly and fairly. I wasn't convinced of this, but I was intrigued by the possibility that things could be better somewhere else. Anyway, I was getting fed up with my family and I was setting my sights higher than hanging out with my buddies from the street. I think the time I spent with Alice and some of my new friends had broadened my idea of how people could relate to each other.

The breakup with Alice left me free to leave the city. My friends in the youth movement had been talking about going to live in a kibbutz in Israel. I decided, after Bert's call, that this was the time for me to go to Israel whether or not my friends would come with me. I might add, however, that an incentive to my leaving was the rumor that Bert and a few of his buddies had gotten hold of zip guns and were going to use them on me.

When officials from the Zionist youth movement offered me a ticket to immigrate to Israel and arranged for me to visit a kibbutz, I took it, even though I wasn't going to graduate high school.

I had written Alice what day I would be leaving from the Brooklyn Pier to go to Israel, and she was there to see me off, along with most of my friends. It was a glorious, sunny day, and Alice looked great, causing me second thoughts of whether I was doing the right thing in leaving. She pressed her body on the railing of the deck and whispered, through her crying that she would meet me shortly on the kibbutz. We all went below to check out my stateroom, which I shared with four strangers; I showed my friends my enormous metal double-decker trunk with drawers on each side. It contained loads of cheap Woolworth type items that my mother had bought on Belmont Avenue from the pushcart peddlers and stuffed into the trunk. She had purchased for me socks, plastic containers, underwear, glass-bowls, artificial fruit, silverware, some cheap jeans and tee shirts, and lots of other inexpensive trinkets and things. They made fun of my collection of valuables.

My friends, knowing that I wanted to spend some time with Alice alone, considerately left the stateroom, agreeing to meet in fifteen or so minutes on deck before they had to depart. Alice was still tearful, and I asked her what was wrong, although I knew she was already missing me.

She looked at me with longing and said, "I don't understand why you're leaving alone and not with the group, aliyah. I also don't understand why you're not finishing school and getting your diploma before you leave."

I leveled with her, replying, "Look, Alice, I never told you the truth about my high school experiences. School always meant a lot more to you than it did to me. For me it was a bullshit experience. I hardly ever showed up there and what am I going to do—be a weaver on the kibbutz? To be honest, I stayed in school this last year to impress your family that I was a serious student like all your friends. I didn't tell you a lot about me." I confided in her that my home and street life were too ugly for me to do more than just hint at. It was hard for her to hear the things I was saying, and it was a sad parting for a number of reasons. When we said our goodbyes, we both, I think, knew that this might be the last time we saw each other. It pretty much turned out that way, though I remember seeing her once more, briefly, after I returned to the States.

I remember the feeling I had as the ship was pulling out of the dock and my friends were waving goodbye. I saw Alice among them, waving also. Despite the tug at my heart of leaving, I found solace in knowing that no matter how bad my life had been at home, I had been able to find a way out. And I had the strength to set out on my journey alone. I yelled out to my friends, "See you soon in the Negev."

Within twenty-four hours aboard the ship, I had become buddies with the working staff. I preferred to spend time with the crew, with whom I felt more at ease than my fellow passengers. I couldn't help trying to sound educated when talking to the passengers; whereas I could be more myself when talking to the ship workers. However, I did spend some relax-time with a cute bohemian girl whom, in spite of my declaration to change my habits with women, I had earmarked for intimate contact. She enjoyed my company but declined my persistent attempts to join her in her stateroom.

In the days aboard ship I had a lot of time to think about my life and my voyage to Israel. I decided not to go to the Negev [a desert frontier in southern Israel] as planned and eventually meet up with a few of my friends from the youth movement. Instead I made up my mind to stay for a while with a friend, Aryeh, at a kibbutz called Beit Hashita in the Amek Valley in the northern part of Israel.

I had first gotten to know Aryeh during summer camp. He, I found out at some point in the summer, was the nephew of the former Prime Minister of Israel, Ben Gurion. His name was Aryeh Ben Gurion. He was one of four or five people affiliated with the Toronto branch of the youth movement who visited the camp when I was there.

We got quite friendly during his visit, and he encouraged me to come to see him in Toronto any time I wanted, before he returned to his home base at Beit Hashita. Some months after camp ended I took him up on it, needing a break from the garment center and wanting to learn more about the youth movement. I hitchhiked from New York all the way up to Toronto. It was my first trip outside of New York State—not to speak of another country.

A few of the drivers who gave me a lift were sort of strange—as is sometimes the case with those who pick up hitchhikers—but I was pretty fearless, coming from where I did in Brooklyn. I made good time on the road and it was not long before I was calling Aryeh in Toronto. He met me, and offered to put me up in a little room in the back of the movement Center. It seemed fine to me. But things did not go that well. Aside from the camp experience, this was the first time I had stayed away from home and been responsible for taking care of my own living quarters. I hadn't realized how much of the household chores had been done by my mother. I had never done my own laundry, cooked or ironed a shirt, so I let things pile up, never bothered by the big mess in my room.

One day Aryeh walked into my room and noticed a stench of garbage and dirty laundry assaulting his nostrils. He was pissed and yelled at me, "How can you live like this? It's a pigsty. I thought you were a mensch—Jews don't live like this. You act like a goy. This place hasn't been cleaned in weeks."

I felt exposed, but covered it up by acting as if it were all a trivial matter. "What's the big deal, Aryeh? It's just a little dirt."

"Your clothes stink. Didn't you ever learn to take care of yourself?"

"My mother took care of that stuff. Isn't that the job of women?"

"What kind of socialist are you? You intend to live on a kibbutz? In our society men and women are equal. Do you think the women on the kibbutz are going to clean and cook and wash your clothing?"

"It wouldn't bother me, if they did."

"Obler, you are as messed up as this room, if you think like that."

The conversation ended on this unpleasant note. It was nice to talk about socialism and living on a kibbutz and sharing duties, but taking care of my living quarters was not something I was used to. I was still the Jewish son who expected women to take care of him.

Aryeh had given me the assignment on my arrival in Toronto to prepare the Friday night Oneg Shabbat (a performance celebrating the next day Sabbath). When Friday came I sang a ditty I had heard somewhere that began, "The working class can kiss my ass, I've got the boss's job at last." I was still angry with Aryeh, although I knew that his criticism was justified. But I came to find out later, in Israel, that I was more of an unregenerate capitalist than I thought myself to be. The exploitative mentality that had become ingrained in me from my home and Brownsville life was not easily expunged. My new friends in Greenwich Village had told me that I was 'full of it', and that I was the last guy to give up the advantages of capitalism. They knew I was cheap, conning and controlling, and that it would not be easy for me to change my old habits.

Mostly to keep Aryeh's friendship I made an effort to clean up my living quarters, and, in spite of my provocative ditty at the Oneg Shabbat, I managed to put together a decent group of performers and a skit of sorts. I think Aryeh was glad to see me go when the two-and-a-half weeks of my visit were up; but I had won a little respect from him, enough so that he invited me to come to see him in Israel after he completed his work in Canada. I didn't think he expected me to take him up on it, probably because he figured I would not be too anxious to bust my ass on a kibbutz, in spite of my espoused desire to live in a communal environment. Aryeh would later regret his invitation as I outdid myself getting into trouble and in exporting the capitalist ethic to the Israelites at Beit Hashita.

At about the time I was beginning to wonder how much longer I could last in the quiet, uneventful days and nights aboard ship—this kind of peaceful, calm on the boat not being the easiest thing to tolerate for a kid used to the excitement of the city streets—word came over the loudspeaker that we were within five hours of our destination, Tel Aviv. The time went slowly; as it does when one wants it to go fast, but eventually a tugboat met us and took us into the landing dock. An anticipatory excitement coursed through me.

CHAPTER FIVE:
THE KIBBUTZ

After disembarking and going through customs, I made my way to a makeshift postal stand on the dock, where I negotiated with a postal worker to send my luggage to the Beit Hashita kibbutz. Then it was out onto the streets of Tel Aviv. I was surprised to hear the familiar sounds of Yiddish mixed with Hebrew spoken in the bustling streets. I came across pushcart stalls at which customers bargained, with gusto, with the seller in Yiddish, some English, and Hebrew, much as I was used to hearing around the pushcart markets in Brooklyn.

After getting my fill of Tel Aviv in a few days, I decided to make two stops at kibbutzim outside of the city, where friends of mine from America had settled. I wanted to get a flavor of kibbutz life before I stayed at Beit Hashita, as if I could get out some of the kinks in my personality before meeting up with Aryeh again. As for sexual activity, I was still hitting on women and ended up having sexual relations with a married woman in both places. My relations with these women preempted my getting involved in kibbutz life before arriving at Beit Hashita. And obviously no significant kinks in my personality were ironed out in these circumstances. I might add, though, that it shook me up to see that these women were not the docile, passive women that I was used to. I had sex with them in my not unfamiliar brusque, self-serving fashion with little attention to their needs… only they let me know in no uncertain terms that I wasn't much of a lover and had a lot to learn about women. It was a turnabout to be with women who were so outspoken and perceived their relationship with men as equal. Then, on the bus to Beit Hashita, I noticed numbers of women in army outfits with guns slung over their shoulders, hitchhiking their way across the country. That pretty much took my breath away...

The bus pulled up to the entrance gate of Beit Hashita, and I stepped out and looked around. The land itself was dusty and sun-baked, some brown shrubs here and there, and small clumps of palm trees—the only green in sight—separated by considerable distances. In front of me was a large olive factory (I knew this by the picture on the wall facing me of men and women pressing olives) and fairly far away was a community of one-family homes that reminded me of the dwellings in Levittown. I caught sight of Aryeh trudging towards me and was cheered to see him. After exchanging greetings and a little chatter about the bus ride, he took me to a lengthy dining hall inside of which were hundreds of people, seated at long, wooden tables, having lunch. There was a lively din in the room; everyone seemed to be having a good time. After we ate a plentiful meal, mostly of foods that it would take me some time to get used to, Aryeh introduced me to Devora, an attractive, chubby woman, who volunteered that she would take me to my quarters. We walked along a cracked-dirt path, for about a quarter of a mile and then came upon a meticulously-cared-for garden. I was impressed how neatly and efficiently the kibbutz was run. On relaying this to Devora, I could see that she looked favorably on my show of enthusiasm. In conversation with her, I learned that she was married with three children; that her husband had just arrived in Russia as part of an Israeli dance troupe touring Eastern Europe; and that he was apparently an important official of the kibbutz. She asked me where I was from in the States, and I labored at the task of explaining to an Israeli what life in New York City was like.

As we walked along, the dirt path gradually became indistinguishable from the dusty, sandy earth surrounding us. We came to a bunch of run-down shacks that were much less inviting than the Levittown homes I first saw. Devorah said that this is the place where newcomers lived during their orientation period. She pointed out the shack I would be staying at, and mentioned that I would be attending Ulpan (language school) after work to learn Hebrew. The inside of my one-room dwelling was bare and shabby, making me think of photographs I'd seen of houses in Appalachia. I felt, as I guess I was supposed to, that I was a second-class citizen, and would have to earn my way up to become a full-fledged kibbutznik. My guide gave me some basic information about how things were run, then said goodbye, adding that she hoped I would like it here.

After two days of relative idleness for me on the kibbutz, Aryeh along with some of his cohorts came to wake me up at six A.M. in my bunk. Looking as though he had lots to do and wanted to deal with me as quickly as possible, Aryeh informed me that my rest period was over and that it was time to go to work. They took me to a tractor with a large platform behind it, which was attached by chains. They asked me if I knew how to drive a car; I said yes and they told me to get up on the tractor and follow them. We headed out of the kibbutz through a field until we came to a large, sandy, barren plot of land full of broken rocks. One of the guys, speaking in rudimentary English, told me to take the rocks by hand, pile them on the platform and drive them about a tenth of a mile down the road to an empty plot and dump them. He handed me a thermos and a lunch box and told me that they'd pick me up at four o'clock. I looked at him incredulously and said, "You got to be kidding." Obviously they were not, because they left me there to start work. I took off my shirt and spent the whole morning moving the rocks by tractor to the designated location. While I worked I felt isolated and lonely. With the afternoon sun baking on my back, I sat down on a rock to have lunch. I opened up the lunch box and saw it was full of fried eggplant, some kind of mushy paste (actually humus), some dried tomatoes and olives, and two pieces of bread (pita). I couldn't eat it; it all seemed too foreign to me. I opened the thermos, which contained a strange white liquid that tasted sour (leben yogurt). I put the entirety of my lunch on the ground and lay back on the rocks, looking at the surrounding hills. I was pleasantly surprised to see a bunch of guys sitting on a hilltop no more than five hundred feet from where I was. I got up and started walking towards them. Something, however, stopped me, and soon I noticed that they were making fun of me. I also saw that they were sitting behind a machine gun. Their army outfits were a different color than the ones I had seen the Israeli soldiers wearing. I followed my intuition, which told me to stop where I was and go back to work. When the kibbutz people arrived at four o'clock, I asked them who the guys on the hilltop were. A confident young man, whose English was fluent, replied: "Oh, you mean the Lebanese."

I was shaken up. "What the fuck is going on? I could have been killed."

"Ah, don't worry. It's just Arabs.

"Just Arabs?"

"They don't know how to shoot. They're dumb. They probably think you're an Arab."

"Do I have to keep coming out here?"

"Tomorrow we bring you out and you move the rocks back from where you got them."

"To what end?"

"Don't question the seniors' decision regarding clearing the land. Do your job. You're a worker, like everyone else. This isn't America. In a couple of weeks I work in the fields, you work in the laundry."

"Can't I switch with you now?"—my Brownsville humor couldn't be repressed.

I saw that things were not going to be easy. I figured that they were just testing me, to see how I would respond to the meaningless task of moving rocks back and forth and to the danger of the armed Arab soldiers on the nearby hilltop. I guess they viewed all Americans as spoiled children who came to the kibbutz full of dreams and idealism without having any recognition of the harsh realities of life here. In the months that followed, the rigidities and aridness and sparseness of life on the kibbutz were such that my hopefulness that things would get better began to ebb; it would not be too long before I had strong intimations that my stay at Beit Hashita would be of short duration.

After some weeks of the aimless rock duty, I was placed in a kitchen job and stayed there for a stretch, eventually transferring to the laundry, the crew for which consisted of mostly women whose hard and firm bodies did not go unnoticed by me. I spent the early part of the day studying Hebrew with other newcomers and worked at my job in the afternoon. It so happened that I was placed in the same unit of the laundry as Devorah. We became friends and more than that. One evening after work, she invited me to her house for a snack. I asked her once we got inside, "Where are your kids?"

"On the collective, children live together in separate quarters from their parents."

"Holy shit, that would have been great for me when I was a kid."

She laughed, but there was no way for her, having lived so long on the kibbutz, to pick up on the grim humor in my remark.

I ended up staying way into the night. Although she was married, she had no qualms about sleeping with me. Once again, I was shaken up by how sexually aggressive and outspoken the kibbutz women were. She said to me, "You don't know much about love-making, do you?"

"That's just what some other Israeli woman told me. What's wrong with the way I make love?"

"First of all you don't spend any time touching and kissing before entering me. And making love usually lasts more than a few minutes. I like to be licked, too... and a woman wants more time to achieve an orgasm."

Even though she was disappointed in me, she obviously liked me and made it clear that she still wanted to see me. She was only in her late twenties, but her marriage, I found out in the following weeks, had lost the intimacy of earlier years. Her husband's dance career and official responsibilities in the kibbutz siphoned off a lot of his energies. She was tired of spending evenings by herself and open to male companionship. She took to me because, as she put it, "I can talk to you." As a lover, even though I made efforts to be less self-centered and more aware of Devorah's needs, there was a large part of me that cut off tenderness and closeness in the sex act and just wanted to satisfy my animal needs. I never seemed to get free of my father coming home drunk and forcing my mother to satisfy his needs... I was like him even though I knew my mother hated his sexual demands. Yet I had a skill for intimacy in conversation: In conversation, I could reach out beyond my own egocentricity, and respond to the other person. Something pushed me to know all I could about the life, especially the inner life, of other people and especially those to whom I was drawn. Devorah was feeling at an impasse in her life and unappreciated, and talking to me touched a chord in her. As her dependence on me increased, to the point where I began to get a little worried about it, outside forces impinged on the relationship. For one, her husband's tour was about over; and two, the elder officials of the kibbutz were becoming suspicious about the relationship, causing us to have to stop meeting at night and pretend that we were only casual friends.

As it got nearer to her husband's return, Dev let me know that she would have to stop seeing me. I knew this was very hard for her to do, but I ignored that and vented my anger: "I thought the collective practiced free love, and that women had the same rights as men sexually. You don't think your husband's banging some of the girls in the troupe?"

"He probably is... but on the kibbutz, married women having affairs is unacceptable, particularly if they have children. It's taboo."

"So that means I can't come over anymore?"

"Don't make it worse..."

Gideon, a friend I had made during my short stint at kitchen duty, introduced me to Racquel, who was born on the kibbutz. I could tell she was attracted to me, maybe because of my body; I was in pretty good shape after my stint hauling rocks. Having been hurt by Devorah's abrupt cessation of the relationship, I now turned to Racquel. This time I wasn't rejected as an inadequate lover. She was a troubled woman—I do not mean to imply that only a troubled woman could consider me an adequate lover but perhaps I shouldn't rule it out—and after every time we made love she would weep long and copiously. I kept asking her what was so upsetting, but she couldn't explain it. Once I spoke to Gideon about her crying and how disturbing it was to me. He didn't know the explanation of her grief, but he reassured me that she had told him that I was a good lover. It was good for my self-esteem to hear this, for I could not be sure, that when she said as much to me, she was not just trying to make me feel better.

After a while, I began to pick up that a number of my new friends in the collective would say things, usually offhandedly and without much conscious intent, indicating dissatisfaction with their life. Even though they had grown up in the caring and controlled environment of the kibbutz, they seemed to yearn for something else, something that they couldn't get where they were—maybe it had to do with stories they had heard about city life, America, or simply reflected some desire on their part to be in an environment which gave more room to individual development. There was something about the parched earth, the cookie-cutter housing and merely functional buildings, and the unchanging routine that gave a gray tint to the world of the collective. Socialist equality made everybody the same: there was little challenge to get ahead or to pursue their individual creativity and uniqueness... or to rebel against the order of things. Even the so-called love among the unmarrieds left something to be desired. They could have as many partners as they wanted without guilt; but sex without love, romance, and commitment grew tiring for them. While I was more than happy to take part in this guiltless sex, I could see that the easy availability of sexual contacts impacted adversely on the love life of the participants. My guess is that the absence of romance and drama took away much of the vitality and passion in the sexual partnerships. And the same was true in the overall workings of kibbutz life, having to do with the sameness of the routine and the downplaying of individuality.

Another thing that troubled me about kibbutz life had to do with the prejudice towards the Arabs. The members of the collective professed that all people are equal, yet they treated the Arabs who worked for them on the kibbutz as inferiors and cheap labor. And non-members, like myself, were treated as secondary citizens. Then there was the hypocrisy about money: the kibbutz ideology stressed that money was not important and materialism, as in capitalism, was destructive, yet I believed that most of the kibbutzniks secretly yearned to acquire money in order to purchase the same things that people in capitalist society wanted. To control this longing among members, the collective paid each worker four pounds (about four dollars) a month, making it clear that there was no point to spending all one's time trying to get a bankroll.

The months passed, and the time came when Devorah's husband returned. He was not too pleased at what had transpired in his absence. Some of his buddies told him about the affair, and word got to me that he was out to get me with an Israeli submachine gun. At least Bert was restricted to a zip gun. I requested protection from the kibbutz elders, and Aryeh, predictably, was very angry with me—here was his invited friend causing trouble in the kibbutz. He brusquely informed me that my status as a pending kibbutz member was in jeopardy. He could not, he said, prevent me from going on trial before the kibbutz council. The issue of the trial was not that I was to be punished for what I had done, but whether I could reform and become an upstanding member of the collective. To me this meant becoming like every other routinized soul there.

At the trial I was accused of being an American male chauvinist and opportunist who was unredeemable. My defense was that I wasn't doing anything different than what was done by a lot of people; the reason I was on trial was that I had humiliated a kibbutz member of high ranking. My argument was rejected. I was given a week's notice to depart.

When I requested the few pounds that I was supposed to have accumulated for work done over the period I had been there, they ruled that I had forfeited my right to it by my transgressions. I told them I didn't have enough money to get a bus out of the kibbutz. They didn't want to hear it.

Devorah did not have to go on trial. But she came to me a couple of days before I was scheduled to leave and begged me to take her with me. I wanted to, but I was nineteen years old and wasn't ready to be straddled with the burden of making it in Tel Aviv with her. I gave her a phony story that once I got settled in Tel Aviv I'd write to her and she could join me. I privately wondered how she could leave her kids, but I guess the answer was that the collective would take care of them.

Using my manipulative skills, I spread the word through my fellow Ulpan students that I would be selling all of my American goods on the Sabbath at noon on the day I had to be out of the kibbutz. I knew that word would get around, and that I might get a few customers. I was in no way prepared for the lines that formed outside my shack, starting at eight-thirty in the morning. They all were waiting to buy American goods. Some thirty-five kibbutzniks were lined up, clenching handfuls of money that they had saved.

They bought everything my mother had packed in the trunk; at the end of the sale tempers flared. Some of those present started to demand that I come up with more American goods. I actually took off my pants and sold my last pair of underwear, along with my watch and a wrist bracelet. Earlier, when I sold the jeans my mother had packed, there were almost fistfights over them. There could be no doubt, in this instance, that capitalism had prevailed.

Things had gotten so bad when I announced the end of the sale that they sent for security to break up the proceedings and head-off further trouble. The security spirited me away and gave me to a few kibbutz members, including Aryeh, who were assigned to escort me off the premises. This little group was furious at me. I still can see clearly Aryeh's scornful expression after I asked him to hold my empty trunk until I could send for it. He turned me down. One of my escorts let me know that it would be in my interests to never show my capitalist face again at Beit Hashita. I thought he put it quite aptly, and I thanked him for his concern. Clearly it did not endear me to him.

CHAPTER SIX:
RETURN

I t was almost two years after being heaved from the kibbutz, that I actually left Israel. And when I departed I took with me my new wife, Dalite, who was four months pregnant with my baby. It wasn't too long after I left the kibbutz that I had met her in Tel Aviv.

I found her attractive—abetted by her being well-endowed. And she had the qualifications that led me to think that she could complete me, along the lines of the psychoanalyst Theodore Reik, who believed that young people are self-duped into falling in love by their feeling that the other person completes them in crucial areas where they are lacking... related to their child-formed sense of self. She came from an educated, middle-class family, she seemed at ease in talking with cultured, knowledgeable friends and relatives; she reminded me of some of the girls from the summer camp and East Flatbush, whose background seemed superior to mine. We bonded quickly, and enjoyed talking and doing things together. Despite my lack of real education and not having a clear-cut path to build an economic future, along with my being four years younger than her and devoid of sophistication, she had no qualms about falling in love with me.

Like Devorah, she let me know that I wasn't very adept at making love, but, contrary to Dev, she tutored me to not just jump all over her and satisfy myself... and after a while I was able to have sex that incorporated a bit of restraint, and conveyed some cognition on my part that it indeed mattered with whom I was sharing my bed.

I imagine I appealed to my future wife, in some fundamental way, because I displayed a confidence in myself, and was able to support myself for almost two years, with various jobs. In retrospect, she was a mother-figure for me and that probably meant more to me than I realized, since I was more scared of being on my own in Israel than I could admit; and to add to that, I also missed my friends—and I'm sure my family, as well. In Tel Aviv people were friendly, and seemingly accepting of me; but I couldn't overcome my feeling of being an outsider.

Part of my attraction to Dalite, in Reikian terms, no doubt had something to do with her coming from well-to-do parents, having completed a degree in architecture, having obtained a good job in her field after serving in the army... which gave her a personal security and sureness that I could latch on to; and not inconsequentially, apart from Reikian considerations, she had a place to live and invited me to move in with her, an offer that I wasted no time accepting.

For the rest of my stay in Israel, she provided an anchor that helped me to grow up and formulate what it might be like to live a successful middle-class life. I was drawn to her but I can't say I ever fully fell in love with her. I should also mention that the same contradictory pattern that I had evolved with my mother, as a child, asserted itself with Dalite. I would be extremely dependent on my mother and, alternately, extremely rejecting and detached. This, decidedly, was a deeply-fixed and not freely-arrived-at pattern. And I asserted it with Dalite. Moreover I was unabashedly self-centered, and the idea of making the relationship better and more romantic was not uppermost in my mind. After living with her in Tel Aviv for quite a long time, I was asking myself heavy-duty questions about whether I wanted to stay in the relationship and leaning toward the negative. And it was at this time, that she told me she was pregnant.

She made it clear that she did not need me to stay with or marry her, and had no problem having the child on her own. To my surprise, I could not live with that idea. The guilt was too much for me. There was something about abandoning my own child, coming from my personal fears of abandonment, that left me with a sinking feeling that I couldn't tolerate. I suggested that we marry in Tel Aviv and fairly soon fly to the U.S. where she could have the baby. She beamed with happiness and assented. In a strange way, the idea of marriage didn't throw me, for I figured I could get out of it if I felt trapped. Great way to begin a marriage.

As for staying in Israel, it was pretty much not a viable alternative for me. I knew I had very little prospect of getting a good job in Israel—I supported myself by having various low-paying jobs with American companies—being twenty-two with not even a high school diploma. Although her family offered to help us, there was no way I felt comfortable with their help and, just personally, I had had enough of Israel. I had failed in the kibbutz and found the country at large to be militaristic, elitist and condescending towards Arabs and non-Jews—none of which sat well with me. But more than anything else, I missed my life in New York City.

After arriving in New York, we went straight to my parents' home on Herzl Street. Walking up the stairs I smelled the old mix of Jewish cooking and funny apartment smell that was so familiar. I knocked on the paint-worn door.

When Debbie opened the door she let out a shriek, "Muttla's here and he's got a pregnant Jewish girl from Israel with him." How she put all that together, I couldn't say. But I introduced my wife to my sister, and quickly made my way into the apartment. I could see that things had further deteriorated in the two years I had been gone. There were crumbs on the kitchen table, clothes strewn on chairs and the floor, the stove hadn't been cleaned for months, and cockroaches were in evidence on the sink and walls.

"Marty, why didn't you tell me you were coming?" my mother asked after I introduced Dalite. "I didn't have a chance to clean up the place."

Even though I had prepared my wife for this moment, the stark reality of the situation was hard for her to take. She was pained at the poverty of the apartment, the grossness of Debbie's initial remark, and taken aback by how old and tired and slovenly my mother looked in her faded smock. But, like the true upper-middle-class woman that she was, she warmly told my mother, "It's a very nice apartment you have here, and I want to thank you for taking us in." Just then Phyllis and my father entered the kitchen and Debbie grabbed my wife's hand pulling her toward the bathroom. As she was pulling Dalite away, I stopped them and introduced my wife to my father and my older sister. I could see my father's glow that I had married such a seemingly dignified woman and he embraced me.

"How come you didn't let us know what day you were returning?" Phyllis questioned.

"I didn't have a chance to. After Dalite was midway through her pregnancy, we decided not to wait any longer before coming to the States. We wound up waiting for the visa in Genoa. Dalite fainted on a bus, and had to be taken to the local emergency room. A local official gave us the visa and told us to leave within twenty-four hours so there would be no further trouble with Americans in Italy."

"Never mind this stuff, let me show her the rest of the apartment," Debbie said and led her into the bathroom. We all followed. Debbie flicked on the light switch and shouted, "See the bulb. You turn the switch and the light goes on. She then turned the bathtub faucet on and announced, "Water, just turn the knob and it comes out." After this, she lifted up her skirt, sat down on the toilet seat and said, "You pull the handle, and flush, it all goes down the toilet. It's not the desert." This was beyond even Dalite's resourcefulness, and she turned red and was speechless.

"Debbie, you idiot. What makes you think this woman grew up like a Bedouin in the desert? What do you mean flush? You think she never sat on a toilet or turned on a light?"

"How was I supposed to know? You never wrote us and told us what life was like there."

"Forget it. Dalite is tired. Should we sleep in the living room?"

"No, you'll stay in Poppa's room, and he can stay in the living room." Phyllis said.

When we were alone I apologized to Dalite for bringing her into my Brownsville home, but I explained that I had no choice, since, as she knew, we were poor.

On my return home I had to get used to seeing new faces on the streets of my old neighborhood. A few of the guys hanging out on the corner of Herzl Street didn't even know me as the Moose. It became apparent to me that I had to find a way to get out of Brownsville and build a life for myself... and not just have another transitional adolescent adventure like the camp and living in the kibbutz had been for me. I was married and had a kid coming. My first priority was to get a job. I worried that all I could do was push clothing racks in the garment center. A ghetto kid, like me, implicitly knew that you couldn't get a decent job without a high school diploma and some college. In some ways I resisted giving up my adolescence, and in others, I was adult beyond my years. Living in poverty and in a dysfunctional family, I had the knowledge forced upon me that life could be harsh, bitter and chaotic, and this knowledge of the brutality of existence made me adult before I was chronologically and emotionally ready to assume this role. It was this precocious adult part of me that fully comprehended that I was up against a stark choice: I would either become a subsistence-wage earner like so many men in the neighborhood or somehow find a way to make a better life for myself.

My marriage, in this period of my life, was good for me even though I was not happy in it. Dalite was older than me and had lived a much more secure life. She did a lot for me by just not worrying so much about our not having money while starting a family. I guess coming from wealthy parents she had the luxury of always expecting, even in tough times, that there would be enough food on the table and money in the bank. She adored me, had confidence in my ability to manage, and wanted so much to have our baby and be a mother.

The phone rang in the middle of the night; I figured it was Cabrini Hospital calling to let me know Dalite had given birth. I was staying for the night at Solly's apartment, which was on the Lower East Side near the hospital. I turned on the light and woke Solly. I really should have been in the waiting room of the hospital, but I was so scared, I guess, of being a father and taking on the awesome responsibility of supporting a family, that I returned to my old habit of relying on magical thinking to help me through anxiety-producing situations. In my thinking, as long as I stayed away from the hospital, everything would be okay and my wife and child would be protected from the malefic forces in the universe.

"Solly, get the fucking phone. It's got to be the hospital."

"Don't you have hands?"

"I'm too nervous to talk." I picked up the phone and handed it to him.

I could tell from what Solly was saying that it was the doctor calling and that Dalite had given birth and everything was all right. Still, it was nice to hear Solly say, after he hung up, "Congratulations, Moose, it's a boy."

A few minutes later the phone rang again and I panicked, thinking it was the hospital informing me that something was not going well.

"Take it, answer it, I can't." Again I handed the receiver to Solly.

They exchanged greetings and a few words, then I heard Solly say: "Maggie, why are you calling Moose?"

(I had given Maggie, Solly's telephone number, and told her that I would be there for the night.)

He covered the speaker with his hand, and said incredulously, "... you fuck, you're screwing Maggie." He passed the phone, "You take it."

"Hi Maggie, I can't talk now, my wife just had a baby."

"I'm in a lot of trouble."

"What do you mean you're in trouble?"

"I missed my period and I'm well into my second month."

"It's not the first time you missed your period."

"... but I'm way past the end of the first month and almost near the end of the second month."

"Look Maggie, I can't handle this now. Too much is going on, I'll call you later."

(Oops... prior to the above conversation, I hadn't mentioned that I was having a thing with Maggie. I had known her before I left for Israel. She had joined the Zionist Youth Movement as a young dancer who wanted to perform Israeli folk dance; we started a friendship, largely on the basis of my initiative, since I was quite taken with her. When I returned from Israel, I contacted her after six weeks and one thing led to another. Looking back at this time, I would say that I was— largely unconsciously—petrified of becoming a father and my affair with Maggie had to do with a regressive wish to return to adolescence, so I could avoid the responsibilities of starting a family... add to that the ambivalence I felt towards my wife. But whatever the psychological push for my affair, I was attracted to Maggie and did not stop seeing her until much later.)

After the birth of my son, Delmore, in 1959, my life began to get very hectic. I quickly obtained my GED high School equivalency diploma; enrolled at Brooklyn College, accelerating my studies so that I got my undergraduate degree in three-and-a-half years. I was spending nearly fifteen to twenty hours a day, seven days a week, working and studying. I had a strange capacity to be able to go non-stop continually at an amazing pace. And I had no trouble finding challenging work and getting through school, summa cum laude, at the same time. I guess I was bright and very driven to succeed and did not allow my fears of failure to supplant the feeling that nothing could hold me back.

On the surface, the turnabout couldn't have been greater... and the ease in which I made my way was hard to fathom, even for me at the time. I just seemed to zip through the work world and the academic world, as if I were a bird flying through air.

After prodding my memory, I am able to recollect how I got my first job that led indirectly to my introduction to the world of psychotherapy. I was standing by a bulletin board outside the registrar's office at the college, where student employment positions were listed. What caught my attention was a listing for a position with United Cerebral Palsy of New York City, working as an aid with severely handicapped and brain-damaged people. I said to myself, I can do this; after all, my parents functioned on a sub-level and I lived with that. The pay for a fulltime position wasn't bad and the job was in a neighborhood adjacent to Brownsville that I was familiar with—in fact, memories came back to me as I was standing in front of the bulletin board of beating up members of a rival gang right on the corner where the Cerebral Palsy Center was located. My major hesitation in applying for this position had to do with whether I could handle being a fulltime student and having a fulltime job. The decision was not hard to make, since a part-time job just wouldn't swing it now that I had a child to support and needed to move out of my parents' home and into an apartment of our own.

At my job interview I met Edna Gordon. She would become my supervisor for the next four years and a dear friend till she died at the end of the century. In that interview I had a feeling that she knew me from somewhere (which later turned out not to be true) and, this feeling scared me a bit because I figured if she knew my background I'd never get the job. She was a warm, nurturing, smart, generous woman, and I am pretty sure that the initial compatibility between us was immediately apparent. She explained to me that I would be an aid to the psychotherapists on the unit and help them with the physical needs of the clients, who were very physically impaired. I told her that I was comfortable with that. Although I was under qualified, with only a high school equivalency diploma, she gave me the job on the spot.

As for the job itself, within four months I was doing some of the work of a therapist, along with my own tasks, and became a key figure in the running of the whole operation—I taught classes, I innovated all kinds of wacky activities for the kids, got them out of their wheelchairs, and forced them to do things physically that they had never done in their life, such as having them jump into the pool with their distorted physical bodies and try to swim on their own and to make fun of themselves, related to their stuttering and physical handicaps, and encouraged the staff to loosen up and have fun with the kids; you might say I was something of the Jack Nicholson character in *One Flew Over the Cuckoo's Nest,* only I was not an inmate but a member of the staff. What surprised me most of all was how easily I got the upper echelon of the staff to go along with me in almost every innovation I tried to incorporate, even when it came to therapeutic matters. Over the next four years the foundation was laid for me to become a psychotherapist, not just because I was good at dealing with people or because I learned quickly and had the intuitive skills to know what people needed to do to get better, but because I seemed to have the charisma and forcefulness that I had as the Moose on the streets of Brownsville and could apply those leadership skills to working in a therapeutic setting.

But I feel the need, here, to explain both to myself and the reader, something of this transitional period, in which I moved from such a raw adolescent to a young man making his way, astonishingly without impediment, in the world.

Granted that I had smarts and was able to present myself well, I do believe it would be much harder in today's world for me to be able to move so rapidly from an uneducated, poor kid to becoming a working professional in the mental health field. The educational requirements would have been prohibitive for me to do what I did. In an odd way, it turned out that the survival skills I had to learn as a child and adolescent helped me to get ahead incredibly fast. I seemed to have been born at the right time.

I finished off my B.A. degree at college in June of 1963; and in September, I began taking a full course load for my Master's Degree in clinical psychology at Yeshiva University. At around this time I obtained a position at The Institute for Orthopedically Handicapped Children, which had just gotten a grant from The National Institute of Mental Health (NIMH). My work at the Cerebral Palsy Center had convinced me that I could become a psychologist. And that meant I would have to give up my work at the Center in order to obtain a position that would lead more directly to meet the State Licensing qualifications in the field of psychology. I would miss Edna and the staff at the Center, I will always think fondly of my time there—especially the freedom they gave me to innovate and use my personality in ways that wouldn't have been possible in the typical professional setting.

I managed to get this new job, fairly seamlessly, which was par for the course considering how my luck was running. Here I was this kid from Brownsville wheeling and dealing again, but with a university and a mental health institute (NIMH). The grant from NIMH was funding me as a full-time employee, providing I only went to school part time (which I was not doing); meanwhile, Yeshiva was paying me a sizeable stipend to attend school full-time, providing I was not working 40 hours a week (which I was doing). For sure, my experience hustling in the streets and pool halls prepared me for the business of wheeling and dealing in the academic and professional world.

And with all of this, I had not stopped seeing Maggie. She had gotten an illegal abortion some weeks after we had talked on the phone on the morning of Delmore's birth. And though she had threatened to end our involvement at the time, she did not carry through with her threat. As a matter of fact, a similar sequence—with a different ending—occurred fourteen months later, when I told her of the birth of my daughter. On hearing this, she threw down her knapsack at my feet, declaring through her tears she was done with me. But this time she did break off the relationship. It hurt me, but I was also glad—at least as I write this—that she was able to stand up for herself.

During the period that I was seeing Maggie clandestinely, I was living on the edge and seemed to have to live that way. I can only speculate that I was confused and moving like a whirling dervish, so as not to have to deal with my personal conflicts, both in my marriage and emotional life. I was probably hoping that by acting out with Maggie the way I had been doing, things would fall apart... and in that way stop me. Or maybe I was really hoping that things would fall apart and bring about an end to my marriage. Yet the more my actions pointed to a serious underlying depression, the faster I whirled.

After Maggie ended the relationship with me, I continued having outside relationships with women and was compulsively driven to do so. In retrospect none of these involvements meant very much to me, in the way the relationship with Maggie had. I found myself thinking about her a lot... contributing to my misgivings about my marriage. In one instance, at the Institute, I got involved with a naïve, female in her late twenties—an intern—who was assigned to help gather data for the grant. She was a fulsome, Southern black woman with severe self-esteem problems, who was given her intern position as a token gesture by a Northern-based philanthropic agency. But her personal problems did not stop me from aggressively pressuring her to have sex with me. She was cooperative in an unhealthy way for her. I did not feel good about what I was doing, and stopped seeing her after a couple of weeks.

My need to juggle my hectic life had to do with avoiding the anxieties I was prey to. My neurotic energy carried me through the frenetic existence I was leading and enabled me to somehow prosper under the most trying circumstances. I was acting on the questionable principle that it would be better for me to plunge into as much activity as possible, rather than duplicate the stagnation and stultification of my early home life.

I must have had some cognition that I was not handling my anxiety too well, for by the summer of 1965 I went into therapy. I chose to enter personal therapy in the hope of relieving some of the stress I was undergoing. However, while it was helpful to me in gaining insight into my inner life, it did little to slow down my escapist behavior... or it may have actually increased it, since the therapy was yet another commitment in my chaotic life. I should have broken down and been forced to confront my life, but, it tells you something about the strength of my survival instincts, that I kept on going and actually thrived in school and at work. I had used my wife, my friends, Maggie, and the multiple women I was involved with for my own purposes—to keep me stable and functioning while holding at bay my vulnerability and panic. When I look back at the pain and suffering I inflicted on my wife and on Maggie, I feel badly how I used them, but I understand I had no choice, given my state of mind.

Part of what pushed me to work twenty hours a day getting a Master's Degree in psychology and working a full-time job was the belief that the only way I would ever get out of the ghetto was to become a success and make a lot of money. Fear of being dragged down by the family genetics never allowed me to let up, to a degree that amounted to a personal neurosis, since my drive to succeed was overdetermined and nothing could alter it. Although I chose the field of psychology as my pathway to middle-class life, I was not using psychology to understand myself—in fact it took me a number of years of working as a therapist and going for a second analysis before I was able to have something of a working grasp of the topography of my internal world.

When it came to psychology, I seemed to know a damn sight more about what motivated almost everybody around me than I knew about what motivated myself... or who I was. (I suppose this is true, in some part, of most everybody, but it applied, in larger part, to me.) I believe that my lack of self-knowledge served a major defensive purpose in distancing me from my fears of humiliation and ignominy stemming from my background. In line with this kind of defensive maneuvering, I sought to separate myself from my family of origin, and ignore the parts of my psychology that I was not ready to face yet and, in some cases, ever. In recent years I am much more aware that in building my own family I am not free of the influence of the family I grew up in, and have paid a heavy price for the psychological distortions (of my personality) that I used for survival—and in time would use me. It was one thing to detach from my family; another thing to try to eviscerate the natural introjections of family that form in childhood. My first therapy was only of limited help because I wasn't ready to fully engage in introspective thinking, choosing to do everything but stop and take a hard look at myself.

I always was of the opinion that I had to be one step ahead of the game and make people feel that I was competent and more successful than they were and in that way I could brush away my past, and, also, manage to try and convince myself that I was now part of the middle-class world.

Perhaps it is not amiss here to bring up the strong impact that Theodore Dreiser's *An American Tragedy* had on me when I read it around this time, largely because of the way that the class conflict dominated the actions of the characters in the book. I remember being particularly caught up in the character of Clyde Griffiths, because he was so anxious at the lie he was living and afraid that his world would collapse.

In time I understood that my sexual acting out was part of my need to feel omnipotent to make up for my underlying fear of being powerless (and impotent) in the external world. No matter how many women I slept with it did not alleviate my primary fear that I was alone and could be extinguished by the horrors of family and ghetto life. Mostly what I sought was a female friend and lover with whom I could lose myself in and divert me from my mounting panic.

And my obsession with success, encompassing the need to appear strong and powerful in the economic and academic world, drove me, at every opportunity, to make sure that everybody knew of my accomplishments—while, at the same time, hiding my deep sense of humiliation at my origins and making light of the fact that, shortly after Dalite and I departed from my parents' home, I had little contact with the members of my birth family. Let me add that in addition to compulsively touting my accomplishments, I presented myself in such a manner that people would also be jealous of me—as if there were some safety in making them experience the envy of others that I routinely experienced as a given of my life. And while I was not unaware of how obviously insecure and needy I appeared, to others, I couldn't stop from my self-adulatory posturing because of the temporary gratification it provided.

Some of the psychological considerations of why I behave the way I do were beyond me in my early years, but this kind of self-critical perception was something that only was opening up to me as I got older... and the major part of which would take place in my sixties and seventies. Still, having the perception was not necessarily bound up with absorbing it and altering the pattern of behavior to which it applied. I seem to have little resource when it comes to changing patterns of behavior that involve painful self-examination. I feel I have some inherent right to indulge myself in whatever keeps my comfort level up... as if my right to self-indulgence is a secret rite that others don't fathom. It had everything to do with my childhood. I bring some of this up now, I suppose, in an attempt to foreshadow concerns to come and the struggles that I will face as time passes. To point the way, as it were. My friend and colleague, Ted, will have a lot to do with my seeing with the naked eye the enormity of my giving myself carte blanche to ignore and deflect some of my most unattractive traits. He is an important friend in my life and will be a significant figure in the book.

But let me return to the concerns of the day. My job at the Institute for the Orthopedically Handicapped did not pan out that well; it just enabled me to finish my Masters. The job itself was mainly bullshit; all the staff quickly caught on that the NIMH research grant was poorly conceived, badly administered, and just served to bring in federal money to the organization. During my two-year stay there, I, like everybody else, practically did nothing and we all got away with it. But it taught me a good lesson: I learned that some aspects of the professional world were no different than the operative motif of my junior high school and high school—in that they were just a means for people to get away with whatever they could. My actual job consisted of going from one community center to another evaluating the effectiveness of how individual handicapped children were adjusting to the typical after-school recreational programs run by the community center. I spent most of my time at work goofing off and flirting—and more— with the women on the staff of the various community-center programs. The main rewards of my work came from this facet of my job, which was not too demanding. But obviously I wasn't doing a bang-up job and my interest in the program was waning. As I was completing my Master's Degree, I began looking for a new job.

Eventually I picked out a position that fit all the criteria of my next move up in my professional career. I was determined to become a working psychotherapist, this in spite of the gravity of my own personal emotional and psychological mess. What is most remarkable is that I had absolutely no credentials or real training to do individual therapy but had no worries whatsoever that I could become a hugely competent psychotherapist; then again, in those days it didn't take much more than having a Master's Degree in some kind of helping profession to start a therapy practice, if you could get the patients. My powerful ego need to be the best at whatever I do, along with my unquenchable desire to parade my grandiosity, would, I had no doubt, propel me upward in my career attainments.

However the head psychologist of the NIMH grant at the Institute got wind of my shenanigans with the Southern intern, and became anxious to get rid of me so as to avoid embarrassment to the Institute. Inevitably, considering my talent for manipulation and making the best out of a bad situation, I worked out a deal with him; I got him to recommend me highly to a well-known colleague of his who administered the therapy program at the Wilson School for Boys in exchange for my tending my resignation at the Institute. Wilson had a reputation for being one of the forward-thinking establishments for disturbed and violent children or children who had run afoul of the legal system. Wilson needed a therapist for their halfway house on East 18th Street in Manhattan and I thought taking such a job would be a good step upward for me. What's more, the job paid a better salary than I was currently earning. So, nothing mediating against it, I applied for an interview with the director at Wilson. After meeting with the director, who was favorably impressed by me, I was scheduled to meet with the head clinical therapist.

CHAPTER SEVEN:
EDITH AT HOME

My attempts to reach Warren following his leaving group were futile. But in about a month he called me. I could surmise from what he told me that he was in the midst of a mental breakdown. I encouraged him to take his medication, which he hadn't taken for the past month. He said that he didn't need drugs anymore and that his relationship to God would offer him more clarity than therapy ever could. I pleaded with him to come in to see me, only to have him angrily say, "It's your problem, not mine if you can't tolerate my ending therapy." And then he hung up the phone.

I called Warren's father and told him I believed his son was having a breakdown. I asked him to go to Warren's apartment and report to me what was going on. His father asked me if he could bring his daughter with him since she had been through similar mental breakdowns with him in the past. Sensing that the father was apprehensive, I agreed that it would be a good idea to have his daughter with him.

Two hours later the sister telephoned me and seemed quite anxious about Warren's condition. She informed me that when they arrived at the apartment the door was flung wide open and inside the shades were drawn up and he was lying naked on his bed, incoherently mumbling something about God and his [Warren's] special place in the universe. She and her dad tried to question him but he appeared unresponsive to their presence in the room. She asked me what they should do. I suggested that they dress him and bring him to my office in their car. Some fifteen minutes later, she rang me back and told me that after they had finished dressing him, he had asked them where they were intending to take him. She said her father replied, "Dr. Obler's office." Then, she said that her brother stormed out of the apartment shouting, "I don't need him anymore."

Forty-eight hours later I received a phone call from Dr. Riva Lakshemi, a psychiatric resident at Long Island Jewish Hospital, in Queens, letting me know that a patient of mine, Warren Tebbits, had been brought by ambulance to the hospital, apparently suffering from a psychotic breakdown. She informed me that Warren was delusional and disoriented, and he was demanding that you be contacted immediately so that he could be released. We agreed to evaluate him over the course of the next few days and make a determination after that time what should be done with him. I called his parents and asked them to pack a bag of his personal belongings and to visit him at the hospital.

After seeing Warren, over the next few days, in the hospital, I consulted with Dr. Lakshemi and we decided to temporarily place him on his previous medication regimen, and at such time that he became stabilized and less agitated, we would transfer him to Jamaica Hospital complex, where I had arranged for a full physiological and psychological work-up to be conducted.

Within two months Warren began to come out of his psychotic state, stopped hallucinating, and began functioning at a less pathological level. He called me one afternoon to let me know that he was grateful for all I had done to help him and felt ready to leave the hospital. I told him that he could not be released unless he agreed to resume therapy under my care and continually stay on his medication without interruption. He readily assented. In a brief conversation with him in his tiny room at the hospital, I got some idea of what had happened to him after he left his apartment on the night he flipped out:

"What happened to you after you left your father and sister in your apartment?"

"Well, to the best of my memory I hailed a cab and went to look for that beautiful girl I had met on my vacation trip to the Southwestern Indian Reservation."

"You mean the girl who did the cooking for the tourist group?"

"Yes, the one who I told you in therapy had a special interest in me."

"How did you get her address?"

"Simple. I called up Dr. Hallard, the director of the excursion group, and he gave it to me."

"So you went to visit her. Did you call and make a date?"

"There was no need to, I believe we had a cosmic connection and she was waiting for me to come see her."

"Did you get to see her?"

"The last thing I remember was that the cab driver arrived on West 74th St. and the driver insisted on my paying him before I went up to her apartment to get the money for the cab fare."

"And…?"

"I argued with him, but he said he'd call the police if I didn't pay him. I told him that I had no money and all that I had was the clothes I was wearing."

"So what happened?"

"I offered to pay him with my clothes but he said, '…just forget it.' "

(Keep in mind, that when patients like Warren have psychotic breaks it's difficult to find out exactly what happened because the experience is fragmented in their consciousness… they can only remember bits and pieces of what actually happened and not necessarily in chronological order. Furthermore, you can see by what he is saying about paying the cab driver with his clothes that his thinking is disoriented, such that the cab driver would accept this as payment or that he could walk up, in his underwear, and ask a woman whom he barely knows from a trip, to welcome him into her apartment.)

"Did you get to see your friend?"

"All I remember was that I was riding in an ambulance and wound up in the hospital. I do remember that I caught a glimpse of the girl talking to the police outside of her brownstone and she looked confused."

(My surmise, with the help of the information from the police report, is that, despite what the cab driver had told him, he ended up taking his clothes off, probably rang her apartment and she, remembering him from the trip, buzzed him in. But when she caught sight of him through the peephole, in his underwear, called the police. When the police arrived, I would assume they rang her buzzer and she went down to meet them… and this is what he saw from the ambulance when he described to me seeing the girl talking to the police.)

"So she was bewildered that her future boyfriend— remember all the women you meet can't resist you—was departing in an ambulance in front of the front door." (My inappropriate humor bringing home to Warren his delusions.)

After a few weeks, Warren was released from the hospital and within ten days resumed working at his job at the New York State Motor Vehicle Bureau and resumed private therapy. However I delayed Warren's return to the group. I felt he needed time to absorb all that had happened and to recuperate. I decided to phase him into group slowly and began to introduce the idea to the other members.

I can still see Edith's look of disbelief at my first mention of Warren's return. For the most part, except for Edith, everyone else seemed reasonably positive about his coming back. There was something in Edith's manner, suggesting an unhappiness and displeasure at the news that seemed to have more to do with her inner turmoil than her dislike of Warren.

At around this time Edith took a half-a-step forward in my work with her because she was admitting that the problems she was facing in her marriage were not soley the result of her husband's inadequacy. She began to open up about her wish to be the darling of her father and the jealousy she felt at her father's attention to his wife. I asked her whether her competition with her mother for the father had caused reverberations in her marriage to Lester, her husband, and father of her two young daughters (currently lving with her parents); she admitted it was a problem and increased some of the insecurity he felt about his place in her life. This was the closest I had ever come with Edith to her even entertaining the notion that she had had some negative impact on the marriage. Usually her ego needs led her to denigrate Lester's contribution to the marriage... as a father, breadwinner, and lover. He took a backseat in the marriage, causing her to compare him unfavorably with her successful and confident father.

The problem was that while Edith showed some progress by being able to see her role in the divisiveness of the marriage, she was too self-centered to not see herself as the injured party because he couldn't live up to her expectations. Clearly she had been in conflict about her marriage, but nothing could induce her to shoulder her half of the responsibility for the divorce. She gave lip service to her faults, but refused to ingest them as failings on her part that should be addressed in therapy. If I cared about her, I would see her as the good daughter. It is the old Jewish princess syndrome. And her good looks and the attention she got from men confirmed her desirability as a valuable female commodity. Only underneath she battled mightily her feelings of being second rate and undeserving of the love of her father—proof of which was her unfair downgrading of her mother.

She was not ready to hear this kind of critical insight, or to appreciate my often-repeated advice to hold off on the divorce. Eventually she turned her ire on me, and ceased coming to my sessions with her, or group. I called her a number of times, leaving messages for her to not run from discussing what seemed to be the conflict between us. She did not return my calls. I was tempted to just forget about the whole thing and let her make the decision for herself. But as an analyst I knew that this easy way out was a shirking of my responsibility. Of course you might think of it as a countertransference problem on my part—by getting back at her by sticking her with the inevitable consequences of her behavior. I liked her too much and respected her intelligence too much to dump on her by doing nothing to counter her self-destructive actions. Instead of waiting her out and hoping she came around, I chose to make a frontal attack and pay a visit to her apartment. I went ahead and sent a telegram to her that I was going to arrive at her apartment the following morning.

Upon my entrance to the (East End Avenue in Manhattan) building, the doorman, after ringing her apartment and not getting a response, refused my request that someone from the building with a key to her apartment come with me. I told him that I was a therapist and this was a medical emergency. He still balked. Finally I told him that I would have to call the police to break down the door, if he wouldn't use his key to open the apartment. He then called the superintendent of the building, who agreed to accompany me to her apartment. He rang her buzzer and when there was no answer, used his key to open the door. Edith was standing with her back to us, in front of a mirror, and turned her head, and nonchalantly said, "Hi, Doctor Obler, I was expecting you."

At this point, the superintendent shrugged his shoulders for my benefit, announced that he had work to do and left Edith with the words: "I'm glad you're okay."

I thanked him for opening the door, shook his hand and said "Goodbye." My guess was that he was from Serbia or somewhere in that region. In a detectable accent, he whipped off, as he headed to the elevator, "Take it easy, Doc,"

I was surprised how messy the living room was considering that Edith was usually so meticulous in her dress and makeup. I had figured that she would give to her apartment the same attention to detail that she gave to her personal appearance. Her clothes were strewn all over the floor, dishes, caked with food, were left on a table, and the rug had a smell of urine from her cat. It was obvious to me the windows hadn't been open for days. I walked over to the two windows and opened them. "We need some fresh air in here."

"Whatever." She turned towards the mirror, resuming putting on her makeup, which she had been in the middle of doing when I had entered. I hadn't trusted my initial view of her face, but I now saw it had been accurate. Her face looked worn and tired; her eyes, tense and anxious; her hair, stringy and uncombed, and her lips au naturel. She did not look like the woman who showed up to my office for therapy. I noticed that she applied her makeup powder over and over again, but only on her left cheek.

"What are you doing with your face-powder?"

"Now you can see why I didn't return your calls or show up at my therapy sessions."

"... because you look so bad?"

"I knew you would insist that I leave my apartment and come to see you. But how could I with this horrible, ugly pimple on my cheek?"

"You're not the only person who has a pimple."

"Think, Obler... do you have any idea of what it means for a beautiful woman like me to walk around with a pimple like this? Last week I went to work with a band-aid over it. I'm not going to go through that humiliation again."

"You mean the humiliation in your mind?"

"So you say. I guess if I were as dumpy as Antonia or as ugly as Warren, with his scarred, pockmarked face, then it wouldn't matter much whether or not I had a pimple. But I'm not. People expect me to look good."

"You don't look so good now."

"That's why, Obler, I'm not leaving this apartment until I'm ready. My standards of what's presentable are higher than most people's."

"I'm sure they are. But what are you going to do to get yourself out of the funk you're in and resume your life. It's not just the pimple that's keeping you in your apartment and preventing you from answering the telephone when it rings."

"No, it's not... and what's keeping me in a funk is partially your fault. It was your idea to put me in the group with a bunch of misfits, and if I continue attending I'll end up losing it like your favorite patient, Warren."

"You seem to be having your share of problems, even without attending."

"I seem to, don't I?"

"That's why I'm trying to knock some sense into that head of yours and not simply go along with the drama you're creating. You're too isolated, too depressed, too into your own thoughts. You have to be careful how much you put yourself through. This is not the first time you've hidden in your apartment when things got rough. I understand it's been a very lonely, frustrating period, but it's not going to help much to blame your problems on Warren or the other people in the group. Ever since the motorcycle accident in California you've been trying to hide the scars on your legs and your slight limp. I guess you didn't want men to get too familiar with your imperfections... and now your jumping into divorce."

"That's bullshit. I'm not leaving my marriage because I'm running away from something. I'm leaving because I don't want to be with Lester anymore. I can do much better than him."

"You mean he doesn't make enough money?"

"What's wrong with that? I think I deserve as much. Without digging into my own finances, the lifestyle I deserve is unsupportable."

"Is this the Jewish princess speaking?"

"You could call it that. I am my father's daughter."

"Is it Lester's responsibility to support your father's image of you?"

"It should be."

"My question is whether Lester has anything to do with it? For many years your marriage worked and you were pretty happy—and if I remember correctly, you weren't too easy to get along with."

"So what are you suggesting Obler? that I stay with him because I can't get anyone else to put up with me?"

"You got it, it's getting late."

"What do you mean by that?"

"You're getting older, your hair is turning gray, and wrinkles come with the territory, and, finally, indignity of all indignities, a pimple appears."

"So because I'm past thirty-five, I am no longer attractive to men?"

"I find you still attractive, but you're the one who is worried that time is running out. I don't think I'm off base to suggest that for a number of years you've been working in therapy on your childhood fear that you will be supplanted by your younger brother as your father's favorite."

"Yes, we have worked on this, but my worry is that, with Lester, I will be supplanted by a beautiful, younger woman."

"Put it this way, when Warren came into group, he took up the group's attention, and before that you had been the focus of the group, so, in effect, you had been replaced. And not by a young woman, but by a troubled, unattractive man. It's not just your fear of aging; it's fear that you don't have enough substance to keep another person interested in you... unless you're a piece of ass."

"Do you have to talk like that?"

I stayed for about twenty minutes more, and the conversation went well. Edith substantially let down her guard. When it came time to leave, I asked her, "Why don't you stop hibernating in your apartment, clean up the mess, get into some nice clothes (don't worry about your pimple), and come back to therapy?"

"I might just do that," she conceded.

CHAPTER EIGHT:
WILSON SCHOOL FOR BOYS

He sat silently for the first fifteen minutes, looking at my resume, and when he looked up at me began blinking uncontrollably in one eye at a time. I didn't know quite what to do, feeling very uncomfortable in the silence. Dr. Terrence Ripkin, head of therapy at Wilson School for Boys and a professionaly-known psychotherapist practitioner with delinquent children in the New York City area, wasn't asking me any questions and I thought that he might be testing my ability to handle silence in therapy, as a patient would experience it. After a while I had to do something to break the tension, so I began blinking back at him. Finally he said something: "You have a very impressive resume, Mr. Obler."

"I do?"

"The problem is that you have no direct clinical experience with patients."

"That's true. But I have had a lot of experience in dealing with the problems of handicapped people and their psychological adjustment. Much of what I did at the United Cerebral Palsy was to talk with my clients and help them with their personal problems."

"That's not quite psychotherapy, Mr. Obler, and the population we work with here is a very difficult one."

"Can you tell me about the clients I'd be working with?"

"You'll be doing therapy with a caseload of fourteen boys, eight to fourteen years old, who have been remanded by the courts for having committed misdemeanors or are in need of adult supervision because of their family situation."

"Where will the therapy take place?"

"At the downtown halfway house facility on the East Side."

"Is this where the courts send them for supervision?"

"No, most of them were placed on a PINS (Person in Need of Supervision) petition and sent to an upstate live-in institution and when the staff determined that they were ready to be reintegrated into society, they were sent to the halfway house. Our staff's job is to facilitate the reintegration."

"Sounds good. And how do these kids respond to treatment?"

"Some do, but many of them are angry, hostile misfits who have very little interest in improving themselves. They are delinquents; after all, most of them are black and Hispanic, with a chip on their shoulder that we have to knock off."

(I immediately sensed that I was dealing with the dean again at Straubenmueller High School. I knew if I was going to get this job I had to strike up a bargain as I had with the dean. Moreover, I knew Dr. Ripkin was fucking nuts and I was becoming nuts too as I was blinking back at him as he talked.)

"Oh, I'm very good at that. I've had years of dealing with tough kids."

"You have?"

"I grew up in Brownsville as a young kid myself."

"You don't look poor."

"Looks are deceiving."

"You strike me as a naïve kid who hasn't got his feet wet in the world, and I'm a little concerned at your stepping into a harsh reality in which you'll feel lost. So my question is, what do you have to offer us?"

"What do you need?"

"I need a shrink who can straighten out these little delinquents so I can spend as little time as possible doing your job for you."

"I can assure you, sir, that I will interfere with your schedule as little as possible. When I take on the role of therapist, I take it on completely, day and night. I'll have these kids under control. Don't worry about it."

"That seems good to me, Mr. Obler, but you're going to need a little help. I'm going to assign to you a 250-pound black ex-football player, named Chuck, who knows how to control the kids when they act up. Between both of you, you should be able to control your unit."

"Thank you, sir. I really appreciate your giving me the job."

Chuck turned out to be everything I could have hoped for. He not only was strong like a bear, but he was bright, sensitive, and totally in charge of the boys on his floor that comprised my therapy unit. We quickly became fast friends, even though I was white, Jewish, and had no experience working as a therapist with this population. He explained to me that the halfway house staff was strongly divided along racial lines. Most of the lower echelon staff at the institution were black and Hispanic, were paid very little money, and were in charge of the children's daily care. They cleaned the rooms, cooked the meals, did secretarial work, as well as doing many of the menial jobs to keep the house running. The higher paid white staff were the therapists and top administrators who set treatment policy, negotiated with the outside community, in addition to controlling the finances of the place. Most of the black staff mistrusted the white staff; they saw them as a bunch of academically-trained dilettantes, who had the right degrees but were out of touch with the kids' lives. Chuck let me know that since Dr. Ripkin had first been appointed chief psychiatrist two years ago, the split between black and white staff had worsened. Things had been better when Dr. George Penn was in charge of running Wilson. I had known of Dr. Penn, who was a leading authority in the country on family therapy and had a great reputation as an innovator in family dynamics, including therapeutic work with dysfunctional and impoverished families. He was still employed at Wilson in the capacity of a consulting psychiatrist, which meant I would be working with him.

Something important that Chuck told me was that the real power at Wilson resided in the hands of Dottie. I had seen her and she was a big, fat 200-pound, black woman who had the look of a no-nonsense person. Chuck related that although her official title was only secretary to the head administrator at the house, she in fact ran the daily operations. It would not do, he forewarned me, to incur her disfavor. And I learned quickly that my stay at Wilson would be short-lived if I did not get on her good side and help her overlook that I was Jewish and white.

"What did you think of your initial interview with Dr. Ripkin?" Chuck asked me.

"Meaning?…"

"I wondered what you thought of him?"

"He's off his rocker, if you ask me. What's all the blinking about?"

"How in hell do I know? Listen, the guy is a prick and a phony. He's made it clear since he's been here that he wants nothing to do with the kids. The more we leave him alone, he's let us know, the better things will be for everyone. All he wants to do is to tranquilize the kids that act out and cause trouble."

At this point in our conversation, a kid came running up to Chuck and pulled on his arm. He saw me and asked, "Who's the white motherfucker, Chucky boy?"

"Mr. Obler, I want you to meet Hector."

Hector placed the thumb of his free hand in his mouth and began vigorously sucking on it.

Six months passed during which I had settled into my job working with the kids on the second floor of Wilson. I liked the work. In addition to daily group meetings I began to conduct brief individual therapy type sessions with some of the fourteen boys in my unit after they finished school for the day. Within a few weeks they started looking forward to our meetings. It was tough getting them to talk about the problems they had with their family, but I had no problem engaging them in conversation about their relationship with each other and their dislike of school.

Chuck often joined me at these individual sessions, and I began to involve him in the therapy with the kids. In my graduate studies I had become increasingly interested in Freudian psychoanalysis and wondered whether it could be used with effect in treating poor black and Puerto Rican kids. To my knowledge very little work had been done with this population, using analytic therapy. As a matter of fact, most of my professors in graduate school suggested that analytic techniques were not applicable to a minority population. This position disturbed me. I was sure that a lot of analytic thinking could prove useful with these kids if I could get the staff to give it a while.

I broached the subject to Dr. Ripkin but he dismissed it out of hand as inapplicable, which I expected. However, I also bounced the subject off Dr. Penn, and as I expected he was enthusiastic about my considering such matters. He however was not in favor of some kind of revamping of Freudian analytical principles to embrace the kids at Wilson; he thought that was too big a stretch. He spoke to me of preferring to use modified principles of Family Therapy, which was a school of therapy gaining favor at this time.

He mentioned that most of the kids here had little communication with their parents or teachers—except of a negative kind—which is why he tried to develop the idea of applying family therapy techniques at our facility, so we could get the kids and the parents talking to each other with the help and cooperation of the staff. He said: "Think of it. Not many people, in the population at large, are willing to take a sustained, hard look at what is undermining in their family dynamic, and this has everything to do with why Freud understood that his psychoanalytic approach was for the few not the many. Family therapy seems much more pertinent to our population here… so they don't have to uncover in one-on-one therapy the dynamics of their family life. After all, their parents rarely communicate verbally with them, and the kids spend most of their time trying to have as little to do with their parents as possible. So it is this imbalance that needs to be rectified in a supervised setting and with the help of informed and skilled psychological counselors like you."

I let Dr. Penn know that I too had little communication with my parents and had preferred hanging out in the streets to being home. And I informed him that I had an internal understanding, crude as it was, about the debilitating dynamic of my family and this did a lot for me in learning how to deal with the world around me... and reading Freud was a major experience for me.

Dr. Penn replied, "There is a lot of room in working with our population to explore the parent-child dynamic." This intrigued me, though I knew that such an idea would not be embraced by Dr. Ripkin. It was hard for me not to think of my conversations with Dr. Penn as tinged with a co-conspiratorial quality.

I seemed to be doing well at Wilson. I got along with the staff and the kids liked me. In fact, I began to get a little cocky and push my ideas of how to work with the kids.

It was not too long before I overreached myself and found myself singled out as a maverick. It so happened that word started to spread through the halfway house that Obler and Chuck were talking to the kids in their unit about their fantasies relating to sexual feelings for their mother... or, non-euphemistically, their desire to fuck their mother. Keep in mind that the rumors being spread about the kind of work I and Chuck were doing with the kids in our unit were distortions of our efforts to get the kids involved in expressing their feelings towards their parents and other family members; this included examining some of their fantasies and dreams... and a mild interpretation of this material. My guess is that some of the staff were put off by my attempt to amalgamate Freudian principles and family therapy. I supposed that what we were doing was threatening to them: it would show them up as not doing any meaningful therapy with the kids and just acting as disciplinarians. Of course this was exactly what Dr. Ripkin wanted from them.

Soon I was invited in for a chat with Dr. Ripkin, in which he warned me that I had better be careful about "the psychological crap" I was into with these kids and if I persisted in discussing potentially sexually-explosive material with them he would bring it up at the weekly staff meetings.

He did just that, confronting me at the next staff meeting with the rumors that were circulating about the approach I was taking with the kids. Before the meeting he talked to me alone.

"I gather you're still trying to work with the kids in your unit as if you're a Freudian therapist trying to get them to free associate about their dreams and fantasies."

"What's my role as a therapist if I don't hold therapy sessions?"

"Your job is to keep the motherfuckers in line and make sure they don't cause any trouble in the house. That's why we gave you Chuck."

"Excuse me, Dr. Ripkin; I didn't realize this was a holding pen. I thought it was a halfway house where we were supposed to rehabilitate the kids, and I was under the impression that was why you hired me."

"If I remember correctly, we agreed in our first conversation that you would take care of things so I wouldn't have to get involved and solve your problems for you."

"That's exactly what I'm trying to do, Dr. Ripkin. I am working towards the goal you want me to achieve."

"Good. Then cut the Freudian crap and make sure our clients follow the house rules."

Our chat ended on that delicate note, and the staff meeting followed:

Dr. Ripkin: What's on the agenda today?

Dottie: How are we supposed to know?— you're the one that sets the agenda.

Dr. Ripkin: I was just trying to see if any of you wanted to add any items to the agenda I had planned for this meeting.

Dottie: What is on the agenda?

Paul: Yeah, I think it's important that we know what's on the agenda for these staff meetings. Every week I'm kind of confused. I come here prepared to talk about the group work with the kids in my unit; but instead we always seem to get bogged down in conflicts stemming from personality issues.

Sally: I agree. We seem to never talk about what's going on with the kids. And I haven't seen a written agenda for any of these meetings during the past two years.

Paul: All that ever happens is that Dr. Ripkin opens the meeting and Dottie takes over. It seems to me the only thing that gets discussed is how to make sure the house runs smoothly.

Dr. Ripkin: Are you suggesting that I relinquish my authority in these meetings?

Sally: I don't think Paul was suggesting that.

Chuck: Can we get past this bullshit and proceed with the meeting? The kids will be returning from school soon and you know what happens then.

Dottie: Can we move on? If I'm not mistaken, Doctor Ripkin wanted to bring up at the meeting today something about the disturbing psychological stuff going on in Obler's and Chuck's unit.

Marty: What psychological stuff are you referring to?

Dottie: Word has it that you are getting into the sex lives of the kids and bringing up all kinds of family garbage. We have enough trouble with these kids without planting wild ideas about sex. I've been watching you, Obler, for these past couple of months and it wouldn't surprise me to find out that you're into some kind of perverted shit. I guess you white folks have it in your mind that sick sexuality is common. But us black folks are too busy trying to earn a living and make ends meet to get into such matters.

Chuck: Dottie, you crack me up.

Marty: What do you think, Dr. Ripkin? Should we educate Dottie and the staff about Freudian drive theory?

Dr. Ripkin: What kind of game are you playing, Obler? The purpose for our staff meetings is very clear. That's why we include the secretary and maintenance staff as well as professional staff. We're here to make sure that the house runs smoothly.

Marty: Oh, is that why we're here?

Dottie: I see you two got some personality differences. Why don't you try to work it out at one of your so-called supervisory sessions?

Marty: You're right, Dottie, we do have regular supervisory sessions, but we never deal with therapy for the kids. The only concern is how to make sure the troubled kids don't make waves.

Sally: What would you have us do in supervisory sessions?

Marty: We have a brilliant clinician and psychological theorist who we hardly ever use in our practice with the kids.

Dottie: Are you referring to Dr. Ripkin?

Marty: Well, Dr. Ripkin too, but I was speaking of Dr. Penn, who started the family therapy program at Wilson. Working with him has been one of the best things about this place for me.

Dottie: So that's why you came here. I thought it was the salary and the side benefits.

Paul: The medical benefits suck, so what are you talking about?

Dottie: I think we have to deviate from our agenda to clarify the kind of side benefits Obler is making use of. Perhaps Chuck or the therapist from unit four could enlighten us at another time.

Dr. Ripkin: Are you getting some benefits I don't know about?

Marty: Aside from the benefit of our supervisory sessions I've been spending a lot of time learning about the world these kids come from. I have to say that Chuck has been extremely helpful in facilitating this.

Dottie: Facilitating or supplying the facility?

Dr. Ripkin: What is going on here?

Dottie: Oh, you haven't heard about Obler's extra-curricular activities?

Dr. Ripkin: Can you be just a wee bit more explicit?

Marty: I think Dottie is referring to the extra time beyond my normal working hours.

Dr. Ripkin: Doing what? You know the institutional policy about working overtime.

Chuck: I think Marty should be commended for the amount of extra work he puts in without compensation.

Dottie: Commended?

Marty: Can we get off my overtime contribution to Wilson, and talk about inviting Dr. Penn to our staff meetings?

*   *   *

Then, on another day, there was this conversation with Dottie:

"Dottie, did you have to put me on the spot at last week's meeting?"

"Don't play with me Obler. You know better than that."

"I get the feeling that you're a little perturbed that I'm not playing with you."

"I'm desperate, but I'm not that desperate. I've had enough experience to know that I don't want a little white schmuck like you."

"It must have been quite a while back. I imagine that since you ballooned up to three hundred pounds a little white guy might be difficult."

"Listen bonehead, I don't care about how many chicks you bring in to screw on the fourth floor or that Chuck has been covering for you. But I do care that you're titillating the kids with this Freudian Oedipal crap… we've got enough problems with the kids as it is."

"Listen, Dottie. Why don't we call a truce? You're one of the few people here I respect, and I think we're both on the same side, the side of the kids. We both know Dr. Ripkin's a joke and most of what we do is to pacify the kids and make sure there's no trouble. I know you care about the kids and so do I. From my point of view what we should do is treat them therapeutically and get them out of here."

"Obler, I like teasing you, but I have to admit you really do care about working with the kids."

"I need your help to take control out of Ripkin's hands and give it to the people who want to do therapy. And without your help I'm not going to succeed. I'm hip to the fact that you run this place in your own way."

"Well, it would be nice if you gave me some respect once in a while."

A meeting with Dr. Penn and the Wilson staff did take place. It was volatile and upsetting, but it brought to the forefront some of the issues under consideration in working with troubled, urban adolescents. Although Dr. Ripkin formally called the meeting, it was quickly taken over by Dr. Penn who, with impressive skill, directed the conversation to where he wanted it to go. Being one of the original founders of family therapy, it did not take him long to realize the tensions and conflicts between the staff and Dr. Ripkin.

One of the interesting things that Dr. Penn pointed out to the staff concerning our work with impoverished black and Hispanic kids, was that the psychoanalytic treatment method was ill-suited and inappropriate for this population. He maintained that the children at Wilson have been educationally and emotionally deprived, which has resulted in a severe deficit in their cognitive development. Living in poverty has further exacerbated their ability to think abstractly. He said that any therapy that focuses on using psychodynamic exploration with this population has proven to be a failure. What has to be focused on in their therapy is helping them to understand that they're angry at their family, at their teachers, and at having been so economically and physically abused. He said that they don't realize how emotionally stifled they are and neither do their parents. They take their problems out on each other and project on to the world their self-hatred and anger.

He was able to bring us together and reduce general tension, and, at the same time, gently reiterated his belief that the best therapy method in our situation was the family-therapy intervention he had introduced at Wilson.

In the months following the meeting with Dr. Penn, I devised a new therapy strategy involving our staff; the kids; their parents; and their teachers from the local public school. My idea was to take some of the precepts from Dr. Penn's family therapy and extend it to the important people in their lives, the concept being that all of these people would have to come together to see how the kids live at Wilson and what kind of problems they had. Hopefully, out of this they could cooperate on an agenda which would remove some of the obstacles from preventing the kids from returning home to their family.

The first line of our new tactic was to bring the teachers from the outside schools our kids attended, into Wilson; the second line was to take our kids on home visits to their family, and be a part of that interaction. All of this fit right into Dr. Penn's conceptual framework of how we should work with the kids.

As usual Dr. Ripkin objected to trying anything new; and it was only with Dottie, Chuck, myself, and some of the staff prodding him that he reluctantly agreed to bend a little. The initial conversation with Dr. Ripkin took place at the tail end of a subsequent staff meeting:

"I would like to invite the kids' teachers to Wilson and have them observe my unit's group meeting after school. That way the teachers can get an idea of some of the children's concerns and how they relate to each other outside of school."

"Understand this Obler, we can't have the teachers come to the institution and be exposed to the deviant behavior the kids at Wilson often display. It could be a public relations disaster," Dr. Ripkin stated. "It's taken us years to build a cooperative relationship with the public schools in the community and have them accept our clientele attending their schools."

"That's precisely why I think it would be beneficial to have them come in and see the way our kids live and the unique problems they face living in a halfway house. Unless the teachers realize the special difficulties our kids face, they're operating in a vacuum as regards our population here. Another idea I've been contemplating has to do with the way we get together with kids' parents. As it is we only see the parents once a month, and when we do, we only get about forty percent showing up. As radical as it may sound, I think we should go to the parents themselves and bring the kids with us, rather than expecting them to show up here."

"What are you suggesting, Obler, that we start doing home visits?" Dr. Ripkin testily asked.

"It might do our lily-white therapy staff some good to see where our kids live," Dottie replied.

"You can't be serious, Dottie. Are you recommending that we hire armored cars and transport our staff and the kids into the ghetto?" Dr. Ripkin questioned. "What about our insurance problem?"

"I think we can handle any insurance problems administratively," Dottie intervened.

Dr. Ripkin answered, "So, then, the important thing to decide is whether or not there is any merit to Obler's proposals."

"I think they're worth trying out," Dottie said. "Not much treatment of the kids and their families has been taking place at Wilson for a long time. Obler at least has a plan. Why don't we let him start with the teachers and then later try out a few home visits?"

"I don't know how Obler persuades everybody to follow his ideas, but what you're suggesting is very risky. The whole thing could backfire on us."

*   *   *

"I want to welcome you all to Wilson and I'm truly grateful that you're willing to devote your own time to coming here and seeing what life is like for our kids, outside of school, here at the halfway house. We've told the children that teachers will be observing today's unit meeting. In our experience at Wilson, the staff has reported that the kids quickly forget that they're being observed behind a one-way mirror. It's very important, however, that you don't converse during the observation because even though the kids can't see you, our walls are not soundproof. After the proceedings you'll have an opportunity to chat with the kids and staff and ask any questions you might have. We'll also serve tea and biscuits that the kids have made themselves. Is there anything you would like to ask me before I go to the meeting room?"

"My name is Mrs. Soltof. I teach English at P.S. 213 and I'm wondering Mr. Obler, what the children talk about at the meeting. In my class I can hardly get any of them to discuss or write about what goes on at Wilson."

"We don't have a set agenda, but most of the time the kids bring up issues around privileges and rules, conflicts they may be having with staff or with each other; and on our part, we spend a lot of time going over with them what is acceptable and non-acceptable behavior. We also sometimes try to introduce a little therapy into the session and push the boys to talk about their feelings, particularly if any incidents have occurred in their unit that they need to talk about. Hopefully, Dr. Ripkin will be joining us later during the question and answer period after the meeting, and he can talk about the therapeutic aspect of our program. Bear in mind that our boys are generally not very articulate and have a long history of emotional and psychological abuse.

I talked to the teachers for about ten minutes in this vein, thanked them for coming, and, then, placed them in the observation room.

Marty: Chuck, do you have anything you want to bring up with the kids in your unit?

Chuck: Some of them are on the verge of losing their after-school privileges if they continue to not show up on time to dinner.

Nathan: You talkin' about me, Chucky? I tol' you I missed my train. Anyway, it was you who sent me to see my parents; it wasn't my idea. I'm not takin' any crap from you or Obler.

Chuck: Nate, you know dinner is served every night at 6:15 and it is your responsibility to be there on time… and there are no excuses.

Marty: Maybe Nathan is trying to tell us that he thinks that some of the rules are unfair.

Nathan: That's right, that's right, Obler… that's what I'm tryin' to say.

Hector: Griffin! Griffin!

Marty: I'm sorry, Hector. What did you say?

Hector: Griffin! Griffin! Griffin! G-r-i-f-f-i-n!

Roberto: You losin' your fuckin' mind, man? What are you saying?

Hector: Griffin! Griffin!

Chuck: What's this Griffin stuff? Make yourself clear.

Hector: Da shoe polish, Da black shoe polish. Griffin!

Chuck: I still don't understand. What is it you're saying?

Jimmy: I know what he's talking about.

Marty: Does this have anything to do with what we're talking about?

Jimmy: You tol' us, Obler, we could bring up anything we want to at these meetings. I think Hector is upset about what happen' last night.

Marty: Be specific. What happened? And does it have anything to do with this Griffin guy?

Hector: Griffin… da black shoe polish… da black shoe polish.

Marty: Chuck, do you have any clue as to what they're talking about?

Chuck: Why don't we take this up later with Hector, and let's get back to Nate's inability to get to dinner on time.

Hector:... that motherfucka, Angel... you protectin' him, Chuck? I want that cocksucka dead.

Chuck: This isn't the appropriate time, Hector, to go into this. I want to hear what you have to say, but let's wait until tonight.

Roberto: I want to hear what happen' last night with Angel. I thought we could talk about anything. You counselors are bullshittin'.

Marty: Roberto's right, but given the special circumstances of today's meeting, I think we should stick to what we originally started talking about, concerning Nathan. If we have time, then we can get to Hector's issue.

Hector: I'm gonna get the motherfucka.... he fucked me in the butt with the Griffin. The faggot used the shoe polish... I'm gonna kill him.

Jimmy: Let's get the fucka. He done the same thing to me.

(Audible noises from behind the mirror were heard by the kids and interrupted their verbal attack on Angel)

I had been immobilized, but when I heard running footsteps from behind the mirror I realized what was happening. The observing teachers, most of who were elderly women in their fifties and sixties and had never heard anything like this in their work with children, were fleeing the premises out of horror and repulsion at what they had just witnessed. I had to do something to salvage the situation or my career at the halfway house would be short-lived. I ran out of the room and saw from the top of the landing that most of the teachers had already gotten to the front door of the building. I zipped down the stairs, hoping to plead with them to stay and return to the meeting. I had the idea in my mind that if they came back and met with the staff, they would realize the difficulties these kids face.

Dr. Penn had cautioned me about the problems of having outsiders observe a therapy meeting with these kids. Dr. Ripkin, for his part, had let me know in no uncertain terms, that my job would be on the line if the meeting exploded. His concern was that Wilson maintain a positive relationship with the community. In fact, when the halfway house was first opened a few years ago a large public outcry had materialized over the prospect of delinquents and disturbed youths being dumped into the community.

By the time I got downstairs and out the door, I caught sight of these elderly teachers all the way down the end of the block. I had to hand it to them, they were truckin'. I gave chase at full tilt until I saw forty feet in front of me Dr. Ripkin casually walking up the street, his head at a one hundred eighty degree angle, looking back at the teaching staff as they hightailed it down the block. I stopped immediately, and as he turned face-forward I saw his face red and perplexed at what he had just seen. When he approached me, he demanded, "What happened, Obler?"

"It's hard to explain. While the teachers sat behind the one-way mirror watching the unit meeting, a fight erupted over an ugly incident that occurred the night before. I don't think the kids' teachers were prepared to hear what happened. Let me put it this way, we intended to serve tea and biscuits that the kids had made, but instead we served tea and buns."

*　　　　　*　　　　　*

I had little doubt that after the fiasco, Dr.Ripkin would find my services unnecessary. Although my long-range plan was to eventually leave my job as a therapist at Wilson I didn't want to do so until I had completed my doctorate. I was now working on a Ph.D. at the New School for Social Research, after having completed my Masters at Yeshiva University. My marriage was crumbling and, financially, I needed the salary from the job to support my family. I had no one checking up on the hours I put in, which gave me the freedom to pursue my academic studies and my nighttime social activities. The latter was very convenient, because I had a place, and an excuse, to stay overnight whenever I needed to. Home, for me, was a place to crash out or play with my two kids, or, infrequently, have perfunctory sex with my wife. As usual, I kept my inner feelings at bay by compulsively acting out sexually with various women. I was adroit at finding women who were looking for a good time and had no qualms having sex with a married man. Also, in my typical fashion, I was doing everything I could to keep busy... another means of avoiding my problems at home with Dalite. I hardly slept, staying up twenty hours a day what with school, my job, and my pursuit of ladies.

The following discussion took place without my being present. I learned about it through Dottie, who gave me her tape-recorded account of what was said:

Dr. Ripkin: I want Obler out. He nearly screwed-up our relationship with the school community. He's impulsive and he's seriously disrupted the routine and structure of this facility. I knew I'd made a mistake from the beginning in hiring him.

Dottie: Why are you so angry at him? He couldn't have predicted such a loaded issue at a unit meeting. He's one of the few people at this place that's open to new ideas.

Dr. Ripkin: Are you inferring that I don't care about ideas?

Dr. Penn: I don't think Dottie is trying to say that; I believe that she is just trying to point out that Obler has made a contribution to Wilson, and, although his idea to invite the teachers turned into a debacle, I don't think we can blame him for that. In any case, what happened at the meeting is not sufficient reason to fire him.

Dottie: I still would like an answer to my question.

Dr. Ripkin: And what question was that?

Dottie: Why are you so angry at him? I can't believe it just has to do with the unit meeting and nothing else.

Dr. Ripkin: It looks as though our administrative-assistant is also turning into a psychoanalyst.

Dr. Penn: Can we get back to the matter at hand?

Dr. Ripkin: I've made myself clear. I think Obler has seriously damaged an important community link that we depend on; he should be let go, or we can work it out so that he resigns if you two are concerned about his future.

Dottie: I think I've made myself clear, also: I think he's a good therapist, cares for the boys, and has made a real contribution since he started here. He's one of the few people who generated some real discussion about what changes need to be made. Our staff meetings were uninteresting and pro forma until Obler started to question our not very successful ways of doing therapy at Wilson.

Dr. Ripkin: It's not his verbal contributions that I'm objecting to. What has been upsetting me has been his behavior in going beyond therapy with those in his unit and projecting himself as an administrator whose role is to set staff policy. One more thing, I have heard that he has abused some of the rules of the house by conducting himself inappropriately in his social conduct... and we don't have to go into the specifics of what is involved.

Dottie: I'm getting pissed off by this vendetta you're carrying for him. He's not as bad as you're trying to paint him. I think your personal concerns are getting in the way of evaluating him. The majority of the staff think highly of him.

Dr. Penn: May I make a suggestion? Why don't we put Obler on probation with the understanding that he will be re-evaluated in a few months? I don't think it's fair to dismiss him on the basis of that single incident, which was really out of his control.

Dottie: I don't have any problem with your recommendation. However I want to make it clear that Dr.Ripkin's vendetta against Obler could limit his effectiveness, especially since he supervises him. Maybe, Dr. Penn, you could take over the role as his supervisor, if that's okay with Dr.Ripkin.

Dr. Ripkin: I don't think that's advisable. Dr. Penn is not available to supervise Obler on a regular basis and in this instance he should be seen daily by his supervisor to rein in his impulsive behavior.

Dottie: It's your impulsive behavior that's disturbing me, but I'm willing to go along with your need to supervise him.

*   *   *

(Conclusion of a meeting with Dottie, myself, and Dr. Ripkin, in which I had proposed making home visits with the boys to talk to their caretakers)

Marty: I'm really very upset that you think my ideas are idiotic, Dr. Ripkin. You know, Dottie, how hard I've worked on this idea.

Dr. Ripkin: Are you forgetting, Obler, how long it took to repair the damage you did to our relations with the schoolteachers. I'm not allowing Wilson staff to travel to the middle of Harlem and venture into doing psychotherapy at our patients' homes. All we need is one of the kids' drug-addicted parents flipping out and creating an incident that will make the papers. Your idea, Obler, to conduct family therapy in the children's homes might work in a well-structured, middle class environment but goes against the principle of not conducting therapy outside of the doctor's office.

Dottie: I think it's a very interesting idea considering that we're not conducting much therapy with these kids' parents because they rarely come in.

*   *   *

(Eventually, with the help of Dr. Penn, Dottie, and Chuck, we were able to wheedle out of Dr. Ripkin permission for a home visit with Hector, myself, and Chuck.)

On emerging with Chuck and Hector from the 116th Street subway station in East Harlem, I was taken with how clean the immediate surroundings looked. It was a cold, windy, winter day and not many people were walking the streets, even though it was five o'clock in the afternoon. I had anticipated, stereotypically, lots of teenage black and Puerto Rican toughs hanging out on dirty garbage-strewn streets, kids who would not take kindly to a white guy in their neighborhood, which was one of the reasons I brought Chuck along for this home visit with Hector's family.

We had been unsuccessful in reaching Hector's parents to set up the visit because they had no telephone. Instead, I had contacted his grandmother who lived nearby and asked her to let Hector's parents know we were coming on this day. I had met the grandmother at Wilson; from what I could make out she was a kind, responsible woman who would follow through on anything asked of her. In talking to her, it became clear that she had taken on the primary parent role in raising Hector and his four siblings. Just to make sure that the parents received notice of our visit, I sent a telegram to her in the morning.

As we neared his apartment building—which was located in a run-down area some blocks away from 116th Street—Hector began to suck his thumb. The building itself was a pre-war, six-story tenement that was dilapidated, and a number of the windows were boarded with panels of wood. Once inside the building door, we could see and smell garbage strewn in the hallway. There were no numbers on any of the apartment doors. I asked Hector which apartment was his, and he pointed, with his free hand, to a door at the end of the hall. I rang the bell and waited. No response. I rang it again and waited some more. No response. I asked Chuck what we should do. He knocked harder on the door. Then, after a few minutes, we heard light footsteps coming toward us. The door slowly opened. A young girl of eleven or twelve appeared looking perplexed and unsure about who we were. A woman from within the apartment, hollered, "Who is there?" When the young girl realized it was

Hector with some adults, she turned and said, "It's my brother, Hector, sucking his thumb with some white man and a big black guy." The woman yelled, "What the fuck is Hector doing here, is the little bastard in trouble again?" The girl asked us, "What are you doing here?"

"I'm Hector's therapist at Wilson and this is Chuck, his counselor. We're making a home visit. We called your grandmother and asked her to tell you we were coming. Can we come in?"

The girl yelled back to her mother, "Mama, they want to come in..."

"Ask them what for?"

"Something about a home visit."

We heard a male voice from inside, "I'll take care of this."

The young girl opened the door three-quarters of the way, and we went inside. We entered a large room, which seemed to be the living room. On the floor there were numerous empty liquor bottles, one or two of which were broken so that shards of glass were strewn over the floor. In one corner of the room, an infant in diapers was crawling around. The room smelled of shit, which was oozing out of his diaper. A man and a woman seeming in their late thirties were sprawled out on separate couches on opposite sides of the room. Hector's mother was a young, light-skinned black woman who had already begun to lose her good looks. She covered her scantily-clad body with a dirty blanket lying next to her. The man, on the other couch, was holding a bottle of beer. He was a heavy-set black man with a big belly. He sat up and said, "Is my son in trouble again?"

I looked directly at him and replied, "No, just the opposite. Hector is doing very well at the home and we're thinking of releasing him soon. That's the main reason we're making a home visit... to check out when you feel you'd be ready to have him come home."

"I made myself clear when I appeared before the judge at the trial. The little fucker don't listen to me and I'm gonna kick his ass until he shows his father some respect. We don't have any

142

SHRINK

money here, and if you're goin' to send him home, you sure as hell better send him home with some money. I have enough mouths to feed."

I replied: "Mr. Conroy, Hector was not on trial when you appeared in court. That was a hearing that we call a PINS petition—a person in need of supervision. He was sent to Wilson for a period of time and when the staff feels he is ready to return home, we are supposed to set up a program for him to resume his normal life."

"What the fuck you talkin' about, man? He's a mean little sonofabitch. You see this strap here, that's the 'normal life' he gonna get."

"Mr. Conroy, I don't think you understand..." Chuck put his hand on my arm as a way of letting me know that we weren't going to get anywhere in this dialogue.

Chuck interrupted, "Look, we're here to see whether or not your son can come back home and live with you. By the looks of this place and the way you feel about him I don't think that can happen. If you and your wife have any objection to our finding a place for him, outside of your home, let's talk about that now."

I felt relieved that Chuck had spoken up. But I knew we were going to have a lot of trouble finding a foster home for Hector. "Mrs. Conroy," I added, "I don't know what you feel about Hector living somewhere else. However, I think your situation is such that it wouldn't work, his living here. In order to get the court's approval to look for a foster home we first have to obtain your agreement and check out whether there are any other relatives he could live with. Do you agree with your husband that it would be best for him to not live here?"

Mrs. Conroy slowly got up from the couch, came over to me and took my arm and walked me into the bedroom. Her step was unsteady and she balanced herself on my arm. She closed the door behind us, disengaged from me, walked about seven feet away, and let the blanket that she had wrapped around her fall to the floor, so she was standing in her bra and panties. My

143

first thought was that she was trying to get something from me, money or some kind of favor involving the courts, but then I saw the needle marks all over her legs and arms. She was showing me that she and her husband were junkies.

"I'm a hooker and that's how we support our habit. This ain't no place for Hector to live or any of my other kids. I pray to God every day that he don't come home. I don't know what to do with my daughter or my little baby; my other two kids are with my mother cause we can't feed them right."

"Can he live with your mother? We're not likely to get a foster home for him, he's too old and has been in too much trouble. Anyone that would take him in is probably doing it for the few dollars allotment."

"Anywhere would be better than here, but mama has a lot of problems now, you've got to talk to her. Do what you have to do to help him."

"Is there anything I could do to help you?"

She picked up the blanket and put it around her. "It's too late for me and my husband, but if you can get someone to take the baby and my daughter, who looks after the baby, it would help."

Chuck, Hector, and I were back on the street, heading towards the grandmother's house. I said to Chuck, "I wonder why she took me in to the bedroom and not you."

"You got the power, man."

"Hey, I'm lucky that I still have my job."

"You know what I mean."

And I did know what he meant, and yet, from my position it was strange to think this way, growing up poor and powerless, a Jew with a crazy family living in Brownsville. As I thought about this, I glanced at Hector, still sucking his thumb and walking as close to Chuck as he could get. I knew what he had just gone through was as potent a message to him as visiting Rachel in the bughouse had been for me... his standing in this bottle-littered broken-glass living room watching and listening to this adult world deciding his fate, nobody asking him his opinion. Imagine routinely coming home from school and being welcomed into that scene in that living room.

The brownstone in Harlem that Hector's grandmother lived in was well-kept-up and in a respectable working-class neighborhood. When his grandmother opened the door to her second-floor apartment Hector's body-language changed noticeably. His thumb was out of his mouth, a lot of tension seemed to flow out of his body and he actually was smiling while embracing his grandmother. It was evident that they were happy to see each other. My guess was that whatever, at least in recent years, had been good and nurturing in Hector's life had taken place in this apartment. His grandmother, Mrs. Baines, took him by the hand, and led him and us into the living room, indicating we should sit down on the couch. We sat down, while Hector ran over to his two younger brothers who were playing with toys on the floor, and hugged them. The grandmother excused herself to get some refreshments for us. The room was warm and nicely furnished, a Bible occupied an important place on a coffee table and over a bureau there was a luminous picture of Christ, which had the feeling of an altar in the room. When Mrs. Baines returned she was carrying a tray of cold drinks and cheese and crackers. After she set the tray down before us, and made sure we helped ourselves, she sat down in an armchair. We exchanged pleasantries for a few minutes, and then she asked us, "How has Hector been doing at Wilson? if you don't mind my asking."

"That's why we're here, to talk about Hector," Chuck answered.

I noticed the heavily-etched lines in her face, lines which bespoke of years of hard toil and worry. Her frizzy, gray hair was pulled back in a bun, and it was not hard to see that she had once been a handsome woman. I could feel her kindness and generosity by just looking at her eyes, and by seeing how Hector had become a part of the room, and not just an onlooker, as he had been at his mother's.

Chuck was taking the hopeful view of things: "Your grandson is doing very well and the staff at Wilson believes that he's ready to get back to the community and be with his family again. We just came from your daughter's house and she suggested that we talk to you about his coming home."

She listened intently to what he had said, and I got the impression that she understood exactly what had taken place at her daughter's house. She knew if there were any chance at all for Hector to rejoin his family and go to school in the community, he would have to live with her and not the mother and father.

"He was always such a good boy, I knew with a little help he'd turn out okay. That's why I sent for the police in the first place. When the judge asked whether he would be better off going to a school upstate with kids who had problems like his or to remain in his mother's custody, I begged the judge to send him away. His parents cannot provide the proper care for their children."

Chuck made his pitch. "That's for sure, Ma'am. We were wondering if you would consider taking him in because we can't release him unless we have a stable home to put him into. A lot of the kids at the facility can't go back to their original home and we have to place them in foster care if none of their relatives can take them in. Believe me, some of the foster care parents don't give a damn about the kids and can be vicious and cruel in their treatment of them. If the kids are not strong to begin with, and Hector isn't, they can be damaged for the rest of their life."

Mrs. Haines quickly turned her head away from us when she heard what Chuck was saying. I couldn't tell whether she was upset at how these children were treated in foster homes or upset at the prospect of Hector living at one of these places. She got up and went over to her grandchildren, setting upright a toy that the youngest had knocked over. After fussing with the little one a bit, she went back to the kitchen.

In her absence I said to Chuck, "What the hell did you have to tell her all that for, Chucky? Look what you did to her."

"I want her to take Hector in, Whitey. I wouldn't have minded livin' in an apartment like this and having a mama like her."

When Hector, who had been looking at us, heard what Chuck had said, he smiled. And I could see how good he felt at our trying to place him with her.

Mrs. Haines returned to the living room carrying a plate of homemade cookies. When the kids saw them, they ran towards her and started reaching for them. As she doled them out, they stuffed them into their mouths. She put the plate on the table in front of us, motioning for the children to continue playing by themselves. She went back to her armchair, falling into it, seemingly out of breath.

I asked her, "Are you okay, Mrs. Haines?"

"Just catchin' my breath. I'm getting on in years and can't keep up with all I have to do the way I used to."

"I hope Chuck didn't upset you by his account of some of the bad foster parents that some unlucky kids wind up with. Usually the system weeds the worst ones out before we send the children to them."

"You know, Ma'am," Chuck added, "it's just that I'd like to see Hector stay with you. It's clear he's happy here."

She took a deep breath and let it out wearily. I could see that the feelings that she was keeping in were taking an enormous toll on her.

"I love Hector more than anything and if I could I would take him, as Jesus took me in, but I don't have much time left. The doctors tell me I have about half a year. You have to help me. What am I going to do with these two children? If I send them back to my daughter, they'll be gone. They don't have Hector's sister's strength. The good Lord has taken their thinking from them and they're like small babies."

What she was telling me was that the two children playing on the floor were retarded. I looked over at Hector, who was with them, and I felt what the loss of his grandmother would mean to him. Thinking about this called up in me the memory of my grandmother being dragged out of the apartment when I was two years old. I glanced at Chuck for help, but he too was sinking. Listening to the heartache of this woman who had given everything she had to raising her family and having to leave this world with her daughter incapacitated and grandchildren unprotected was too much for us.

We sat in silence, not knowing what to say. Eventually the conversation resumed on a less bleak note, having to do with how Hector was doing at Wilson. When it came time to leave, I tried to console her by saying, "We'll do all we can, Mrs. Haines, to place your two youngest grandchildren in a good home." But she and I both knew that nobody would accept them, and they were headed for an institution for retarded children. Chuck, on the way out, reassured her that he would do everything he could to see to it that Hector ended up in a good home. She thanked us warmly, and said goodbye. In my heart, even though I hadn't been facing it, I knew that Wilson was no longer the right place for me to be working. I was becoming more of a social worker than a psychotherapist. Placing kids like Hector in foster homes took up more hours of the day than working with the kids. And the little bit of personal therapy I did with the boys paled in comparison to the insurmountable problems I had to deal with as a social worker-interventionist involving the schools, welfare, the court system, and placing the children in foster homes after they left Wilson. When I complained to Dr. Penn that I wasn't doing family therapy with our kids but was merely applying Band-Aids to their serious problems, he half-heartedly tried to encourage me to go on with my efforts to implement family therapy. When I pushed him about his role at Wilson, he hedged and I could tell that he was planning to leave soon. And he pretty much surmised that I would be doing the same.

After Dr. Ripkin learned that my trip to Hector's had been a failure (from his perspective I came back from the visits empty-handed, with no place to send Hector to live), he lost no time in reminding me that my job was on the line. However, during the conversation, I let him know that I had been seriously thinking about applying for other positions. Soon he was blinking repeatedly. This took me aback because after the first meeting with him, he had more control over his eye-blinking in my presence. Was it possible that behind all of his threats to dismiss me, he needed me as a whipping post and was anxious at the idea that I might be leaving? I was so pissed at his giving me such a hard time over the past few months that I couldn't refrain from blinking back in synchronicity with his blinks.

We both agreed we would not mention anything to the staff or children until I actually handed in my resignation. But I couldn't resist conveying to Chuck how Dr. Ripkin had increased his blinks per minute, after I told him that I had decided to look elsewhere for work... and how I had responded in kind. And an outgrowth of informing Chuck what had taken place was that the staff started playing the blinking game out of view of Dr. Ripkin; and soon the kids too began blinking at each other in unison. When Dottie asked me what was going on with all the blinking, I told her I might be leaving and it looked as if Dr. Ripkin couldn't take it. She laughed heartily, though underneath the laughter I could discern she was disappointed that I was contemplating leaving. We had become friends over time, and she considered me an ally.

During the next few months, I went through the motions of trying to launch the family therapy program by doing more home visits. I knew, however, it wasn't going to work. In many ways it just repeated the hopelessness and futility I experienced when visiting Hector's family.

In March 1967, I received a feeler from my college Alma Mater, Brooklyn College, to become a counselor in an innovative educational program (SEEK) for mainly black and Hispanic students. Some of the staff at the college had heard about my work at Wilson and thought that my pursuing a doctorate in clinical psychology in conjunction with my therapy experience at Wilson might prove useful in helping minority-kids in the program overcome the obstacles faced in making it at a predominantly white college. When the college finally came through with the offer of a job, I handed in my resignation.

Even though I assured Chuck that we would try to stay in contact, I had the feeling that our friendship would dissipate once we ceased working together. When it came time to say goodbye to the kids in my unit, I felt regret and a pang of guilt, knowing that I was not going to be able to provide for them two of the things they most needed: constancy and follow through. On saying goodbye, I kidded with them, but whether they kidded me back or let me know they would miss me or played it tough, I knew and they knew I was leaving... and it confirmed their unworthiness.

Just before my departure, I stopped in at Dottie's office to say farewell. I gave her a big, fat kiss right on the lips, and she pushed me away, and said, "Obler, you're impossible." I hugged her, and left.

BOOK II

CHAPTER NINE:
MAKING MY WAY (I)

Even though I had worked as a therapist at Wilson, I did not as yet have the formal credentials of a psychologist. It was during the next few years of my life that I did the intense, supervised work with patients and completed the rigorous academic training that led to my Ph.D. and New York State license as a psychologist. In September, I started the job at the College.

I was assigned to do psychological counseling in the SEEK program, while also teaching courses in psychology, some of which were comprised of both SEEK and mainstream students.

I pressured all of the students, within the structure of my psychology courses, to look at their family life and question the values and prejudices that they grew up with. I was brash and I had no problem pushing students to speak up about their home life and personal problems. I turned the classroom into a sort of huge group therapy session in which I taught the textbook psychology in connection to their lives and experience and not just out of the book. Surprisingly, the kids loved it and some of them saw it as the best class they had ever taken, because of the confidences they shared with each other.

Also I could bring to bear my sense of humor that was nourished in Brooklyn. I got a kick out of making fun of a number of the quintessentially Bronx and Brooklyn types (who put me in mind of the Brooklyn teenagers depicted so well, ten years later—1977—in the movie *Saturday Night Fever*, starring John Travolta), with their values, prejudices and narrow view of the world beyond Brooklyn. But I could zing them because I knew their world and I liked them. I remember making fun of the Italian Guido's preoccupied with their bodybuilding and their macho image. In one class, I was speaking about the lengths people go to disguise their insecurities. I brought up the bodybuilders in the class and their obsession with their physiques, interpreting it as an inversion serving to allay their fears of being weak and vulnerable. And when a few of the muscular bodybuilders in the class protested that I didn't understand what body-sculpting was all about, I couldn't resist saying, "C'mon, you know you're all latent fags," and the whole class broke up including the weightlifters.

And I was popular with the faculty in the psych department, for similar reasons. I made fun of their dependence on their presenting themselves to the students as scholars and intellectuals, and needing to be called Doctor or Professor. And I would talk in my Brownsville argot, peppered with curse words.

I did things with the students that impressed the faculty, like simulating group therapy experiences in the classroom; I introduced some of the new therapies that were trendy at the time, such as sensitivity training—sometimes touchy and feely stuff—and psychodrama, in which the kids acted out their family stories; and, most in the public eye, encounter groups, involving, for example, the 'hot seat,' in which one student sat in the middle of a circle and the other students confronted him with their feelings about him.

I can't even quite tell you how I assimilated all this new therapy stuff, some of which I picked up in the Master's program and, later, in the Ph.D. program and some of which I picked up because it was in the air at this time... but I was willing to try most anything, even if I had no prior training in or experience with it.

For instance, I took groups of students and faculty away for weekend retreats, and somehow I bungled through the interactive activities I engineered for them and the weekends were hugely successful. In spite of being a very insecure person on the inside; on the outside I was fearless, and I would make up, on the spur of the moment, encounter exercises for the kids to do. It also helped that I was brazenly confident that nothing I tried would explode in my face—this in spite of the supra-disaster I went through at Wilson.

One thing that still kind of amazes me is how, in terms of formal authority at the college, nobody questioned what I was doing, despite my being quite forthright about the new stuff I was trying with the students. But of course this was years ago, and colleges were anxious to expand curriculums to meet some of the demands students were making to update courses. I had no trouble fitting into this emphasis on making courses more relevant to the lives of the students, since I had been having my issues with the narrow strictures of academia for years.

By 1970, I completed the courses for my Ph.D. and had to choose a subject for my Dissertation. I was quite put out by having to decide on a subject, since I wanted to do something that would attract attention and not bog me down in painstaking scholarly research. After some hit and miss attempts to arrive at a subject, I came across what seemed to be the perfect fit for the kind of thing I wanted to do. It helped that it centered on sex.

It so happened at this time that I had been reading Masters and Johnson's latest research work, *Human Sexual Inadequacy*, and immediately saw an opportunity to develop a topic that would be acceptable to the committee members. Part of the Masters and Johnson book focused on comparative sex therapy techniques with sexually dysfunctional males and females. I got the idea that I could develop a similar sexual research comparing different psychotherapeutic interventions with an equivalent population. The techniques of Masters and Johnson mainly had to do with sexual stimulation methods and partner cooperation in the stimulation of erogenous zones in order to overcome sexual dysfunction.

The study I decided to work on focused on the psychological aspects of primary and secondary orgasmic dysfunction in females; primary and secondary impotency in males, and premature ejaculation and ejaculation incompetence. My techniques would center on various interventions with these disorders in order to help overcome the dysfunction. By way of example, I had female patients who suffered from inability to achieve orgasm watch films that aroused them or fantasize about sexual situations… and I taught them to relax and get pleasure from these activities rather than being made uptight. I won't go into the technical aspects of the research other than to say it involved fairly complicated physiological measurements of erogenous zones.

The committee approved my dissertation topic quickly and unanimously. My own speculation is that they saw the potential for the college gaining national attention for sponsoring this type of research, which was currently being popularized by the media… and the committee members were helpful in finding funding and searching for laboratory space for me to conduct the study.

As usual, things worked out for me for reasons that were less than noble. There was no laboratory space left on the fourth floor, which was allotted for graduate student research. But the graduate school had attracted one of the top social psychologists in the country and he insisted on taking up all the floor space for his research assistants. Without gaining greater faculty support for my research, I would not have been given any space for my study. The way it got resolved was that I advertised for subjects for the research and when the predominantly male faculty on the staff saw that many attractive females were showing up—as I expected—to be interviewed, they put pressure on the administration to give me space. I wound up with a small lab room about 20 by 30 feet, which was adequate, if cramped, to conduct my work.

On the marital front, my sexual life with my wife continued to go downhill, and staying home was more difficult than ever. Predictably, I acted out and increased my extra marital sexual activity, with most of the burden falling on a few of my fellow students at the graduate school. I frequently slept with them at the lab and avoided being home, using the excuse that the demands of the research required me to be there at all hours of the night. Shades of the situation I had set up at Wilson.

As I had mentioned previously, I was conducting weekend retreats, which I sort of considered to be an extension of my new teaching job; on one of these retreats I met my future wife, Margaret. She had heard of my work from one of my students, and was there with her boyfriend because they were having trouble in their relationship. She was great-looking, young, and I right away fell in love with her (she was one of the dark-haired, model-thin, Jewish-beauty types I had always fantasized about). On the weekend, I made a move, and invited her into a private meeting with me, in which we kissed and embraced. It was apparent to me that we were both looking for a way out of the unsatisfactory relationships we were in. After the weekend retreat we began seriously seeing each other.

Falling in love with Margaret brought home to me how unchecked my sexual life had gotten. Not only was I cheating on my wife but I did not discontinue the practice of sleeping around while seeing Margaret. I felt I was out of control and had to wonder whether I could ever have a normal, healthy relationship with a woman. I really did believe that some essential romantic feeling for my wife was missing, but I used it as justification for my engaging in multiple sexual encounters. And I also used it to act unfeelingly and insensitively to Dalite. I allowed myself to be irritated and impatient with her, and to ignore her complaints about my emotional distance and my reduced physical interest in her. I would defend against her complaints by saying I was too tired, I had to support a family and do my doctorate; and to head off further discussion, I was quick to get ugly—i.e., if she didn't like it she could go out and get a job to help support the family. I was shameless in my self-defense. Of course she couldn't get a job since she was raising our two young children. I knew that she sensed that I was sexually involved with other women but she never confronted me on it, probably out of the need for self-protection. I further rationalized my promiscuity by seeing it as part of the sexual-freedom movement that was taking place in the culture at large. I would often discuss with my colleagues at the college and with my students the concept of Open Marriage, and the benefits of sexual freedom. If I were going to be part of the so-called sexual revolution, then I had to act accordingly. How convenient... and how shallow and self-serving of me, to say the least. It would be an easy way out to chalk it up to the follies of youth, but that would be really hypocritical. Using women has been a constant in my life, from the time of adolescence. Just writing about the way I talked to my wife in this paragraph makes me shudder. I was not a very edifying creature.

Things were not simple with my feelings about Margaret. I had not stopped screwing around but I was in love with her—in part, I was playing a game on myself.

When Margaret went off to Europe with a female friend in the summer of 1971, I fell apart. I missed her inordinately. And although I hadn't spoken to her about any immediate plan of breaking-up with Dalite, I knew my marriage was over. Margaret never actively pressured me to leave my wife, but I could tell she was growing frustrated at having a prolonged affair with a married man. The fear of losing her became so strong that after she departed on her trip many of my old symptoms—restlessness and anxiety about being alone, magical or superstitious thinking, including my old standard... touching walls for security—flared up again. Fortunately it was the summertime so I didn't have to work at the college, but it was a major effort simply to get out of my apartment and conduct the research at the New School. I even created some new rituals revolving around magical thinking... the gist being that as long as I carried them out to the letter Margaret would return to me and I would not lose her. I started to get seriously depressed and found it difficult to eat and sleep. I convinced myself that if

I could extricate myself from my marriage and live with Margaret, I would return to my normal self again.

Several weeks later I announced to Dalite that I was leaving her. I had a hard time with the guilt I was feeling at informing her of this; the only way I could tell her was to cut myself off from the pain and anguish I was causing her. I presented it as a fait accompli, from which there was no turning back. She went along with my decision, perhaps feeling too hurt and too betrayed to oppose me or make an appeal to get me to reconsider. I accepted her capitulation, short-circuiting as best I could the kind of farewells and tears that could weaken my resolve and open up my guilt. I managed this by adhering to an all-out pragmatism, thinking only of myself and what was good for me. Of course this was not exactly new behavior. Temporarily I moved into a friend's apartment a few blocks away and immediately started calling every woman I knew with whom I had had a relationship. I couldn't deny to myself how desperate and anxious and lonely I was, but neither could I face how compulsive I was becoming sexually—for that matter, maybe the frequency of my thoughts about sex itself, along with my elevated sexual activity, amounted to a magic ritual.

It was extremely rough telling my eleven-year-old son and ten-year-old daughter that I would be moving out of the apartment. Despite my attempt to reassure them, that the only change that would affect their life was that I would no longer be living in the apartment with them, it did little to relieve their anxiety that I was abandoning them and their mother. I had the feeling that, if anything, my attempt to coat the pill only made things worse. By playing down their fears, I reinforced their sense of the magnitude of what was happening, for obviously I needed to deny to myself what loomed large to them. The best I could do was to convince myself that my leaving might, in the end, benefit the children as well as me. As it was, I was hardly ever home for the kids and I jumped at the idea that if I could establish myself with Margaret and stop running away from my home life, it might improve my fathering of my children. But that was the plan for the future, for the present I kept up my compulsive philandering.

At the lab at the Graduate School, I began to enjoy my research project a bit too much. Part of my doctoral study involved hooking up subjects to electronic devices that measured their body responses to sexually stimulating material. The most sensitive of the machines was the Galvanic Skin Response (GSR); it could calibrate both conscious and unconscious anxiety and libidinal responses to erotic visual and auditory stimuli. This was helpful in detecting in the subjects of the study, physiological responses to sexual material that they couldn't consciously admit stimulated them. It was particularly applicable to women, because they tended to feel more conflict around their 'improper' sexual fantasies. For example, pictures of anal penetration repulsed some of the women subjects consciously but in more than a few cases the GSR indicated otherwise, on an unconscious level. I would think this conflict was more than a little engendered by culturally-induced inhibitions. I have to admit that I myself got turned on at the idea of being able to determine, electronically, what stimulated a woman when she herself denied it. Men, too, had their share of anxiety... around size issues, performance issues, and comparison-with-other-men issues.

Part of what I was trying to do by the experiments I was conducting on the subjects was to demonstrate my theory that if I could reduce their underlying anxiety to sexual stimuli that produced discomfort and tension in them, I could make a change in the kind of interference that was causing their sexual disability or dissatisfaction. The results of the research indicated that the treatment I utilized was effective in reducing the majority of the problematic symptoms of the subjects; in 1975 I published an article on my research in *The Journal of Experimental and Sexual Research*.

As for my propensity to find women who were sexually available, and desirous of commingling, I would say that it had not deserted me in my research efforts. This connected to my observation that "I was running as fast as I could," which had everything to do with the way I was leading, or should I say avoiding, my life. For me, there was nothing new about plunging into sexual encounters as a means of relieving tension; but this was outside the radar of the GSR.

Margaret returned from Europe by summer's end. After she arrived at Kennedy Airport, she called me at work and asked me to pick her up. On hearing her voice on the phone, I was thrilled that she was back in my life, and relieved of the anxiety of having to think about her alone in Europe and what she might be doing. I beelined it to the airport. When I saw her there, waiting for me at the baggage claim with her suitcases, I couldn't contain my happiness; and as we embraced, I knew that she was as happy to see me as I was to see her.

Still, I was a guy, and on the way back to the city from the airport, despite the joy I felt at our reunion, I couldn't help myself from asking her up front, whether she had slept with anyone on her trip. Her answer was of the variety that every man hates to hear and cannot help wishing that he hadn't asked the question. Without hesitation, she told me that she had one affair with an American tourist her age. He was traveling with a male friend, and his friend paired off with her traveling companion. The four of them had spent a week together in Italy. Naturally, I couldn't just let this information sink in without having to ascertain how she felt about the affair... and, of course, what was the sexual experience like. I was reassured at the casual way she seemed to talk about the affair, and accepted her characterization of it as being something that didn't amount to much. She didn't forget to ask me, however, "What about you, during the time I was away?"

I did my usual shuffling and prevarication, by way of denial; but, in addition, I had an added incentive—of not wanting to let her off the hook by admitting straight out that I had been sexually active too. So the route I took was to pile on how much I missed her and followed that with the news that I had left

Dalite and was now living at my friend's apartment. I figured the substance of this latest news would rescue me from Margaret seeing through my not having answered her question and could instead get us talking about our new life together. It worked… in the half-satisfactory way that such pathetic moves work, leaving me with the feeling that Margaret didn't feel it was worth it to press the issue, and could control her jealousy much better than I could control mine.

Within a week after Margaret's return, I moved into her apartment in Brooklyn and lived part of the time with her. I also took a small studio of my own which was located a block away from where my wife and kids lived in Manhattan. I did this for a number of reasons, among them: to maintain the facade with Dalite that I wasn't living with another woman, so as not to antagonize her and to make sure that she wouldn't be inspired if we got divorced to ask for half of everything; and also I took the apartment to cover myself with Margaret, because even though I was committed to her, I still was driven to see other women and I might need a place to fall back on. And probably another reason that motivated me to have my own apartment was that it would allow me to keep all my options open—in order to dispel my childhood fears that everyone would abandon me and I would have no place to live.

Let me say this: I myself am abashed at the cold, calculating and narcissistic way I conducted my affairs. Even in the most generous view of my behavior, I could only say that I was out of control and extremely vulnerable to the fear and panic that dominated my life. However, what continues to amaze me is that while my life was in such disarray—having to do with my running full tilt away from my inner life and conscience—it never interfered with my uninterrupted success in the outer world. I was able to support my family; rent a studio; work towards completing the doctorate; teach a full course load at the College; and spend time with my kids.

Moreover, when the economics of supporting this lifestyle became difficult, I set up a small private practice. And while the practice started slowly, after four or five months it began to take off. I myself was surprised at how relatively easy it was for me to get patients, by word of mouth, without having had much experience doing individual therapy.

On a personal level, I began to have an increasing sense that success was a double-edged sword for me... that it buttressed my self-worth while it allowed me to keep running from myself. As long as I could see myself as this kid from the ghetto making it in the real world, I could keep from examining the morality of what I was doing and the way I was using people for my own ends. I was not exactly a *mensch*. And the more I felt this, the more I needed to compulsively sing my praises to everyone and anyone. I was pretty much a case of grandiose delusions hiding a scared little boy. Help. I needed help. But how to get it, when the shell encasing my fears was so thick and impenetrable? My problem, for one, was that I was so damn good at making my way in the world. If I was that good, what could overtake me?

In a sense, the real issue of my life at this time, and probably forever, was how much would I continue to operate in defense of my defenses and ignore the need for change and confrontation of my reality. What kind of a person would I become, knowing this and continuing to ignore it? More and more this is becoming the crux of the book—which is how much change am I capable of? I see that but I have put up with the child Marty Obler I am for endless years. I'd like for the sake of the book to become a better person, and for the sake of cleaning up my act as a shrink... even though I know I am doing good work with my patients.

The trouble is that I bullshit myself about myself, so I'm a very poor shrink to myself and of course that has to carry over to my patients, one way or the other. But my pragmatism also takes the form of self-acceptance... and feeling certain that I'll always get by. That I say this outright, I suppose puts me in the category of having one foot in the mire and one foot out. Is that surprising, coming from the family I came from? You can see that as an excuse... or an overwhelming truth, from which there may be no escape.

But let me get back to my story.

For about a year I managed to get by without much change in the way I was handling my life. Among the list of my accomplishments, I now could boast of having handed in my dissertation, and successfully defended it; received a next-step promotion at the College, to Assistant Professor; and did an internship at Brooklyn Community Counseling Center, which was part of my responsibility in completing my doctorate. Still, with all of the impressive activity, more holes began to appear in my armor: In the summer of 1973, I was invited to give a paper at the annual convention of The American Psychological Association. Not too long before leaving to the convention, being held in New Orleans, I started to fall apart... bodily. I developed acute back spasms that made it difficult for me to be up and about; sometimes I had to use a cane or a walker to support me. I could only sleep in one position, and even then I was in pain. I consulted a back specialist, at the Rusk Institute, who assured me, after doing comprehensive testing, that my condition was primarily psychosomatic—mainly the result of the intense stress in my life—and that it was his recommendation that I see a psychotherapist. He said to me, "You're a shrink, get some help." But it took a rift with Margaret to move me from thinking about getting help to actually getting myself to therapy. Fortunately, after a few weeks, my back spasms abated and I could walk almost normally again.

At the convention, I met a young, attractive female psychologist and proceeded to do what I have always done. But while I was having dinner with her and some other colleagues the next day, my sixth sense told me that something was wrong. I felt panicky at the dinner, excused myself and went to call Margaret, who was staying at my studio. I called late at night and nobody answered; I right away booked a flight to New

York, went back to the table to excuse myself to everyone, not even taking time to say more than a few private words to my new companion.

The flight got in at 2 A.M. I drove my car back from the airport, went up to my studio and unlocked the door, but it was chained from the inside. I heard Margaret say, "Oh my God." I said, "Open the damn door." Then she came and unloosed the chain, informing me, "Someone's here." I pushed my way in and confronted the two of them.

"How could you do this to me, in my place? I can't believe it."

"We didn't have to use your place; she was only waiting for your phone call."

"Don't you have any sense of respect, it has to be in my bed? You (him) get the fuck out of here, and you (Margaret) just sit there and don't say anything." He did leave, and she said little.

I spent the next seven hours cleaning the apartment, bawling, crying, and putting her through hell, accusing her of the worst betrayal of my love for her. This was not the controlling, manipulative, self-confident, dominant Obler who was pretty much impervious to the needs of his partner and centered on his own needs. This was a sniveling little child Obler, doubling up in pain and self-pity, feeling that I had lost my power and seeking relief at all costs.

It's not that I was not in touch with that little, frightened, vulnerable child in me, it's that my need for Margaret, as a mother/wife figure, was so powerful that the thought of losing her stripped away my masculine defenses I had relied so heavily on for most of my life. Consequently, I felt insecure and forced her to promise me over and over again that she wouldn't see this guy anymore.

Certainly, during this time Margaret seemed to be doing okay, while I couldn't sleep at night because I was obsessively ruminating about the incident.

At no point, however, in my dependence on Margaret and trying to reestablish the intensity and intimacy of our relationship, did I ever bring up my sexual activity in New Orleans. What I make of that is simply: I was a huge hypocrite, there's no getting around it. Beyond my hypocrisy, however, which was fairly native to me, I felt that I couldn't afford, in my present condition, to be truthful about my own sexual activity in New Orleans because I couldn't take a chance of losing Margaret. Obviously, if I let it be known, after all the grief I had given her over her affair, that I myself had slept with a very accomplished, pretty woman, she would not be looking at me too favorably. And, if I went so far as to come clean, in a weak, anxious moment, and confess to her how many women I had seen during the time I was with her, she might have left me. I was in bad shape and needed to talk to someone about how shaky I was feeling. I turned to a relatively recent close friend who was a colleague of mine in the psychology department at the college. His name was Ted. And he was capable of being perspicacious about my personality and problems, and, in general, would not just feed me pablum to make me feel better.

Ted had been the only person I had confided in, early on, while I was still living with my wife, that I was having a major affair with Margaret and I trusted him partially because he had confided in me openly about his difficulties with his steady girlfriend. We met in an Upper West Side coffee house. I filled Ted in on what had happened in New Orleans and the painful details of my catching Margaret in my apartment with her friend. Of course Ted was very interested in some of the details of the story, simply as a male who could put himself in the position of being betrayed sexually by his lover.

"I don't believe it. You actually caught Margaret in your apartment with this guy?"

"Yup, in my fucking place."

"For me, that is exactly the nightmare that I worry about. I have had enough trouble hearing from my woman about her sex life in the past, before I knew her. Forget about catching her in my apartment with a guy. That would be too big a stretch for me."

"That's why I called you, I'm not dealing with it too well. I feel humiliated, embarrassed, and afraid of other people finding out what happened… and I'm like an idiot who can't believe this just happened to him."

"I totally sympathize with you, but I can't help thinking about how regularly you cheated on Dalite and on Margaret. Don't you think, maybe, what Margaret did had something to do with your screwing everything you could get your hands on, even if she never actually knew what you were doing?"

"Logically, I completely understand that her behavior had everything to do with mine. But the logic doesn't make me feel any better. I fucked up and I am frightened and panicky and afraid she's gonna leave me… the weirdest thing is that I had a premonition some weeks before New Orleans that something like this was going to happen."

"What triggered that off?"

"I wracked my brains to figure out what led me to this premonition and the thing I came up with was a recollection of an incident that happened in her apartment with some of her fellow students in anthropology. I was there. One of her male classmates hadn't shown up at the meeting to study for an exam, and when a girl asked her to call him, she right then and there dialed the number off the top of her head. Her friend seemed perplexed, and asked her, 'How did you know his number?' She said that she had recently called him, but I could tell it was bullshit. I suppose that is why I hopped on the plane when I had not been able to get a hold of her at my apartment. Obviously, it was the same prick that I had the pleasure to meet in my studio."

"Sounds to me that you hopped on that plane because you had a feeling that you deserved to be cuckolded. Even while you were down there, at the meeting, you were cheating on Margaret. You know, one could make the case that you engineered the whole thing in New Orleans, and your frenetic screwing was an attempt to get caught and be stopped."

"I hear what you're saying and I'm sure you're right. But I still am wracked with anxiety that she prefers him over me… and that I've lost her."

"I appreciate that, but to tell you the truth, I would be having a more difficult time than you seem to be having over all the male ego stuff… like, Was he a better cocksman than me?"

"That worries me, but nowhere near as much as seeing myself left all alone in the world and it is irrational, since I have loads of numbers I can call of women that are available."

"I think that *thought* is irrational. It's not about that. It's about what you've done to yourself by closing off your feelings and downplaying what Margaret offered you. It sounds to me, if you can gather yourself together, and not fall prey to the masculinity stuff of someone bopping your ol' lady, you really have an opportunity to stop messing your life up and establish a different kind of relationship with Margaret."

"I fully agree with what you're saying."

"Yeah, but the real question is, Do you want to be an asshole for the rest of your life?"

"I'd prefer not to be, but I seem to be moving in that direction."

"Rapidly, I might add."

"What can I tell you that might offer a ray of hope for me?"

"Nothing. Your hopeless, Marty, you never learn… face it."

"Great. Anything else you have to say to cheer me up?"

"Forget it. It would be a waste of time."

"Anyway, at least I know I can always count on you." We both laughed.

A couple of weeks later, as I was beginning to get over Margaret's betrayal of me, she let me know that she wanted the freedom to see other men—not, however, the guy I caught her with. I was happy to hear that she wasn't going to see him, but I wasn't too pleased to hear that she wanted the freedom to see other men. I would have liked to present her with an ultimatum that if she was going to go out with other men, then that was it for me. We were finished. Only I didn't have the *cojones* to threaten her with that. Instead I agreed to a limited open relationship in which we would both be free to see other people as long as we kept it to ourselves.

Not too long after the above agreement took place, I spent a weekend visit with the psychologist I had met in New Orleans. On my return, Margaret called me and seemed very anxious to see me. I made an appointment to meet her the next day at my apartment. I figured she knew that I had been with a woman, and I assumed she had at least spent some part of the weekend with a man. It was all okay according to our agreement. She appeared at the apartment and, when I asked her what was wrong, she remained silent but I could tell from her sullen face that she was fuming inside. On the way back to her apartment, she bolted from my car at a red light, walking quickly down Eighth Street in Greenwich Village. I parked the car in an illegal parking spot and ran after her. When I caught up to her, I grabbed her by the shoulders and could see her tears. She blurted out, "I can't take this anymore. You have to stop seeing other women."

"But you're the one who wanted it this way."

I felt great having retrieved the power in the relationship.

When I think of the turnabout, from my feeling so vulnerable and tenuous in the relationship with Margaret, to feeling buoyant and in control again, it surprised me, not that the shift occurred, but how easily I was able to bring it about. It reminded me of how easy it was for me to gain control over the kids in the gang in Brownsville. Similarly, in my family, I was adept—as an older teenager—at assuming a position of power in which they all listened to me and eventually capitulated to my wishes. Of course I was also aided in this aspect by my position as the only male child in the family and, especially, given a weak father. With Margaret, I pretty much knew that I was the best prospect for her economically, and in terms of a career, since I was able to provide the tuition and support for her to go to graduate school... and pull herself out of her lower middle class origins. At this time I was making a good living as a college teacher and a therapist and could offer her a chance to move into Manhattan. When she insisted that I give up seeing other women, I calculatingly jumped right in to look for an apartment together with the unspoken condition that she would have to be completely faithful. The way I looked at it was that for an extra four hundred a month I had complete control of the relationship. Furthermore, I wasn't really thinking that I was going to give up my promiscuous way of life.

(Note to the reader: It might be useful at this point to re-read the Introduction before concluding that all hope is lost for me.)

CHAPTER TEN:
MAKING MY WAY (II)

Margaret and I found a two-bedroom apartment in Greenwich Village and moved in. However, the increase in rent didn't bother my economics since I managed to convince Margaret to let me use the apartment, additionally, as an office for my private practice; before long, I was able to almost double my income, with all the new patients I got from the university population in the Village.

So, I would say this: that having wormed my way into power in the relationship again, I had no problem, going from the shaky child, I described when I came across Margaret and her temporary lover in my quarters, to resuming my old role of dominance in all situations. Once I could see that I had room to manipulate and control things, I was back in business.

So, at least, I thought. Only, while I continued to shake and bake and run from my problems, my anxieties increased and I began to have a growing feeling that it was only a matter of time before Margaret would find out that I was screwing around. Losing her was not something I was sure I could handle; moreover, I worried that the way I was going, I could have an anxiety attack and end up needing to confess my infidelities. I felt I was presented with a choice: to wait until my life crashed or seek help in the present. I would like to say that it was moral responsibility that pushed me to give up the games I was playing, only it was fear of losing my security with Margaret and fear of cracking up that led me to get help.

Being fairly sophisticated by now—partially having to do with having completed my Doctorate and having a private practice—I was able to set up a plan to go for post-Doctorate certification in psychoanalysis; and this program required that students embark on their own psychoanalysis—which I did with positive feelings that it would force me to work on myself on a deeper level than I had done before. I was assigned to see Dr. Myra Henderson, a well-respected psychoanalyst in the program (she was also a member of the Karen Horney Institute). She was an older woman of seventy-five and she agreed to act as both my supervisor and personal analyst.

In session with Dr. Henderson, we started working on my relationship with Margaret and what it said about how terrified and desperate I was in my relationship with women. The following dialogue took place:

"Margaret is just a young kid of twenty-two and is discovering herself in her relationship with men. Her affair with a young person from her generation is very different in kind than your repeated multiple affairs while you are involved with her. You have to face your own ambivalence toward any woman you are with who takes on the role, for you, of lover and mother. It should be clear to you by now, after having dealt in your first personal therapy some eight years ago, that your problems with women persist into the present. You still have a lot of unresolved, deep ambivalence towards your mother which is manifesting itself in your relationship with Dalite, with Margaret, and with me in your analysis."

"So you don't see any difference between the way I feel toward Margaret and my feelings towards my mother and women in general?"

"Oh, there is a major difference in your conscious feelings toward the women. Some of them are mere sex objects that you didn't care about, some of them are love objects whom you use to fill the emptiness you feel, and still others, like your wife Dalite, are more directly transferred mother figures whose sole purpose is to take care of little Muttla's needs."

"And Margaret?"

"As we've tried to establish, she is your long sought after, idealized mother whom you yearn for but is unattainable...

unlike Dalite, who really did take care of you—in a way that your mother couldn't—and liked the idea of mothering you. Perhaps the very fact that you believe the mother-lover is unattainable is at the core of your compulsive womanizing and it serves the purpose of being a decoy enabling you to avoid your underlying depression."

"What about Margaret's affair with her classmate?"

"What about it?"

"It *hoits*, right in the *kishkes*."

"Why does it hurt so much, since you, if you remember, were having an affair, and had many before, while you were seeing Margaret?"

"... part of the reason I have had these affairs is to protect myself from being destroyed by the woman l love."

"You're entitled to have affairs, it seems, without worrying about destroying her."

"How many males wouldn't feel destroyed by their woman sleeping with another man?"

"True, it is different for men than women, but don't take refuge in identifying with other men. What do you feel is so devastating about Margaret sleeping with another man, when you've done the exact same thing, with other women?"

"Even though it sounds infantile, she should love me so much that she wouldn't want to be with someone else. And if I don't have that total devotion, I am afraid of feeling hollow and empty... unable to face life alone."

"So why is your capacity for healthy projection so limited that you can't suppose that Margaret could feel similar fears and insecurities at your behavior with other women?"

"That's a hard question to answer, maybe I'm just too egocentric?"

"... and self-indulgent."

"Why is that so important?"

"It's important because it shows your complete lack of ethics when the issue really hits home. You talk a good game about Margaret but you are completely self-indulgent when it comes to you… and resort to platitudes about why it's harder for men to accept adultery than women. Is it just possible that Margaret is feeling a lot of what you went through? Or do you ever stop and think about what Dalite must have felt?"

My analysis with Henderson did not just focus on my relationship with Margaret and my wife. It took in the personality problems I was having at the Post-Graduate Institute. It troubled me that I had barely begun my studies and analysis, and already I was inordinately contentious with those around me. I found myself arguing over theoretical issues, power issues, mainly centering on the Institute's strict adherence to the Freudian line. Of course when I entered the program I knew this was the policy; but I was young and arrogant enough to not let that deter me from being unabashedly critical of the faculty, and my classmates, for not embracing a more eclectic approach.

Henderson tried to get me to examine my tendency to create controversy wherever I went, as I had in junior high school; in Israel on the kibbutz; at the Wilson School; at Brooklyn College; and now in my psychoanalytic training at the institute. "I am willing to admit that I seem to create problems wherever I go, but I also think in large part that is due to the need for change in the way institutions are run."

"Can you apply that to your post graduate training and what bothers you so much about how that institution is run?"

"Yup, I'm not doing too well on personal or theoretical grounds with Doctor Barton and Doctor Waite, in my Freud theory class."

"What's the problem?"

"Well, I'd like to get to that, but, to be honest, I'm a little afraid that, if I share it with you, in my personal analysis, you might bring it up with some of your peers in the Administration and it could effect my standing at the Institute."

"I can understand your concern, but everything that goes on here is confidential."

"It's supposed to be…"

"It will be…"

"Okay. I'll explain my side of things, I'm sure you'll hear Doctor Waite and Doctor Barton's take on it. But let me say beforehand that I hope you don't end up lecturing me."

"I hope I don't have to."

"Well, here goes. For the past three months I sat with my hands crossed as a model student, while listening to case after case of student presentations and have had to swallow what I really feel about the bullshit intellectual games people are playing. At the last class meeting I finally lost it. I guess you're going to hear about it soon enough, as word spreads through the rumor mill, about my personality problems."

"And how were the so-called personality problems evidenced in this class?"

"As Doctor Cavaletti finished her presentation on the subject of her patient's hysterical sexual symptomatology emanating from her Electra complex, Doctor Barton came out with his typical explanation of Freud's approach to female hysteria."

"What was the technical explanation he gave?"

"… that her globus hystericus and vaginismus are classical representations of a sexual-conversion disorder based on her Electra fixation."

"And what is so disturbing about this explanation?"

"My response."

"Continue."

"I blew up."

"At Doctor Barton?"

"Not Quite. I asked why Doctor Waite and Doctor Barton invariably attribute every female difficulty to women's unconscious desire to have sexual relations with their father. When Doctor Waite intervened, and she confronted me with the problem I was having accepting Freud's basic Oedipal theory, I answered with my usual cynicism."

"In your colorful Brownsville argot?"

"You got it."

"Spare me."

"I volunteered that not every woman's difficulties in performing fellatio is traceable to her fear of swallowing her daddy's semen and becoming pregnant, which is also her wish. I went on to point out that her patient's throat constriction, which was labeled globus hystericus, might be due to having a sore throat on that night. Doctor Barton attacked me as obviously not having overcome my simplistic psychologist training in graduate school."

"And what did you say to that?"

"I said I could accept the globus hystericus symptomatology as having an Electra-based ideology, but it's extremely hard for me to accept the tight muscular constriction surrounding the vaginal walls in vaginismus as being derived from ego and id conflicts during the Electra stage [in Freud's later theory of psycho-sexual development in women, he switched the emphasis somewhat from sexual desire for the father to wanting to be impregnated by him]... though I think what I actually said was that most of the women I've known who had a tight vagina had trouble with the guys they were making it with, and, as far I could tell, none of these females were having sex with their daddies."

"Very nice, very endearing."

"I'm afraid I used a more colorful term for the word vagina."

"What else?"

"I thought I was trying to wake up my classmates in the hope that they would join me in taking issue with having to parrot Freudian theory at every turn. You and I both know that the students keep quiet out of fear of being denied the credentials to practice analysis. However, I wonder whether in following the narrow Freudian dogma so aggressively we're doing a disservice to many of our patients. On the other hand, I have to wonder whether my main purpose in making myself outlandish was to get attention. I ought to confess that I was intent on impressing Dr. Waite."

"Why her and not Doctor Barton?"

"It should be obvious."

"Oh…"

"I even suggested to her after the class, when she indicated that a supervisory session with Doctor Barton and her might be helpful at this juncture, that I meet individually with each of them."

"Did she go along with that?"

"Yes, we met a few days later over coffee."

"Am I to expect more disclosures of your immaturity?"

"I exceeded myself in that department, rest assured."

"I am not feeling comforted, I can assure you."

"After we sat down Doctor Waite asked me, 'What is on your mind, Dr. Obler?' "

"I told her, 'It's been a great experience being in your class. I've learned a tremendous amount and I would like to get to know you beyond the student-teacher relationship.' "

"She saw where I was heading and asked, 'And how do you propose to do this?' "

"I answered, 'Just sharing some of where we've been and who we are.' "

"You were very forward."

"Her reply was that the training institute had very clearly-defined positions concerning student-faculty fraternization and that she thought it only proper for us to refrain from getting to know each other on a personal level. She suggested that we limit our discussion to analytical issues."

"I said, 'I have no problem with that. But I admire you and would like to know what motivated you to become a psychoanalyst.' "

"She asked me what was motivating me to become an analyst?"

"I asked her whether I could expect that all my questions will be turned around so that I am asking the question of myself?"

"She came back with, 'I thought you were pleased with the way I conducted class.' "

"This is where I really outdid myself. I said, 'I am,' and then I asked her, 'By any chance did you ever hear of the Glass Water theory of sexuality?' "

"What are you talking about?" Dr. Henderson asked.

"It will become clear.... Then Dr. Waite said, 'No, but I'm curious.' "

"I wasted no time in satisfying her curiosity. I proceeded to explain: 'Well, after the Russian revolution, Lenin, Stalin, and Trotsky decided to introduce measures designed to remake the way men and women related to each other sexually. Lenin suggested a modern Marxist society should completely reject bourgeois, romantic love and replace it with a more natural, pre-industrial sexuality. Trotsky proposed that children be educated from the earliest years to be receptive to having sexual relationships with anyone they were attracted to on demand... very much like, if someone were thirsty, he wouldn't hesitate to request a glass of water and it would be the responsibility of the person asked to give it to him because he needed it. Stalin worried about this, not surprisingly, given his paranoia; he couldn't help worrying, that in such a free sexual society, many people, especially men, would exploit this social philosophy to satisfy their own sexual desires. Lenin and Trotsky countered with the argument that sex and water are necessary to life and the working class should not be prevented from having free access to both necessities. I wonder if there isn't a deep connection between Marxist philosophy and Freudian drive theory. After all, think of Wilhelm Reich's Orgone Box theory... as one man's attempt to open up sex to everyone and take it out of the hands of the church and government; good sex was a classless entitlement. Even Freud, in *Civilization and Its Discontents* recognized a terrible price was being paid for society's demand that we inhibit our sexual instincts in order to maintain a stable social order.' "

"Doctor Waite was very articulate in her reply. She said, 'I think, Dr. Obler, I get the drift of where this is going. But let me say I agree with Freud, both as a married woman and a psychoanalyst. For there to be a stable social order within our analytic institution, some clearly set forth sexual restraints have to be in place between training students and faculty and, of course, between therapists and their patients. I suppose that I should also mention that the Institute, unlike Marxist institutions, establishes unambiguous hierarchical distinctions that are fixed and unchangeable. It does not do to have the faculty and the students enmeshed in one great proletarian mass.' "

"I asked her, 'Does that mean I will not get an opportunity to know you better?' "

"She replied, 'I think you can draw that conclusion.' Which wrapped things up pretty well, wouldn't you say?"

"I certainly would. No ambiguity there."

"I know I made a fool of myself with Doctor Waite, but I couldn't help it."

"Why couldn't you help it?"

"As you have indicated on many occasions I can't tolerate feeling helpless in the grasp of the all-powerful mother. My aggressive need to conquer her and take away her power over me had become almost an obsession. I took a big risk and I knew it every moment I was with her at the coffee shop. And even though I felt relieved when she put me down and rejected me, I felt really strong sexual desire while I was with her. I knew in the back of my mind that she was treating me like a little boy, who was acting inappropriately."

"Isn't that similar to the dynamic with you and your wife?"

"Maybe at the beginning, but later I took more and more control as I sensed her dependence on me."

"I have to let you know how disappointed I am in the way you came on to Doctor Waite. This is outside the analytical issues that your behavior with Doctor Waite brings forth. What right do you have to act like a seventeen-year old rebellious child with Doctor Waite and take advantage of your teacher-student relationship with her? There is nothing amusing or charming about your gross behavior... and you demean yourself and the Institute by what you have told me. Let me be clear that this is my personal response apart from being your analyst."

"I agree with you. I was out of line, and I am sorry. Should I apologize to Doctor Waite?"

"That is up to you."

"I planned to apologize to her, but somehow never got around to it."

In the weeks to come, Dr. Henderson played her part as analyst, in examining with me, and for my benefit, my acting out in the inexcusable way I did with Dr. Waite. Two short dialogues stick in my mind. The first,

"If we look at a key element of your mother and father's sexual relationship, we can't get away from the underlying dynamic of your father's abuse of and aggression towards your mother... and your internalization of it."

"Can you clarify that for me? It's hard for me to get a handle on some of this primal material because it applies to me."

"Your father took your mother sexually whether she welcomed it or not, just like a male chimpanzee forces himself on a female chimp in estrus. She even screamed and cried while he imposed himself on her and you witnessed this primate-like scene many times, a scene which you replicated in spirit if not in actuality with your wife and Margaret... and you would have liked to have done the same with Doctor Waite."

"I didn't force myself on them."

"What do you call having sex with your wife and Margaret five to seven days a week, year round?"

"I call that having fun."

"Do you think either of them welcomed that kind of compulsive sexual behavior?"

"I would like to think so."

"Did you ever ask them what they feel?"

and the second,

"What in your mind did you think might happen if Doctor Waite had welcomed your coming on to her?"

"Well, I guess that if I was able to get her to need me, then I could gain power over her; but if she doesn't need me—as she doesn't—then I might revert to the little child whose neediness and vulnerability knows no bounds."

"Exactly, and your fear of that is so great that you superimpose this situation of you and your mother in your relationships with other women. And the fact that Doctor Waite didn't need you and wasn't interested in you was so anxiety producing that you had to test whether or not you could gain power over her or whether you could survive if she had the upper hand."

"That sounds right to me. And, if my situation with my mother became too fraught and too anxiety producing, I would withdraw from my mother and identify with my father. But of course the problem with that was that he was a depressed, helpless, weak, frightened man who had to suppress much of his anger for fear of the consequences. And I identified with his fear and probably, on an unconscious level, wanted him to abuse my mother."

"It's better than being dependent, helpless, and rejected…"

"… which explains why I had the confidence all along that I could play the fool with Dr. Waite and still land on my own two feet. It was my way of asserting my brashness with her."

"… with only Dr. Waite? What about with the way you are seen in the program, and certainly you knew that this kind of grossly immature behavior with a colleague of mine was not likely to impress me highly… though you might have seen it as a way of getting on equal footing with me, if you could lay claim to having been intimate with her."

"You have to admit, I've provided a good window, in my account of what took place with me and Doctor Waite, through which to see my psychological hang-ups with women."

"Yes, for what it's worth. I'm sure Dr. Waite was not oblivious to the kind of interpretation we've been doing. You can take heart from that."

"You mean that I could hardly have done more to lower myself?"

"… something like that."

*   *   *

I was a good intuitive analyst with patients and others, but, as the reader can see I was a rather raw recruit when it came to my own behavior. Also, clearly I was resistant to doing the kind of analysis Dr. Henderson was pushing me to do. I dragged my feet out of self-indulgence and not wanting to do the hard work that was called for—hey, I'm Martin Obler, let the world take me as I am. What was the point of becoming so adroit at getting ahead and manipulating the system, if I had to go back to ground zero and relive the pain and dependence of my childhood years? I earned the right not to have to go through that… even with Dr. Henderson, or, someone as sharp as Ted. Life still had to beat me up some more to alter old habits of defense. If my current activities were any barometer—I was heading for trouble.

Unfortunately, time with Dr. Henderson was not my ally. Skipping ahead:

I looked at Dr. Henderson after two more years of personal and supervisory analysis and wondered how much more time we would have with each other. She had confided in me that she was suffering from emphysema. Her face looked drawn and pale and it occurred to me that over the time we were working together I had never seen her as an old and physically vulnerable woman. I guess my transference required that she fill my need for the early nurturing mother whose face I perceived, in my infancy, as shining and beautiful. Now I was seeing her from a different angle. I began to think about her mortality and how she was dealing with her frailty. I also began to think about her countertransference toward me. Dr. Henderson on many occasions had voiced her feelings about my behavior and my personality, but it was always at a professional distance, accompanied by appropriately-timed interpretations and insights. Did she like me? Did she care about me? Was I just a patient to her or did I play a role, in her countertransference, of the son she'd never had?

We began to talk a lot more about how we felt about each other, which made sense within the circumstances. I knew within myself that Henderson was dying. When the subject of her dying of emphysema did come up, I took it very badly. I could feel my body trembling and I did all I could to prevent myself from bursting out crying. I know now that I chose not to let in the impact of the many times that I witnessed her struggling for breath, in order to protect myself from seeing someone so knowing, caring, and nurturing fatally wasting away.

It was not long before the mother-son bond was acknowledged between us and we both conceded our dependence on each other. I began to see with her help, that I could be, in spite of my self-reference and childhood deprivation, a caring and empathetic human being... who was capable of being a nurturing therapist. I had felt this about myself but now I was able, more often, to cut it loose from my need to inflate my self-image and impress the world.

In the next couple of months before Dr. Henderson died, we worked together on the transference and worked at creating some kind of closure. She also helped me in setting up my first formal group therapy practice. She made it clear that she believed in my potential as a therapist. She saw that I could utilize, in my profession, the strength I had amassed in withstanding the downward pull of my childhood and even in keeping in check the pathologies that were no stranger to me.

After her death, I contemplated leaving the Institute, but decided not to because I concluded that I needed to continue my analysis and refine my skills as a working therapist. Moreover, Dr. Henderson had pointed out to me that I thrived on opposition—even if, sometimes, for the wrong reasons— and that I would do better having an aggressive and assertive outlet than to isolate myself.

This much about Dr. Henderson: She was a solid clinician and a genuine caretaker, a combination not automatic in an analyst. And like good therapists everywhere, she served as a role model. Part of her contribution to me in this area had to do with the way she was able to combine the warm surrogate mother and the exacting professional psychoanalyst.

I didn't attend Dr. Henderson's wake and funeral; I very much wanted to, but my personal pathologies surrounding death hadn't been worked through sufficiently for me to feel comfortable being there. In my phobic way of thinking, I feared that somehow magically I would be vulnerable to death if I entered the funeral parlor. My way of dealing with the lingering guilt I felt at having let Dr. Henderson down in not partaking of the ritual obsequies was to plunge into activity, in this case my private practice. It was helpful, however, that she had done so much work with me to bring me aling as a therapist, for it enabled me to feel close to her in the work I was doing, and that I had her approval.

CHAPTER ELEVEN:
EYE LEVEL WITH HER BREASTS

I never did get over my analyst's death. This was actually progress for me, since it indicated I had established a relationship with her which did not exclude my feeling grief and mourning. One of the serious things that seemed to be missing in my character was that I never really let myself feel loss. The distance I had created between me and my mother when I started public school resulted in my moving away from the strongest bond I had in my life. And at the time I hardly thought about it. What I did think about, often, was my embarrassment and shame at the way she looked and dressed, and her inability to assimilate as an immigrant—she couldn't even get around the city and, at best, spoke in simple English mixed with Yiddish… not to speak of her isolation and dependence on the family. By adolescence I had rejected my sisters, Debbie and Phyllis, as well; they too seemed stuck in the home and unable to adapt to the changes that could lift them out of the children-of-immigrants mentality holding them back. And while I felt closer to my father, I was ashamed of him too—at his ineffectuality. At age twenty-nine, I literally ran away from his deathbed at Brookdale Hospital, when I saw him lying in the hallway on a gurney, recuperating from his post-operative surgery on his prostate. He lay there, an indigent immigrant, not even able to afford a room to die in. I was so cut off that I wasn't even alarmed at my own lack of feelings… or my fear of my feelings.

Another example of this syndrome in me, in which I really exceeded myself, was with my break-up with Dalite. I emotionally withdrew from the strong attachment I had to her, and dealt with her as if we were handling a logistical problem rather than facing a momentous disruption in our lives. Mine as well as hers. The feelings for her were there, somewhere under layers of denial, but were not available to me. To enact the separation I had even built up such a residue of resentment towards her that I saw myself as the injured party in my years of the marriage.

My experience of Dr. Henderson's death was quite different. I missed her and I felt grief that she was no longer in my life. And while there was a selfish component to my grief, inasmuch as part of the loss was that she would no longer be around to guide me as a mentor in the early years of my practice, it had no appreciable effect on the warmth of my feelings for her. I rejoice that this was the case, for I recognize that I have a limited capacity—even today... but less severely—to let myself feel the pain of separation from those I love and have depended on. I know I didn't attend her funeral, but that I believe had to do with my fear of death and my magical thinking, from way back, that any willingness to encounter death, or illness, even by coming across the words themselves in a magazine article, would open the door to my worst fears. But this said, my feeling for Dr. Henderson remains intact, and I am thankful for that. She was a large figure in my life, as someone who saw me, understood me, and believed in me... and held her ground in not letting me bamboozle her.

But considering a more general application of my syndrome of cutting off from those I depended on, I have to believe, in those rare moments when I'm up to engaging in thought about it, that the cost to me was great, since it had the effect of leaving me more alone in the world, which was the last thing I wanted. This kind of reverse effect, in bringing about the thing one is trying to avoid, goes a long way in explaining why people need to see psychologists. And there are the accumulations, or call them side effects, of giving in to one's injurious patterns. The layers of harm accumulate, making it exceedingly difficult to dig oneself out of the hole one is in.

For instance, in childhood, I was only able to leave home, during the day, when I replaced it with my life in elementary school; and later, with junior high school and the life of the streets. Still later, I could only leave Dalite, my wife and the mother of my two children, when I had replaced her with Margaret. I acquiesced to this pattern of replacement, in my separation from Dalite, by blocking my awareness of how I was operating. Yet I know, somewhere inside myself, I have hidden the guilt I feel over this behavior. I was old enough to perceive what I was doing. It is one thing to fall into such a pattern in childhood because I had no choice in what I did... I was just responding to what I had to do at the time. But it is another thing to do so in adulthood, and having recourse to the adult mind. (Of course the distinction between adult and child mind can be a false one, in that the adult mind is often the continuation of the child mind.) With Dalite, I had an opportunity to come to grips with my less than gallant behavior. Which I declined through my subversion of conscious inquiry. And, if I had been less *oblivious*, I could have handled things in a way that would have been much better for my kids and Dalite and myself. In some of what I put forth in the last two paragraphs, I am trying to justify the profession I practice; and in some of it, I am trying to use myself as an example of the pitfalls of constructing a life of building myself up and denial. I mention the latter now, as an insurance that I won't fail to pursue my 'injurious patterns' throughout the remaining part of the book... and as part of the hard seeing of myself that needs to be done. I say this as someone who has a long way to go... or to use an image from my kibbutz days, my moving of the rocks, which still brings to mind the myth of Sisyphus.

Some five months after Dr. Henderson's death, I left the formal structures of training to become a therapist and went off on my own, and the only institutional involvement I had was my job at Brooklyn College. These were the years where my private practice took off and I also thrived as a teacher at the college.

Dr. Henderson had done all she could to keep me in line as a traditional therapist, while giving me leeway to make use of my past and personality... she really did have an understanding that the forcefulness of my personality and my willingness to think and act independently were some of my best assets as a clinician. However she had remained adamant about her disapproval and intolerance of the stuff I pulled with Dr. Waite... and to a lesser degree with other staff members. So she had pushed me in the right direction and kept me in check.

But shortly after she had expired, I started to get more than a little bent out of shape by the constraints imposed on me by my supervisors and instructors at the Post Graduate Institute, and my colleagues and administrators at the college. I was tired of being instructed on proper procedure and wanted to be on my own. It had been some fifteen years, since returning from Israel in 1959, and over that time I had been in a whirlwind of working and training, switching jobs and getting credentialed. Granted, I may have been a little arrogant in assuming that I didn't need supervision or couldn't benefit from advice from my peers, but the kid from Brownsville wasn't going to be held back by his family, or the junior high school principal, or the leaders of the kibbutz, or Dr. Ripkin, or a marriage that was unsustainable; he was going to force change and go his own route, fortified by his ultra-confidence in himself. If people saw him as a maverick, so much the better. Of course this was all from my youthful view of things.

By 1974 I had received my state licensing certification (as a clinical psychologist) and had established a full-time private, psychotherapy practice. And my work as a therapist had become a cornerstone of my life, something that made me feel good about myself and helped me to superficially overcome my feeling that I was bluffing my way through life.

For the rest of this chapter, I have chosen to focus on three patients who started with me early on in my private practice. The first, Mark, is pretty much only known to the reader as someone who was in group therapy; the second, Cora, is new to the reader; and the third, Warren, is someone with whom the reader is familiar. The three of them encompass three major categories of mental illness that a majority of patients fall into. Mark was a neurotic who suffered from a severe neurosis of sexual deviancy; Cora suffered from a serious personality disorder, which was highly resistant to treatment; and Warren was a psychotic, who was often detached from reality and suffering from intense self-delusions. But for the purposes of this work what unites them has to do with how their problems caused me to deviate in my work with them from the traditional role and training as a psychotherapist.

Mark. On the surface, he was easier to work with than Warren and Cora because he, unlike them, was a firm believer in psychotherapy and its values and loved the intellectual challenge of self-examination along psychological lines. Warren and Cora were much more tenuous in their motivation for self-inquiry, wanting instead reinforcement for their ill-arrived at convictions... and it was always a form of combat to get them to see this about themselves.

But the ongoing problem with Mark is that he would use all his intellectual astuteness and awareness to defend against change and perpetuate his dysfunctional Oedipal fixation with his mother.

Case in point: Mark told this story early in therapy about him and his mother:

Mark, in his early adolescent years, came home from school one day and found his mother lounging in the living room in her bra and panties. It was a hot day, and he began to perspire as he looked at the scantily clad figure of his mother, whose body was highly exciting to him. She noticed an impressive zit on his face and beckoned him over to sit on her lap so she could attend to it. Reluctantly he came over to her and sat on her lap, like a good boy. This meant that he was at eye level with her breasts and could feel the curvature of his body against her. Moreover, she seemed to be turned on by his awakening of desire. He got overwhelmingly aroused and as much as he tried to hide this from her, he could see that she recognized the turmoil and arousal he was experiencing. It was not long before he was out of control. He attempted to embrace her and kiss her on the mouth. This, in turn, poured cold water on her response. She pushed him off her lap, in revulsion, causing him to feel humiliated and rejected.

He spent the next twenty or so years obsessing daily about his sexual attraction for his mother, bringing her in fantasy into every sexual situation he engaged in, whether onanistic or with older mother figures. Eventually he got married but rarely had satisfying sex with his wife or with other women, without conjuring up his seductive mother.

He came to therapy with me after having relatively unsuccessful couple's therapy with his wife as well as individual treatment. His Oedipal fixation weighed so heavily on him that he developed a whole bunch of other psychological problems that included alcoholism, pill addiction, and obsessive entanglement with aging women who brought to mind his mother.

Although he acquired insight analytically and intellectually into the origins of his problem, going back to early childhood, it didn't do much to alleviate his condition. In my treatment of him I was growing increasingly fatigued listening to him talk about the older women he was involved with and his rationalizations about his destructive and compulsive behavior.

Tired at having to be a party to his verbal dance, I kiddingly proposed to him that a more active solution to his pathological obsession with his mother might be available: "Why don't you consider creating an actual replication of your mother rather than depending on your wife or elderly women as mother surrogates." He looked at me bewilderedly, "How would one do that?"

"Well, some people who have trouble finding the partners they envision have taken recourse to purchasing life-size rubber, inflatable dolls, built to specifications from a photograph of the desired person."

"And you think that will solve my Oedipal fixation?"

"... more than your seventy-year-old girlfriends."

To my incredulity, Mark diligently followed my advice—which never was intended seriously... mockingly, if anything—to a tee and was able to purchase such a representation and make use of it with some regularity. It only faded in value when, over time, the rubber doll sprung a leak and deflated permanently.

While I was amazed and amused that he had taken my suggestion to heart, I understood that, from my end of it, it was not just playfulness and sardonic humor that caused me to mention the rubber female. I just didn't have the resources within me to effectively subdue my annoyance, impatience, frustration, boredom, and play the part of the supportive, empathetic, dutiful listener. Also, I felt that Mark, by utilizing me the way he was doing was rendering me inconsequential as a therapist, some kind of appendage to his psychological needs. In terms of my history, this was not the best position to be put into—it certainly did not lend itself to the grandiose vision of myself that seemed necessary to my idea of well-being.

I finally got to the point where my patience with Mark's verbal overkill wore so thin that I began to take him to task for wasting his and my time with a lot of talk and intellectual analysis that didn't lead to anything. I swung into my confrontational mode. This way, at least I was doing something that made me feel better and something that disrupted his comfort zone, since nothing was going to change as long as he was trying to talk away his problems.

At one fairly typical session with Mark, he began his obsessive focus on the elderly-females whom he was presently courting by phone... and was about to launch into actual conversations that titillated him, when I stopped him... I was determined not to be outmaneuvered.

Here is a little piece of dialogue from the session with Mark; it occurred a few minutes after I had let him know that I was unwilling to sit quietly by while he wasted the session filling me in on his provocative phone conversations. The conversation took its own turn, but I pushed my agenda throughout.

"It seems to be that your libidinal excitement is reserved for women that you're not married to. Granted you use the excuse that it's not you but your wife who has the problem and you'd be more than willing to put the wood to her if she was more zealous."

"I've tried for years to overcome her sexual inhibitions. She's not turned on by me."

"Neither are you by her. Then again, it appears as though the only women you are turned on to are those who reside in old-age homes.

"So the couples therapy you're doing with my wife and me to improve our lovemaking is to get us to feel passion and not just base our relationship on love and security?"

"That's theoretically what you want, isn't it?... or, what you say you want?"

"I'm always up for bringing passion and good sex into the marriage."

"... and that leads you to dissect intellectually every aspect of your lovemaking? would you call that passionate?"

"I may be analytical when it comes to sex but it doesn't prevent me from appreciating the wonderful sensations of a woman achieving orgasm or a man ejaculating."

"Yeah, I can imagine the feelings you have as you're searching with a magnifying glass what portion of your wife's clitoris is most responsive."

"That's hilarious."

"I'm not trying to make fun of you, Mark. I just want you to begin to comprehend how much your compulsive need, in childhood, to prove to yourself that your mother desired you became the central feature of your compulsion for sex. It's more important to you that Beatrice gets turned on by you and has an exciting orgasm than it is having one yourself."

"What's wrong with that?"

"In and of itself, nothing. It's actually quite healthy to want your partner to get excited and all that. But if you're obsessively preoccupied with only her response and not your own, then something is missing."

"I get turned on by turning her on. Is that unnatural?"

"No, not at all. But let's be real. When you're talking to one of your elderly lady friends on the phone and trying to titillate her through your version of phone sex, you get really excited and masturbate yourself to orgasm. In this situation you're narcissistically in control. But if you're actually with your wife or a woman in a sexual situation, you're never as fully involved and complain of losing interest. When you're not in your little, narcissistic cocoon, it's not a lot of fun for you. Unfortunately, giving yourself love, while thinking about your mom, was the best you could do. Which did not point you in the right direction."

"On top of everything else, my mother enjoyed stimulating my interest in her, but rejected me if I tried to be overtly sexual with her. And as you well know, nothing has proved to be more exciting for me, erotically, than overcoming in fantasy her resistance to the libidinal desires I have for her. So much of my sexual energy is prompted by the thought, *What if...*

"... and it's that misdirected or misspent energy that takes the fun out of normal sexual activity."

Mark, over the next few years, worked hard on these issues in his therapy, and eventually succeeded in building a much better marriage with his wife—though he never overcame the crucial Oedipal attachment to his mother. I can't instill in him the will to change; he has to want that badly enough to fight for it. He doesn't want to give up what he has. He loves his sessions with me. I'm afraid that will have to suffice.

Cora. In her situation, I was confronted with a patient who had a major narcissistic personality disorder. The only thing that mattered to her was her; it became clear to me, in working with Cora, that if I were going to establish a successful therapeutic alliance with her, I could not rely on battering her ego, in the confrontational way I needed to do with Warren, since her defenses required that she be treated as the special person who was seen by me in much the way she saw herself. That meant I couldn't confront her on her delusions and distortions because she needed to feel she was such a good, bright, and sensitive person... and, more importantly, she would have bolted from therapy if I had been too heavy in my criticism of her.

I had made the decision at the end of my training with Henderson to deviate from the traditional way the Institute dictated how therapists work with patients. This meant that I would work with each of my patients, fitting the therapy to their needs and not the other way round. In Cora's case, it meant I had to tread lightly in the first year of therapy. Her insecurities and skepticism were such that she required enormous support in order for her to forge the requisite trust in me. There was no way I could use a conventional Freudian take on her childhood issues to breakdown her defenses and illusions. Her resistance to this kind of treatment would have been too great. So in initially working with her, I made her feel that she was very special to me... and I dismissed that my supervisors, including Henderson, would have been opposed to my manipulation of her. Instead I chose to use what I had learned in the streets with the gang... that "if I let on that I liked them, they would do what I asked of them."

I understood that in manipulating Cora for therapeutic purposes, the Freudians might criticize me for interfering with the natural progression of the transference. But I did not concur with them, assuming that Cora would project on to me problems she had in childhood with her parents—no matter what I did. Whether I was supportive or confrontational, this transference would take place; however, by being supportive I insured that she wouldn't drop out of therapy before the real work began. If I didn't build up her ego, she would have written me off as someone who was preoccupied with his own perceptions and unsympathetic to her needs. She would have placed me on her long list of not-to-be-trusted males—just like her father. To avert this unproductive outcome and foregone conclusion, I was willing to brush aside much of the irritation I felt at her self-involvement and cynical dismissal of others, particularly those of the male gender. I made a concerted effort to shift into pragmatic mode with Cora, doing what it took to make her feel good. I often made reference to the tender, loving little child Cora who tried, without success, to please her father. I not only saw the hurt little girl within the adult, but I believed in her essential goodness... and tried to communicate it. I, in essence, twisted things around so that I was overtly in her corner. I justified the role I took on, by adhering to the questionable principle of the ends justifies the means. And, anyway, when you come down to it, nearly every therapist resorts to flattery at times to ameliorate the patient's positive sense of self.

Still, I wonder about the falseness of my being so nice and so praising of her, downplaying my negative response. Why couldn't I have been more myself, sometimes tough and critical and sometimes warm and encouraging? Play it as it lays, as it were. I suppose I like to feel I am a skilled practitioner... a good player at the game.

A dandy example of Cora's egocentricity and self-reference came during a dialogue I had with her in her second year of treatment. In the specific situation she was trying to manipulate me to see her for free. She kept repeating that she deserved it because of all the people that she had referred to see me.

"So what you're suggesting is a sort of kickback system in which you send me patients and I give you free therapy?"

"If you care about me, you'll do it for me."

"Given that assumption, I should do it for all the patients I care about. So if I'm a caring therapist I won't be able to pay my bills."

"Why don't we try it this one time with me and we can see how it goes?"

"You're reminding me in your total self-absorption of an incident with my sister many years ago in which she too felt that her needs were the only ones that mattered. I was on my way home with her after picking her up from a routine visit to an outpatient clinic, where she had received her medication. I had gone out of my way to go to her house and get her, drive her to the clinic and then bring her back, and my time was very limited since I had to collect my kids from school. I made it clear to her that we were on a tight schedule. On the way back she asked me to do a slight favor and stop off at the local supermarket so she could buy a couple of things.

"I said to her, 'Debbie, I made it clear to you when I told you I'd pick you up that I was in a big rush. My kids are waiting for me outside the school. So I can't stop off anywhere.'

"We drove a few more blocks and she started in again. 'It will just take a few minutes and I'll even buy less than I originally intended to. It's not really very much out of your way.'

"I reiterated my point to Debbie, 'I thought I made myself clear. I'm in a big rush. Can't you see anybody else's needs but your own?'

"She said, 'Of course I can. But it will just take a few minutes and I'll only get two items.'

"I said, 'Debbie, did you hear me? I got two young children, my children, waiting for me outside the school and there is nobody with them. I drove out of my way, left my job, to come and get you so you would have your medication, because you're too crazy and scared to go by yourself. Do you appreciate that? Do you think you might be able to do something like that for me one day?'

"And she answered me, 'Of course, you're my brother. But this will only take a minute or two. I'll only get one item.'

"I slammed on the brakes, and said, 'I'm gonna ask you for that big favor right now. I want you to get out of the car, walk to the supermarket, buy your items, have them pack it for you and then walk home by yourself all alone in the streets and in that way I'll be able to save time and pick up my kids.'

"She replied, 'You know I can't do that. You know how terrified I am of the streets of Brownsville.'

"I said, 'Think Debbie, you and mom moved a couple of blocks over to East Flatbush, it's more of a Jewish neighborhood. You don't have to be so afraid. Out. Get out.'

"Cora looked at me quizzically and said, 'What has all this got to do with me? I recommend patients to you because I think you're a very good therapist and I like you.'

"I answered coarsely, 'Don't bullshit me, Cora, I know better. You're not so different than my narcissistic sister.'

"Cora went into another of her little ploys: 'A therapist shouldn't talk to a patient the way you just talked to me.'

"I replied, 'Let's talk about business. I have a counter offer to make: How about you giving me an increase of twenty-five dollars a session?… you make a hundred grand a year… so that shouldn't be a problem.'

"She said, 'You have no right to increase your fees without giving your patients adequate notice.'

"I said, 'Cora, you're taking this too seriously. I'm not about to raise your fee, but I'm also not going to abolish my usual fee.' "

With Cora, I had to keep the alliance between us going while taking her to task for not looking truthfully at herself; I did this by using humor, analytic psychology, a pinch of confrontation, and the forcefulness of my personality. But Cora is a tough cookie, and I can't imagine her ever fully catching on to what I'm trying to get her to see about herself. Sooner or later I will affront her and she will stop coming to therapy.

Warren. In his case, despite his having had exposure—before I knew him—to many different kinds of therapy and therapists, it didn't prevent him from cracking up every few years and being hospitalized because of his psychotic regressions. (The reader will remember that Warren was hospitalized while seeing me early in my work with him, but after that, with luck and maybe my approach with him, he has not been hospitalized again for some thirty-five years.) His previous therapies did little to force him into reality and keep him from mental breakdowns. I began to doubt the efficacy of working with a delusional-bipolar psychotic in a way that predominately relied on talk, on psychoanalytic inquiry into childhood, and on insight... as the tools to lessen his psychotic delusions. If I sat and listened to his delusional accounts of his interactions with other people, without forcing him to face some basic truths about how distorted his thinking was, my efforts with him would come to naught. And beyond this, I knew from the outset that I would have to take over this man's life and completely control it if I were going to help him to learn to function more competently in the world. Drugs alone would not do the job. In this case, I chose to get some supervisory guidance. However, my advisor was quick to let me know that my impatience and intolerance with Warren was my personal problem and that it could prove dangerous to force him to confront reality all the time and break down his delusional structures. According to him, he was such a fragile man that I should make sure that he took his medication and avoid disrupting his equanimity.

Yet, if this kind of minimal therapeutic treatment was the best I could do with Warren, I would not have taken him on as a patient. As I have mentioned earlier, Warren's pathology was on the order of that of my parents and other of my family members. As an adult I believed that I was left with two choices: to have nothing to do with them or stick by them and try to change them. I—sadly, for the family and myself—chose the former out of my fear and desperation and need to survive, believing that if I stayed the course with them they would take me down.

But with Warren, I was not limited in my thinking, in the way I was with my family... and was willing to take him on. Clearly, I had a wish to do with Warren what I wasn't able to do with my family. I made a critical decision to take complete control over his life—more than I had ever done with any other patient—forcing him to constantly deal with reality instead of letting him off the hook by considering him too vulnerable and psychotic to engage in a knockdown battle as to what was real and unreal in his delusive responses. And this will to battle with him over what was delusive and what was not, and my faith in him that he could handle this confrontational approach... over time proved to be the main therapeutic ingredient that kept him within the boundaries—though on the edge—of sanity, which meant that he did not have to be written off as a hopeless patient whose destiny was to be zapped out on anti-psychotic drugs and relegated to periodic breakdowns and incarceration in mental institutions. Amazingly, Warren for some years now is something remotely close to a functioning member of society, even though his battle for sanity is ongoing and probably will be with him for the rest of his life and may someday overtake him.

There is a big difference between working with Mark and Cora, and a delusional psychotic like Warren. And no matter what I have done with Warren, there is always the possibility that he will regress and again be hospitalized. It may be helpful to add here something more about how strong a delusional system is in place with him, and how resistant his defenses are to change. This reality is omnipresent with Warren, as you can see in the following interchange with him.

The interchange involves a regression on his part back to his earlier days at his civil service job where he was immensely delusional about the women wanting to make love to him. I didn't abandon my usual way of working with Warren... I still employed humor, confrontation, drama, even exasperation in a highly personal way to jolt him out of his paranoid projections. In this instance he was dealing with a delusional system he created with an individual who lived above him in his apartment building.

Here is a dialogue out of Warren's storm:

"So let me get this straight, Warren. I want to be sure that I'm hearing you right. You're telling me your neighbor, Derek, is flushing his toilet late at night, or early in the morning, because he's angry at you?"

"I can't be entirely sure that he's angry at me, but it's definitely in response to whatever has been going on between us lately. And it's not just the flushing of the toilet. When he turns on his shower full blast, it makes an awful screeching sound. He has to know if he turns it on only half way then it won't screech."

"So he's turning it on because he's angry at you and wants to punish you?"

"Exactly."

"The only thing that puzzles me is why he is angry at you?"

"Well that's a long story."

"I'm not going anywhere."

"For weeks now whenever we've met on the street, he doesn't say hello or acknowledge my existence. This is after we were on somewhat friendly terms since he moved into the building."

"Why do you think he stopped greeting you?"

"That will become clear if you give me a chance to continue…"

"Do go on."

"About two months ago he started bringing one of his white girlfriends up to his apartment. They obviously were having sex a lot."

"What made it obvious?"

"I not only could hear the springs of the bed going up and down and heard her panting and her begging for more, but as they would get close to climaxing she would let out a scream of pain as if he were hurting her."

"How could you tell it was pain and not pleasure?"

"I can tell the difference."

"So, what you're saying is that you've been listening to your neighbor having sex with his girlfriend, imagining that he's into some kind of sadistic sexual abuse of her?"

"Not only her, there have been others too."

"All of them white?"

"No, one or two of the other girls are black."

"Are they attractive?"

"I would say so, although the girl I've been telling you about is a little heavy."

"Let me ask you something else, Warren. You must have unusual hearing to be able to pick up so much of what's happening in his sexual encounters. Do you put your ear against the wall?"

"Funny, Obler. You can't help hearing what's going on in that apartment."

"Well, have any of his neighbors commented about it?"

"You know the problems I have with the nonverbal stuff with my neighbors. How would you think I would talk to them about such things?"

"Okay. Let's assume that you have very acute hearing and you're picking up accurately the hot, steamy S & M going on between him and his girlfriend. It still doesn't explain why he's angry at you."

"I'll get to that."

"Okay."

"I tried sound plugs, pressed my pillow against my ears, put up the radio full volume and I still couldn't block out what was going on. The only thing that worked at all was my going into the shower and turning it on full blast so I didn't hear them."

"Well that sounds like an effective solution, and it certainly keeps you clean. Still, you think he's angry at you because you're taking showers?"

DR. MARTIN OBLER / JED GOLDEN

"Maybe the noise from the force of the water hitting the tub interrupts his sexual activity."

"Seems unlikely."

"It doesn't end there. In order to get back at me, he started taking showers late at night or in the wee hours of the morning, knowing that I would be awakened by the screeching noise that the shower made. And he would turn the water on for twenty minutes at a time. It was tit for tat. Who takes a shower for that long? I bet he wasn't even in the shower all that time."

"How does the toilet come in?"

"To get at him I started flushing my toilet because it makes a racket every time I flush it. And to show you that I'm not living one of your 'ideation of reference delusions,' which for years you implied I was doing, he started flushing his toilet to get back at me."

"In synchronicity?"

"Don't be a smart-ass. If he took a dump every once in a while, I wouldn't connect it to my flushing, but who the hell flushes a toilet ten times before going to bed? How many times can you go to the bathroom?"

"So you both entered a kind of folie a deux agreement?"

"Folie a deux?"

"That's French for when two psychotic people collude to somehow share their craziness. But I'm just teasing you, Warren. I seriously doubt that Derek has entered into a personal war with you. I think you're imagining his part in it."

"So you think I never heard the noises?"

"No, I'm not saying that. It's your interpretation of what the noise means that I'm having trouble with."

"He's not angry at me?"

"Why do you think I might feel that?"

"For the same reason you questioned that the women at my old job were coming on to me."

"You yourself have begun to see the possibility that you were reading a lot into their responses."

"Believe me I have no attraction to Derek and his girlfriend and no interest whatsoever in their kind of sex."

"None whatsoever?"

"You think I want to be in Derek's shoes. That I want his woman?"

"The thought crossed my mind."

"Well, erase it."

"You seem to be titillated by what you hear, or imagine you hear, over there."

"I'm so lucky to have a therapist who thinks I'm a creep."

"We can always go back to medicating you."

"I'd rather not. At least you talk to me as if I'm almost a real person."

"Bipolar real."

*   *   *

"So how are things going, Warren, in your battles with Derek over the last few weeks?"

"Much better, especially after you helped me to see that I desired to be like him and do the things I imagined he does with his women."

"Especially the white woman."

"I am attracted to some of the blacks and Hispanics also."

"So am I right to assume that the toilet flushing and shower noise isn't bothering you as much?"

"Not nearly as much. But I still maintain that he was a contributor to the game we were playing with each other and his thoughts were entering my head and my thoughts were entering his."

"How come you keep holding on to that idea? You believe everything people do is connected to you?"

"There is always a possibility it's true. You may be right, but there is a chance that I'm right."

"Were there any incidents of late with Derek?"

"Only one."

"Uh, hum."

"I overheard a conversation he had in the hallway with our upstairs neighbor, Millie, in which he referred to me, I believe, in their conversation."

"So what did he say: that he heard jerking off at night?"

"I couldn't hear exactly what he was saying, and the only words I heard were 'cracked up.' "

"Why did it mean that he was referring to you if all you heard were those words?"

"Well, after all the things that have been going back and forth between us, is there anyone else he would be talking about?"

"I don't know, but you don't know either. And it's not him that's coming up with the idea of someone cracking up, but you."

"He may be as obsessive about me as I am about him."

"Don't you think it's a little peculiar that you can't make out any of the conversation between Derek and Millie except 'cracking up?' He could've said 'shacking up' or referred to 'cracking up,' meaning laughter. But the 'flipping out' type of cracking up is on your mind. You get the picture, bubbala?"

Mark, Cora, and Warren give a picture of how I used my personality and psychological make-up as components of my therapeutic treatment of them. And I believe that this approach served me and them well. Who knows how long it would have taken for them to entertain some of the things about themselves that I brought out, if I hadn't short-circuited the process with my need to be abrupt, confrontational (less so with Cora), intervening and controlling? Not only would it have prolonged the time that it took to get anywhere with them but it might have also entrenched them in their defense systems... as well as driven me crazy. I like to think that I did a pretty good job with each of them, managing to convey, importantly, how much I care about them, while fighting them every step of the way.

It is my hunch that the reader could use a break from my work with my patients, and it seems a good time to fill the reader in on what was taking place in my life, both in terms of my family life and personal psychology.

CHAPTER TWELVE:
AN ADDITION TO THE FAMILY

The big thing in my life was that Margaret was pressuring me to have a child with her, and when that couldn't happen, to adopt a child. Before we get to the adoption of Danny, however, it would be relevant to go back to my honorable and dishonorable behavior with Dalite during her pregnancy.

I did the noble thing with Dalite when she was pregnant in Israel by insisting that we get married and she come with me back to the States. I suggested this fully knowing I wasn't in love with her, and she went along with it. However, to her credit, she never pushed me to take this position, making it very clear that she was willing to have the child and take care of it, with the help of her family. I turned her down, preferring to take responsibility for my actions and assume the role of the upstanding spouse.

And that was meritorious; but on the downside, I didn't wait long to start misbehaving; by the time she was six months pregnant, I was already diverting my interests to younger women and was resentful that I wasn't free to follow my dictates. Two months later my frustration and depression was so great at my feeling trapped in a marriage I did not want to be in, that I took it out on her. When she came to me eight months pregnant, vulnerable and upset that she was unattractive... and sought assurance that I still cared for her, I responded to her need for affection by showing little warmth. By any standards it was an unforgivable response on my part and obviously tapped into a wellspring of anger over which I had little control. Nor did my cruel and solipsistic behavior stop there. At the time of

Delmore's birth I was having an affair with Maggie (she was the woman who called me on the night Delmore was born, worried that she had missed her period, which I had mentioned earlier in the book). I was behaving like a self-centered, hostile and rebellious adolescent who couldn't see more than two inches in front of him.

I was acting out in a very loose way with any woman who seemed lively and enticing... and I believe that this was a way of exacting revenge on my mother and also on myself for not deserving a better mother than I had. What I didn't acknowledge to myself was the extent to which I was dependent on Dalite and benefited by the stability she provided. Her responsibility and maturity helped me to become increasingly successful. And I owed her a lot for this, and for the grounding my family gave me. But at the time I couldn't take this in, other than in a remote, logical way. I don't know whether I would have left Dalite had I been more appreciative of her contribution to my welfare, but no matter what I should have been more considerate of her. She deserved more support and affection than I could muster. As it was, when I began to make my way in the world, my need for her was diminished. This freed me to seek the romanticized women, embodied in the svelte, thin, black-haired, dark, Mediterranean Jewish beauty... going way back to my yearning for the mother who bought for me the charlotte russe in Woolworths on Pitkin Avenue... a woman whom I could fantasize would lead me out of my dreadful life at home.

I'm sure that my friends wondered at how I stayed locked into my marriage with Dalite for so many years, since I had affairs, took every opportunity to get out of the house, overextended myself in my practice, and was a full-time teacher at college. In leading my life in this manner, I was doing a disservice to Dalite, my two kids, and to myself. I spent little intimate time with my children, something which weighs on me now, even though I have been more attentive to them since I have been out of the marriage. I know they suffered psychologically from my inadequacies as a parent. I guess I thought that everything would be okay, simply by my providing a nice home and ample food and clothing. Sometimes when I was with my son Delmore, I was very entertaining and playful; in those moments he probably felt as if I were a terrific daddy. However, I was very inconsistent. And, to this day, it is painful for me to think of the disappointment he must have felt in the times when I had little to do with him.

As a therapist I saw over and over again in my work with patients the damage that was done to the child's psyche when one of the parents doesn't really want to be in the marriage and is unhappy and depressed at being home. Invariably that parent is going to be more and more absent from the real emotional and psychological experience of involvement in the family, leading to a position where he/she is there but not there. It was apparent that my two children had longtime, harmful effects from my being a part-time parent. Delmore's biggest difficulty has been establishing a working relationship with a woman, which I attribute largely to the tensions he experienced in the home... and his needing me to be an intact father and thus not seeing my failings or feeling free to vent his anger towards me.

Dina, my second child, for her part, was perhaps not as adversely affected as my son by my negligence as a parent, but obviously it had serious consequences on her as well. She likes to think that she's not been significantly damaged by the divorce (she was eleven at the time), but I certainly feel that she paid the price for what took place... and had to be depressed at what she was seeing, which was that her mother, after so many years of service as a homemaker and child caretaker, was being devalued and discarded. In her relationship with me she often plays the caring and sometimes put-upon mother as a way of reaching me; and in this respect, she takes on some of the role her mother played in being the dutiful wife. She also, however, denies to herself that she is still the little girl that wanted a lot more from her daddy than he could give her.

My relationship with Margaret had been proceeding fairly well for some time... since the middle of the seventies to the early eighties... but we faced a crisis when she gave an ultimatum to me that either we have a child or she would have a child without me. I knew that if I didn't give in to having a child with her, it would be the end of the relationship. Naturally that didn't make me feel too good. But I was unwilling to face another disintegration of a long-term relationship... and this time with someone whom I truly loved. I acceded to her wish, or should I say demand, to have a child despite my reservations (I already had two children in their twenties). After a year of trying unsuccessfully to conceive a child, she decided that we go the adoption route. Whatever my demurs were about having a biological child they were minor compared to my reluctance to adopt. I questioned whether I could feel the same way towards an adopted child as I could to my own biological offspring. That worry weighed in very heavily, when it was combined with my fears that I may be doing the wrong thing having a child at my age. I also wasn't buoyed by Margaret's lack of concern about my anxieties in all of this. I felt somehow I was alone in what I was going through.

She proposed that we adopt a child right away, to be followed by adopting another child within three years. This precipitated a crisis between us. I argued, "I'm forty-six years old, I've got two kids of my own whose lives are not free of problems, and I don't relish the idea of adding two new kids, and think of it: by the time they reach mid-adolescence, I'll be in my sixties. And for that matter, you and I have our share of troubles that we haven't fully acknowledged, never mind, resolved. All we would be doing by adopting would be burdening ourselves further... and that could be a whole new set of problems; I think that by going that route we would be agreeing to mask our problems by escaping into parenthood...." Of course I was playing the therapist card for all that it was worth.

We argued and fought for our individual positions. I was a master at trying to get my way... and testing Margaret's resolve to thwart me. But in this instance I chose to avoid a long, protracted battle between us. It was a little too much for me to deny Margaret her chance to be a mother. After all, I already had two children and she had none. Still, out of stubbornness I refused to give in to her right away. I somewhat lamely would come back to one or another last-ditch attempt to avert surrender. I can remember at one point having this particular conversation with her:

"No matter how much you want this adoption thing, it isn't going to work anyway. I've told you that."

"So what are you saying?"

"I'm too old and they are most likely going to turn us down because of that... and also the thirteen year difference in our ages."

"You're talking as usual about stuff you don't know anything about. You know a great deal about therapy, but you're ignorant about everything else."

"Oh, really?"

"I've done the research, and, as I've told you before, there is a very good chance that we can get approved as adoptive parents in spite of your age or the difference in our ages... if we apply to countries like Brazil, the Dominican Republic, or Colombia."

"I thought you yourself have been saying for the last six months that couples are having trouble adopting because of not meeting the criteria set by a number of countries."

"Once again you're distorting what I've said. This holds true in certain countries like Taiwan, China, and Korea... where everybody is trying to obtain kids. In Romania we can adopt a child easily in a few months, all they care about is the money. And it may be harder in Brazil and the Dominican Republic, but it can definitely be done."

"How much would it cost in Romania?"

"Great. Now you're showing your true colors."

"I'm just kidding. I read in the pamphlet you gave me on Brazil that we can't adopt in that country unless we're married. Isn't that true?"

"Yes, that's accurate."

"So?"

"We're going to get married. We need to do that anyway, if we're going to have children."

"Yeah, suddenly you want me to marry you... because it serves your purposes."

"Marty, you really have to make up your mind, whether you want to do this with me or you don't. You're just trying to wiggle out of the whole business. Why don't you tell me what's really going on with you?"

"If you want to know, I'm petrified, I'm scared of adopting. Let's be real. I didn't do that good a job with my own kids."

Margaret could tell, however, that I was gradually weakening and that my resistance was more token than adamant. She let me express my misgivings as a way of pacification. Her hopes and spirit started to rise, and I am sure she knew that I did not have the heart or the desire to put a damper on her excitement of what the future had in store for us. Most men are not quick to sacrifice the rewards of being considered champions by their female partners.

Eight months later we were married, and I could see that something had changed for the better in our relationship and in me. Predictably, it had to do with the commitment I had made to her and to our future together. The bottom line was that my giving in, in this conflict, assured Margaret that I loved her in a way that nothing else could have. And thinking of Margaret first helped to convince me that I really did love her and helped me to feel that I belonged in the marriage, despite my questionable activity with other women and my historical doubts about the viability of marriage as an institution, going back to my parents' less-than-ideal connubial involvement.

It was ten months before we were in Brazil finalizing the adoption process for getting a baby boy of eight months, whom we had already named Daniel (shortened to Danny).

We landed in Sao Paulo airport and were met by Carmela Di Santora, the social worker contact in Brazil for the adoption. She had been in charge of Danny's care since a few weeks after his birth and was responsible for taking us through every step of the adoption. She was quite a well-built and attractive middle-aged woman, with black hair and a lovely smile. She greeted us warmly in English; she reminded me of an accomplished corporate executive who had developed considerable social skills in her profession. To my surprise, she told us that we would be staying with her and her family. I asked her where the baby was and she said that we would be picking him up from relatives of her parents who had been caring for him shortly after his birth; then he would be staying with us at her house so we could begin getting used to him.

I asked her, "Don't you think it might be upsetting to him to be taken all of a sudden from the people that he's been staying with?"

"Don't worry about it; that's not a problem here," she said, dispensing with my concern.

When we got to the house of the original mother's relatives, I saw poverty that was worse than anything I had seen in Brooklyn. The house they lived-in was only two steps up from a tiny, flimsy shack and with no glass windows and a few pieces of basic furniture. Carmela introduced us to Danny's aunt and her husband, and told us the names of the small girl and boy playing on the dirt floor. The family members seemed to be a mixture of native Indian and Brazilian descent. I got the feeling on seeing the aunt and brother-in-law that they, in their youth, had been very attractive but poverty and hard work had lined their faces and taken its toll on their looks. After the introductions the aunt took out of the knee-high refrigerator box a platter of ham and cheese and bread along with slices of papaya. It was my feeling that the spread that they put before us had been provided by the social worker in order to make us feel that Danny had been well-taken care of. This impression was further confirmed when an elderly lady came out of the only additional room holding a lovely, calm and seemingly good-natured brown infant in her arms, who was Danny, and handed him to Margaret who gladly but nervously received him... I noticed an American-type disposable diaper on him, which could only have been for our benefit and not something that they would have purchased on their own.

When I saw Danny in these surroundings I got a sense of what Carmela meant when she said we needn't worry about Danny's adjustment to being taken out of the house he had been living in. In the dramatic poverty of these people, children were expected to adapt to whatever were the exigencies of life around them... and I suspected the children were resilient, as if somehow internally they understood this requirement of their environment. This was not a situation in which hours would be spent discussing with the parent, the adopting parents, the relatives, and social worker, what would be the best approach for the child.

We all sat around the living room eating and exchanging pleasantries, with Carmela translating back and forth. Soon Carmela announced that it was time for us to leave and Margaret walked off with Danny in her arms after thanking our hosts for everything they had done for us, and we exchanged warm goodbyes and best wishes.

On the way back to Carmela's house, as she drove in her car through the city, I sat in silence while the two women chatted about the baby and what we needed to do to complete the adoption process. I was barely able to concentrate on what they were saying because I was taking in the significance of what had just transpired. In one moment I was a father again and feeling very uneasy about this new phase of my life. I could see that Margaret was and would be all caught up in the mothering of the baby and that it would be expected that I would just fit into place in my role as father. But I was feeling strange and alien to the circumstances I was being put in and I wondered whether I was cut out to be a father again.

We got to Carmela's house, which was a small, middleclass, ranch-type home with a little garden in the front... and the neighborhood looked like a Latin American version of American suburbia. Inside the house, the hall, living room, and what I could see of the kitchen were meticulously clean and everything was in its place. We were introduced to Carmela's three children and to the two servants, one of whom was a day worker and the other was a live-in cook and nanny. The nanny took Danny from Margaret and beckoned us to follow her to the room where he would be staying. She held Danny in her arms with easy confidence and maternal warmth, and he seemed to have no problem undergoing the exchange. She stayed with Danny in the room, while Carmela took us back into the living room; we sat down with her and listened as she outlined the busy day we'd have tomorrow in the government offices, where we would go through the adoption protocol—this would, we were assured, take forever. Carmela's husband came home later and he was a squat, friendly, cigar-smoking man who was a customs inspector at the airport in Sao Paulo. He seemed very comfortable and very hospitable as host. Towards late afternoon the nanny came in to the living room and informed us, in Portuguese, that it was time for Danny's bath and asked if we would like to watch. Carmela translated for us, and Margaret, surprisingly to me, declined the offer, preferring to remain with Carmela to continue the conversation. I excused myself and went with the nanny to watch her bathe Danny. She picked him up out of the bassinet and I followed her to the bathroom, which, like the rest of the house, was neat and perfect, with attractive blue ceramic tile on the floor and walls and blue porcelain sink and bathtub. The water was already drawn and, after testing it with her hand, she placed Danny in the water with her hand beneath his back. Danny, like most babies, loved being in water and started kicking his legs and thrashing his arms with delight... in the way babies do. He seemed like a fine and healthy baby. However, when he calmed down for a little bit and the nanny soap-sponged him, I could see that on his genital area and his upper thighs there was a nasty-looking rash that went beyond the typical baby diaper rash. I figured that the relatives hadn't changed his diapers often enough and probably didn't have the bacitracin-type ointment that helped to prevent and do away with diaper rash. When we got Danny back to the States, it took a number of visits to the pediatrician to clear up his rash and it came back time after time, after that. Anyway, it was fun watching Danny in the tub; I was pleased that he looked like a happy, strong, well-coordinated fellow.

Carmela, Margaret, and I spent the next few days going from government office to government office accumulating all the documents necessary for the adoption—which we would have to present at the Attorney General's office in Rio De Janeiro to get final clearance before we could leave the country. I was impressed with Carmela's adeptness at negotiating with the various government and police officials and managing to avoid some of the long lines that had formed in various departments. This was particularly notable in the Sao Paulo family court where numerous people were sitting on benches waiting their turn to see the judge in the courtroom. Somehow we managed to get to see the judge in half an hour and we were out of the building not too long after that. I was beginning to wonder what magical touch Carmela had, to be so effective in working the bureaucracy. The conclusion I came to, which was never confirmed, was that some percentage of the $12,000 we paid for the adoption was being siphoned off in graft payments. At least that was the only way I could explain the preferential treatment we got. Even in my limited interaction with various petty officials in Rio and Sao Paulo I found myself paying money to get what I needed. For example, I wound up getting a room in a hotel in Rio that was "completo" by slipping the desk clerk a few bills in response to his not-too-subtle indication that there may be a room opening up in a half hour, depending on something.

On having acquired all the necessary paper work in Sao Paulo for the adoption process, we celebrated by taking Carmela and her husband out to dinner in a restaurant that was recommended by a guidebook. Midway through the meal my anxiety about Danny's parental background and biological heritage surfaced and I started to press Carmela to tell me about his parents. So far we knew practically zilch about anything connected to his progenitors and we were not allowed to contact either of them. Carmela had consistently avoided replying to any question related to the parents' economic situation or whether Danny's mother was married or how old she was, her health history, etc. Finally, at dinner she cut me short and curtly told me that she was not at liberty to disclose any information about the orphan's history, and this fiat was enforced by the courts. Case closed. The restaurant, however, was deserving of its good rating, and Carmela and her husband profuse in their thanks to us.

We spent the night in their home, and later, in our room, with Danny, I had the feeling that our threesome was a family. The next morning we exchanged warm goodbyes with Carmela and her family, and set off.

We arrived in Rio de Janeiro about noon and found a relatively inexpensive hotel near the beach. Without Carmela there to help us make our way through the various government agencies, I found myself getting increasingly anxious about accomplishing what we came for and exceedingly impatient to get out of the country. Quite notably, I was lacking my usual confidence in myself out in the world. Even as a kid, I had little trouble traveling with my mother and taking her around to apply for economic assistance of one sort or another. I was only eight years old, but I knew how to present my mother and me so as to make a favorable impression on the office workers we needed to assist us. Of course it didn't hurt that I was so young and clearly capable. But, now in Rio, I was nervous and stressed; I had gotten accustomed to relying on Carmela to take care of everything. I kept worrying that I would mess things up and delay our departure. In the States I knew how to deal with people who were looking for bribery payments; but in a foreign country with a very strong police presence and a government that seemed to be comfortable with bribery as a built-in part of the bureaucratic system, I was worried that the system operated under different rules. I was fearful that I'd be put in a position where I would offer a bribe and end up in the pen.

However, the first couple of days in Rio, things went pretty smoothly and no problems developed, partly because no one—except the hotel clerk in the second hotel we stayed in—had been seeking under-the-table payment. I started to wonder whether I had manufactured in my mind that Carmela was paying off the various officials to get preferential treatment for us. It was only at night when the three of us were alone in this second hotel that my anxiety returned. It had to do with my need to protect my family and be responsible for them in a strange land with people that might be hostile to us. I assume this fear went back to my early childhood; in those days, in pre-school, I felt the outside world was dangerous and I clung to my parents for security. In all likelihood, I probably had absorbed the fears that they had, since my mother spoke terrible English and didn't know how to negotiate something as simple as public transportation; and my father was uneasy about his role inside the house and outside the house. So I suppose I was a very frightened little boy who sought the security of his family, while knowing somewhere inside himself that he might not be able to count on them to provide it.

By the end of the week I was very edgy and did not feel that I would handle things well if we had to prolong our stay for any length of time. The big hurdle was coming up on Monday morning when we would have to meet with the attorney general of the whole country to get final approval for our departure. Once we got that we could apply for a visa at the American Embassy to return to the States. I anticipated that the attorney general would scrutinize us carefully and put us through a rigorous question and answer procedure in order to determine whether there was anything amiss or illegal in what we had done. When we arrived at the attorney general's office we were told to sit and wait until he was ready to see us. There were a number of people ahead of us. When our turn came we were ushered into the room of one of his assistants.

His assistant was a middle-aged, gray-haired, bespectacled, light-skinned, English-speaking woman who made a big fuss over Danny and assured us that everything would be all right. I hadn't expected this calming sort of reassurance, and I couldn't help myself from asking, "Is there anything I should know when I see the attorney general?"

"Like what?"

"Well, like what kind of questions will he ask me?"

"Don't worry; everything has been taken care of."

It flashed on me that here too extended the long arm of Carmela—everything was taken care of. The assistant congratulated us on our good fortune in getting Danny and took us to the private chamber of the attorney general. Once there, she bid us a cheerful goodbye.

The attorney general beckoned us to come in and sit down, but first relieved us of our documents. He was a tall, slim, partly-bald man of about forty-five; he was wearing a lightweight, tan, three-piece tropical suit and seemed very much at ease at our entrance. He too spoke English. After an opening conversation about our new baby and about how we liked Brazil, he excused himself and began to look through our documents; in a bit he looked up and, speaking only to me, said, "I have just two questions to ask you: What do you do for a living and how much do you make?"

"I'm a psychologist with a private practice and I also am a professor at a college. My income, which is listed in the papers before you, is a hundred sixty thousand dollars a year."

"That's a very nice income, and I'm sure that Danny, as you call him, will be well-taken care of by you and your wife. And I hope at some time in the near future you will come back with him to visit our country. Everything seems in order here; you can pick up your papers from my secretary in a half hour. She is in the room next to this one on the right as you come in."

Margaret flushed with delight and happiness and thanked him sincerely for the privilege to adopt a baby in his country. He stood up and bowed graciously, wishing us well.

We picked up our papers from the secretary at the prescribed time and off we went straight to the American Embassy to get Danny's visa to enter the U.S. We encountered no problems there, so we were all set to leave the country with our newly-acquired baby and return to our home in New York City.

At the airport early the next morning we had all our papers with us and were ready to go through what we expected to be the perfunctory airport procedures. When it came our turn to hand our papers to the Brazilian custom's official, he took them, quickly perused two or three documents, and placed the pile on the counter before him, saying something in Portuguese that I did not understand. I asked him if he spoke English and with a look of irritation, he said, "A little." I began to get nervous.

"Is there something missing in our documents? Can you explain to me what seems to be the problem? Yesterday we got the approval of the attorney general and we thought everything was okay."

"Yes, everything is in order, except this one document has not the official stamp that is required." His English seemed pretty good.

"But our plane is leaving in an hour and fifteen minutes," Margaret let him know, with urgency in her voice and no small worry in her manner.

"These are our regulations, madam."

"Can't you do something to get us on the plane without the stamp? Contact the attorney general, if necessary."

"We're not in a position to do that," he answered her. But at the same time he very pointedly lifted the bottom stack of papers and placed it on top of the pile, while leaving the whole thing on the counter. Relieved, I understood what he wanted. I pulled Margaret aside and told her to move away with the baby, not to worry, and that I would take care of the situation.

She asked, pleadingly, "What can you do?"

"Trust me."

She moved off a little, and I turned my back, took out my wallet and fished out the last of my Brazilian currency and added some U.S. dollars to it, turned around and placed the money between the two piles. Then I pointed to the top sheet and said firmly, "Oh, here is the paper you've been looking for."

He glanced at me, relieved, and said, "Yes, you can proceed now."

CHAPTER THIRTEEN:
MARGARET AS MOTHER...
AND A TALK WITH TED

Margaret thrived back in New York City in her capacity as mother, and I don't think I ever saw her happier than she was during the next four years. She became totally immersed in nurturing Danny and her fulfillment spilled over to almost every aspect of family life. As for Danny, he was a warm and affectionate child and adored his new mom; they were a perfect pair. If there was any damage that accrued from his life before we had adopted him, it was not apparent to Margaret or me at this time. Contrary to my fears in anticipation of the adoption, I found myself not being troubled by Danny's non-biological tie to me. If anything, I over-identified with him... and just as I had created magical rituals for myself as a child in order to feel safe, I now transferred the rituals to include him. For instance, I took his birthday date—and I had done the same thing with my biological children—to be a lucky number and, if I accidentally came across the day, the month and the year in some form of print, that would be an omen for me that the child would be safe for the upcoming year. These are fairly classical symptoms of an obsessive-compulsive disorder (OCD), although I never saw myself as seriously impaired along those lines. However, in looking back at my years of psychological treatment, I sometimes wonder why my therapists underplayed this aspect of my behavior. But I suppose I had a hand in this. Instead of admitting the significance of the OCD symptoms, I used my skills at manipulation to avoid their being given the weight in treatment that they deserved. What this shows is my unwillingness to face up to my weaknesses against my own interests... for example, it turns out that my four children manifest some variation of this disorder, and perhaps it is not coincidental that my compulsiveness, to protect myself from crippling anxiety and insecurity, has filtered down to them.

When it came to Danny, fatherhood was turning out to be not as much of a burden as I had anticipated. I would even go further, and say that I felt a sense of well-being and delight in family life. Little was required of me—except to keep the money flowing—inasmuch as Margaret was flourishing as a mother and pretty much took care of everything.

Margaret also handled Danny's schooling, finding a good pre-k program for him available in our area. And she rightfully insisted that I set up my practice in an office outside the home, not in our living room as had been the case before Danny came on the scene. I rented an office nearby and this meant that she no longer had to vacate the premises or hang out in the bedroom in the blocks of time when I was seeing patients. Good grief, even my recognition of the needs of other people was increasing.

Margaret was so busy and so deeply content that she did not continue pursuing her career. Four years before Danny was adopted she had enrolled in a doctoral program in anthropology and by the time he was living with us, she had begun work on her dissertation. She was a top student. However, as a diligent therapist, I pointed out to her that she may well be using motherhood to sidestep her fears of not having what it takes to be successful in the work world. She didn't want to hear it.

Later on, her having back-pedaled in her career would aggravate problems in her self-development and our family life—especially when Danny was an adolescent and young adult. I saw the negative potential in what she was doing and understood there would come a time when she would require self-fulfillment in more than just motherhood—particularly since she did have high expectations for herself. For my part, I said my piece and shrugged my shoulders. My position was too comfortable and her happiness too great for me to create a rift between us over the issue of her completing her dissertation. Or maybe I shrugged it off, because I don't always fight for a relationship as hard as I should. In my family, people didn't change much.

I liked being consulted on all the matters concerning Danny's development and gave my opinion unhesitatingly, without having to do much in the way of taking care of him, since I was overloaded with teaching at the college and carrying on my practice. I was more tied to family life than ever before, but I still needed to get away from household and child-rearing responsibilities by throwing myself into my work.

Yet it didn't escape my consciousness that Margaret and I were evading some serious issues in our marriage because we had a common purpose, which led us to concentrate on our parental and family concerns as opposed to our conjugal concerns—and this was fine by me, and I suppose the same was true of her. I still was not ready to give up the defenses and habits that I had cultivated in my first marriage having to do with my absenting myself, on any number of levels, from family life. Margaret was so involved in parenting, and getting so much joy from it, that she wasn't too upset by my absenteeism; it was okay as long as she could make most of the decisions concerning Danny and rationalize to herself that I was working very hard to take care of the family.

While my second marriage was much better than my first— for any number of reasons—I still hedged my bets and tried to keep my options open. I didn't trust Margaret, or any woman, to be able to satisfy my enormous needs and deprivation in a way that would induce me to make marriage and home life the center of my existence. I would say that this narrow, self-serving view had stemmed from my projecting on to women my mother's pathologic self-enclosed approach to the world. My experience with Dalite and Margaret to the contrary, I could not help but to see women as serving their own self-interest before they would serve mine. I'd say this distrust of women dovetailed rather nicely with Margaret's distrust of men. Neither one of us was anxious to give up a great deal of our life pursuing a romantic ideal. And while both Dalite and Margaret were devoted mothers, it didn't relieve my mistrust of women. However, I was no longer persuing extra-marital affairs. Miracle of miracles.

A year after we adopted Danny I had a freewheeling conversation with my close friend and colleague, Ted, which picked up on and extended his view of my problems, and my questionable defenses in the marriage. I cherished Ted because he was astute about my psychology and pretty merciless in his attempts to dent my arrogance and armor. If someone couldn't see through me, I tended to devalue him or her—and the same was true, if I could belittle or manipulate someone. Neither was a problem with Ted: if anything, he belittled me, in thinking I was psychologically impossible. For instance, he always told me I was a hopeless person to be married to... and anyone who would engage to take on this role was, ipso facto, disturbed and incomplete—given that my personal habits were atrocious; that I was an incurable skinflint; that I was manipulative and invariably created a major dependence in my spouse on me; that I didn't want to be home all that much; that sexual and romantic intimacy in my marriage was not a priority for me (though the lack of it could send me out in search of an affair)... and the list was endless. And he found pleasure and humor in parading my inadequacies before me. He also let me know at every turn how culturally stultified I was, apart from my knowledge of my profession. And his attacks on me never were mean-spirited but always good-natured and offered as an antidote towards my grandiosity and self-infatuation. He also found a few redeeming qualities in me and, I might add, not infrequently turned to me for analytical help with certain of his psychological patterns that continually upset him. But on to the conversation:

"I can't believe it; Margaret is doing so well and is so happy with Danny that she has proposed that we start thinking about adopting another child."

"It never ends."

"It's too much. I'm gonna be fifty-one years old and I'm going to be running around the playground and hanging out in the sandbox for the next seven years. My father was in his late forties when I was born and never had much energy to keep up with me. It's fine for my wife, she's blooming with the joys of motherhood, but she's thirty-eight and she's not thinking of me."

"C'mon, Obler, you have boundless energy."

"I don't think you appreciate how hard I work."

"That's my point... you don't feel safe unless you're making more money all the time."

"It's easy for you to make little of my security needs, coming from your middleclass childhood, but I can't get the memories of poverty out of my head."

"Marty, you got more money than Scrooge McDuck.

"But that is beside the point. The point is, I know I sure don't want any more children."

"I certainly think you have every right to say no. But how that will play out in your relationship with Margaret is another matter. Would it be so bad if you agreed to adopt another kid?... you seem to be enjoying your family life in a way that you didn't anticipate. Maybe you'll enjoy your life with another kid twice as much."

"And by that way of thinking, if I adopt two additional kids, I could enjoy it four times as much."

"Your math is pretty good."

"Think about it, Ted. Margaret is already totally occupied with Danny, and often oblivious to my needs in the marriage... and this with only one adopted child."

"I think you're missing the target. The reason you're not getting more from your marriage hasn't to do with whether you adopt another kid or not."

"What does it have to do with?"

"It has to do with you're not being home half the time... and, additionally, it has to do with your compulsive sexuality and needing to relieve yourself seven days a week, even if it means that sex is perfunctory."

"Isn't it enough that I'm not screwing other women any more?"

"Why don't you ask Margaret? But the real issue is, What would it take for you to really see Margaret and believe that you can get and give a lot more than you're resigned to?"

"To be honest, I don't know."

"You don't know what I'm talking about?"

"Look, Ted, you and I are different. To be blunt, I don't expect as much out of life and relationships as you do. The difference between you and me is that you keep plugging away—the eternal idealist—hoping that the next woman you get serious about will be the right one. And you believe that if you're good enough and sensitive enough and caring enough, the fates will reward you."

"I do think like that, and, what's more, with all my idealism and belief in doing the hard work that relationships require, I'm discouraged and no closer to meeting the kind of woman I'm looking for."

"If you ask me, I don't believe the candle is worth the game. The women you're meeting can't really appreciate you. Your expectations are too high."

"In a certain way we're similar. We both latch on to hopefulness as a way of doing something or in lieu of doing something. My hopefulness has to do with believing what you said, that in being a good, caring person I'll be rewarded. And your hopefulness has to do with the idea that if you don't ask for too much, and you're willing to compromise, you won't have to face the disintegration that awaits... and, perhaps more important, the depths of your fear of Margaret seeing you as the small little shyster you are underneath all the bravado. The salient thing is that in either situation, yours or mine, change doesn't take place, all that happens is a continuation of hope. In yours, hope provides a buttress so that things don't collapse and, in mine, hope provides a necessary belief that everything will work out."

"… only I'm willing to live with whatever I can get from my relationship with Margaret and even feel it's more than enough, since it's more than I expected to begin with; but you are not willing to live with an imperfect woman."

"At least we've established that we're both sad sacks in our core psychology… and that hopefulness is a cover for hopelessness. But I'm still interested in hearing your response to my original question about what it would take to improve your relationship with Margaret so that you both can move away from the fixed positions that you have established… that don't allow enough of the real love you have for each other to come to the fore. You're not going to give up the habits of yours that are annoying to your wife and you are certainly not going to diagram for her the ways you retain control in the relationship. You always talk about collusion when you talk about the marital stuff with couples, but there is no small degree of collusion between you and Margaret in not opening up your innermost desires with each other… out of pessimism that it won't matter, even if you do. She distrusts men and you distrust women. But I blame you more than Margaret."

"Naturally."

"Put it this way, Margaret has set up a defense against processing the kind of stuff we've been talking about—so that she really doesn't have to hear your innermost voice… or her own; but you know all this stuff that I'm saying, I've been saying it to you for years… and you deal with couples' problems every day of the week in your practice. Only you choose to ignore the very same thing in your own marriage."

"What else would a pragmatist like me do? I'll bet if you take a hundred shrinks, ninety-eight of them would be as unwilling to go the whole nine yards as I am."

"Well, who knows? What I'd like you to talk about is the fear that prevents you from truly encountering your problems with Margaret. You never talk about that."

"Listen, I learned from my father's life that it isn't going to matter much what you do or don't do—nothing changes. The secret is to make the most of what you've got, which is exactly what I tell my patients."

"Your pessimism is part of it. But that I would think is just the first line of defense against the fears that you want to keep locked away in the family attic."

"You won't rest until I end up in the psycho ward, cringing before my demons."

"More likely, you'll end up running the psycho ward, like Jack Nicholson."

My conversation with Ted was very helpful. It set my mind working about the lifelong grasp my fear and pessimism had on me. It had been so easy to coast along being myself and not dealing with the stuff Ted confronted me with. Always so much work to do on my psychology and personality. I could upset people with my gross humor and manners, especially women. The damned thing is that I like who I am or fool myself that I do so. And here again I have to put so much effort into being me and making everyone think I have everything all sewed up… and that I am unique and funny and sharp in my blunt offensive way. Underneath I have great disdain for myself, and perpetually worry that someday my whole persona will just collapse and I'll lose everything I've worked so hard to achieve. I know I talk a lot about making changes in my personality and character, and I'm sure the reader is getting impatient with me. But I feel I am more aware of my shortcomings, more aware of my self-indulgences and excesses… and that I am growing up, slowly but steadily. I am becoming more of a family man all the time. I really listen to what Ted has to say and take it seriously. But change is hard for me. I am over-confident by way of defending against my insecurity; and my insecurity is so threatening that I need to go beyond insecurity into grandiosity. And I am able to prop up this tin structure by being absurdly capable and successful in the practical world. And I am also humorous and charming in my rough Brooklyn way. And, on a practical level, you can't fool me. I know what's what. Ted, bless his soul, has a bullshit meter that sounds me out and I can't put over anything on him. And he doesn't let up; he is a real friend. Margaret has the capacity to see deeply into me and can be bitingly critical of me but she gets bogged down in her own neurotic behavior… and can't hold me to account. I am able to play the daddy figure with her and outmaneuver her—which is too bad because it benefits neither of us. I don't fool her, but I manage to be very stubborn about preserving the personal traits she objects to in me. All of this leaves her very hostile towards me, which takes some of the joy out of my life and can't be very good for her, physically or emotionally. But it is a part of our relationship. Just as my efforts to defuse her anger towards me are not likely to strike a receptive note in her, something that has to be pretty discouraging to me.

After all, not surprisingly, the child in me is still present and spills over to my relationship with Margaret—and neither of us is very willing to pursue the disabling things in our childhood that cast a long shadow over our relationship. I can refer to them, but putting in the hard work to make changes in the way the past infringes negatively on the present has been beyond me all these years. And while my past is flamboyantly in evidence in me, Margaret, in a much more hidden way, suffers from the same syndrome of child in the adult… in her case, depleting her capacity for joy, achievement, and fullness of personality. We collude to give each other the space not to have to give up our dependency on injurious patterns. As a professional, I see this all too clearly; seeing isn't enough, however. Margaret and I do have a very workable relationship… and do love each other in an insular way. In many respects, we have earned the right to think of ourselves as a good couple. We do combat; we also begrudgingly admire each other, after many years together.

CHAPTER FOURTEEN:
WARREN'S WORLD

Warren's world as a bipolar had dramatically changed over the years of his treatment with me. There was less danger that he would slip into a psychotic state or regress to a point where he was practically nonfunctional. I give myself a lot of credit for that. He would go to work every day; at my urging, he would sometimes go to AA meetings; and I pressured him to socialize with some of the people from group therapy. The main goal was to divert him from getting too involved in delusory and hallucinatory thinking. Left too much to himself he would have to create imaginary conflicts with other people as a means to feel engaged, even if it had to be on a negative basis. Bipolars like Warren, who are so disengaged from their inner life and are isolated from other people, constantly have to create interactions with those around them in order to avoid the reality that they're incapable of having real relationships. Part of the problem is that Warren views others as being there to satisfy his needs, very much like a two-year old would view his parents. This outlook is a very narcissistic and one-dimensional view of other people and the world, but unlike the average two-year old, the bipolar remains stuck in this self-referential phase of development, which often leads to distorted, delusional thinking.

Not all bipolars are as disturbed as Warren, but those who are tend to become very desolate, and believe that those around them are the source of their difficulty rather than they themselves. Warren can't see that other people have needs just as valid as his. And he can't see himself through other people's eyes. Most people experience him as a troubled, defensive, dull, humorless person—sort of the way Edith saw him years before in his early group therapy experience.

Warren's life was routine and boring; the best that could be said about it was that he tried to keep busy. But no matter how many AA meetings he attended or how often he got together with people from group, it was still Warren who was present and that meant he was always burdened by being himself and most people thought he was strange. Nevertheless, being active was a lot healthier for him than staying home and thinking. The aim was to get him to learn how to interact with people and try to build a continuity of friendship. The same goal was established at his job; he had switched jobs some years ago, going from one position to another in the state civil service system, but the latest job was turning out to last a little bit longer. We targeted in on a number of individuals with whom it seemed there was some potential to build a social life outside of the office. In this job too, his history with people at the job was fraught with conflict and paranoia and it took a tremendous effort on my part to break down his delusory thinking in respect to them.

The problem I faced with Warren, fifteen years into therapy, was that I had done as much as I could with him to keep him afloat and make sure he would not have another psychotic break under my aegis. Yet I knew that the marginal life he was leading, while improved, was still tenuous inasmuch as he could easily breakdown at any time. Without a solid foundation to buttress him he would, inevitably, slip into his form of pathology. What he needed—on the most practical level—was a woman to fill up his emptiness and boredom and to provide the day-in, day-out home life that he had lacked for most of his life. A woman who could provide this for him, hopefully, could keep him from dwelling on his morbid thoughts, which would attack him as long as there was no center to his life. What Warren needed was a normal life, even though he wasn't normal.

Obviously it was one thing to talk about Warren's need for a woman in his life; it was another, to find the right woman (if such a person existed) and put the package together. Considering Warren's historical problems with women, it would take Divine intervention to get him to successfully build a relationship with a woman. While Warren had dated women and had made attempts to engage in the singles scene, he never lost his terror of emotional and sexual intimacy. In fact, the only successful sexual relationship he ever had with a woman was with a paid sexual surrogate under the auspices of his therapist at the time. From what I can make of it, this surrogate partner supplied an environment that was nonjudgmental, supportive, and non-threatening. Yet his success with the surrogate did not transfer to the women he started dating. In a couple of instances he was able to work up to the point of engaging in sexual intercourse, but became so anxious about his ability to perform that the women bailed out. On one occasion, he actually was able to penetrate a woman but then he froze for some minutes. When she asked him what was wrong, he mumbled incoherently but still did not move; she sensed that something was drastically wrong and recoiled, explicitly telling him that he was a freak. It took months of therapy after that to overcome the devastation to his ego before he would even attempt to date another woman.

As a consequence of my pushing him to meet women, he started dating again and met a young light-skinned black woman, Colleen, whom he was very attracted to. He was able to bring Colleen to an orgasm, even though he was unable to do the same for himself; he did this for her by maintaining his erection during intercourse... but it was mechanical as if he were an automaton.

Things went okay with him and Colleen for a while, but it was not long before he developed a new obsession: he feared getting involved with her because he believed that his inability to come would lead to her rejecting him. In actuality, she did end the relationship but not for the reason he thought, not for his inability to reach orgasm; it had to do with his passivity and his disturbed personality, at least as much as I could make out from Warren's account of his interaction with her.

Finally, I reached the conclusion that if I were going to succeed in this area with him, and help him with his woman problem so he could lead a more normal life, I would have to set up the relationship for him, choose the right person who could tolerate his abnormalities, and control what transpired between him and her so that he could have some chance to have a quasi-relationship with a woman. It would be the closest thing to Divine intervention

He was now forty-nine years old. His window of opportunity was narrowing. With this in mind, I decided to take a step with him that would prove to be one of the most controversial I had ever undertaken in therapy. I would assume the role of the *shadchan* and arrange a marriage for Warren, in which a partner would be chosen, largely, on her capacity to tolerate his compulsions, fears, self-doubts, paranoia, delusions, etc. Strikingly, here I was bent on setting up an arranged marriage, which returned me to my own parents' arranged marriage... and their relationship had turned out to be disastrous. To say that I was walking on thin ice is to put it mildly. But I didn't let the hazards stop me.

"Let me get this straight, you're suggesting that I get involved with a woman who would be accepting of me, and if we hit it off, I marry her?"

"You got it."

"Why should I do that? I thought, with the work you've been doing with me, I've been making progress in my relationships with women."

"I don't deny that, but it's a too-slow progress as is the slight reduction of your anxiety in dating women. There is no question that you've become less afraid to meet a woman through the personal ads or even on a blind date."

"So, then... ?"

"The problem is that it doesn't go anywhere because of your sexual difficulties and fears of intimacy. You're just spinning your wheels."

"It's odd that you say that; I think I performed sexually much better with Colleen."

"... better than what?"

"... better than in the old days."

"It still boils down to when you're with a woman you can't perform because of your great fear that you won't be able to come inside them, and you believe that completely turns them off. Of course I'm referring only to those women who are willing to date you more than once or twice, that is the ones with whom you have some possibility of overcoming your intimacy problem. The only woman in your whole life that you've been able to have an orgasm inside of was a professional who was totally patient and understanding and was able to guide you through your fears. You're not likely to find that kind of woman in the dating scene."

"So why would this woman who you're going to choose for me be any different?"

"I can't say it will be. You want to know my hope?"

"Yes, I do."

"My hope is that if we go foreign and seek to match you up with a financially hard-pressed Asian woman who is religious and has not been able to find a man to marry, she would be a lot more accepting of your sexual and emotional difficulties and not dump you if you couldn't perform right away."

"That's a pretty big if... What's in it for her?"

"A green card... and since we'll choose a devout Catholic, she can finally have sex—after marriage. Even more importantly, Warren, once she marries you, she can't divorce you, so you'll have an infinite amount of time to work out your sexual problems."

"Listen Marty, I agreed to do the personal ads... to satisfy you; but this is a little too much. They don't do arranged marriages any more. I grew up in Queens, not in Bangkok.

What's the chances of my falling in love with this woman? Who knows whether I'll even be attracted to her?"

"Love... ? There's a lot more important things than love."

"... like what?"

"... like having someone to come to home from work to and having someone to be with on weekends."

"There's been many a Saturday night that I have something to do."

"Look, you fucking *mischugina*, wake up. You've been all alone most of your life, you're isolated and removed, cut off from any real affection or warmth from another person. A woman like the kind I'm talking about would provide you with company and make it worthwhile for you to live in the real world."

"Well... what if I agree to go along with what you're proposing, and then once she gets to know me and my problems, she turns off? What do I do then?"

"We can deal with that when and if it comes up. But, to me, the more immediate question is, What do you do now, given your reality: stay put or take a chance?"

"What I'm having trouble with is the need to make a decision so soon that could change my life forever."

"Well, we don't have six months to debate it. Sometimes you have to take a risk in life."

"And this is one of those times?"

"I'd say it's now or never."

No one in his right mind thought that this was a good idea as part of the psychotherapy process for Warren. Even people that cared about me and knew my work cautioned me strongly against it. To my way of thinking, this arranged marriage was the only possibility Warren had to change a basically hopeless situation. Honestly, I haven't seen much going on in the field of psychoanalysis and psychotherapy with this type of narcissistic, delusory, bipolar personality other than anxiety-reducing drug treatment, or the kind of traditional insight therapy that can't bring about the change that I was seeking for him. I understood the liabilities and the risks of this bizarre solution to Warren's problem with women. After all, Warren wasn't the run-of-the-mill businessman who doesn't have time to find a woman; he was psychotic. And this isn't the kind of solution that therapists typically come up with. I understood the unorthodoxy of my remedy, but still remained undeterred in my conviction that it was a chance worth taking. For one thing, I had confidence in myself—that I could make it work; or at least avoid total disaster, if it didn't. I did not feel at a loss when I asked myself the question, What could come up between him and his future wife that I couldn't handle? If anything, the consideration that Warren would be in a real relationship with real problems made it much more likely to effect positive change in his life than if he were to stay in the uncommitted dating scene where he had recourse to fantasy when things didn't turn out well. Better to force him into the real world, I calculated, than to let him stumble along in his fantasy-ridden world.

If there was anyone who put pressure on me not to go ahead with this idea of mine for Warren, it was Ted. Let me say a few words about Ted before I roll into our conversation. Ted at this point was single, his wife of twenty-five years had died of cancer. Ted was 54 at around this time, and so was I. In terms of surface personality and looks, Ted is tall, thin, and quite good-looking; he is sensitive and intellectual. I, on the other hand, am 5'11", stocky, not conventionally good-looking (but had a solid body), not particularly intellectual, and offensively blunt at times. He is romantic and idealistic (along with an ingrained cynicism); I am practical and pessimistic. But, despite the differences or perhaps, in part, because of them we get along quite well together. We both were psychotherapists; and teachers at the same college.

However, when I talked to him about my plan to arrange a marriage for Warren, he not only laughed at what I intended to do but thought it was unethical, dangerous, and professionally indefensible. As much as I argued to the contrary, and made my case in terms of what was best for Warren and not the profession, Ted did not let up in his attempt to dissuade me from going ahead with it.

"Hey, what's up with you and the arranged marriage for Warren? Are you still working to bring Nasi over?" [Nasi is the woman that I had targeted for him to marry.]

"With all due haste."

"I can't believe it. Do you realize how unethical what you're doing is? And I don't mean only professionally, but just in terms of the two people involved?"

"I imagine you're talking about Nasi more than Warren. For after all, it's probably more of a concern, ethically, to put her in a position of marrying a psychotic than any concern over him marrying her. "

"Well, I'm glad to hear that it is of concern."

"Of course I'm troubled about fixing up a woman with a delusional bipolar, but bipolars, like Warren, have a right to get married too."

"And what about Nasi, what about her rights?"

"Thousands of people marry individuals who are delusional and have psychotic features… people for the most part who don't have the benefit of seeing a therapist before marrying. I think I am being ethical by letting Nasi know before she makes the decision some of the difficulties she'll be facing with Warren. It's not the kind of arranged marriage my mother and father had where the rabbi didn't consider at all the mental state of the couple he was marrying. It was enough for him that they both were Jews."

"So what you're saying is that because you're not as ignorant or unconcerned as the rabbi in the case of your parents, that everything is fine."

"I'm just making the point that Warren and Nasi are going to know a lot more about each other before they get married than most people do in the world at large."

"C'mon Marty, don't bullshit yourself. Warren can't make it with any woman and you're banking on the fact that this is a foreign woman who is unfamiliar with the extent of his psychological illness. And no matter what you say, you are using your position as Warren's therapist to assure her, once you outline his problems, that this is a good thing for her to do."

"I think you are giving me more credit than I deserve. I can't say that I intend to outline in full Warren's extensive disabilities because frankly I myself don't know how much the extent of his disorders will impede the marriage."

"You mean it's a crapshoot?"

"That's right. Only I look at it this way. Bipolars like Warren are not dangerous, they're fragile, vulnerable people and are not more of a threat to others than the normal population. Even schizophrenics are statistically no more a threat to commit dangerous crimes than the average person."

"Are you making up these stats as you go along, or do you know something?"

"I'm making it up. But I really feel that when I first started therapy with Warren, I would have been reluctant to fix him up with anyone, never mind marrying him off. But he's made tremendous progress, he hasn't had a breakdown in fifteen years. What's more, he has gone on dates with women since then and has shown no signs of untoward aggression or threatening behavior."

"So you don't worry about his paranoia as a condition that disqualifies him for marriage?"

"Of course I do. But one of the major focuses of his therapy has been to keep it under control and I've been extremely successful. That's why I believe he is ready to be married. Furthermore, if you want to talk about ethics, the best way to protect the society is if he is married, because then he will be less lonely and desperate. I don't think you're suggesting that paranoids and paranoid schizophrenics should be prohibited from marriage?"

"What about psychopaths, would you marry them off, too? For instance, John Dillinger, would marriage have kept him from a life of crime?"

"Who knows, if Dillinger had gotten more home-cooked meals he would have been less prone to violence. But the bottom line is that Warren is not a danger to others—he is more of a danger to himself—and is, in actuality, a frightened little boy who has wanted someone to love him all his life. The only chance he has of participating in what resembles a normal life is if he is living with a woman who cares about him."

"Well, I hear what you're saying and I do feel for him. But what about Nasi? The big risk is hers. Aside from Warren's major delusions and paranoia, he is unaware of how other people see him, unaware of their psychology and thinking, and is isolated and removed in ways that are incalculable as to their effect on others. Would you marry Warren, if you were a woman? Obviously not, so you are making a judgment that she has no alternatives and she's better off with anything she gets. Who gives you the right to make this judgment about her and the right to sacrifice her for Warren's benefit?"

"You know me better than that. You know I am a good analyst and everything I've been doing with him has been to help him become more aware of other people's needs and feelings. Of course, you're right about my convincing a woman like Nasi to marry him. But I would like to give her an opportunity to get to know him and see that he is a pretty good guy, someone who now has the capability of being almost present in a relationship; and considering that she is a woman in her late forties, a strict Catholic, very much desiring to find a husband so that she could have sex and have something resembling a domestic life, this is the best she can do."

"We'll see. But I'm not so sure that your playing God is going to work out the way you think."

I had a friend who knew a Thai woman whose sister (Nasi) wanted to come to New York City. It was possible to arrange for Nasi to come for a three-week visit to the city. Without going into the correspondence and phone conversations that took place between me and the sister and Warren and her, the groundwork was done and the purpose of the visit clearly enunciated, which was for Warren and Nasi to get to know each other. Nasi had the ingredients of the type of woman I was looking for, for Warren: She was a heavy-duty Catholic, getting on in age, looking to get married and her prospects in her home country were extremely limited; she saw her mission in life to serve her future husband, in a self-sacrificing way. Also important, she was economically self-sufficient so that eventually she could find work in the United States and the two of them, together, could live in a reasonably comfortable fashion. And, finally, from her pictures she did not appear to be an unattractive woman.

Warren grew extremely apprehensive when it finally sunk in that Nasi was coming to see him in a week. It was no longer something that awaited him in the distant future.

Nasi and Warren began the process of getting acquainted over the first week after her arrival. He reported in his sessions that he found her to be a pleasant person but very passive; he was at pains to make sure I knew that he wasn't at all physically attracted to her. Still, he was willing to give it a shot, having partially accepted my spiel that he could have a good relationship with a woman even if he wasn't passionately in love with her. I asked him what he found was unattractive about her. He stated: "I like women with big breasts." I questioned him about her personality and he indicated that she was nice but uninteresting. He said that she spoke in a low voice and that this, combined with her language difficulties in English, made it hard for him to understand her. In spite of this, he managed to learn a lot about her, especially since I kept pumping him to get more information.

Nasi came from a very large family in a rural area of Northern Thailand. Her mother converted to Catholicism early in her marriage and raised her children as devout Catholics.

Nasi became very involved in the religion, even entertaining becoming a nun.

The family by American standards was poor; they grew most of their own food and raised chickens and other livestock as the backbone of their livelihood. But Nasi told Warren that while her family was poor, she always had enough to eat and okay clothes to wear to school. Early on in her schooling, the nuns recognized that she was a bright girl and gave her special attention, encouraging her to study hard so that she could get a job that paid fairly well. Being by nature a reserved, shy girl she welcomed the chance to concentrate on her studies since she felt awkward in the social world.

Over the years she stayed with her studies, left her village to go to college in Bangkok and eventually became a nurse and was able to support herself and provide some help to her family. But socially she never overcame her early shyness, which translated into her never being in a relationship with a man; at forty-seven, she was still a virgin.

I asked Warren whether anything physical had taken place between him and her during her visit so far. He made it clear that he had no desire whatsoever to touch her, and let me know that he was just going along with my plan in order to pacify me. I strongly urged him to attempt to become physical with her, explaining that I believed that he was fearful and defensive when it came to performance with women and this was just another example of it. I also mentioned that Nasi would be particularly threatening to him because she expected that they would be in a permanent relationship. It would be one thing for him to be sexually inadequate in a short-term relationship, but another thing for him to be locked into his failure forever.

In order to try to alleviate some of his worries, I got him to agree to bring up the subject of a physical relationship the next time they met.

Warren came into session after their having seen each other again, and he was overtly agitated. When I asked him what was bothering him, he angrily denounced my whole scheme, claiming that it was idiotic and doomed to failure from the beginning.

"So tell me what happened."

He told me that he had brought up the subject of sexual relations with her, and she explained that in her religion sex was discouraged before marriage.

I had suggested that he point out to her that while in the Catholic religion it is taboo to have sexual intercourse before marriage, it is not a sin to have sexual foreplay without being married. I didn't know whether this was true or not, but it sounded good so I said it. Warren was not of a mind to hear this, and determined that it would be better if they canned the sexual stuff and got more comfortable with each other—and that maybe then he would be less turned off. I went along with that, although I didn't agree; actually it made sense, of a sort.

From what Warren told me the remainder of her visit was spent in his showing her around the city and their spending amiable time together. At their last meeting before she returned to her country, they agreed to keep in contact regularly. She further indicated that she enjoyed his company and hoped that they could work things out so that they could be together in the future. Warren, for his part, was flattered at her positive feelings for him, but was very hesitant about continuing the relationship beyond a correspondence. When it came down to it, he couldn't overcome his sexual disinterest in her.

I, for my part, was very outspoken: "Listen, *moch schaffer*, you may want a pen pal, but I want you to have a mail-order bride."

Over the next months it took a great deal of pressure on my part to get Warren to sustain an ongoing communication with Nasi. I had to push him, cajole him, and order him to keep up his end of the correspondence… and had to constantly remind and badger him that he needed a woman to live with—and Nasi was as good as he was going to get considering his ocean of problems—since, as long as he lived alone, he would be prey to the full force of his paranoia… and he should keep in mind that he can't count on me forever to be there to pull him back when he starts going over the edge. And being the manipulative and powerful figure that I am, I was able to get Warren to reluctantly do what was best for him.

Initially there was a period of nice-enough correspondence, pretty pro forma, but in time Nasi began to voice some of the concerns she was having about what to do with her life.

Nasi had a secure job as a nurse in Thailand, which she hoped she could parlay into a job as a nurse in New York City. Also, she had the basic instincts of an avid shopper and loved New York City for what it offered in that domain: when she was here she had dragged Warren off, at every opportunity, to check out the clothing stores and the expensive department stores on Fifth Avenue. She liked the way the American women dress and conduct themselves, and admired their seeming independence. All of this added to her already existent wish to come to America to live. And, perhaps, most tellingly, she was embroiled with her parents about her fledgling plans to move to the United States without having an in-place commitment of marriage.

Curiously, Warren was not put-off by Nasi's seeming willingness to think about coming to this country without assurance from him that they would be married. He seemed, if anything, pleased that he could assume a different role with her other than that of prospective husband.

In keeping with her new idea for herself, Nasi made an effort to research, at the Thai and U.S. embassies, what would be involved in getting a visa to come to the United States to live for a few months.

This prompted Warren, surprisingly to me, to get caught up in the legalities of the immigration and visa process and begin doing research on his own as to the options available to her. He was able to compartmentalize her problem of getting over to this country and living and working here, treating it as if this concern was unrelated to their pursuing a conjugal relationship.

It didn't dismay him that he was splitting one concern from the other, which is characteristic of a bipolar position. Nasi, however, was making it clear in their correspondence and telephone calls that her efforts to come to the States, without pursuing a conjugal commitment, was causing a disturbance within her family. Predictably, from a cultural standpoint, her parents were opposed to her returning to America without some formal agreement of marriage.

Nasi proceeded on her own, apart from her parents' wishes, to move along the business of obtaining a visa. With Warren's help and encouragement she found the stamina to act in her own behalf and in opposition to her parents' preference, not such an easy thing to do in an Asian culture. Nasi, though, had not given up on her plan to make things work with Warren; she was willing to come to the States in, more or less, good will and trust that the two of them could make a go of it. Warren was not of the same mind. He simply split-off, preferring to think of himself in the role of a facilitator rather than a lover/husband.

It took about eight months for the paperwork to be processed by the American embassy. Nasi didn't succeed in getting a work visa but was able to obtain a visa that permitted her to stay in the country for an extended period of time, under the condition that Warren would take economic responsibility for her while she was here.

Nasi held on to the idea that she was coming to this country in order to test the job prospects for the future and that she and Warren would continue their attempt to see if marriage was feasible for them. Naturally, I had to hammer Warren into submission to at least agree to remain open to the second part of her agenda, a difficult proposition, considering the extent of his disinclination. I convinced him on a mental plane that the three weeks she had been here previously were not sufficient time to enable him to make a valid decision about whether things could work out between them. As for Warren, his heart was now in his role as facilitator, since he had helped her to get into the country; he got caught up in his own egotistic need to see himself as altruistic savior helping a third world woman make it in America. This type of self-image boosting is not uncommon with bipolars and is used as an antidote—usually short-lasting—to their feelings of weakness and helplessness. A central facet of the manic condition, in the bipolar disorder, is the need to shore up the damaged ego so as to avoid disintegration of the personality.

Once Nasi returned to America she and Warren agreed to meet three or four days a week to see how things went between them. She moved in with a friend she had worked with in Thailand and managed to cover her own expenses, which was more than fine with Warren. For the first six weeks things went very well for them. She and Warren spent full days walking around the city, going to department stores, visiting the parks, museums, eating out. They had enough to say to each other because everything was centered on their activities. Warren loved the role of the tour guide and for the first time in a long time was able to be relieved of some of his depression, largely as a result of his having something to do much of the time and someone with whom to do it.

At the end of two months I decided to confront Warren with my observation that although Nasi and he were feeling good about being together, it didn't sound as though they were sharing much intimacy beyond the external activities they took part in together. When I said as much to him, he replied testily, "What's wrong with our enjoying ourselves and my helping her to get to know the city?"

I replied, "It's what's not happening that is bothering me."

He asked for clarification, and I said to him that it was my understanding that the purpose of bringing Nasi over to this country was to decide whether or not to get married to each other and not for you to use the experience as a training ground for a tour guide.

Warren smirked and asked me what I thought he should be doing differently.

I responded, "Very simple, if you're going to decide whether you want this woman as a lifelong companion, you're going to have to check out if you can emotionally open up to each other, can enjoy sex together, and are attracted to each other's personality."

He seemed flustered by what I was saying, so I asked him about his feelings as to what I had said.

After a long pause, in which I could see Warren's dejection, he said, in a lowered voice, "You have to understand, she has a lot of trouble expressing any emotion or feelings of a personal nature and I have to drag it out of her, if I'm going to get anything from her; and if I do get something, she speaks in such a whisper that I can hardly make out what she's saying. It's very hard for her to talk about anything that matters to her."

"Could that possibly be a cultural thing?"

"I wouldn't know."

"Why don't you find out?"

"How?"

"I'll bet if you bring up the issue of your relationship with her and where she wants it to go, she'll start letting you know what she feels and thinks."

I saw he was a bit taken aback by this pretty mild statement of mine, so I remarked to him, "You're not so sure you want to hear what she thinks and feels."

I went on to explore with Warren his resistance to go through the natural steps of building a relationship with a woman. I let him know I could understand how much I was asking of him, since his history did not include much in this department. I explained to him that to build such a bond with a woman he had to go through the painful steps, learning by trial and error, as most people did in post-adolescence and their twenties. And that many of them had parents who modeled at least some of the necessary skills for them. He was not so fortunate.

Warren said, "If that's the case, we should have chosen a woman like my surrogate sex therapy partner to get involved with, someone who is experienced in these matters."

"Warren, think about it: What woman who has her act together is going to be with you?"

He obviously wasn't too pleased at what I said and the way I phrased it, but seemed to accept the truth of what I was saying.

"So, then, what's the point of working with a woman who has as much trouble with intimacy as I do?"

"... good point. My only answer is that I feel Nasi is the kind of good person—and good nurse—who could accept your problems, as long as she believed you cared for her."

"I hope so. But I still don't seem to be attracted to her."

"Give it time. And think, Warren, it might be good for you to be in a position with someone who is less experienced sexually than you—if that's possible—and therefore there would be less of a chance that she'd see you as deficient as a man since she hasn't much of an idea of what men are supposed to do."

I could see that he was pleased by this idea and relieved. And I decided to use the next few sessions to outline to him my plan of how he should go about working out their emotional and sexual problems. I saw the sexual problems as considerable on both their parts, and I knew it would require my coming up with a step-by-step manual on how to proceed.

Warren was still very ambivalent about the whole marital question but was interested in working out his own sexual hang-ups with anyone he could find to do so. And he appreciated that in this situation I would be there to take him through some of his sexual dysfunction in a practical way.

CHAPTER FIFTEEN:
A LITTLE MORE ON THE SEXUAL EDUCATION
OF NASI AND WARREN

I knew from her prior visit that Nasi would be resistant to becoming heavily sexually involved with Warren without a commitment of marriage. Yet I felt to open the subject of their sexual needs and problems could potentially contribute to their becoming closer with each other, which would help them to put more of their personal issues on the table. And this might ultimately induce Warren to be more attracted to her.

Initially, when Warren put forth to her some of my thinking on the subject, she was silent and had very little to say about it. She did not commit herself one way or the other and indicated that she would think it over. But it did lead to them conversing about the whole subject of sex and intimacy when they got together, and this was the necessary step that they needed to take. In session, Warren ranted and raved at Nasi for procrastinating over having some kind of sex with him. He wanted to believe that any woman, given the opportunity, would jump at the chance of engaging in sex with him. When he carefully broached this notion with me, I reminded him of all the work that we had done previously in getting him to see the unreality of his thinking and that it didn't reflect his experience with women, now or ever. As usual, he only partially agreed with what I was saying but, again, as usual, I ended up hammering him into submission for his own good. I convinced him that he would have to go slowly with Nasi, and that he should be respectful of her having had no experience with men; if she did participate, he should keep in mind that she probably was doing so mostly because she felt she had no other alternative. He would have to ease her into a sexual involvement with him… for her own good. Warren liked the idea that he was acting out of the noblest of motives. On most days that they met, some part of the afternoon or evening would be relegated to going back to his apartment to further their sexual acquaintanceship.

As their sexual encounters unfolded Warren's account of what was taking place appalled me—I couldn't help thinking that a couple of savvy ten year olds could do better than they were doing. As he related their pattern, on every occasion they were together to have sex, he would undress down to his boxer shorts and she would undress down to her bra and panties; then they would lie down next to each other on the bed and each one would wait for the other to make a move. I asked Warren why he didn't grab her and start making out. He simply stated that her tits were hardly existent and that the only time he would ever grab a woman was if she had a big pair of tits.

"So what do you do with her?"

"Eventually I would get so bored lying there that I start kissing her."

"Yeah…?"

"But she doesn't know how to kiss. She never opens her mouth, so I can't stick my tongue in."

"So…?"

"I finally asked her what was wrong. And she told me that she thought that people closed their mouth when kissing. So I showed her how to open her mouth and kiss."

"That sounds pretty good.

In following sessions, Warren and I worked on his need to take the initiative and move their sexual life forward. At least now they were routinely French kissing. From what I could make out from what Warren told me, she was very passive but hadn't explicitly refused to engage in more heated sexual activity. I urged Warren to overcome his hesitations and get into heavy petting and further explore mutually-satisfying sexual activities.

Warren's face reddened. I assumed he was embarrassed but in actuality he was irritated by my suggestion. When I inquired what was so bothersome about what I had said, he angrily replied, "By now you know that what turns me on is a woman being aggressive with me and not the other way round. We've been talking for years about my masochistic fantasies. This woman is the exact opposite type from my fantasy woman. She is passive, just lies there, and waits for me to do everything. I want someone who is active, who will make demands on me, and excite me to do things sexually to her. It's never going to work with her."

"You're not giving her a chance. Maybe if you learn to turn her on she'll begin to lose some of her inhibitions. Part of her passivity may be just inexperience and her cultural upbringing. How do you know that once she discovers lust and passion she won't be a firecracker?"

"I doubt it. I can tell when a woman is aggressive sexually and is hot. She's not the type. I asked her what she had done with men on the few dates she had and she told me that the most she had ever done was a light kiss and holding hands."

I could see Warren was being defensive. He was fearful of getting what he wanted, fearful of having to face his own sexual inadequacy, fearful that his own sexual inexperience would be painfully revealed. He preferred to set up the situation so that his lack of interest was her responsibility, her fault. That way his performance would not become the issue.

I knew if I were to confront him with this perception, there would be a good chance that he would become even more defensive and possibly back away from the whole involvement. In order to insure that this didn't happen, I played into his egotistical need to see himself in the situation as a teacher, mentor, and facilitator, someone who could help Nasi overcome a lifetime of social and sexual withdrawal.

I said, "Nasi is a very deprived woman who could use all the help you can give her. I would guess that part of the reason she wants to marry you is that she sees the generous nature of your personality. And even though you have had your share of trouble sexually with women it takes a certain amount of courage to act in the face of fear." These calculated words represented just how controlling and manipulative I could be; but from my perspective, they were a necessity if Warren was to make some headway with his lifelong inability to engage in a loving and sexual relationship. I had no illusions that Warren would not have enormous problems with anyone he tried to get involved with and I was equally sure that if I did not oversee everything that went on, as I was doing, nothing would ever happen—he would remain a social and sexual semi-basket case for the rest of his life. I had pushed the Warren antidotal, button and he had made some effort to comply.

"With all my problems there is only so much I can do. But if you think I can be helpful to her, I'm willing to try."

"Warren, I know you don't see it this way, but I think you can be helpful to each other. I think it's worth putting in the effort. The question you have to ask yourself is, What else do you have going for you?"

In their subsequent sexual encounters, both of them started to relax with each other and he became much more cognizant of her needs in his new teaching role. As they participated more and more in heavy kissing and bolder touching he began to ask her how she felt and what she liked. And his questioning helped to get them talking at last about their sexual responses. It seemed to be turning out that Nasi was a lot less inhibited than Warren had contended. To his surprise he found that he even enjoyed sucking on her nipples, despite her not having big breasts. And she too enjoyed it and got aroused.

Needless to say, there were still heavy-duty sexual problems that were not amenable to quick improvement and I had expected that Warren would always be bogged down with sexual hang-ups.

When it came down to it, Warren's sexual difficulties stemmed from a severe anxiety about his performance as well as a fear of his own aggressive impulses. While I was working on these long-term sexual problems with Warren in therapy, I had to monitor and address the day-to-day sexual difficulties they were experiencing. It was not easy, since Warren's need to distance himself from intimacy with women, and Nasi, in particular, kept him from a basic understanding of what most men took for granted in how to proceed sexually with a lady. For sure, poor Nasi could have used a less screwed-up mentor.

He came into a session, some weeks later, discouraged: "I give up. This is not going to work out, I'm not attracted to her. I can't teach her what to do, she's a virgin. I have my own sexual fears, how can I help her with hers?"

"Did you try to get her to do anything to you?"

"You mean like jerk me off?"

"Yeah, and other possibilities."

"No, I didn't have any interest in continuing at all."

"How did you leave it with her?"

"We agreed to meet on the following day, as previously decided."

"What are you going to tell her, then?"

"You're the director."

"Listen, bubashkite, you and Nasi are very inexperienced sexually; what's more, both of you have your problems with sex. It's going to take time to get used to being with each other and learning how to get pleasure from sexual intimacy. Not everyone starts out their sexual life enjoying sex. It often takes time and experience before you get to know how to proceed in the rhythms of the other person." The reader must be getting a laugh at my talking to Warren about taking time and trying to get a feeling for the rhythms of the other person in the act of sex. It was certainly a case of do what I say, and not what I do. At least I do *sound* sensitive.

"So what should I tell her?"

"Why don't you tell her that it was courageous for both of you to attempt sexual play at all?"

In the next session I explained, "Look, if you're groping around her and having trouble touching her vagina, and are disoriented and unsure of what you're about, you're not going to excite her."

"What should I be doing?"

"Well, it would be good if you could become a little familiar with what turns women on, as you discovered when you sucked on Nasi's nipples. Both of you enjoyed it. For instance, it would be beneficial if you could play with her clitoris in a way that turns her on."

Let me say that he wasn't too enraptured at my suggestion of clitoral play.

"I think we have a lot of work to do. If you play with it or lick it or kiss it, she is likely to get pretty hot."

"You're asking me to go down on her?"

"Yes, that's the idea."

"And what would that accomplish?"

"If she gets excited and you're still turned off to her, then at least we'll know that it's not her failure to be aroused that is the problem."

"Then, I'm the problem?"

"I think so. I think you'll find fault with any woman you're with and it's going to take you a long time to feel comfortable sexually with her. The truth is that very few women would even consider being with you given the seriousness of your emotional, psychological and sexual problems. What you should be worrying about is finding a woman—and I think Nasi can fit the bill—who could accept your limitations and still want to be with you."

"Can't I find someone who fits my sexual fantasies more?"

"If you haven't found a woman till now, what makes you think you're going to find one?"

"I'd like to try."

"Warren, you need a woman now, not ten years from now; my advice is give Nasi a chance, and start going down on her."

In spite of not having made that much sexual headway, two months later Warren and Nasi agreed to live together and a year later, they were married. But keep in mind that it had taken three years short of two decades of relentless work with Warren until he was able to take his chances with Nasi—and tie the knot in 1999… God bless him.

CHAPTER SIXTEEN:
THE GROUP AND WARREN'S WEDDING

Warren invited everyone from group therapy to his wedding at a Unitarian church in Manhattan. He and Nasi had argued for months about the religious ceremony: being a devout Catholic, Nasi was set on getting married in the church of her religion; Warren, being of the Jewish faith, made it clear that in no way could he and his parents consent to a Catholic wedding with a priest conducting the ceremony. In terms of the religious importance of the ceremony, Nasi was the one more fixed on having her way. She only agreed to compromise and have the wedding at a Unitarian church, with both a Rabbi and a priest officiating, because she knew that Warren was less than enthralled by the marriage and might use the problem of the ceremony as an excuse to back out. She had no qualms about marrying Warren, even after my being forthright about the extent of some of his mental problems. Though I probably withheld as much as I disclosed. Her willingness to marry him reduced my guilt at the fears and condemnation expressed by Ted and others.

Even with the compromise on the ceremony solidified, it took months of my pressuring Warren for him to accept the marriage. He maintained his resistance and came up with excuse after excuse to delay the proceedings. One of the more outlandish proposals, to this end, was that he be allowed to have an experience with a voluptuous lady of the kind he dreamed about, to test whether he still had the sexual problems that I maintained he would have with any woman he chose. I told him: "Go ahead, Yankila, you have my blessings. But it's going to be immensely difficult for you to find the woman of your fantasy, and I'm not getting her for you, even if I could."

He replied, "I'm not asking you to. I want to do it on my own."

"Warren, your insurance coverage for two-days-a-week therapy will not continue indefinitely; and considering the success rate you've had so far in finding a woman, eight to eighty, blind, crippled or crazy, I doubt whether you'll succeed in what you're proposing within any reasonable time limit. I think you should be grateful to Nasi that you have even those little nibs to suck on."

"Ha, ha. I got news for you, Obler, I'm not going ahead with this insane plan of yours to marry a woman who I don't desire."

"I got news for *you*. If you don't get married it's only a matter of time before you seriously regress. I mean that Warren, you need to get out of yourself and be with someone else in a real and not fantasized way. It may seem to you that you've become healthier, and in some ways you have, but don't delude yourself: if you continue to live in isolation, it won't take very much stress, what with your paranoia and masochistic fantasies, for you to regress again. I can't keep holding you up forever and you need the day-in, day-out support of someone who can be part of your life."

Despite his resistance, Warren crumbled before my insistence that he go ahead with the marriage. The day was set and he actually showed up at his own wedding. Amidst relatives and others, seven of the ten members currently in group therapy with him were at the service as well. The core of the group had remained the same over the years, but a few people had left group and were replaced by new people.

Only Edith, out of the core members, did not attend. That Edith failed to show up was of course predictable. Some of the group members brought their spouses along and I brought my wife and my adopted daughter. Warren's father and mother and sister, along with his sister's husband and two children, were the only members of his family that attended the wedding—his parents had lost contact with other relatives many years before. The rest of the wedding party consisted of two people from work; Nasi's sister and her American husband; and a couple of Warren's friends. It was not hard to see that Warren was unhappy at his own wedding. He was anxious, worried, skeptical, and preoccupied with misgivings about getting married. But the ceremony took place, and married he was.

Group met four days after the wedding while Warren and Nasi were on their honeymoon. Predictably, the discussion revolved around the wedding. Edith began the proceedings by asking the others how the wedding went.

Mark: We missed you, where were you?

George: I wondered why you weren't present.

Edith: I had my reasons for missing the wedding.

Maynard: ...and they were?

Edith: You want to know the truth?

Doris: I would.

Edith: I know how all you softies feel you need to support him because he's so vulnerable. Like you Mark, 'Oh, it's so wonderful, Warren, that you found a woman that you can get along with to marry.' If you people want to play along with Obler's great solution for Warren's immense personal problems, that's okay with me. But I'm not fooled one bit by this arranged marriage idea. Anyone who would hook up with a misfit like Warren must be really desperate.

Maynard: You sound angry, Edith.

Edith: I'm not angry. I'm just pissed at our therapist toying with our lives.

Alex: Sometimes it may be necessary for people to be helped along if they can't undertake a relationship by themselves, as Warren can't.

Antonia: I agree. I don't think Warren is capable of being in a relationship with a woman without Obler's help. He's a lot like my husband in this respect: if Marty and I hadn't forced him to confront his sexual dysfunction and to own up to it, we probably still wouldn't have any sex at all... not that it's very good, even now.

Mark: Edith, if Marty hadn't encouraged you to marry Lester, you might still be going to bars and complaining about the men you met.

Edith: I got involved with Lester because we had a romantic connection, not because of a green card, or Marty trying to keep me from cracking up.

Obler: That seems to be working for you, but not everybody gets married for love and romance. And many folks end up not getting married at all; I believe some of them might have lived happier lives if they had gotten help from a directive therapist.

Maynard: Edith, you're assuming that Warren's marriage to Nasi is a complete farce. I'm not sure that their marriage is so hopeless. Warren may not be head-over-heels in love with her, but I could see at the wedding that they seemed friendly with each other.

Heidi: At the reception, they were holding hands.

Edith: Were they holding hands because they cared for each other or for mutual security because they're both certified misfits who are terrified of other people?

Obler: Edith, what's your problem with people bonding together out of insecurity?

George: That's a good point.

Edith: Obler is so willing to subject his patients to making compromises in their relationships, as if passion and love were the last things to be concerned about in a marriage. I doubt that he made these kind of compromises in his last marriage. Did you?

Obler: Less so in my second marriage.

Heidi: So your current marriage is more of a love marriage?

Obler: You could say that.

Doris: Then how come you keep pushing us to make compromises with our romantic needs?

Obler: Let's be clear. It wasn't me who pushed you into being with your partners. You made those choices based on your realistic view of what you could get considering your sense of yourself. Market value.

Mark: Pragmatism trumps romanticism.

Edith was not the only one having strong questions about the morality and efficacy of my solution for Warren. I could tell from my therapy with Doris that her defiant stance towards my approach to him was really deriving from the jealous little girl in her that had wanted me to become the wished for father. She could see how much time and effort I devoted to Warren. Now, some years later, not only did I get him married but I hadn't helped her in a similar way... to find a marriage partner. As bad as it may sound to the reader, I would have had few qualms about finding someone who might have jelled with Doris— obviously, not in the arranged-marriage, dictatorial format that I employed with Warren—but simply suggesting that she consider getting together with someone I thought she would enjoy meeting. Doris, however, emphatically rejected my offer. I took it that if she were to submit to my intervention in this personal domain, she couldn't help thinking of it as having relinquished control over her own life, and might make her think of herself as a weak and submissive person. I desisted, on this basis, pushing her to let me fix her up, preferring to work with her on the psychological issues that were interfering with her capacity to find the 'right' person.

So as I see it, when Heidi asked me about whether my marriage was a love marriage, one of the things she was trying to find out is can people really change and is there some hope that we're not doomed to repeat the same mistakes, relationship after relationship. My feeling is that the question that Heidi presented was representative of what the group needed to be about, having to do with hopefulness that by hard work and cooperative effort people can make better choices in their life.

Obler: Let me say this about Warren's resistance to Nasi. You know, she wasn't the type of woman he fantasized about most of his life, a woman with big tits and a typical American good-looking woman. And that's one of the liabilities that he has to face: he's not going to get that kind of female.

Antonia: You think, ultimately, everyone here is severely limited, almost like Warren, and we have to make these kinds of great compromises, if we're going to get anybody?

Obler: Yup. But I would like to think that they are informed, healthy compromises. My wife may be beautiful but I have my share of dissatisfactions. I'm not going to go into them, however. Let me just mention that it is very hard to find a mate who lives up to your fantasies and, if you don't want to be alone, you have to make compromises—as couples soon find out when they start living together. And for that matter, it's not going to be easy for you to live up to someone else's fantasies, either. In choosing a partner, you pay a price one way or the other.

Edith: Marriage is more than making a business deal.

Obler: I believe that, but I also know from experience that many people, underneath, view themselves as commodities and think in terms of what their value is and what they can get. If you, Edith, valued yourself more, you might be less demanding of Lester. Nasi and Warren don't have that opportunity.

Maynard: It seems to me, I also didn't have that opportunity.

Obler:.... but that doesn't preempt you from working on a relationship and getting a lot more out of it, even though it can't fulfill your dreams.

George: So what we really need is a sharp shrink like you to negotiate the best deal for us?

Obler: Yes, I am very capable, but negotiation doesn't mean that I'm making the choice for you, as I did with Warren and Nasi. It simply means that I'm trying to get you to act out of real personal considerations, and not deprivations from childhood.

Doris: It would be nice if you could temper your need to control us. It seems as if when we look and act the way you want us to, everything is fine; but if we behave in ways that you perceive as inept and counterproductive, you have no hesitation about directing us as you see fit.

Obler: Look, I don't relish being the manipulative shrink. I feel that some of you force me into it by devaluing yourselves and retreating into passivity. I also contend that some of you have a sense that Warren has more hope to make a life for himself than he had before the marriage, and that has set you to thinking about your own choices.

George: I wouldn't disagree with your point, but I prefer to hold on to my romantic dreams... even if they have been derived from unresolved problems going back to my childhood.

Edith: Everybody needs the hope of romance...

Mark: I'm with you, but where does it end up? This discussion is, as I see it, basic to the patient-analyst exchange. It's not just about Nasi and Warren.

Antonia: I like what you said, Mark. For many of us, it feels as though our fate is in the balance... of a complex issue. Maybe that's what's causing so much tension in this discussion.

Doris: We don't know much about your love life, George. Am I right to assume that you are in love with your girlfriend?

George:... was in love, unfortunately

Maynard: So you are no longer in love with her?

George: She used me, and when that was no longer feasible she dumped me. That's where it ended up. Score one for Obler.

Doris: But would you still be with her if it were not for Obler's influence on you? I've always had difficulty separating out my feelings about my relationships and Obler's idea of them.

Edith: That's because you're unsure of yourself... and feel more secure thinking that Obler knows you better than yourself.

Mark:... as opposed to Edith who understands everything, but is not so happy with her husband of late.

For a shrink with my kind of interventionist approach there was no alternative. A preponderant number of patients in group came to therapy with me because they were frustrated by the decisions they had made and felt helpless and trapped to do anything about it. My strong personality and willingness to direct them at least offered a way out of their predicament and their reliance on past coping mechanisms, even if it comes at the expense of their individuality. I couldn't help thinking that this was a necessary corollary of my providing some kind of escape to their self-imprisonment in a disappointing and depleting relationship. I remember once giving this group an exercise to close their eyes, hold hands and imagine that they were watching a little bird sitting in a birdcage on a trapeze bar with the door of the cage open. While they were imagining this I asked them to get in touch with what came to mind. Maynard reported identifying with the bird, and, that even though he could leave the cage, something compelled him to stay fixed on the bar. Some of the other members nodded in agreement, indicating they could relate to what Maynard was saying. I interpreted this inability on their part to take flight to freedom as being connected to the safety and security need that they couldn't give up.

George emphatically identified with Maynard: "I completely sympathize with Maynard. I too felt in my relationship with Gabriella imprisoned in a cage that I couldn't fly from. No matter how much she took advantage of me, I felt stuck in my craving for security and continuation of what we had together. Obler, however, would say, "You were stuck in your destructive dependency collusion with her, the way you were stuck in your dependence on your abusive and destructive mother and father."

Antonia asked, "How did you get out of it?"

"I didn't, she dumped me," George replied.

George's relationship with his parents in childhood was so bad that he had to develop a dissociative defense mechanism in which he cut off one part of himself from another part of himself to maintain any sort of equilibrium in his family life. His need to get away from his parental home and the need to remain in it reproduces what I was saying about the dilemma of the bird in the cage.

In my view Gabriella, underneath her veneer of reasonability, could become as disparaging and cutting as his mom in certain situations—for instance, her repeated attacks on him not to whine and act like a baby. He was, in relation to his mother, acting out his alcoholic father's response to her, which fluctuated between passivity and detachment and unexpressed fury and rage.

I couldn't see how to get around George's ongoing dependence on Gabriella other than to intervene in the process. I saw it as my job to influence him not to try to hold on to Gabriella, since she was destructive of him in the mold of his mother; and try to steer him towards finding a more giving less self-serving mate. Left to his own, he would just repeat the pattern of attaching himself to a lover who would end up driving him to despair.

In one week, Warren returned from his honeymoon and I let him know that the group had been discussing his marriage at the meetings he missed; I suggested that he should be prepared to have this come up at the next group session. He wasn't too thrilled to hear that his marriage might come under scrutiny; his honeymoon hadn't gone well and his doubts about the marriage were consuming him, in true bipolar fashion.

He talked to me about his having felt trapped in his marriage during his honeymoon, and I let him go on for a while, before I mentioned that it might be useful for him to hold back a bit his resentment towards me for having forced him into the marriage, and to bring it up in group. I also told him that as for him being trapped in his marriage, he should not forget that he was much more damagingly trapped in his psyche all of his life; and, if anything, his marriage is a possible way out of his imprisonment in his own delusive thoughts. And, as always, I took every opportunity I could to inflict on Warren my unyielding view of his distortions of reality. Again, the repetitive factor comes into play. Repetition was certainly a major weapon in my arsenal when dealing with Warren. His defense system was such that his brain turned everything I said, that ran counter to his obsessive thinking, into Swiss cheese. His dependence on me, and his willingness to assimilate what little he did of my advice to him, was probably driven by his anxiety of having to be hospitalized again.

The group welcomed Warren back, congratulated him on his marriage, and told him what a nice time that they had had at his wedding. Mark had brought a bottle of wine and offered a toast to a happy, successful marriage for him and Nasi. Warren went along with it, but had a long face and looked as if he'd rather be someplace else.

"You don't look too cheerful, Warren. Did the trip go all right?" Antonia questioned.

"It sucked. I couldn't wait to get home."

Maynard asked him, "… that bad?"

"Yeah, real bad. I knew this marriage was a mistake. I shouldn't have listened to Obler."

Edith wasted no time in letting the group know that this was confirmation that whatever Obler recommended, one should do the opposite.

"So does that mean, Edith, that if I suggested you and Warren were totally incompatible, you should marry him?"

Antonia grew impatient with my attempt at levity, and asked to hear more from Warren about the honeymoon.

Before Warren could answer, I posed the question to the group of what they thought went wrong on his honeymoon. I was curious as to their construction of what might have taken place.

George said, "I had reservations all along about his marrying a woman who he wasn't sexually attracted to, no matter what the practical benefits of the marriage. Marriages don't work out if you don't have, at least at the beginning, a strong sexual desire and romantic feelings for your partner."

I should have let the group respond to this good point George had made, but somehow I didn't want to get from them the same old flack. I had no qualm indulging myself in this way. As I have mentioned before, I think it's all right, or even desirable, for the therapist to be human rather than a blank slate. But also the therapist has to be open to his patients' criticism and not automatically deflect it. But in this case, I chose to ward off what promised to be a prolonged criticism of me that had already been expressed in an earlier group meeting. To effect this, I jumped in with another question, pertinent to what George was saying: "How many of you when you committed yourself to the person you chose to be with, felt the romantic feelings George is talking about?"

Maynard volunteered, "I did the first time around, when I was twenty-one; but certainly not the second time and still don't."

Edith delivered herself of the opinion that Warren's and Maynard's experience was exactly why she was reluctant to make compromises in her idea of what a marriage should be. She insisted that she would never subscribe to "Obler's pragmatic approach towards marriage" and if that were the only alternative, she'd rather be single. Edith was not going to let the opportunity go to rub salt in my wound.

"Edith," Antonia said, "I disagree with your idea that everything has to be in place at the beginning of a marriage."

I mentioned to Antonia that I thought what she was trying to tell Edith was reflective of her own warm and hopeful personality, and was not unmindful of her own wish that she lived in a world in which her maternal feelings and her yearning to give to a man would count for something.

I added that, while there was nothing wrong with Edith wanting to hold out for passion and romance in a relationship, her inability to make compromises with her husband may be putting stress on the marriage. And I have told Edith, more than a few times, that this difficulty in compromising reflects her pessimism that her much-desired intimacy and sharing are not possible for her... as it wasn't for her parents. So why fight for it?

Doris said, "In a way, this is Marty's answer to all questions, and while it is a good answer, it opens the door to Marty's controlling personality as a therapist. It downplays passion and romance, and plays up practical considerations, which he excels in... and everything leads to childhood issues."

"I don't have a problem with what Marty is trying to do here," Mark reflected. "He's trying to get us to take a look at the expectations and self-deceptions we bring to our relationships... and how we reproduce our stuff from childhood, one way or the other. And I seem to be someone who needs to be reminded of it all the time."

"Reminded or hit over the head?" Edith added

Mark rejoined, "I suppose a knock in the head wouldn't be a bad thing for me... and you too are hardheaded, Edith."

"Maybe I am, Edith answered, "but I'm not going to pay someone to do it."

I rejoined, "That's true to form, Edith."

"So is your need to outdo me," Edith said.

I said, "If you say so."

But the most refreshing and uncharacteristic remark belonged to Warren when he said to me, "Be real, Obler," spoofing the way I talk to him. I cracked up along with the others.

Edith in her most disdainful manner said, "I'll bet he starts charging *extra* for his dating service."

Doris looked right at me and earnestly confided, "You know, Marty, you're not a *shadchan*."

"I think my days as a *shadchan* are over."

Well, maybe I'll retract that last remark. As a therapist I'm increasingly confronted with the reality that my patients are frustrated, unhappy, and dissatisfied with their close interpersonal relationships. (Of course this common thread was one reason why I selected these particular people to be in this group.) In my attempt at treating these patients, I found that their resistance to working on their deeper psychological issues remained intractable unless they first made headway in their personal relations, and usually secondarily, in the practical concerns of their life. Most psychotherapies, such as the Freudian derived schools, subscribe to the opposite approach: if you alleviate the neurosis and pathology, the interpersonal and practical stuff will invariably get better. I take the reverse position.

So, as I see it, my theoretical approach, based on pragmatic considerations, leads to my becoming a nuts and bolts counselor and fixer-upper, in my patients' dating and love life... and jobs, insurance (to finance their therapy), and plumbing if necessary. But one of the reasons I can be confident in stressing the ultra-practical approach is that I push very hard on the pure psychological stuff. For me the two go hand in hand. And I don't pussyfoot about what my patients have to confront psychologically, for instance, my conversations with Warren, Mark, etc. I have many beginning patients with me tell me that I have done in a couple of sessions more than their other therapists have done over a long time. I certainly don't assume that the patient is here to have me hold his or her hand and be a cheerleader for them. I often push them as far as I think they can go right from the start. Of course I have to determine how far is too far, and avoid that, until they are ready. But you would be surprised how much patients will uncover about themselves if you approach them with an assumption that they are here to get down to business... and if that means that patients do a lot of crying, even in a first session, so be it. Patients often respond in a way that corresponds to the assumption I bring to the therapy. Again, I have to know what I'm doing. It's not about guesswork. And I recognize that, even in my own personal analysis, I could not deal with my childhood issues effectively until I started examining the unhappiness of my first marriage and the complications of my second marriage. Dr. Henderson had to help me come to grips with my choice of mates and my problems of communication and power struggles and escapism. I wasn't able to change my escapist solutions until my second marriage was reasonably satisfying. That is a personal example from my life of the dividend of putting the practical ahead of the psychological—though of course it doesn't always work out that way... and the Freudians would not see things as I do (though I am a very Freudian therapist, since I think the root of most people's problems are related to the family nexus).

So I recognize that a lot of therapists would have difficulty in my taking such a practical approach with my patients. But I feel I have no alternative. If I did not fix up Warren to get married, my whole therapy with him would have been keeping him out of a mental hospital. With Antonia, I had to help her find a way to overcome her fears of marriage before we could address her sexual abuse in childhood. And I couldn't do this until she, with my help, got married and had a child.

In short, it is the practical consideration of the unsatisfying relationships—or lack of any relationships—that patients have engineered for themselves that brings them into therapy. And once here, until these issues are ameliorated, there is not much incentive on their part to do the necessary introspection... which is often initially upsetting and depressing and threatening. They want to feel better, not worse—that is, they want to relieve their pain, not increase it. Psychoanalysis, as a discipline, is increasingly fading as a treatment technique in favor of short-term therapies because of the pragmatic demands. I don't really think that I would be doing as well as a therapist, if I did not alter my formal training and address the immediate concerns of my patients.

BOOK III

CHAPTER SEVENTEEN:
LOSING SIGHT OF BOUNDARIES

By the time I turned fifty, I started to relinquish some of the rebellious adolescent in me. Two years later Margaret and I had adopted our second child, Leah—who was born in the Dominican Republic—four years after our adoption of Danny. Once again I had a family with two children. I began to assert some control over my old pattern of getting involved with other women. In a huge turnabout I stopped having affairs and from age 52 on (for over two decades) I have not bedded down another woman other than my wife. And even as a father, my role began to change. I didn't want to make the same mistakes I had made with my two kids from my first marriage: in those days, I was hardly home; was not a particularly good role model for them, having been so caught up in my life outside of the family... and left the child-rearing almost entirely to Dalite; and was an inconsistent figure in their life—someone who entertained them roundly when I was there for them but such times were punctuated by long periods of unavailability.

With my adopted children, I still was not home that much, what with two jobs and socializing, but I tried to be more fully present when I was with them. I had a heightened awareness of the potential of the potential for problems with them, being adopted children and children of color. Moreover, I had a very strong—too strong—identification with them, fearing that they would be outsiders and alienated from the society at large, much as I had been as a little boy. And, now, becoming more of a family man, I didn't want to incur the risk of my philandering undermining my home life; and the idea began to take hold in me that Margaret could well be my partner for the rest of my life. That was really a formidable conception on my part.

I like to believe that in middle age I started to make some positive changes in my way of looking at things that reflected some long overdue maturation and strength on my part, but I would also have to admit that I was not readily giving up some of my major faults, such as my grandiosity and my need to feel superior; my belief that, no matter what my excesses, I could control and manipulate people and situations to get the desired result; and my belief that I could ignore the criticism of my wife and close friends with impunity. It is a not an inconsequential list.

What it comes down to is that Marty Obler is still Marty Obler, despite positive changes. The boy in me was such that I still delighted in being the center of attention and loved feeling that I had the power to shock and disturb people by my behavior. A good example of this need to upset people for my own purposes was my enjoyment in telling dirty jokes to make a point in my psychology courses, even though some of the students found it offensive. In one class where I was discussing treatment of phobias, I told the joke in which a therapist in order to help a patient overcome fear of exposure unzips his own fly and says, 'This is a phallus.' The patient responds by saying, 'Oh, it's like a prick, only smaller.' And if some students were offended by such humor, I wrote it off as their problem—which was pretty arrogant of me.

And even in the early years of my relationship with Margaret, who had a short modern dance career until injuries forced her to give it up, I took to name-dropping dancers and choreographers all over the place... in an obvious attempt to promote myself as an intellectual, ignoring Margaret's advice to curtail this distasteful trait.

I suppose I was conflicted in that I liked the idea of having some of the veneer of a Greenwich Village intellectual shrink. Yet I was very resistant to Margaret's justifiable attempts to get me to spruce up my bargain basement wardrobe, not flaunt my

Brooklyn argot, and not slurp my soup. Ted laughed at me when I told him about Margaret's pleading with me to dress better and spend a little money at a good restaurant, and try to eat with something like good manners... commenting that it was like trying to tame an orangutan.

I couldn't help myself from taking every opportunity to impress others with my success, my smarts, my accomplished acquaintances, my know-how... and on and on. But underneath I had strong feelings that I was an inveterate buffoon and pretender; or just the little child that suspected that his family was inferior and nothing he could do or dream of would change the ignominy that would follow him throughout his life. The pain of being forever that little boy did drive me to change and take refuge in building my own family as well as toning down some of the provocative behavior. But I was reluctant to invest in doing the hard work that could have helped resolve some of the basic conflicts in my childhood issues; I also withstood the pressure to make headway in this area by declining to select a new therapist after Dr. Henderson's death.

I could work long days at two jobs, the college and my private practice, but working on myself was not my forte. Not a pretty admission for a psychotherapist, who bludgeoned his patients to do what he resisted doing. Obviously forces were at work, since childhood, that were deeply imbedded in my psyche and caused conflicts in me that were hard to overcome. Still, by any barometer, I was much less averse to the thought of change than in my earlier days.

So in a roundabout way this is all prefatory to the change, during middle age, of outlook, whereby I would be more receptive to Margaret's needs with the family in mind. In an unlikely scenario for me, I eventually succumbed to Margaret's orchestration of our moving to the Long Island suburbs.

Like a moderate percentage of New York City mothers, Margaret, when the children were nearing school age, began to talk about moving to the suburbs. I put up a good fight against it, feeling it was a betrayal of my origins. But I was also under the sway of Margaret the great mother and Margaret the one who thought about the children every second of her life. It is hard for the male in such a situation to not buckle to the sphere of influence of the dominant mother. The day came when I folded my resistance and delaying tactics, accepting my fate. The family moved to Sag Harbor, near the Eastern tip of Long Island, in 1992, when Leah was two-and-a-half-years old.

I certainly did not feel myself to be a candidate for middleclass Long Island. While growing up, I was not like the working class Jews in (East New York, East Flatbush, Canarsie, and Brownsville) whose ideal of upward mobility was to move to Long Island, a distance away from the ghettos of Brooklyn. As a teenager, my notion of getting away from my immediate neighborhood was to cross the Brooklyn Bridge into Manhattan. And after I moved into Manhattan with my first family, I stayed in that borough for the next thirty-four years of my life. Over that time the concept of the 'burbs' was abhorrent to me. I saw myself as a New Yorker who dreaded the thought of living a *Man in the Grey Flannel Suit* type of existence. I remember reading John Cheever's short story in *The New Yorker*, "The Swimmer," and later seeing the movie version with Burt Lancaster, and vowing to myself that this would never happen to me—winding up an alienated, forgotten man in a superficial, suffocatingly-homogenous, Westchester community. I identified myself with the neighborhoods I had settled in, first the Upper West Side and later Greenwich Village, a Manhattanite, a hip New Yorker giving and attending parties, visiting the museums, going to foreign films, and bookstores; the funny thing is that my more sophisticated friends knew damn well that I wasn't much of an intellectual or a very convincing dilettante... Ted particularly would take me to account in this respect. He could not resist delivering himself of his barbs at my pretenses and grandiosity; my mental sharpness mixed together with my boorishness and ignorance of highbrow culture. I should mention that Ted took evident pleasure in laughing at himself as well, for his pathetic and hopeless expectations and aspirations, his psychological burdens and incongruities, and his social insecurities, and so forth. His four brothers and he took pleasure in debunking themselves and each other. So that was part of their family life. I bring this up about Ted, here, so the reader may keep in perspective, as the book progresses, that he is not less harsh on himself than he is on me... oh, well, maybe a few degrees less harsh, as I seem to be a more deserving candidate for being the butt of his humor than other of his friends, considering the excesses of my personality.

It was very stressful for me to leave New York City after having spent over fifty years there. The city was a place of continual excitement, things to do, friends to hang out with, and women to ogle and flirt with... and for a guy that didn't like to be home too much, it was the perfect place. Keep in mind Lenny Bruce's routine about not storming out of the house, over an argument with the wife, if you live in the country or suburbs, because there is nothing to do. And I should mention that I was running from myself as well.

But in the 'burbs' I did not fail to assert some of my old social patterns that were not the most admirable; for instance, I started getting enmeshed in my neighbors' lives, utilizing my skills as a therapist to make my friends dependent on me.

The first house I lived in with my family was a forty-year-old ranch-style house that we rented. It was a flat, one-story green wooden house with faded carpets and a small kitchen, three bedrooms and a living room. The neighborhood is called Azurest, and it is on the eastern tip of Sag Harbor, slightly out of the main section of town en route to East Hampton. We rented the house from a racially-mixed couple whom Margaret knew from the dance world. We visited them at the beginning of the summer to check out the Sag Harbor area for a house. They posed the idea that we rent their house for the summer, with the possibility of continuing on in the fall if we liked it. We stayed there a few days and felt so comfortable in the community that we took them up on their offer and rented their property for the summer and the beginning of the school year.

Azurest is a bustling, vibrant community during the summer, composed mainly of urban black middleclass families. For almost all the residents, their home here is a vacation home. Since we too were there during the summer, we really didn't pay much attention to what community life would be like after Labor Day. Sure enough the place emptied out after Labor Day and on Danny's first day of school at Sag Harbor Elementary School, he asked me while I was driving him to school, "Where is everybody?" I didn't have much of an answer for him, but it certainly set me thinking about what life was going to be like the first winter in Long Island.

Margaret was the one who had it roughest during this period, since I was more of a weekender, living in the city and conducting my practice, while she was alone with the kids until I returned home on Friday. In a way, it fed my ego to have a place in the city and in the suburbs: I was the prosperous shrink. But, in a more telling way, it was upsetting to me to have to give up my weekend social life with friends in the city, a life that I had built up over many years. The Sag Harbor area had only a few thousand full time residents and I didn't know anybody, anyway. But Margaret jumped right into the social life of the area, made a lot of new friends connected to Danny's public school and Leah's nursery school. She and the kids were thriving, and I certainly didn't have the heart to force a change, though it didn't stop me from complaining. I would make sure I took every opportunity to belabor what I was sacrificing in the move, figuring when future disagreements occurred I would be a leg up. I was not above such covert tactics.

By December we bought a home in North Haven, an adjacent community, which had more year-round residents. I became a weekend soccer dad and spent a lot of my free time shuttling the kids here and there. I was equally at ease in the all-white village of North Haven as I had been in Azurest.

Still, I didn't take to suburban life, like a duck to water. I missed the crowded streets of NYC and hanging out with my old buddies. However, I would have to admit that I was somehow reassured living in North Haven, where I was a homeowner, living a suburban life with a barbecue in the backyard, transporting my kids around, mowing the lawn, shopping at the mall, even occasionally helping Margaret with the garden. I could fit in to this suburban wealthy area.

To counter my lack of social interaction in the suburbs, I started to bring together neighborhood people who could fill the empty space, and satisfy my need to be a central figure in some way or another. As usual, I managed to inject myself into the forefront of the life that was going on around me.

Not only did I start developing friends, but I became an informal, resident shrink. The latter endeavor served two purposes: it made people dependent on me and, more crucially, it supplied a drama and excitement to what otherwise would have been a mundane, boring, trivial existence in Long Island. It was not so different from my jazzing up my therapy sessions with my patients, by creating intensity and drama and humor... so I wouldn't be bored out of my skull. I was bent on doing everything I could to call attention to myself... or blow up (in the photographic sense) my persona to anyone and everyone. Perhaps the most questionable conduct I engaged in, related to my social interaction, had to do with my blurring the boundaries between my professional and personal life.

I set up with a couple of my best friends in Sag Harbor a time when I would meet with them on a one-to-one basis at the local coffee house, Java Nation, and eventually I turned my get-togethers with these individuals into a group hang-out at the coffee house several times a week. And, naturally, I was the driving force behind the get-togethers—the comic relief, the enthusiastic raconteur, the one who pushed interesting ideas into controversy, and the resident psychologist. It was my form of holding court and being in control. Or you could say I had the largest investment in making others think I was the big cog.

And by having a group to feed off, and individuals who relied on me, it provided some assurance that if things turned bad at home or I had a scary bout of loneliness, I had something to fall back on.

With my friend Branch, I set up an exchange of services where he would supply his skills as a handyman to complete all kinds of odd jobs in my house. My thinking was that I would save money on repairs; in return, I would provide my services as a counselor, guiding him in his problems with his live-in girlfriend.

For the first few months this arrangement worked superbly for both of us. Considering my proclivity to be a cheap bastard, I saved some money and he got some benefit from the counseling. Moreover, it had for me additional perks, in that it lessened my boredom and built me up in the eyes of my neighbors. It only became a problem when the relationship with his girlfriend started falling apart and I had to become more deeply involved as a psychologist in their conflict.

To make matters worse, after I helped him through this trying period, I worked with him on finding a new girlfriend... and when trouble started between them, I began counseling her too. While I was enjoying the self-importance I felt in this role and the drama it supplied, I had enough sense as a professional to ask myself: What the fuck was I doing?

The involvement only got worse when she asked me if I could see her aging parents because I had been so helpful with Branch. I won't go into how the whole thing played out but suffice it to say, it was a mess... and I continue dealing with the repercussions some fifteen years later—I still get phone calls from him and his second girlfriend trying, once again, to get me involved in their lives. For that matter, I occasionally run into his original girlfriend, who attempts to engage me in discussion about her life.

Around this time I was spending an afternoon with my friend Devon when I noticed that he recognized a disheveled-looking man, with a noticeable limp, who was walking towards us. Devon knew that this was a fairly well-known entertainer, residing in Sag Harbor. My friend was attracted to people in the public eye, because he secretly wished he too could have been famous. In his case, I always thought that he was at heart a secret Walter-Mitty type.

The man in question had been talking to himself as he walked along. As he neared us, he inappropriately started talking to us about some very personal things in his life (he seemed to be addressing us, but you couldn't really tell). One of the things he said was that he had made a great mistake by going along with his wife and moving from Sag Harbor to another nearby town. He went on, mentioning further, that his professional career was going downhill—as was his health.

I impulsively went into my shrink mode and questioned him as to some of the specifics of what he was talking about. He went into some detail, but then caught himself up, wondering who was this person who seemed to so knowingly be questioning him.

"Who are you? Do you live around here?"

I said, "I'm Martin Obler."

Devon, however, couldn't resist and added, "He's a shrink, and he lives in North Haven."

When he heard this, he eagerly asked, "Can you help me?

I answered him, "No, I unfortunately can't. I'm not taking on any new patients at this time."

I was wary of becoming involved with him, because I only recently had gotten disentangled from Branch and his latest girlfriend and thought it would be best to cool it with the local residents.

He shrugged his shoulders, and said, "Never mind, and walked off, continuing to talk to himself.

I hollered after him, "Have a good day."

Devon wasted no time in letting me know how callous I had been: "How could you turn him away like that? You're supposed to be such a humanitarian."

Devon may have felt what he was saying, but he was also taken with the idea that his good friend could have been treating this moderately-renown public figure. And of course, as a layman, he felt that shrinks should treat anyone in extremis.

"It's bad enough that I'm treating Branch and you for nothing, leave this guy out of it."

A few weeks later the man's spouse called me, begging me to see him. Although my best shrink judgment told me that he was too far gone to be treatable as a patient, I took him on because it gratified my ego to do so. While the treatment was initially fairly effective, in time his condition was so severely regressed that he stopped coming to see me. I found it quite a relief when he ended therapy with me, because he was unable at this point to benefit from it. Within a relatively short time, his ongoing wish to end his days took over.

Yet a third example of my impropriety in crossing boundaries had to do with my friend Devon. Devon was a six-foot, blue-eyed, easygoing fellow whose parents originally settled in Montauk, Long Island. Devon had a troubled marriage to a short woman, of striking good looks, whose heritage was Ecuadorean on her father's side and Spanish on her mother's. Devon was a fairly successful home landscaper in and around Sag Harbor. We had developed a close friendship over years, and this led to a transgression on my part: I got involved in doing informal therapy with him—which I shouldn't have done. It was antithetical to my professional responsibility in that I crossed boundaries between my therapeutic role and personal life. This encompassed not only my treating him informally, but my getting involved in his family affairs, to the extent of giving him advice as to how to conduct himself in his embattled relationship with his wife. Add to this, I did a somewhat formal diagnosis of her based only on Devon's account of interactions between them. To say the least I should have known better.

Even in writing this, now, I can't avoid flinching at the intrusiveness of my behavior. It is hard to escape from the conclusion that in doing what I did with Devon, I was trying to redo unresolved issues I had with my father Saul, since Devon reminded me of him. As I saw it, both of them had woeful marriages, about which they constantly complained; and irritated the hell out of me by their nebbish behavior and their inability to alter the circumstances they tirelessly objected to, leaving them forever dependent on their spouse. No matter how I look at it, I can't help but acknowledge that my overreaction to Devon's self-imprisonment in a bad marriage had to do with my own powerlessness in childhood.

When I confided in Ted what was going on in my friendship with Devon, he was not bashful about giving his opinion of the mess I had brewed.

"Marty, what's with you? You can't stop talking about this idiotic marriage Devon is in with his wife."

"What do you want me to do, Ted? he is a friend of mine and he needs help… he's in a disastrous situation. I have many friends, of both sexes, in a similar predicament and I can't just turn my back on them."

"You're missing my point."

"What's your point?"

"My point is that you're totally consumed with what's going on in his life. What is going on that you are compelled to talk about him all the time? If you spent one-tenth the time on your own marriage, you'd be blissfully happy."

"I'm too practical to even think about bliss."

"Then think about me. I'm bored shitless hearing about Devon all the time. Seriously, can't you stop yourself from obsessing about him?"

"I don't seem to be able to. It's a feeling I've had all my life. With some people I know, I can see exactly how their symbiotic pathologies and collusions within their marriage are going to play out, and it is as if I'm writing the script."

"I think you're getting off on your power over him and at the same time you're indulging in what amounts to voyeuristic fascination with his relationship to his wife."

"To be honest, it's not that glorious. I think I'm a *yenta* like the women in the streets in Brownsville."

"That sounds pretty pathetic."

"Pathetic or not, I get pleasure being privy to information that somebody shares with me that nobody else has heard. It gives me a sense of importance along with a sense of power by impressing other people with the confidences that people impart to me."

"Do you have a life of your own or are you just feeding off those who think you're the great Martin Obler?"

"Well, to tell the truth, the more my life is enmeshed in my friends' life, and this one knows this about that one, and that one knows this about this one, and I know everything about everyone, the more I feel I exist."

"Have you ever explored where this bottomless deprivation comes from?"

"My first analyst helped me to see that in early childhood I was so full of fears of isolation and so embarrassed by my family that I welcomed anything that makes me feel I'm part of a group. Anything was better than being excluded and living in a void."

"Obviously your childhood was extremely painful and lonely. But remember you're not just his friend, you're an experienced analyst. And it's not Devon's job to provide vicarious pleasure for you by the way he mishandles his life."

"As an analyst, for the most part, I do have control of crossing boundaries with my patients; it's in my personal life where I lose it. Neurotic or not, I get great pleasure out of indulging myself in the way I do with Devon and it fascinates me to be part of his life in such an intimate fashion."

"So there are no worrisome consequences to your actions?"

"Did I say that?"

"Then why not desist in your interference?"

"I am not contesting the correctness of what you're telling me. But I have to say, I do feel more alive being enmeshed in the soap opera of the marriage of some of my friends. I've always been this way. Can't you remember even with you, years ago, when you were having problems with your wife and she consulted me on what she should do?... and I got all caught up in your lives. I loved it; I felt that you both needed me."

"I question the comparison with Devon."

"I'm not trying to compare you to Devon, I'm trying to make the point that to become involved in my friends' life, and to be needed by them, is something I long for, partially because it helps me to sidestep my own fears of isolation and dissolution.

"But there is a major difference between your role in my situation and in Devon's. In my situation you were feeling good that Loni and I were talking to you about our marital stuff, and that makes most people feel good... being included in that way and relied on. But with Devon, you're not simply presenting back to him his options and being a good listener; you've taken it further."

"I admit I like gossip... I'm not above being titillated by hearing from Devon the latest story about his embattled marriage."

"Even that wouldn't be so bad if you maintained neutrality."

"That's exactly what it's hard for me to do."

"You're in this situation now, Marty, because you ignored the advice your psychoanalytic supervisor and I had given you for years about your tendency to become over-involved with your patients and friends, in disregard of basic protocol."

"Here it comes, I can see it coming. More criticism of how immature I am."

"What did you expect?"

However, in recalling some of these examples of my working with individuals in the community, it brings to mind my involvement in a case where I did not inappropriately cross boundaries and acted as a consummate professional—but through circumstances beyond my control, the patient came to a tragic end. Sometimes a therapist can do everything right and circumstances overtake his efforts.

Gregory, a medical professional, had been arrested by the police for sexual misconduct in public. At his court hearing, the judge agreed to not prosecute, providing that he enter private psychotherapy for a period of not less than one year, at which point—if there was no further misconduct— the case would be dismissed. His lawyer, whom I had worked with previously, asked me to take on the case. And I did so. At the end of the year, the original charge was reduced to a misdemeanor, while Gregory voluntarily decided to continue on in therapy, which lasted for a year and a half more.

After this period, Gregory stopped treatment, telling me that he felt cured of the behavior that led him to have to enter therapy. I went along with his decision to stop, with the proviso that he contact me immediately if there was any problem with regression.

Over the next five years I would periodically run into him around town, and he would always give me the impression that things were going capitally. I had to admit that I was relieved because I had become a bit hesitant about whether I had done the right thing in allowing him to stop treatment when he did. I wasn't entirely sure that if I were working with him as a regular patient of mine in my NYC practice, I might not have gone along with his discontinuing as easily. I very likely would have explored his decision in greater depth.

One day I received an emergency call from him, in my NYC practice, telling me that he was in deep trouble and needed to consult with me immediately. At our session he informed me that after he left therapy, he took a new job locally in the prison system in an adjacent community. He had become part of a scandal in which it was claimed that he was trading drugs for sexual favors with inmate prostitutes. The scandal was about to break open because the newspapers and media had gotten wind of the internal investigation that was taking place in the prison.

He was fearful that once the story broke nobody would believe his side of what happened. He maintained that he had been manipulated by a few female inmates into sexual play and that they tried to coerce him to give them drugs; but he never went along with it. He was panicky that once the scandal came into the open, his career would be finished and his family would be devastated by the publicity.

I confronted him with his breaking our agreement to contact me if he got into trouble. All he could say was, "I screwed up."

I went into high gear... had him contact his lawyer and that we formally resume therapy. I suggested that he work closely with his lawyer and me and not overreact to the public outcry. But it was too late. He did not take my advice and succumbed to panic when the story broke. On the evening before he committed suicide, his wife called me, in great distress at my New York City office, pleading with me to see him immediately in Sag Harbor. I agreed to see him the next day, but by the time I returned he had killed himself. And when his wife called me to tell me of his suicide, she let me know that the night before he told her that he could not face the world anymore.

I think he would still be alive if the media hadn't hounded him and made him a sensational news story.

While I had been successful in the duration I had worked with him, circumstances overtook what I could do, in large part because he hadn't told me the truth of what had happened to him. Even though I didn't cross boundaries with Gregory, as I had with Devon and Branch, I felt inhibited and constrained in my work with him. It makes me wonder about my own personal difficulties with boundaries; I seem to be drawn into tearing the boundaries down but end up feeling the need to extricate myself from the involvement; it makes me wonder, especially professionally, what drew me so strongly into becoming enmeshed in other people's life, as if I didn't have a life of my own. Though I do.

CHAPTER EIGHTEEN:
DEBBIE, ET AL.

The phone rang. I was having dinner with my family at home, and drinking my usual one glass of red wine, which made me a trifle tipsy. I picked up the mobile phone on the nearby kitchen counter and I heard a voice that came from the past. I had the feeling that this wasn't really happening... it must be a dream.

"Hi Marty, it's me, your sister Debbie. What are you doing?"

"Having dinner, Debbie."

"What are you eating, Marty?"

I looked over at Margaret and asked, "What are we having for dinner? It's my sister Debbie. She wants to know."

"I could see by the puzzled expression on Margaret's face that she was flabbergasted by the incongruity of my sister's mundane question after not having been in touch with me for years. My ten-year-old daughter Leah asked, "Who is Debbie?"

"Debbie is my sister."

I registered what I saw on the dinner table and told Debbie that we were eating meatloaf with mashed potatoes and string beans. I asked her what she was having for dinner. She didn't answer the question but asked me, "Why don't you ever come to visit? You know where I live, it's the same place."

Her whole approach and tone was as if we had been speaking weekly for the last twenty years and I had neglected to return her most recent call.

"Debbie, I'm wondering what prompted you to call me this evening, anything special?"

"Yeah, I just spoke to Phyllis in Phoenix and wished her a happy Rosh Hashana. And she asked whether I spoke to you."

"What did you tell her?"

"Oh, you know Marty, he's always so busy."

"Debbie, where's Alice?" [Alice is her daughter]

"Oh, she got married, she lives in Florida now."

"Do you see her, Debbie?"

"Not really, she's been all involved with that husband of hers and doesn't have time for her mother."

"Why didn't you invite me to the wedding?"

"What wedding?"

"I assume she must have had a wedding."

"I don't know. If she did, she never mentioned it or invited me."

"Debbie, instead of my visiting you, Why don't you get out of that little apartment of yours in Brownsville and put on some of those silk stocking of yours... remember Betty Grable and the war ads?..."

"You remember those stockings?"

"Yeah, I used to love watching you putting them on—but what about it? You could come up to Sag Harbor... just take the subway to Penn Station, get on the Long Island Railroad and make a day of it."

"Oh, I don't do that anymore."

"When was the last time you left your house and went out of town?"

"I'm an old woman now; I haven't done that for a long time. Are you going to visit me with Delmore and Dina? They're so cute."

"Delmore is forty-two years old! He weighs 250 pounds, he's six-feet-two. Dina is thirty-nine years old. I'm a grandfather, she's got two kids, a boy and a girl. They're your niece and nephew. Clean out your cobwebs, Debbie."

Margaret shook her hand at me, signaling me not to make fun of Debbie and to tone down my voice. It was true, I was speaking in an aggressive manner to my sister, as was typical of me.

"How is Phyllis doing, Debbie?"

"Don't you speak to her?"

"Rarely. As a matter of fact, my last contact with her was about eight years ago... oh, actually I did talk to her more recently, now that I think of it. She called me when she came in for a wedding of a friend of hers in Plainview."

"I remember that. That was the last time she visited me. You didn't see her then?"

"Nope, couldn't make it. But we had a nice conversation. You know what, Debbie, if you won't visit me, I'm gonna visit you. And I have a nice surprise for you, I'm going to bring my two adopted teenage children with me."

"Oh, my God! Phyllis said you have a boy and a girl."

"Danny and Leah." ("Hey, Margaret, I just mentioned to Debbie that we're going to visit her in Brooklyn and bring the kids with us. You remember where she lives in Brownsville? – not far from where your parents lived.")

Margaret—not amused by my remark—stood up, went over to the TV in the living room and turned it on.

"Would you do that? I'd love it, I hardly get visitors anymore."

"I wonder why?" However, I caught myself in my knee-jerk, mocking remark... and a sadness came over me. I thought about my mother and my sister, sitting together in that old apartment, year after year until my mother went to the old-age home; I often wondered whether Debbie ever left the apartment anymore, for anything other than shopping for her basic necessities. I asked her whether she still went to the hospital to get her medicine.

"Yeah, I go to see that nice black lady."

"I'm glad to hear that. You need to get out of the apartment."

"I try to, I go to the store, sometimes I bring back Chinese food."

"Good for you... Listen, Debbie I got to go now. Thanks for calling. And I'll try to get down to see you." I doubted, however, that that would happen. Shamefully, I still needed to avoid my sisters.

In the days that followed, the telephone conversation I had with my sister made its way back into my consciousness, overriding my predictable reaction, which was to forget about the whole thing and think of it as a joke. The telephone conversation kept coming back to me, and pushing me to reflect on it. Somehow I wasn't able to file the conversation away in some meaningless draw in my mind the way I usually did when it came to thoughts about my family. I would always tell friends and people close to me that I had no regrets and no guilt at completely separating myself from my two sisters. But after such a long time of dismissing them, as if they really had nothing to do with me, it seemed a pretty lame way of behaving. Ted, for one, berated me when I would explain to him how little my family meant to me and that it didn't bother me at all that I had almost no contact with them. He would take me to task, saying something along the lines that he thought I was running away from myself, more than them, and that while they weren't Manhattan intellectuals, they were still family.

Ted was, as usual, right. Only I didn't choose to delve into his criticism of me. But for some reason, now, the telephone call with Debbie upset me and got me thinking about my need to belittle my sister. As a therapist, I would invariably ask my patient to examine such an upsetting phone call—as if it had the significance of a dream that should be looked at. So applying this process to my own experience, I asked myself what hadn't I been looking at and hadn't been looking at for a long, long time in what transpired between my sisters and me.

I tried to comb through my conversation with Debbie for material that linked to the deeper levels of my psyche and what came up was an association to my sister Rachel at the time they dragged her off to the institution. I was very confused at the way she left, and, then, later at her scratching my face when my father brought me to visit her. It was very hard for me to process the abrupt shift in having a caring older sister and then to have her carted off, have her furiously attack me, and finally have her disappear entirely from my life. I was very much the helpless child; there was nothing to do; I couldn't get back the connection with her no matter what I did. It's hard to say how much this experience has impacted on me. Here I had been very attached to this important person in my life; then she was suddenly uprooted, entirely changed, and, finally, not to be heard of again—and, as far as the family was concerned, it was as though she had never existed or had gone up in smoke. So for me it took on the form of a mystery in which I could never be sure what had happened to her.

There were shades of that kind of mystery in my attachment to Debbie. After the departure of Rachel, I depended on her as the central sibling caretaker of me. She was a pretty hard-boiled bird, but she provided a motherly touch when my mother was at work or shopping. As a three or four-year-old, I liked Debbie; however, the older I got the more I came to realize that Debbie was not only out of it and dippy, but I could see that she didn't care about anybody else. And my mother, too, as she aged lost her ability to go outside of herself and think about me. She became increasingly anxious and fearful—finally sinking into paranoia and delusions in her response to the world around her. By the time I was sixteen, the two of them had become locked-in together in their fear of the world and their persecution complex. After my father's death, when Debbie was thirty-two, they retreated into an apartment in East Flatbush where Debbie still lives, much as she lived forty years ago. I couldn't count on her as I had when I was a little whelp; she seemed to have mental lapses that I couldn't quite comprehend.

I remember once when Debbie and I went to the corner grocery store where my family had a line of credit, which had been used up weeks before. The owner of the grocery was trying to explain to her that he couldn't give her any more credit. It was hard for her to extend her thinking to take this in because she had trouble getting beyond the immediate thought that she wanted and needed food. More and more as I grew up,

I began to discern that I was different than she was; I could grasp things about the reality around me that she couldn't.

It was on my return to the States from Israel, when Dalite and I had temporarily moved in with my family, that my exasperation at Debbie's narcissism, selective reasoning, and sometimes inane responses was compounded to the point, for me, where I would become increasingly irritated with her. So when she asked, "What are you doing?" at the outset of our telephone conversation, I relapsed into my dismissive, impatient and mocking manner of dealing with her. Reflecting on this, I had to admit that I was angry at her... for her mental decline, for her selfishness, for her lack of interest in me, for her not continuing to be the caring person she had once been when I was a baby, and then, later on, for her succumbing to the family disease of isolation, ineptness, pathology, etc. After our mother's decline, Debbie had never come to visit me, it was always the other way round; she had very little interest in my children, and about the only time she ever contacted me was when she wanted me to do something for her. It angered me that she just didn't get it; she had no idea of how self-centered she had become. Couldn't she realize that if she treated people the way she did, they wouldn't have anything to do with her?, which is why I didn't have anything to do with her.

But I also understood, on reflection, that a lot of my dismissal and mockery of her, Phyllis, and my mother when she was alive, came from the distrust I had towards them. I thought that if it served their purposes, they could abandon me the way they had abandoned Rachel. They had never visited her, and by the time I was in school, no one brought up her name, and, in that respect, she ceased to exist, almost historically. Obviously, the obliteration of all vestiges of Rachel's and my grandmother's presence in the family had a lot to do with my childhood fears of my own obliteration.

In thinking about the individuals in my family and their total self-involvement (Phyllis, was something of an exception in this respect), it brought to mind a bizarre situation with Debbie and myself. When I was in my late twenties and already married with two children and working towards becoming a psychologist, I received a phone call out of the blue from Debbie asking me for assistance. "Marty, I need your help. You got to help me. They're trying to take the baby away."

"Baby? You mean Alice?"

"No. Gerard.

"Who? Who is Gerard?"

"Gerard, my baby."

"Oh, you mean my nephew, someone you've never told me about, someone I didn't even know existed until this moment. What is this all about?"

"Marty, I thought I told you."

"How old is he?"

"He's three years old."

"Debbie, I want you to hear me clearly, I haven't spoken to you for over three years. How would I know about this kid? And who knocked you up?"

"Who else but the fucking fat pig?"

"You mean your husband?"

"He never made any money. So when we had Gerard, things got worse. And I had my hands full with my Alice. I put Gerard in a foster home in Long Island with a nice Jewish family. Now they don't want to give him back to me, they complain I'm an unfit mother."

"I wonder how they reached that conclusion?"

"Marty, I told the social worker that my brother is a psychologist and he'll testify for me that I'm a good mom. She's gonna call you next week."

"Debbie, let me get this straight. After discarding your kid, you want me to testify that you're a good mother and you have a right to have your child back? Let me ask you one question, one simple question: 'What is different about your life now than three years ago?' "

"He was a baby then and I couldn't take care of a little baby. The social services hardly gave me any money in those days for the care of a baby; now he's three years old and they give more money."

"Debbie, what's in it for me?"

"Don't be funny, Marty. [She always had some ability to catch on to my sense of humor.] You know what I mean."

"I know exactly what you mean. But I'll tell you what, Debbie, since you're my older sister and you've been so good to me over all these years, I'm going to talk to the social worker and I'm going to find out more about this."

"But don't forget, Marty, I could have given up the kid for adoption if I didn't care and you know how much kids go for, for adoption. I could have gotten a lot of money."

A week later I got a call from Debbie's social worker, who was distressed. She pleaded with me that they ought not to give the kid back to his mother because the only family he's known is the foster family, and added: "In point of fact, if your sister fights the agency's decision, the court would no doubt rule in her favor. Unless you testify that she's an unfit mother, Gerard will be uprooted from the only family he's ever known and placed in the midst of poverty and with an unfit mother. It would be devastating to him."

There was no doubt in my mind that giving the child back to Debbie could damage him for the rest of his life.

I asked her, "Why didn't you enlist my help, back then, to get Debbie to put the kid up for adoption and then get the adopting parents to offer her a sum of money? and that would have taken care of the whole thing."

She couldn't give much of an answer to anything I was trying to get at, so I let it go. The conversation went on, and she again reiterated that taking Gerard away from his foster parents was not a viable option. I told her I would do my best.

Then I called Debbie: "Debbie, let's not play bullshit games. You're not fit to take care of anybody, not even yourself. You gave the kid up in the first place because of your selfishness and thank God you did. Your daughter is a drug addict and is fucked-up beyond belief; your husband is a mental case, and you're one step from in-patient status at Creedmore, and, really, what you care about is the money, anyway."

She contested this for a bit, but it didn't take long for me to prevail. It ended up that she let the foster parents adopt her child, and took the money they offered.

In my dealings with Debbie in this situation, I was angry at her, and hostile and arrogant in my behavior; but underneath it affected me that my family was such that I could have a nephew I would never know, just as I had a sister whom I had known and never saw again. I suppose I myself could have found out about my nephew, when I was older, but that is not the way the family operated. And you don't come from a family like mine without partaking of some of the insularity and craziness of the family model.

There was never any shortage of craziness in my family. There was this addendum to the phone call I initially received from Debbie, after not having heard from her in such a long time. My sister Phyllis called my home and spoke to Margaret, informing her that Debbie's daughter, Alice, had passed away, at age forty-six, in Florida. The circumstances, according to Phyllis, surrounding Alice's death, were that she had been in a car accident, which resulted in severe back pain. Various painkillers were prescribed by a number of doctors, none of whom knew about the other prescriptions and, apparently, Alice had overdosed on the pain- killers and other drugs. Phyllis was calling to let me know that there would be a memorial service on the following Sunday in Staten Island, where Alice had lived with her husband.

When Margaret relayed Phyllis's message, I was shocked. I also felt guilty, because I had known that Alice was a deeply-disturbed child and as a young adult had become a heroin addict. Although I went through the cursory motions to get her some help, I didn't follow through in the way I should have. I did hook her up with a rehab program, but I pretty much absented myself from my involvement with her after that. From time to time Alice called me, and I could tell that she was in some trouble, or that Debbie was in some trouble, but all I did was go through the perfunctory motions of offering help; I really wasn't there for either one of them.

I called Phyllis in Phoenix the next day to find out more details about what had happened concerning Alice's death and how Debbie was doing. When Phyllis told me that Alice had died three weeks earlier, it was hard for me to take in.

"What do you mean she died three weeks ago? I just spoke to Debbie a week-and-a half ago. She told me that Alice was living with her husband, and was doing okay."

"I don't know about that but Alice lived in Florida with her husband, and she died there and was buried there. She used to live in Staten Island, that's where her husband came from."

"Oh, I see. How did it happen?"

"I'm not sure… her husband told me that she was taking these painkillers that her doctor prescribed, after she had an automobile accident. She then apparently took other painkillers on her own, which she wasn't supposed to do, and she overdosed. Her husband warned her not to take other pills, but you know Alice—she never listened to anyone. They buried her in Fort Lauderdale, and her husband arranged for a memorial service this Sunday in Staten Island for her friends and family."

"I'm all mixed up. As I said, Debbie phoned me a week-and-a-half-ago to wish me a happy Rosh Hashana."

"You're mistaken about that. She must have called you before Alice died."

"But Phyllis, even so. Why didn't anyone call me at some time to tell me that Alice died?"

"You know, Debbie. She's funny."

"Phyllis, one more thing. Who is coming to the memorial service?"

"I can't go because I have a sinus condition that affects my esophagus and I'm not allowed to fly. I had a serious surgery over a year ago because I couldn't eat solid food."

"Is anyone else going to be there from our side of the family, besides Debbie?"

"Well, Debbie can't come either. She doesn't feel well."

"What about Gerard?"

"No one has any contact with Gerard or his foster parents."

"No one has any contact with anyone.

"You mean you don't have any contact with anyone? I'm in touch with Debbie and I used to call Alice every so often."

"Don't you think somebody might have called me to tell me something about what's going on?"

I needed to present myself as the injured party in my conversation with Phyllis, and this is an old habit of mine when I am criticized. It's my way of piling up points for when I might need the other person. Not very pretty behavior, but I think people who feel guilty at the core tend to be very sensitive about their shortcomings. Phyllis, to her credit, had cut through my defense when she had let me know very directly: 'You mean you don't have any contact with anyone?' She was absolutely right, but I'd never tell her that. And what Phyllis didn't say was that if there were anyone in the family who could have brought the family together a little, it was me. I had the skills to do that; what I didn't have was the motivation. I was perennially in flight from my family, and up till now I never seemed to require any justification for this. Strangely enough, sometimes I even saw it as a badge of character: my ticket to freedom.

At the last minute both Phyllis and Debbie changed their plans and came to the memorial service. Although it was fifteen years or so since I had seen Phyllis, I was taken aback when she and Debbie came to greet me at the memorial service in Staten Island. She had aged so much. My last image of Phyllis was in her late fifties when she lived in Plainview, Long Island, before moving to Phoenix with her family. My image of her was of a capable, active, mobile person who was middle-aged, blond and relatively fit. The person I saw before me, now, at the service, was wrinkled and stooped. She clearly had gone through a lot in her life, and it took its toll physically and emotionally. Debbie's

DR. MARTIN OBLER / JED GOLDEN

appearance was disturbing in a different way: her looks were distorted—her stomach jutted out in an unsightly way; her back was hunched; some of her teeth were missing, as my mother's were for the last two decades of her life; her face was drawn and hollow-looking; and though she had put some effort into making herself up, it didn't alter her worn-out appearance much. Her clothes hung poorly on her body and her lifeless gray hair was tied up in a bun, which, instead of sitting squarely in the back of her head was slightly off to one side. This was a seventy-six-year-old woman who had not aged gracefully: the years of poverty, mental anguish, isolation, and the effect of a half-century of taking psychotropic medicine for her anxieties had worn her down visibly. Yet here my two sisters were in front of me, greeting me with such obvious pride in their robust, successful younger brother. As they greeted me, some of the twenty or so people in the room, mostly friends of Alice's from AA and NA, gathered around to watch the family reunion. In looking out at the people in attendance, I could see that the majority of faces reflected years of storm-filled life. I was not a great believer in class distinctions, but it was hard for me not to feel that my sisters and the people at the service were from a world I had left a long time ago... and their faces, their manner of speech, and their bodies betrayed an existence of hardship and struggle. But instead of feeling uncomfortable in this scene, I felt right at home where I was, and managed to take over and be the center of attention as I had done in my old neighborhood in my teens... to the delight of Debbie and Phyllis, who expected no less. When Debbie burst out inappropriately in the middle of a "sharing," apropos of the meetings (which was the form that the service had taken)— "Marty, Marty, look at the pictures of Alice that Stanley [Alice's husband] found at my house"—I hushed her quiet. But what impressed me was that no one in the room was in the least startled or disquieted by her outburst... and there was a warmth and acceptance, which was palpable.

During and after the service, I noticed how caring, patient, and gentle Phyllis and her daughter, Helene, were with Debbie and I didn't lose sight of how impatient and dismissive I was used to being with both of my siblings. I was very aware on being here, with my two sisters, that there was something quite askew in the view I had retained of them. The words of my daughter, Dina, came back to me. She had often, when we had conversations about my family, pointed out that, for my own needs, I had negatively mythologized my sisters as being hopeless, insensitive strangers with whom I had nothing in common. My doing that was obviously necessary for my emotional and psychological survival, but was sad and unfortunate. My daughter Dina told me that I could not see my two sisters as they actually were, especially Phyllis.

Phyllis, if I allowed myself to see it, was a warm, relatively stable (she had, however, made a poor choice in her husband), good and nurturing mother and wife and deserved a lot better from me. She was limited by her acceptance of the mediocrity of life in the world around her, but she was, within the family, a kind of oasis of sanity and reasonability; only I chose to ignore her virtues, and dwell on such negatives as her tiresomeness and predictability, and unquestioning acceptance of my mother and sister's depressed and narrow lives. All I could see was that she was pushing away from herself the reality of the disjunction in our family life. She was in denial of why I might need to put as much distance as I could between my family and me. Seeing her now as a frail, but caring and concerned, elderly lady, I could finally tune in to the distortions that I had needed to create. The best I can say of it is that I had acted towards Phyllis pretty horrendously, but to my way of thinking I had had no choice. I was shaped by my environment in the home in such a way that I never had a conscious choice... and that absolved me from guilt.

While I absolved myself from guilt, I had trouble defending against Ted's insistence that I was deluding myself that my lifelong choice to detach from my family was a necessary step in my emotional survival.

For Ted, the issue was not my culpability but my psychological misrepresentation of the reality of what had taken place. Ted would say that, given my family, I was guilt-free for my entire life—no matter what I did; his point, however, was that the psychological damage in refusing to examine my dismissal of my family was harmful to me. "How could it not be?"

CHAPTER NINETEEN:
"A SCHMUCK, A *SCHNORER*, A *HAZARAI*"

Maybe it would be helpful for me to take a little time here to give some sense of the origin and basis of Ted's and my friendship.

We were first introduced to each other through a mutual friend, who taught with Ted and me at the college. Ted and I quickly got close, and began to share intimacies about some of the problems we were having in life. It was he that I turned to when I began my affair with Margaret. He was the only friend I had in the profession whom I could confide in and not have to maintain the role of the informed, well-balanced psychologist. We were both tough on each other and tough on ourselves without losing the humor in all the stuff we were going through. And we could enjoy the competition of trying to establish who was the more incapacitated and neurotic of the two of us.

For one thing, Ted disqualified me as a decent spouse of any woman, on the basis of my immoderate sexual compulsiveness, my awful manners, my boorishness, and my controlling and manipulative personality; and I, in turn, dismissed him as a romantic idealist, naïve as to how the world worked, and hanging on to an exaggerated middleclass morality, unable to make practical use of his talents—for instance, never moving up the academic ladder—... and is still buffered by having been a rich kid.

Aside from Ted's importance to me as a friend, I feel the need to provide some sense of him as a person, so that he does not seem like some good angel who mysteriously comes and goes in the book. He is flesh and blood, a fast friend who sees me as I really am and still believes in me. It is Ted, more than

anyone else, who has pushed me in the direction of change…
and this for years.

If writing this book has done anything for me, it is to
crystallize how far I have come and how far I have to go. Over
the years—especially the lasts few years—I have expanded into
a more sympathetic person (to the travails of being a person on
this planet) than I was for a good part of my life. Ted does not
fail to let me know just how much I've changed—particularly in
the area of taking responsibility for my two adopted kids; but he
also doesn't let up about the extent of my willingness to run
from my problems. When it comes to addressing my
weaknesses, he pushes me more than I think is realistic.

But let me include the following conversation I had with
him, related to my devaluation of my two sisters:

"How is it that you have such a hard time letting go of your
patients when it comes time to terminate… and yet you don't
seem to question at all your lack of involvement with your only
living sisters? Don't you see the imbalance of that? What would
it take to get through to you what the resistance to your family
has done to you?—that far from escaping from them, you have
made sure that their effect on you is enormous and
omnipresent, reaching to every relationship you have. The more
you deny them as people, the more you deny yourself. It doesn't
get anymore fundamental than that.

"You mentioned that Debbie called you a few days ago and
you had your typical conversation with her. What does that
mean, that you put her down and poke fun at her? that you
don't make any effort to go over there and see her? She's your
sister. Do you automatically become little Muttla if you go over
there and speak with her, maybe give her a few dollars to
brighten up her apartment?"

"You vant I should do a mitzvah?"

"If that means something good, a favor, yes."

"You'll never be a real Jew."

"But what about making amends to your sisters?"

"How did that get in there?"

"Are you serious? It irks me, put it that way."

"From where I stand, breaking away from my family was one of the best things I did to keep me sane and from vegetating in front of the TV all day long."

"That was never an option for you."

"That's because you didn't live in my family and maybe because you can't really imagine what it was like. You feel that by denying my familial ties I am doing some kind of great damage to myself. Whereas I see what I did as necessary to my survival."

"... and what about the price you're paying for it?, not to speak of the unconscionable treatment of Debbie and Phyllis, as if it's okay to turn your back on them."

"Even though a part of me feels that there is truth to what you're trying to tell me, another part of me feels that I can cut my ties with my biological family and be better off for it. Why do you think that I tried to discourage Debbie from taking Gerard back from his foster family—because Debbie is such a good mother?"

"You know my philosophy, Marty. The thing that may save one as a child, when carried over to adulthood, may be the thing that prevents one from a necessary stage of growth. I know from my experience that my defensiveness against my mother was something I just took on as a child and held on to well into adulthood... to the age of probably fifty-five. But somewhere along the line I began to feel that I would be doing a very bad thing to myself if I did not make a major attempt to reach out to my mother before she died. And I was right."

"Well you've always been a jilted mommy's boy. However, with all your mother's shortcomings, I still think there was enough good stuff in her that you benefited from making a real connection with her, no matter how late it came. But I can say in all honesty, that I don't feel the same thing about my sisters or my mother... maybe a little bit about my father, at least he had some deeper sense that his relationship with me mattered to him. With my mother, she may have loved me, but by the time I got to junior high school, she was too nutty, too out of it, for me to retain my attachment to her or think of her lovingly. And I am not a believer that just because you come from your biological family that you have to live out the familial attachment for the rest of your life. My friendships have always been more meaningful to me than my relationships with my family members. I'll never forget the time at my father's funeral when my mother and Debbie were wailing at his grave, when in fact they hated him."

"If you ask me, your inability to come through and give Dalite some token of money, of which you have an abundance, is just another instance of your myopia or emotional failure."

"Who asked you?"

"I'm asking myself, I certainly haven't been able to get you to think about the inhumanity of your omission in this case. And I'm not a particular fan of Dalite."

"Well, let's hear it, do your worst. I'm a bad human being."

"I wish I could say that, but the reality is that I don't understand the extent of your denial of your familial obligations and what makes you think that you can just walk away from the care and responsibility that goes with being a brother or a husband? Is that what you've learned over all the years you've been a shrink?"

"… that and a few other things. Look, you came from a family where there was a lot of tough stuff but there was also a lot of good stuff and that makes a world of difference as to whether one should escape from the ravages of a dysfunctional family or stay connected and incorporate one's experience. As a shrink, I am faced with the same choice for my patients as I am for myself."

"What side would you come down on if you were treating a patient like yourself, with your family history?"

"That is a question that really stymies me. I will say this: I firmly believe that if I didn't escape my family they could have pulled me under. I completely saw myself at risk. That is how I justify my own behavior. Yet, what I did to myself is almost an equivalent of taking a child away from its mother. The ramifications are hard to contemplate."

"Only you haven't contemplated them, in disavowing your family, old as you are. You retain the position towards your sisters that you employed as a late adolescent with your mother."

"That is a very good point. However, I do think, in part thanks to you, I'm a little less resistant than I used to be. At Alice's memorial, I could see that my sisters weren't as hopeless as I made them out to be. It struck me that there was a lot of humanity to them."

"What's stopping you then from acting human?"

"...because, down deep, I still haven't been able to overcome my shame and humiliation that I was an Obler. I confess I want to be seen like you and your upper-middleclass family, not like the losers in Brownsville. I remember how fearful I was when I introduced Dalite to my family that she would judge me negatively. It was very surprising to me that she wasn't fazed by my family; in fact, she reacted to them as if they were normal."

"I understand what you're saying, but you're not taking into consideration how much you've impaired your own development by casting off your family, a point that I reiterate all the time, but which never seems to seep into that brain of yours."

"Being identified with my family was no easy matter."

"True, but underneath you can't really like yourself for your behavior, and it keeps you defending yourself in multiple ways, some of which work against you."

"For instance?"

"For one, you really don't see how others see you and you don't care about how gross you come across. You seem to be content being just the way you are, with your impervious and screw everybody attitude."

"Did it ever dawn on you that I like being this way?"

"So you say."

"What do you want me to say... that I'm a schmuck, a *schnorer*, a *hazarai* ?"

"It's not bad, not bad at all. It's athletic."

"... up your mother's twang."

CHAPTER TWENTY:
"WHAT KEEPS YOU FROM JUMPING?"

Esther was a patient of mine whom I took on reluctantly at Warren's prodding. He had worked with her for some years in his civil service job and over time they had become friends. He had spoken a lot about her during his years of therapy with me, and at one point brought up his concern about her mental deterioration after her boyfriend of fifteen years had died. She was, apparently, talking a lot about suicide and Warren felt that she was giving up on life.

He was eager for me to see her, counting on that I could help her in the way I had helped him. I have to admit that the thought of Warren referring a psychotic patient to me was on the face of it pretty funny—a sort of the blind leading the blind. But, more seriously, I understood there was a multiplicity of motivations, and issues, in his wanting me to work with her; however, I chose to bypass them. I'm not sure my getting into the complications of his dependence on me, and my getting into my countertransference considerations with him, would be the best thing for his therapy. Better that he think of me as the all-knowing, all-caring, dictatorial father. So I simply told him that I was hesitant to take on another patient with the severity of his problems, but I would have no problem seeing her for a few consultation visits.

In my first meeting with Esther in 1999, I learned that she was born in 1949 in Flatbush, Brooklyn, the eldest daughter of Naomi and Hymie Buchholz, the mother suffering from clinical depression and the father disabled by periodic psychotic regression. In talking about herself to me, Esther let me know that she had been depressed all her life. As she put it: "I don't think I've ever known a moment in my life when I was not depressed." And judging by her appearance, I had no reason to disbelieve her. She looked spaced out and distant, almost unconnected to life. Even though she didn't wear cheap clothes, her apparel was poorly coordinated and didn't fit. Her face was inherently attractive but had overtones of her disturbed mental condition. She fidgeted quite a bit.

I asked her why she was seeking a new therapist. She explained that her years of therapy had consisted largely of taking one drug after another; and while it kept her going from day to day, it hadn't done much to make her life more tolerable. She then added that she still thinks about killing herself every day. She said, "I can't erase from my mind the bleak, green, hallway of the mental hospital." She said that she had been hospitalized a number of times over a twenty-five-year period. I asked her if she had a plan to commit suicide and she said that she often opens the window in her apartment and considers jumping.

"What keeps you from jumping?" I asked her. She told me that she was fearful of the mess it would make and she worried about how her parents would take it. Everything that came out of her mouth reinforced her wish not to live. Yet, to my mind, her words didn't match her affect—they were too strong, too implacable, for the feelings I had about her. There was something tender, something hopeful about her manner that I took to be an attachment to life. I viewed this as a counterforce to her death wish and it gave me some hope that she could make improvements in her condition. However, it was hard to not succumb to the disconsolateness and defeated presence of the person sitting in front of me. Her affectlessness and her unceasing depression, I would surmise, convinced her doctors that she would not benefit from traditional psychotherapy. I wondered whether she was quick enough to have internalized their bleak view of her and reflected it back to them. Maybe there was more to her than her therapists and psychopharmacologists supposed?

Towards the close of my second consultation session with her, I was faced with the tough decision of whether or not to take Esther on as a patient.

She had been depressed for most of her fifty-one years and, besides this, her genetics dictated that the prognosis was not good for her ever getting out of her depression. Her father could barely function, her younger sister I gathered was an obsessive-compulsive with deep layers of depression, and her mother, although less afflicted genetically with depression than her two children, was riddled with cancer. The gravity of her mother's illness was compounded by her inevitably dwelling on what would happen to the family without her. If you boiled it down, they were all basket cases, and my family of origin didn't lag far behind them.

What was I doing even thinking of taking Esther on as a patient, considering how exhaustive it has been to work with Warren? But nevertheless I took her on.

I guess, partly, I attribute it to Warren pushing me to see her and that his concern for her was a good thing for him. In addition, I had reason to think that she was capable of making some modest headway, despite the severity of her condition. I was basing this opinion on things she had told me about herself, such as having had, when she was considerably younger, a few stable relationships with guys; and, more significantly, having had, as Warren already told me, a long relationship with a caring man who died shortly before she came to see me. Another thing that she had mentioned, which I found hopeful, was that she had been able to stay in the work force for over twenty years. And lastly, I noted in my consultation with her, that she had a nice sense of humor, despite the severity of her chronic depression.

Then there is yet another factor that influenced my decision to see her. I have to say, for better or worse, it is generally my pattern not to turn away patients after consultation. Truthfully, it doesn't take much time for me to connect to the person I am seeing in consultation, and I also am able to quickly, sometimes amazingly quickly, ascertain her problems. I see her past and what needs to be done and what I know I can do for her... and that vision is so arresting to me that I can't not take her on— especially, when you throw into the hopper my messianism and my wish to be omnipotent; or, perhaps most significantly, my identification with the would-be patient and my not having the heart to turn her away. I suppose I want to rescue her the way I wanted to be rescued as a child. (Whew! this whole paragraph doesn't sound too ennobling about my countertransference issues... but it does give some indication about what might lead me to be a motivated and sympathetic practitioner.)

I did, however, lay down, as with Warren, specific conditions as part of my working with her. They were: I would have complete control of her therapy and she would have to go along with everything I recommended; and I would have to involve other patients of mine in her life because a major problem in her getting better was overcoming her self-imposed isolation and withdrawal from social contact.

She displayed no hesitancy in agreeing to my stipulations; but I could see in her face and body language a resignation that upset me, so I asked her what was bothering her about the conditions I had imposed. She said, "What choice do I have?"

During my first two months of working with Esther, I was hopeful of what might be accomplished. After all, the job I did with Warren had been so successful that I couldn't help thinking that I could have a parallel success with Esther. Sure she was seriously damaged but so were Warren and some other of my bipolar and psychotic patients; and if I found a means to help them acclimate in some fashion to the world they lived in, why couldn't I do so with Esther? I was beginning to feel at this stage of my career, in 1999, that I was blazing a trail forward. It didn't take much to stir the grandiose feelings that accompanied me wherever I set my hat. Could I become another R.D.Laing? In the late 1960's and 70's Laing had gained a reputation for having some success treating schizophrenics and other seriously disturbed patients as if they were not totally unlike ordinary people; he saw psychosis as something of a journey through difficult terrain rather than purely as a bio-chemical illness.

It didn't take forever for me to have a reality check; gradually over the next months and years, Esther began seriously regressing and I started to feel discouraged and frustrated. I could see that I was developing the dismissive attitude towards her that I had fallen into with my family members. Into the second year of treatment, I was pushing myself just to find the wherewithal to continue working with her... which of course is the polar opposite of my high hopes for her (and myself). However, I had to be very careful that Esther did not clue-into the extent of my discouragement, for her fears of being hopeless needed no reinforcement by me.

What went so wrong? I suppose in my enthusiasm for thinking of Esther as another difficult case in which I could overcome a lot of hurdles, I was too quick to put aside some of the crucial negative history of her mental illness. This was a failure on my part to face the imposing reality of her life experience. Somewhere inside myself I was determined to make a difference in Esther's life. I suppose there is a resemblance here, on my part, to Warren in his flying high period. But, my saving grace was that underneath I was eminently practical and was very capable of evaluating what did and didn't work. And reconstructing my approach. I had allowed myself to get carried away by optimism and self-importance, but in the back of my mind I was not discarding Esther's checkered past. I ended up juggling the hopeful and the hopeless side of her.

Early in Esther's life it began to become clear that her psychological problems relegated her to a life of depression and anxiety and terror. By the time she was an adolescent she got in trouble with the law, started to show signs of volatile changes in mood and behavior, which foreshadowed the onset of her bipolar illness. In her early twenties, she became a full-blown bipolar and started to use drugs and alcohol heavily, in part to mask her problems from herself and others. Despite the severity of her condition she somehow managed to keep herself afloat—emotionally, psychologically, and monetarily. This pattern of being able to survive in the midst of chaos and disintegration continued for the rest of her life. As bad as her life was during her twenties, she managed to finish college and eventually land a permanent position as a New York State employee. Her heavy drinking lasted about ten years and she described it as "walking through life in a fog state, barely present in her own experience." Through thick and thin, she was able to keep her job and was able to support herself, eventually retiring in her early fifties and going on social security disability.

One of the life skills that kept such a marginal person as Esther going was that she had an impressive capacity to find and reach out to people who were willing, for their own collusive needs, to take care of her and cover up her disorganization and deficiencies in various spheres of her life. Even of late, her boyfriend of fifteen years had paid her bills, done her taxes, and helped her with her daily functioning; and, at her job, when she was unable to handle certain of her responsibilities, her co-workers would come to the rescue.

But this ability to make use of people on her behalf, did not preclude her mental deterioration and bouts of becoming unhinged. Her first serious mental breakdown occurred in her mid-twenties after she had an abortion. At this time, she slipped from a clinical depression to a more regressed psychotic state. She began hallucinating, went to a local emergency room, and was diagnosed mistakenly as a paranoid schizophrenic (paranoid schizophrenia is a psychotic thought disorder while bipolar psychosis is a disorder in mood shifts) and was put on anti-psychotic medication which began a thirty-five-year stint of prescribed drug dependency.

Since the initial breakdown she has had several additional hospitalizations and been seen by numerous psychopharmacologists and other mental health professionals. The picture I ascertained in her treatment with me was that the professionals taking care of her were prescribing drugs in an incompetent and irresponsible way, so that one didn't know what the other was doing and nobody controlled her imbibing alcohol while taking drugs, and, incredibly, was often given highly addictive drugs without being appropriately medically supervised. A simple instance that will give some idea of the confusion and irresponsibility in her treatment was that one of her physicians put her on a highly-addictive drug, fiurnal with codeine, while a psychiatrist prescribed valium, which is also highly addictive and has a negative interactive effect with fiurnal.

The following dialogue sums up pretty well how things not too long ago deteriorated for Esther, culminating in the decline of her taking care of herself and the intensification of her depression:

"So am I to assume that you have been feeling crappy?"

"Crappy is too mild a word to describe what I've been through."

"Tell me what you've been through."

"I sleep most of the day away; I have to force myself to bathe and when I do bathe it's a painstaking ordeal. When I contemplate brushing my teeth I feel as though I won't be able to muster up the energy to move the brush back and forth. By the time I finish bathing and my ablutions all I want to do is crawl back into bed."

"Do you eat? Do you have any appetite?"

"Practically none. I have to force myself to eat a little yogurt or gulp down a glass of Ensure or I wouldn't have anything in my system. It's an effort even to chew."

"Do you try to do anything to feel better?"

"Like what?"

"Call some friends, watch TV, rent a movie, converse with your parents."

"I don't call anyone and nobody calls me, except for my parents and sister. Even the few friends I have from AA have stopped trying to get me to go to movies or out to dinner. I guess they get turned off at how down I sound. I don't feel much like living. It's the same way I felt right after John died.

Until he passed away I hadn't realized how much I depended on him to have a feeling of wanting to be alive."

"… and how much was that?"

"Looking back now, though I didn't realize it while I was with him, almost totally. He took care of almost everything. You know, I was thinking one night while lying in bed, unable to fall asleep because I had slept all day… that even though he was slowly dying of emphysema we had hardly focused on his fears and needs. Everything was about taking care of me. And it dawned on me that it had been like that for all the years of our relationship. If I felt lousy at work, he would come to get me and drive me home. Yet he was the one that couldn't get around easily because of his breathing problem. He bought the food, cooked the meals, hired the cleaning lady and would make sure that I made my doctors' appointments. And if I wanted to be alone and not have any sex with him, and believe me we didn't have much of that to speak of during the last six years of our relationship, it was okay with him. I never thought much about how he felt about it. I can't believe how self-preoccupied I was. What's the matter with me, Dr. Obler? All I can see are my needs… what I want… it's all about me."

"Let me ask you a question, darling: How did it feel while you were going through this stuff with him and all the focus was on you?"

"It felt great. It felt as if I was the most important person in the world."

"What was in it for him?"

"I wish I knew."

"Well, one thing I could say is that if he was dying of emphysema, and there was no way of getting around that reality, then to have someone whom he could look after and do things for gave his life a purpose… or, at least the illusion of a purpose."

"And I'm on the other side of it: I feel I want to die when I don't have someone to be there for me; if, however, I have someone totally devoted to me, I feel great."

"In spite of what he was going through?..."

"I'm afraid so. Sad to say, I didn't give him anything. I made it clear toward the end that I wasn't very sexually responsive to him."

"Really?"

"Really."

"Were you punishing him for caring so much about you?"

"Why would I do that?"

"I think you would, on some level, find fault with any man that would see you as anything more than a convenience and as someone to gratify his sexual needs. You needed to debase him for his willingness to be with you. Was John this devoted to you before he got the emphysema?"

"No, not at all. He was the one that insisted in the first couple of years that he see other women... and it upset me, though I went along with it."

"I bet you very much wanted to sleep with him during those years."

"You're right."

"In the later years when you lost interest in him sexually, did he beg you to help him get off?"

"He did and it repulsed me."

What I was trying to do during these sessions was to test out whether Esther could do serious psychological exploration in spite of her mental condition and depression. I could see that she was a bright woman who was capable of such work but had been so damaged and worn down by her years of crushing mental illness that whatever progress she could make in insight therapy was unsustainable.

I became very discouraged by her condition and how it impacted on me. I needed, for me and for her, to do something that offered a bit of hope to counter her pervasive despondency. Here is that conversation:

"It's not really working out too well, Esther. You're becoming more and more incapable of moving out of yourself.

In fact, you're living out your self-destructive wishes, but you don't want to jump out the window and make a mess. Instead, you're making the worst mess possible of your life. And if you don't start getting the desire to do something about this with me, then it comes time to reconsider the loony bin. That's what those people are in there for; they become babies again, they want to be taken care of. Life is too tough, ya gotta work, ya gotta clean up, make your bed, and eat a little. No more supervisors at the job making demands on you. No more forcing yourself to go to AA meetings, having to listen to all that shit, whether it's good for you or not. Just a little old crib you can crawl into. And since we can't make this office into a crib, like a Skinner Box—where all your needs are met... the perfect infant environment, totally, all the time—you run the risk of ending up in a state mental institution."

"No thanks. I never want to go to a place like that."

"But you would be completely taken care of, like with John."

"It's hardly the same."

"I noticed that until two seconds ago, when you said 'no thanks,' you were in your zombie state."

"Now I'm a zombie?"

"Yup, that's the way I see you, even though you don't see yourself that way. You just sit there, telling me how terrible you feel while staring off into space; what little energy you display goes into feeling sorry for yourself and talking about how empty your life is... and, typically, by the end of the session you look at me with those sad, childlike eyes and ask me, 'When is my next session?' After I tell you, you get up, looking lost and disoriented, and wonder which direction you have to go to get out of the office. Did you ever notice, Esther, that at the end of almost every session I lift my hand and point to the front door?"

"Of course I do. I never thought anything of it."

"That's right. You never did. You don't want to see that I'm treating you like a baby and that you want to be a baby. It's not lost on me that you get me to play that role for you."

320

"But you don't understand, I see that I'm doing this with you and don't want to do it, but I can't help myself."

"It interests me that you constantly use those words 'I can't help myself.' Do you want to help yourself?"

"I do, but I don't know how."

I had to recognize the validity of what Esther was telling me about herself: she was losing the will to live. The life force that I so depended on for her to maintain herself was rapidly fading and I was worried about losing her. From what I could make out, she felt best when she became a baby and had people take care of her. So I decided to create the conditions for that to happen... something that might resemble the situation she had with her boyfriend John and her office coworkers. I drew from the theories of D.W.Winnicott and Margaret Mahler, who advocated a revisiting of conditions of infancy, allowing the adult child to be given the love and nurturance denied earlier.

My plan was to create a miniature family constellation for Esther, enlisting the help of Warren, who referred her to me, and Mark, who liked the idea of helping people... and he had been active to this end in group therapy. I convinced Esther that she could no longer live alone. Initially she balked at the idea, but eventually she came to see that it probably was in her best interests to go along with it. Esther and I successfully solicited her parents and sister to let her live with them; and I got them to cooperate so that they would be a part of the intended family constellation, which meant taking care of her, if it came to that, as if she were a newborn baby coming home from the hospital. At least so went the theory, as I set it up.

The parents were invited to periodically attend her therapy sessions; however her sister became part of her weekly sessions for a period of several months. Mark and Warren were instructed to visit her at home biweekly, individually or together, and were directed to get her out of the house and into the outside world. Esther, with my okay, rented out her apartment on a monthly basis to a friend, so that if she made a big improvement, she could resume living in her own place...

this I hoped would provide some incentive for her to do what she could to make progress.

In the beginning everybody was upbeat about the challenge of helping Esther recuperate. I also felt invigorated by the plan I had put into motion.

Eventually, however, the novelty wore off, and Esther did not seem to be responding that well to the plan; inevitably, the enthusiasm of those I had enlisted to help her began to wane… even her family members retrogressed inasmuch as they began to recreate the negative conditions in the original family dynamic. I suspect that the old patterns that had been in place for so many years proved to be more powerful than the novelty of my new treatment plan. Her father withdrew into his semi-catatonic state, her sister revived her old obsessive-compulsive symptomatology, and her mother resumed her tyrannical control over all the family members, yelling and screaming at them. In this unfortunate repeat of the family pattern, Esther withdrew into her own world even more. I tried to get Mark and Warren to increase their contact with her, hoping that this might help matters. It didn't.

Years later in one of Mark's psychotherapy sessions, he reminisced about a visit at this time to her family's apartment in Brooklyn. He rang the buzzer and was let into the apartment by her father, who was in his usual foggy state. Mark asked him a few times whether Esther was home, and finally was rewarded by an arm pointed in the direction of her room. He relayed to me that he knocked on her door and announced himself. He was expecting her to come out wearing a nice outfit, that her hair would be brushed, and that she would have bathed and made herself up. He was all set to spend a nice afternoon with her walking in the park and getting a bite to eat. That prospect was dashed when Esther emerged "looking like a derelict and smelling like one too." Not only was Mark terribly disappointed to see the state she was in, but he was ashamed to be seen with her in this condition. He ended up playing cards with her at home. On reflection, I have to laugh at my idea of recreating the ideal Winnicott and Mahler family environment.

For the next few months I continued to modify my family plan, but clearly it wasn't working. It would start off promising but after a while familiarity would set in and Esther would slide back to where she had begun as my patient. Eventually her sister had stopped attending sessions with her; Mark and Warren saw her less frequently; and her father remained in his leaden state; the mother tried to hold things together but her physical and mental problems beat her down... and she made it clear that she wasn't able to keep the family functioning anymore.

This kind of deterioration, on the part of Esther and her family, brought back vivid memories of my own childhood; and, just as I had wanted to run away from my own family, I now could catch myself starting to want to run away from Esther and her family. Since that was not practical, I switched to a new plan, which by all measures would be considered extreme. I moved from the family plan I had constructed to a last resort intervention, consisting of hospitalization, the new-type electro-convulsive shock therapy (ECT)... to be followed by halfway-house residential care. Seen from the most unkind—and inaccurate—perspective, what I was doing was not unlike what my parents did by shipping Rachel and my grandmother into a mental hospital because they couldn't deal with them. I mention this only because it would be impossible for the comparison not to enter my mind. For that matter, I was also reminded of my sister Debbie having a mental breakdown in her early fifties and receiving electro-convulsive shock therapy, to which I had agreed when the Kings County staff notified me that they planned to go ahead with the treatment as a last resort for her massive depression. And, finally, my desire to jettison Esther called up, associatively, my need to run away from my father as he lay dying in the hallway at Brookdale Hospital. So much for the kind of haunting memories that leave me thinking the worst of myself. From a realistic, practical standpoint, what I was proposing for Esther, might just be the only type intervention that could get her out of her dangerously-depressed state. So I went against my inclination as a therapist in what I recommended for her, because from what I was seeing about her condition, she might well be at a dead-end and conceivably give in to her suicidal impulse. I listened to the practical rather than the theoretical side of me.

All in all, I believe I initiated this new blueprint for Esther because I was looking out for her as best I could, which is not to say I was free of unsettling thoughts. If there was something I deserved to feel guilty about, it was that when my grandiose image of myself was deflated by the failures of my therapy interventions, my enthusiasm for treating her decreased. In any case, I presented to her my plan of what needed to happen.

"Look, Esther, we're not getting the results we want, you're still not bathing, still not getting out of the house on your own, you're still frightened, anxious, and depressed most of the time. And, if you remember, the aim of our therapy was to get out of the drug mentality and for you to become somewhat able to function in the world."

"I told you I was hopeless."

"C'mon, let's not go back to that. It's a tired old song for you. But we do have some serious problems here and we have to alter our course of treatment."

"You're in charge."

"Well, let me tell you what I'm thinking. Although I have a queasy feeling about it... and this is going to initially upset you... I am entertaining the idea of your going for modern-day electro-convulsive shock therapy. It could have better results than we're getting with what we've been doing. And let's face it, all the years in which you were heavily medicated didn't diminish in any real way the seriousness of your depression; and, in our work together, while I believe you initially made progress you have been slipping backward for some time. All in all, I would have to admit that you are not doing as well as I had hoped. There is a growing body of evidence that with your kind of depression and anxiety, electro-convulsive shock therapy often helps when nothing else does."

"This is very hard for me. I've always been terrified of shock therapy. I always had the feeling this is what it would come down to."

"Listen, Esther, the idea of shock therapy frightens me also, but the truth is that even though we've modified your drug regimen, taking anti-depressant and anti-psychotic medication is shaking up your whole body anyway. Every time you pop one of those Serotonin-reuptake and Benzodiazepine pills it changes the whole balance of neurotransmitters in your brain. And that's exactly what shock therapy does. I'm not suggesting this course of action frivolously. But it can work where other things don't. It may have a real effect in changing your mood and that could make a significant difference in your life."

"I'm frightened."

"That's natural but this isn't the old shock therapy; it's become a rather benign procedure. They put you to sleep and you don't feel a thing. The worst part of it is that when you wake up, you have a temporary loss of memory. But I'm going to be here for you, and Mark and Warren and your family will be here for you, too."

"That's good to know. But what scares me the most is that if this doesn't work, there's nothing left."

Esther was right. I felt the same way: if it didn't work, there was very little left to try. If electro-convulsive shock therapy didn't work, I could see her future ahead of me by looking at her father.

Esther finally agreed to go to shock therapy at St. Vincent's Hospital, in Greenwich Village—the same hospital where she received treatment for her first mental breakdown. She was very reluctant for months to take this step and I only got her to do it by reassuring her that I knew what I was doing and that she should trust my judgment—all the time having doubts myself about the efficacy of the treatment for her condition. But I did believe that something needed to be done to combat her devitalized state and this had some possibility of doing that.

The initial plan designed by the St. Vincent's psychiatric staff, together with me, called for a series of twelve shock treatments, after which we would evaluate whether further treatments should be given, depending on the level of her progress.

At the end of the first three treatments there was no success in achieving a convulsive seizure, which is an absolute response that must occur if the treatment is going to work. However, it is not all that uncommon that some people react to ECT the way Esther did. The general practice is that the ECT treatments are continued until the patient responds favorably or, if not, the treatment is abandoned. The second series of treatments proved successful in producing the necessary seizure (and after that, it was expected that she would not have a problem with the treatment); she was told, however, that she would have to prolong her stay at the hospital for an additional few weeks in order to complete the twelve originally-prescribed shock treatments. To put it mildly, this did not please her. She opened-up to me how distraught she was feeling, and what a horror this whole experience was turning out to be. It wasn't actual pain connected to the shock therapy she had undergone, but, according to her, the aftermath of the shock treatment was a nightmare. She said that her depression had escalated into a prevailing wish to end her life. Her dark thoughts were casting a shadow over her will to live. Some of the secondary symptoms were short-term memory loss, disorientation, and mild nausea; the most upsetting of all, she reported, was that she felt no energy or desire to do anything but lie around and vegetate: this fed into a deep fear that she has carried around for many years that she would be reduced to a catatonic state—which she had witnessed her father go through.

I have to say that I was discouraged at not having anticipated the severity of her response and had spoken positively about her taking the treatments... and convincing her to do something she had strongly resisted all along. I had underplayed some of the aftereffects she was experiencing because I was running out of treatment options. I can't help feeling guilty for relying on her dependency on me to convince her to do something that was greatly feared by her. In some ways it was a pretty self-serving thing to do.

Soon after the sixth treatment, her mood improved and so did her attitude towards completing her stint at the hospital. Whether this uplift was a result of the treatments or had to do with new social considerations on the ward was hard to ascertain. I will say that some of the patients on seeing how depressed she had been, or having heard snatches of doctor-nurse conversations about her, started to spend more time with her and she thrived on the attention.

More tellingly, around this time of her stay at the hospital she had somehow managed to forge a bond with a male patient who was homeless, and, like her, had gone through a series of mental breakdowns over the years. He grew dependent on her as a source of security and hoped that he might have some kind of a life with her after they both left the hospital. Mark and Warren, who reported to me daily after their visits to the hospital, wondered how I viewed her relationship with this homeless fellow. I said, "I don't give a damn whether she gets involved with a robot if it helps her to get out of her depression and start to feel alive."

As time in the hospital passed, and Esther continued to improve, her resistance to taking the final series of treatments hardened. She was frightened that this ECT nightmare would go on forever and she would end up catatonic like McMurphy in *One Flew Over the Cuckoo's Nest*.

Despite her fears and dread, the changes in her daily activities were somewhat remarkable.

Esther evidenced signs of moving out of her self-encapsulation. She started to bathe regularly and when I asked her why she was able to bathe in the hospital and not at home, she replied matter-of-factly, "What would people think of me if I didn't bathe?"

A noteworthy signal of her improvement was that she began to be outspoken about the "terrible food" at the hospital and about the number of patients who sat around all day watching TV, hardly ever engaging in conversation or reading a book or taking a non-required stroll.

While I was heartened by this change in Esther, it did not cause me to wholly revise my notion, based on my experience with her, that unless the ECT resulted in major change, she would continue not to have much of a life. Her core pathology of depression and pessimism was still intact; soon she would be released from the hospital and would be repeating the circumstances in her life that had led to her falling apart.

Before Esther left St. Vincent's, I had to meet with the staff to formulate a plan of follow-up treatment. I could see that she was functioning better in the structured hospital environment than she had before starting the ECT treatments.

This reinforced my idea that maybe a halfway house would be a good thing for her. While there she would be living among residents many of whom had problems as debilitating as hers, guided by a trained staff working with them in a controlled environment. This kind of group setting might be a better situation for her than therapy with me once or twice a week and staying with her family.

I posed this concern to the hospital staff and they agreed with my thinking, given that so far the efficacy of the ECT had been hopeful but far from decisive. For it to be more conclusive, the depression—most importantly-would have to lift for a prolonged period of time and her overall mood, affect and demeanor would have to continue improving. After Esther's last ECT treatment, I met with her at the hospital for a private session in which I posed the idea to her of the halfway house.

"Let me say, Esther, a little about how I see your situation at this juncture. You and I have tried a number of types of social intervention stuff over the course of your recent therapy, but none of them did much for you... which led to my suggestion of ECT. And you agreed to go along with it in spite of your serious misgivings. Of course it is too early to say what the results of the ECT will be; we won't know that for some time. But here and now we have to make some decisions about where you're going to live."

"... as long as it's not an institution and no more shock treatment."

"We're not talking about hospitals or an institution, Esther. What we're talking about is a halfway house in the community with people not so different than you... where you'll be part of a group, and a caring staff. Maybe in this kind of a setting, life will be more livable for you. The truth is that what you do when you're home with your family is to resign yourself to living in an emotional void where one day is exactly like the next, and then you start thinking about suicide. At least there is a chance, maybe small, that you'll feel more alive and less hopeless in a halfway house."

"If you've taught me one thing, Marty, it is that the feeling of hopelessness and emptiness is within me and I carry it wherever I am, whether it's in a halfway house or in the apartment in Brooklyn."

"Look, Esther, you know me. If you want to give up that's up to you, but I'm not going to encourage you to do so. I think there's still hope—you're a bright woman and in the right setting people would take to you."

"Thank you, Marty, but it was always apparent to me that you were willing to fight harder for me than I was willing to fight for myself."

"That tends to be true of the way it is in most therapy situations, patients are loathe to give up on the defenses they depend on... and the therapist has to push hard to knock down those barriers."

329

"Marty, I like to believe that I could change in ways that would make a difference. But, underneath, when I look at my family, I have no illusions about who we are. We're all unfit for this life. We live a fringe existence, and it's no accident that we're so dependent on each other."

Even though I pushed Esther not to give up and to consider the halfway house as an option, I had a pretty strong feeling that she would end up back with her family. I learned a long time ago that persons like Esther and my sister Debbie were so emotionally incapacitated, by their genetics and life circumstances, that the best they could do, as they aged, was to live out a minimal existence and remain dependent on other people to take care of them.

Be reminded that my recommending Esther for ECT treatment was very definitely a last resort. I couldn't say, at this juncture, I was all that optimistic about the possibility of her making large changes as a result of the treatment.

It was rare that I gave up on a patient, but there was something constitutionally in me wherein, if nothing I tried was working, I felt a strong wish to detach from the patient and move on.

I would do what I could for Esther, but I knew my investment in her was dwindling. I believed that the halfway house experience would be better than my attempt at therapy; but it still was, in effect, along the lines of maintenance therapy. Maintenance therapy, of any sort, did not appeal to me, and maintenance was about all I imagined could be done with Esther in her present condition. I shared with Mark and Warren my thoughts about placing Esther in a halfway house; and I encouraged them to keep in contact with her and let her know that they liked the idea—if they did—of the halfway house. Mark had no difficulty with this... he liked the prospect of meeting all the folks in the halfway house and visiting her there... but Warren, picking up that my interest in her was waning, was more concerned with this than her placement in the halfway house. Warren knew that my continued work with him, over many years, had resulted in turning his life around, beneficially, and he must have wondered why I hadn't retreated from him the way I appeared to be retreating from Esther.

Just before Esther was to be discharged from the hospital I received a phone call from her in which she stated pretty forcefully—atypically so—that she had decided that Petrovich, the homeless alcoholic whom she had met in the ward, would be moving-in with her upon her release from the hospital. As much as I was stunned by the content of what she was relaying, I was equally stunned by the forcefulness in her voice as she delivered her message. There was a determination to do this that I did not think, by any stretch, she could muster in her present state. But here she was telling me what she was going to do, and not asking me for permission.

"My plan is to make him stop drinking and get him off the streets."

"I thought he was in the hospital?"

"Oh, no, I thought I told you a week ago that he left the hospital and was assigned to live in a homeless shelter, which he refused to do."

"I gather you stayed in contact with him?"

"He was calling me, drunk, and pleading with me to take him in when I am released from the hospital; he promised that if I would do that, he would stop drinking."

"You believe that?"

"That's what he said. His actual words were: 'If I can stick it to you regularly, I'll quit drinking.' "

"This doesn't sound so good, Esther."

"I've made up my mind to help him."

"Don't you think it would be sensible to resume therapy and talk this over, maybe at some point bring your new friend to a session? How do you know that he's not a psycho?"

"We've made out a little in the hospital and I can tell he's not psychotic. You're not giving me much credit."

"You don't know this guy, and he's probably very unstable."

"I'll come in to talk it over with you, but I am not going to let you talk me out of my decision to invite him to live with me."

"At least defer his living with you until we can start to make some sense out of the whole thing. You don't have to act like a girl of seventeen."

"What do I do in the meantime: let him live in the streets?"

"That's not your problem. You can't let him pressure you into this by making you responsible for him."

"It makes me feel good to have someone depending on me for help."

"Look, before you went into the hospital, you were hardly able to take care of yourself; that's why we moved you from your apartment to your parents' apartment. What makes you think you'll be able to take care of yourself now?"

"Now I have a goal. You know me; I never did anything unless I had a purpose, a goal… and wanted to do it. Like bathing. I wouldn't do it for myself alone, but I would do it for other people."

"Well, why don't you just hold off making any major moves, like giving him the key to your apartment, until we start our sessions again? And until then, my advice is to live at your parents' apartment."

What impressed me about Esther's declaration of intent was the energy that she conveyed, which seemed to me to have completely dried up, prior to the ECT. However, my way of looking at it, which is, admittedly, biased and inconclusive, the change had more to do with the residual effect of my therapy than with the ECT. My emphasis on interaction with people, getting out in the world and being a part of it, and forming ongoing friendships, must have sunk in somewhere within her. And when this gent came along—disturbed as he surely is—she jumped at the opportunity to rescue him and herself. Maybe I had failed to see the most obvious thing in front of my face: people need love… even crazy people. Petrovitch may not be the right person for her, but the idea of working on forming a relationship might be a step in the right direction.

I can't help thinking that when nothing was working in therapy and Esther was deteriorating, all that was left for her was ECT. And then—bang!—along comes a guy who is on the skids and she comes back to life. How do you account for that in the annals of psychological theory? And now, I had to admit, my interest in her was rekindling.

One thing I should not pass over is how Esther, in the dialogue of this chapter, is doing the work of therapy… and is saying some really moving things. Wow, it makes you think.

CHAPTER TWENTY-ONE:
FALLIBILITY

In the year 2003, I was sixty-seven years old and had been practicing this business of psychotherapy for about thirty-seven years. As I have mentioned previously, I might be seen as leading a typical prosperous, middleclass, professional life in prosperous Sag Harbor.

While I appeared to be eminently successful and I liked coming off that way, changes were taking place that began to reduce my overblown self- image. These changes had to do with my two teenage adopted children; my relationship with Margaret; and changes in my physical well-being as a result of aging. I can recall two years before casually walking into my local social security office to apply for benefits and being told that not only would I get benefits for myself but money for my two young children as well. As I walked out of the office, I thought to myself, "I'm a senior citizen, all right." For most of my adult life l tended to think of myself as being much younger than I was, but here was concrete and undeniable evidence that I was soon to be sixty-five and no longer a kid. During my late sixties I could see physical differences taking place in me that belied my invincibility. My skin started to wrinkle, my waist was working on a roll of fat, my pate was almost bald; and I could feel it getting more and more difficult for me to do the gym workout that I was used to. Just in terms of physicality alone, life was beginning not to be so kind to me.

Part of what was happening to me from around 2003 onward was that I had to acknowledge and deal with some of the limitations that I had assiduously dodged previously. My son Danny was in deep trouble in his teenage years with a serious

Attention Deficit Disorder that was interfering with his school life and his social behavior. I kept trying to minimize the extent of his problems and reassure Margaret—who had no doubt of the worrisome nature of his immaturity and cognitive difficulties—that most of his adjustment inadequacies could be considered age appropriate. Of course this was the kind of minimization that fit my needs since I was reluctant to devote a good portion of my time to the care of my children… and I was still supported by the feeling that if they really did badly, I could step in and turn things around. Margaret had been pleading with me for years to deal with Danny more effectively. In his last two years of high school he was jeopardizing his graduation by hardly ever studying and by aquainting himself with pills, grass, and alcohol. My attempts to reassure Margaret that Danny would be okay weren't holding up. I couldn't escape the fact that if I didn't get more involved in his life he could get into trouble with the law and not make it through high school. It was up to me to become the principle caretaker of my son. Margaret was not able to relate to Danny well during his difficult teenage years; she so couldn't tolerate his hostile social behavior that their conversations were more inflammatory than reassuring.

I picked up the slack in Margaret's declining effectiveness with Danny, but it took its toll on me. I sensed that I couldn't keep up fulltime teaching, a fulltime practice, and writing this book while raising a troubled teenage son. Ted perennially implored me to give up my professorial position at the college and be available more for my family. He was right, but the fears that I had of giving up the security and pleasure I had as a tenured associate professor kept me from retiring.

It took a car accident in which I broke my femur bone and was laid up four months, for me to finally retire from the college. When I saw that Margaret really took care of me in my convalescence and held the family together—something which I had had some uncertainty about out of my own problems—I felt an affection for and commitment to her and the family, which gave me the push I needed to retire from teaching.

But it was the physical deterioration of my heart valve that brought to the surface how tenuous my omnipotence delusion really was. After recovering from the car accident, I started to notice I was having more and more difficulty breathing when I climbed stairs or walked rapidly. Initially I attributed it to the recovery process and my having been laid up four months without exercising. Yet I knew that something more was happening that was affecting my breathing than just the recovery from the accident. There had been other times in my life when I had not worked out for months and never had this kind of a breathing problem before. My internist referred me for an echocardiogram and a stress test. The echo showed that I was having a leak in the aorta valve of my left ventricle. I consulted a cardiologist who suggested that we wait a year, repeat the echo test and see how much further deterioration took place. This was pretty much normal procedure. The results of the test when I took it a year later were not good. I had the test sent to a renowned diagnostic cardiologist and a week later I met with him in his office. He looked at the earlier and later echo test, and confirmed that over the year my situation had worsened. He concluded by saying, "You need to replace the aorta valve."

I asked, "What do you mean, within a day or two, or a month or two?"

And he replied, "...more like a week or two."

I questioned him whether there was any other procedure that could be used to ameliorate the problem other than replacing the valve. His answer was, "No." Once I agreed to have the operation, he set up an appointment right there on the spot with one of his colleagues at Columbia Presbyterian Hospital in NYC. The doctor he had chosen was well-known as one of the best heart surgeons in the city.

I went down four floors to the heart surgeon's office. I was feeling all the fears and shakiness that one might expect. I spent only something like ten minutes with him but I came away feeling tremendous confidence in him.

Over the next four weeks I experienced a calmness that was strange and unpredictable, considering that I was facing open-heart surgery... even the name of which terrified me. Maybe I was covering over my fear and trembling through this mantle of calmness that was so welcome at this time. It was like me to find one way or another to appear to others as if I were in charge of my emotions and handling this new reality in exemplary fashion. It was also like me to convey a feeling to others that I was handling a scary situation so well that it made them jealous. And obviously I must have had secondary gains in needing to come off this way. But more to the point was my need to find a placebo that I could rely on to get me through the valve surgery. The placebo (or, more accurately, the placebo effect) in this case was not a pill—though I have used that in other less threatening situations; it was convincing myself that I had found the best doctors, the best hospital, and that I was, for my age, in good shape, I had a strong heart in spite of the valve problem, I had an immune system that still worked well. However I managed it, I was calm and serene about the ordeal to come.

I survived the operation, and within a month I was practicing psychotherapy again with a full load of patients. I also resumed work on this book. I had a helpful conversation with Ted towards the end of my recuperation in which I brought up some of the life changes that I was going through in recent years. Parts of this conversation are given below:

Before I proceed, let me say that Ted had moved to California in 2004, a little over a year before my operation. I confess to ambivalence about his move, since along with feeling good for him, I missed him and felt alone and abandoned... much like patients often feel when their therapist retires... or even goes on summer vacation in August.

So, the conversation I am referring to with Ted was a coast-to-coast telephone conversation. At one point in the exchange, I mentioned to Ted my fear that as the operation drew closer I would dissolve into unbearable anxiety; but, amazingly, I continued to feel okay. And that carried through till the operation itself and my recovery. I did, however, confide in him that I had succumbed to the somewhat humorous worry— exacerbated by his move to California—that, if I died, who would be at the funeral?—… and the thought slipped into my mind of Willy Loman's sparsely attended funeral in *Death of a Salesman*. Somehow the words "liked, but not well-liked" came to mind. I rhetorically posed the questions: *Was that Martin Obler as well? Would even his patients show up for his memorial service? And how much of an impact did he really have on them?*

Being a therapist, Ted picked up on my Willy Loman reflection and asked me what I made of it.

"I know what it is about. Just prior to going completely under the anesthesia I had the thought that eighty years down the road, after my grandchildren are gone, I wouldn't be in anyone's consciousness…."

"What a relief."

"… maybe for you, but that is a fate I can't stand. The great man won't be remembered. That's intolerable. That is why I am writing the fucking book."

"Sounds like you're having the Philip Roth syndrome— overwhelmed by bitterness that you can't live forever."

"You're right, I am *The Dying Animal.*"

"Only, dying animals don't have the unbridled pathos for themselves that you have for yourself."

"You seem to think that if someone expresses his self-pity it shows his inferior character. I can accept my inferior character. I never thought otherwise."

"Why is Willy Loman the object of your identification? You make more money in a day than he made in a month?"

"Truthfully, like Willy I am getting tired. Maybe I have too much responsibility and I feel I'm getting two steps behind my own life."

"What is happening to you that you are going from thinking that you are leading the best life possible to leading a mediocre, unappreciated life? One of the most salient features of your life in the last five years is how much responsibility you've taken on and how that has grounded you. Much to your credit."

"Look, I am taking more responsibility for my family, but I feel drained as if it's never-ending. And there is one major difference: my body is starting to break down and I am fully aware that I might die before my kids grow up and start to appreciate their parents."

"What about taking on the responsibility for Danny just because it's the right thing to do and the kid may go down the drain if you're not there for him?"

"That's the assumption I've been making for some time now, but I keep waiting to see whether my efforts are going to make a difference with him. Only it doesn't happen that way. I get a glimmer of hope to be followed by more of the same discouragement. And it wears me down. It's not just Danny. I have problems with my older kids as well. Delmore was out of work and I had to help him get a job and Dina is worried about her kids. This, in addition, to Margaret's battles with Danny. It's gotten to the point where she can't stop herself from criticizing him and he has less and less to do with her. There is no relief in sight. And I can see this going on until I'm in the grave... with R.I.P. carved on my tombstone."

"This too will pass. Danny will be leaving the house and soon Leah will be going off to college and then you and Margaret will start to have more of a life."

"We'll see."

"You're pessimistic."

"It's not about the kids and my family. I'm a good-enough analyst to know that by focusing on my weariness I'm displacing what is frightening me most. All my life I've been living with delusions of omnipotence to feel that I was in control of everything, as if by having this kind of power I could go on living forever and nothing could happen that I couldn't handle, even death. And in the last couple of years I was forced to face that my body is not holding up, I've had a serious operation, and who can predict what's gonna fall apart next? Before you know it I'm dead. The great man's fallibility is coming home and he is afraid that there will be no one at his funeral. Would you fly in from California?"

"If I have enough frequent-flyer miles."

"I figured as much. Look Ted, you're the one that attempted to convince me that I had to stop ignoring Debbie and Phyllis... and I left Sadie and Saul when I was seventeen because I couldn't control the world they lived in. But I see how much I have created a myth around myself to mask my vulnerability, or more accurately, my fear of death. Yet, putting all this out there does give me some relief... as if the game is finally up."

"I think that is a big step forward, but I don't think we've seen the last of the Joker yet."

CHAPTER TWENTY-TWO:
THE CONVENTION

It was good talking to Ted on the phone about some of the stuff in my life, and we usually had a long intimate conversation once a week; but I was looking forward to seeing him in person next month. He was coming in to NYC from California to attend the annual clinical convention sponsored by the same institute that I had trained at and been affiliated with since my post-doctorate. This time around, I was going to make a presentation at the convention. We agreed to go to dinner after I gave my talk.

As to the presentation itself, it would be, predictably, about what I see as some of the particular features of my work that individuate me... using a number of my patients in this book as subject. That is a lot of what I covered at the Convention; but the reader is somewhat familiar with this material, since I've covered it in the book. What I would like to do here is to jump to the question and answer period, where members of the audience ask questions about my work. The questions were of interest to me, and I welcomed the opportunity to stray a little from the case studies to try to get across how I as a therapist think about my work. However, let me first start by giving a couple of paragraphs from my opening remarks:

"I venture to say that at my current age I am a little wiser, more simpatico with and tolerant of my patients, more open to self-criticism, a very tiny bit less sure of myself and less caught up in my need for recognition and adulation... and yet I still resist a hard and determined look at my countertransference problems and assorted personal-development problems—of which the most knowing person would be my wife. And yet if I know anything, it is how I am ensnared by my resistance to what ails me going back to patterns set in childhood. It is not for nought that one of the titles I had consideried for this book was *The Onslaught of Childhood*, a title which gives Freud his due, even though much in the book sets myself off from orthodox Freudian precepts. My devotion to what works, or what I see as needing to be done in the practical world of my patients, has everything to do with my growing up in poverty in Brownsville and coming from a dysfunctionaal family. Controlling my world and paying great attention to practical matters was seen by me as vitally intertwined. It also gives me a private permission to follow my own dictates as a therapist, since I have to assume that I am responsible for figuring out what works and what doesn't, and without that knowledge I may be putting my patients in harm's way.

"My determination and ambition has led me to be more successful in the world than I could have dreamed as a child. But success has also been a good cover to sweep some of my major problems under the rug. While I try to convey to my patients that it is never too late to grow, mature, be more understanding, and make needed changes, I often don't act accordingly, out of my deep-seated pessimism. I have a long way to go. If that reassures the young people here and the older ones like me, that one can make a contribution as a psychotherapist, and be a positive force, even though one is half-baked, then maybe my talk will prove worthwhile."

Questions and Answers

Context: for the first question, having to do with my discussion about Mark. The question is related to my having continued to treat Mark, even though he had gotten too old and wasn't able to do much serious analytic work anymore.

A: Why didn't you gently terminate him if he couldn't use analytic therapy anymore? Therapy is not social work?

M(arty): For most of my career that is the way I would have operated… when therapy has reached its natural conclusion and the patient can't go any further, then it's time to call it quits. However, in recent years, as I've gone through my own medical and family problems, I now look at therapy differently than I did when I was younger. I now see therapy more like a marriage. You know, you go through different phases, and as the years go by, an emotional bond is established, for better or worse, and after long-term therapy, you should do whatever it takes to make things more tolerable for someone like Mark. It's more of a human decision than a therapy decision.

A: But you don't inform him of the decision?

M: One of the reasons why therapy continued for so many years with him was because he wasn't really willing to give up the Oedipal connection to his mother and its transferential manifestations in his relationship with me. He preferred me in the role of the good parent more than an agent of deep change in his life. Essentially, after years of intense therapy—on the issues amenable to change—why couldn't I do this one for him? Wasn't he telling me what he needed by not bringing up some of this stuff himself? Who is to say that part of a therapist's job is not just to be a good friend, a good parent, but also a good pastor as well?

B: You seem pretty lax in your therapeutic approach with Mark, as if therapy is whatever you want it to be. Could you speak to that issue?

M: I'd like to think that therapy is whatever I want it to be, but I can't erase from my mind that there is a patient involved. It's my belief that most practitioners adapt their therapy to the particular needs of the patient with whom they're working. And that is what I did with Mark. I saw from the beginning of my therapy with him that he would respond to treatment more positively if I had a strong personal relationship with him and then used the real friendship as the basis of my right to hammer away at his Oedipal neurosis and fantasies. Pushing him in this direction was my way of looking out for him. Moreover, in some primal way, he and I shared a common bond: we were still sad little boys trying to get from our parents what was not there to be gotten. I see no reason to not indulge Mark by relaxing the impetus to do meaningful therapy at his age and let him off the hook. I think the therapy of recognition, if not change, was a boost to his life and his feeling of having acquired a pretty good understanding of his personality, his lifelong issues, and lived out his passion to thoughtfully examine what made him the way he is... and I suspect that it was one of the bright spots of his life that he had an enduring friendship with his therapist that was not lacking in humor, reflection, and affection. By accepting his need to slow down and prepare for death, I did my share to help him cross that threshhold... and hold his hand in the process. All of which is age appropriate and conforms to my idea of what therapy sometimes needs to turn into, according to the circumstances of what life dictates.

Addendum (to the reader):

I think there are many examples in my work where I handle my feelings of closeness to the patient quite well, and I cite Mark in this category. But I feel a compunction to add more about my countertransference concerns. In my childhood I longed for close family relations that would continue forever, and this need was rarely fulfilled. In my own personal psychoanalysis it became clear that part of the reason that I chose to become a therapist was because I craved, as a child, close familial ties. I recognize that because of my unresolved emotional need for intimacy, I sometimes overstepped the boundaries and kept therapy going when it was appropriate to terminate.

With Mark, my countertransference problem was present but I think I did the right thing. We became good friends, and, as he once put it, when I approached the subject of termination, "Why should I give up therapy with you, when it's the highlight of my week?"

I replied, "Maybe you don't have to." And he came in from time to time for something that might qualify as half friendship and half therapy.

Someone at the convention, when I brought some of this stuff up about my aging patient, Mark, questioned me whether I charged him for these sessions. I said no.

And it does not escape me that I am having a great deal of difficulty moving towards retirement, partially because I don't want to let go of the close relationships with my patients and my personal sense of value that I am doing work that matters. I joke with my friends that I am probably going to die in the office with my last words to my patient, being, "I'll see you next week."

Questions and Answers

Context: My next patient, under discussion, is Cora. Cora suffered from a borderline personality disorder with narcissistic features. Her parents lived together but were incompatible; as a result she and her brother endured a lifelong unhappiness in that they reproduced in their respective marriages a similar lack of intimacy and trust. Cora identified strongly with her mother and consequently took on the mother's burden of feeling emotionally and psychologically abused by her husband.

As her therapist, I chose to center on Cora's problems with her husband and people in general rather than go with the modern-day trend to focus on the neurological and characterological (the latter being more biologically induced than induced by personal relationships).

It is sometimes said that neurotics build castles in the air while psychotics live in them. I would say that Cora's personality disorder was somewhere in between… you might say she was in the front door of the castle.

Contrary to Mark, Cora was unable to form a long-lasting connection with me in therapy. Even though Mark only went so far in resolving his core issues in therapy, he was able to form a meaningful working relationship and an ongoing close bond with me. With Cora, it was only in the beginning stages of therapy, where I was very supportive of her, that she was cooperative and enthusiastic about therapy. Once I started to confront her with the deeper issues of her defensive behavior, she turned me into another male who let her down and couldn't be counted on. This kind of abrupt transformation in which a patient initially starts out highly enthusiastic about therapy but over time becomes disenchanted and distrusting is not unusual for therapists to encounter with such patients. Cora doesn't trust anyone. She seems to have an entrenched flaw that prevents her from seeing people as having the same needs and requirements as she does. Not for nothing, professionals in the field have had great difficulty in coming up with treatment strategies that have proven successful with personality disorders. It is hard, consequently, to establish a truly working relationship with this kind of patient; they resist the give and take that is essential to therapy. Their egocentricity stands in the way.

A: You say that borderline and narcissistic personality disorders are not successfully treated with talk therapy. So what was different about your strategy with her and what did you hope to accomplish?

M: It took me a while to diagnose her accurately, but once I came to the conclusion that she was borderline and extremely narcissistic, I had to formulate limited goals of what therapy could do for her. I decided that individual therapy could help her gain insight into her role in creating problems with her husband, and could increase her social skills and responsiveness to others—since people with borderline and personality disorders most often lack empathy in their interaction with people. I chose to make this concern the central focus of her treatment. Initially some progress in establishing a closer connection with her husband and friends actually occurred; however it proved to be short-lived and in some cases reversed. This is an inevitable problem with borderline personalities because their problems are so deep-rooted, stemming from early childhood... that whatever goes wrong in their relationship with others invariably ends with their blaming the other person for being at fault and never being able to take responsibility for their contribution to the difficulty. It is as if they are fixated at the age of three and that's the way a child of that age sees the world. And that is what has taken place with Cora. Her marriage started disintegrating; she fell into blaming her husband for their economic difficulties and felt no empathy for him when he was laid off from his job. When I pointed out to her that her husband was not at fault for having been laid off and that she was largely responsible for their money problems because of her need to overspend, she turned on me with rage. Not long afterward, she informed me that she was done with therapy.

B: I have a hypothetical question to ask you, but I really would like you to answer it. My question is if another Cora type came to you for therapy, would you take her on, knowing what you do?

M: Now there is a question that gets right down to business, even if it is hypothetical. A good question poses a vital challenge for the recipient, or an opportunity to bring forth something that the recipient wants to bring out... but may not have been entirely formed in his mind. So I hope my answer will do justice to your question.

Let me say, that my answer is mixed... that it contains a lot of ambivalence. It's like so much in life that is shrouded with uncertainty and ambiguity. Cora, both in terms of looks and personality, is an attractive lady: she easily draws people to her. Predictably, Cora reversed her position towards me when I began to stop playing into her game: when I rightly pointed out things critical of her for the purposes of therapy, she would show her displeasure by attacking me and letting me know how disappointed she was in me. After many months battling with her, I found her a turnnoff. You might say that this was something a therapist had to guard against. But it was not her anger and dismissal of me that caused me to tire of her; it was her unwillingness to see the direction I was trying to take in the therapy and the knowledge that she was going to make me pay by leaving therapy. In her mind, I had only one way to go and that was to be entirely supportive of her. If I acceded to this cardboard image of hers, little of major substance would occur.

It is very hard to reach such an ego-driven patient since I as therapist now became the enemy rather than the ally. I used the word *predictably* some seconds ago because she overinflated my value when I became her advocate and deflated my value when I did not ride along with her blaming her husband for everything that was wrong between them.

In the end she left treatment, preferring to believe that I was the problem not her. She refused to take responsibility for herself. The ambivalence I feel as to whether I would take on another Cora is best answered: it depends on how good I am feeling about myself, knowing what I know. If I am feeling inadequate and needed the gratification of my early work with her, I probably would take her on; if I were older and wiser, and understood the limitations of what could be accomplished with such an intransigent and willful patient as Cora, I would not agree to taking her on. At this stage of my professional career, I also recognize that there are therapists who are better equipped than I am to integrate the new neuroscience strategies with a psycholgical approach. I hope I would refer this kind of patient to them.

C: So much of what you have to say about your patients has to do with how you're feeling about them... or how they make you feel about them. One of the advantages of the traditional

Freudian and post-Freudian approach to working with patients is the adherence to the idea of the psychotherapist remaining neutral. Part of this approach depends on the therapist maintaining an objective stance. The way you describe your work with Mark and Cora, a lot hangs on your feelings about them; in other words, you are the central figure as opposed to the patient. Is this a liability?

M: What you bring up has been an issue that has been plaguing me for most of my career. I can recall for years struggling with myself over whether my resistance to taking on the neutrality role meant that I had serious deficiencies as a therapist. In recent years, I lean more and more to the object relations school of thought which puts emphasis on the countertransference issues of the therapist and utilizing it effectively as part of the patient's treatment. In my opinion, it is one of the most effective agents for change that therapy offers. However, with the object relations school of thinking, it is important for the therapist to disclose his personality and flaws, too, not just the patient. The strict Freudians contend that the blank slate is the best way to bring about the countertransference since it allows the patient to make the therapist into whomever she needs him to be. From my experience, I don't quite go along with this. I tend to think if I push the patient off her comfort zone, by insisting that she work on the stuff that she would rather avoid, she will of her own make me into the person or persons that are key figures in her life. That transformation, you might call it, will happen because I am pressing her in a way that will call forth other people in her life. But Cora would not tolerate this kind of a ride if it got bumpy, which it did ultimately get.

Addendum:

On the side of non-neutrality, Cora brought out in me my family dynamics... and it was my subjective response to her that enabled her to change what little she could change. When I repeatedly pointed out to her that I couldn't stand her manipulation and selfishness, I liked to think that it helped her to gain some slight insight into what her self-preoccupation made other people feel. But this didn't change her resistance to treatment. Or didn't cause me to feel less discouraged about my inability to fix in her what I couldn't fix in my own family.

A question I often encounter has to do with wheather the therapy is about the therapist or the patient. The incentive behind the question implies I am occupying too much space in the conversation between me and the patient, thereby putting my needs on the same footing as the patient's.

However, the thought that comes to mind is of a different nature: It leads me to remind you that therapists, like all of us, remain children at heart.

Questions and Answers

Context: I proceeded at the convention to describe my work with Warren, amply conveying a good part of what the reader already knows about him.

Warren suffers from a bipolar disorder with psychotic features that included bouts of paranoia, ideation of reference, and delusional thought processes.

I have come to think that working with Warren will prove to be a lifelong proposition, which makes treating him highly impractical and pretty kooky. It's hard to imagine that there are more than a few practitioners, if that, working with this kind of patient as I am doing.

A: Under the conditions you're describing what would be the incentive to work with a 'lifelong' patient like Warren?

M: The only incentive I can think of is that it offers a lifetime annuity. Kidding aside, my incentive is that I have made a big difference in his life. And I have done this by controlling his life and doing real therapeutic work with him—even though, he will always be a bipolar, and subject to extreme mental distortions. But to me, treatment means just that, not maintenance. And I do with Warren a lot of what I do with most of my patients—involving breaking down their defensive postures... so that they have some degree of freedom of choice in their responses to life and are not locked in to unproductive, predetermined, repetitive ways of dealing with the issues in their life. With Warren, however, I have to crank up exponentially the control that I exert in treating him. And crank down my expectations. He is who he is, and can only do so much.

With Warren there is no other way to break down his resistance unless some of the time you tell him the truth even if it temporarily humiliates him. What are the choices? To indulge him in his delusions or hold his hand and tell him he's a lovely human being? But none of this will do the job. To be honest, it doesn't hurt for me to sometimes get off some of my aggression towards Warren, since he can be exasperating and unappreciative of the enormous effort I make on his behalf.

Let me tell this little anecdote about Warren's self-preoccupation.

He recently came into a session, and I announced to him that I had had an exhaustive day with patients, and I hoped he wouldn't mind if I made myself a cup of coffee in the kitchen, and I offered to make a cup for him as well. He responded indignantly, saying: "Can't you wait until after the session? it's cutting into my time." I blew my top: "I can't believe this. How many times have I pointed out to you that Medicare only covers 45 minutes of your session and I have given you a full hour for 25 years and, in addition, I spend almost an hour-and-a-half each week, of my time, without getting paid for it discussing with your psychopharmacologist your medication regimen... not to speak of your contacting me numerous times during the week, in one crisis or another, the time for which I don't charge you. And here you are begrudging me a fucking cup of coffee that I need to be more effective in your session. Don't you think that's just a tiny bit over the top? Warren answered, to placate me: "I was just fooling around, don't get so huffy-puffy."

But the important thing in all of this, and this goes to the very center of the patient-therapist relationship, the reason I can be so hard on him is he knows how much I care for him and how much I am invested in seeing him do well. It's all about the foundation you establish with a patient. In the end, I believe in Warren... believe that he can take what I'm saying and make some use of it.

B: How is your approach replicable in the field? From your account of your work with this patient, you seem to be saying that the amount of time, effort, and energy you put into your treatment of him was almost a fulltime proposition. You need to be in control of every aspect of his life and you have to be on-call twenty hours a day, and, as you mentioned to him, you're underpaid. It is as if in administering to him, you have become a kind of psychological life-support-machine. I certainly applaud your willingness to do it; and, in your estimation, it appears to be working. However, when is he going to be able to begin life on his own? And what happens if you retire and move to California?

M: I guess he'll have to move to Los Angeles. I made a decision early on to control him and make him dependent on me, as the best hope for anything resembling normalcy in his life... and the best hope against insanity. Better dependency than insanity. I had to do this because if I left him alone, with his distortions and delusions, it would not be long before he lost it. It is my conviction that the best way for him to function semi-normally was to control his behavior, confront him with his perversions of reality, and model for him appropriate responses and behavior... as a good parent would. Eventually some of these changes that I modeled have been absorbed by him and take on a functional autonomy of their own.

Only that is looking at my work with him from the positive side; seen from the negative side, I have to face up to the fact that a lot of Warren's dysfunctional behavior and thinking was not amenable to change and I need to constantly be there to keep him grounded. And sometimes that meant forcing my opinions on him... or, in effect, beating him down. In answer to your first question, Is my treatment method replicable? I would say yes, providing the therapist is willing to get involved with him, as I did? Practically speaking, it's not that replicable because few therapists would be willing to go that route. I'm the abnormal one. My philosophy is you do what it takes; and with most of my patients, it doesn't take anywhere near this kind of superhuman effort. I feel very good working with Warren, knowing how much improvement he has made and factoring in the reduced expectations of what he can accomplish. And it is hard for me to describe the sanguine feelings I have when I think about his coming home to his wife for the last six or seven years as opposed to vegetating alone in a tiny, shabby apartment, mired in obsessional thoughts. As for your question about whether he will ever be able to begin life on his own, I'd say I don't know, it depends on a lot of things I can't predict; but that he has been able to live something of a normal life, at all, means a lot to me. And, finally, your question, What if I move to California? That's something that's hard for me to think about. As they say in AA meetings, take it one step at a time.

Addendum:

A patient like Warren represents to me my connection to my own family... that I had abandoned in early adulthood. During my first and second personal analysis, I continuously dealt with the reality that a large part of why I became a therapist and took on psychotic patients had to do with my unconscious feelings of guilt and betrayal that I left my family behind, especially my sister Rachel—I never did try to find out what happened to her.... I also had no interest in my grandmother once they dragged her off to the looney bin. And I had a less-than-perfunctory relationship with my sisters Debbie and Phyllis, and just went through the motions of being involved with my parents when they were aging. One doesn't abandon one's family in the way I did without it having a major effect on one. I'm pretty sure that I took on patients like Warren, whose level of psychosis is so severe that most therapists wouldn't work with them, in order to make up for ignoring my family.

One question I have to ask myself is, Why did I invest so much in him? I now know that it was my way of trying to ward off a major fear of mine. No matter how successful I have become I live with the fear that I could be as crazy as the people who brought me up… if I can save Warren then in some convoluted way, I might not succumb to the family heredity. How can I ever escape the fear when there is madness in the family, that it is waiting for me? I continue to worry about this no matter how illogical and irrational it may seem, given how strong and practical a person I am. I worked this through in my personal therapy quite intellectually, but the emotional gut fear never went away. In my case, it got sublimated into working with a few patients like Warren. In some ways, he is my deserved cross to bear.

Questions and Answers

Context: Esther, like Warrren (who got me to see her) suffered from a bipolar disorder, but her primary symptoms included, typically, periods of severe depression, which afflicted her so badly that she was barely able to function. Although she is bipolar, Esther rarely had bouts of mania and wasn't generally delusional. She had never grown emotionally or psychologically independent, and had spent most of her life relying on her family—much like a child—and subsequently the men with whom she lived. It was only after her shock treatment that she became somewhat more independent and reversed roles with her caretakers. I am choosing to pick up Esther's story from after she left the hospital, since it takes me further into the mysteries of patient development that are an important aspect of therapeutic possibilities.

Esther, eventually as the reader knows, booted the derelict—the homeless person she had met in the hospital—out of her apartment, but as I anticipated it wasn't too long before she found another lover, who was as dilapidated and psychologically crippled as the previous one. The funny thing about this new involvement was that she and he were so miserable that their dual misery tended to work for them. At least they had each other. As she often said to me: "I can't be alone. At this point in my life, taking care of a man is the only reason for living I have."

A: Something that is troubling to me is how you deal with Esther's condition, which involves depression, dependency, occasional bouts of mania, and her childlike behavior. Doesn't the sheer weight of her problems bring you down... as it might with any therapist encountering this severity of illness? I know, I would worry about getting too caught up in her hopelessness.

M: I like what you're saying about Esther living in psychological extremes; the way I look at it is that the duality of craziness and non-craziness exists in all of us, but that Esther, and obviously Warren too, are on the high end of the spectrum. With their form of rampant bipolarity and its debilitating characteristics, the learning curve is so poor that it takes nearly a lifetime to make a modicum of progress. There is no point talking about their overcoming their mental problems. They're crazy and they're non-crazy, and I can't say it better than that. As for your specific question, I myself have a long history of family depression and I almost take it for granted. I can't speak for other therapists. But I will say that if you're not driven to work with someone like Esther, you're better of not doing it.

As to how I deal with the back and forth of their mental states and does it leave me frustrated... and make me crazy too, as if I get pulled into their madness, what comes to mind is something Robert Lindner talked about in his classic work *The Fifty Minute Hour*. He describes his years of frustration in working with a schizophrenic patient who was half the time crazy and half the time sane. And he explained that it took him years to realize that if he were going to be able to help him, he would have to enter his world and experience it in the way his patient did. That sounds a lot easier to do than it actually is, I think I could safely say.

In talking about Warren and Esther's mental state, I should mention that a basic condition that they suffered from was depression. There is a duality in the experience of depression that is often overlooked in our profession... that depression can be a good thing or a bad thing. For Esther and Warren, who are largely dysfunctional people, it is a bad thing—they can't use depression in any kind of productive way because they can't learn from it and it erodes their life. Before I got into therapy with them, they were using only anti-depressants and antipsychotics as their main form of treatment. I tried to do serious therapy with them and lowered considerably their dosage of medication. And they felt good that their therapy consisted of more than just pill-popping. A large part of what I did with them was to help them to learn to manage their depression despite life's hardships. Let's face it, depression is a part of life and there is no escaping it. Even you normal suckers in the audience are depressed. And I'm getting depressed just looking at you, not to speak of making this presentation.

[Luckily for me, the audience found the humor in my last two sentences and I was not jeered at... in fact people clapped and laughed. I told them: I will field one more question, if any brave soul will risk asking it, having seen what a disagreeable person I can be.]

B: (a female student): I'll take my chances. I like you in spite of yourself.

[More, spirited laughter.]

M: You seem to be a most generous young woman. Thank you. What might be your question?

B: The question is less affable. You see, I am at a loss as to how you could allow such a psychotic and depressed person as Esther make decisions about whom she's going to live with, when clearly the person of choice is even more derailed than she is. And you're a therapist who prides himself at how completely in control he is in handling the lives of patients like Warren and Esther. Yet when it comes to what most anyone would conceive as a horribly doomed decision that she makes, you seem to think it's a good idea. What about that?

M: A good question, and asks me to explain something that warrants further comment. I welcome the opportunity to do so. However, from my point of view the answer I am going to give reflects some of the complications and other considerations involving my work with Esther that de-simplify my thinking about the step Esther wishes to take. Try to bear with me.

As I've already indicated when Esther planned to leave the hospital, I strongly tried to dissuade her from what she was about to do, but she was adamant that she was going to live with this first derelict no matter what I did. But I could see that she seemed stronger and more together than I had seen her for years, so instead of fighting her I decided to go along with it and see how it panned out. I didn't have any plan to go along with it indefinitely, if it proved, as I expected it would, to lead to a dead end. When things disintegrated, she got rid of him, so that showed progress on her part. She didn't wait till the bitter end. In my work with her before she went into the hospital, I had assembled a supportive cast for her, I tried to do confrontational therapy, I did some behavior modification, and other type interventions; this approach met with limited success for a period of time... but always the depression and her feelings of futility reasserted itself. ECT was my last resort. But she only started to pick up her spirits, and make more noticeable headway with her despair and suicidal ideation, after she left the hospital and began living with the boyfriend. Ever since, it hasn't been a smooth track, it's been up and down. However the overall trend has been that her depression has lessened, she's taking better care of herself and is less dependent on other people to take care of her. I can't help feeling that, even though I gave up on her at one point, the kind of therapy I was doing with her—instead of the usual handholding and pill-pushing—has benefitted her in rather dramatic fashion.

The thing about working with Esther that I enjoy most is those moments when she comes out of her nightmarish regression and sees how chaotic and unfulfilling her life has been... in those moments she displays such a nice sense of humor and humility that all the hard work I've put in has been worth it.

I guess I should mention in discussing the feelings I have about Esther, the terrible mixture of sadness and hope I feel when she's in the room with me. She has such a lovely face, and such a beaten-down face, she's so fragile a person and has experienced such depths of torment and defeat... and I have been a part of moving her towards seeing herself as she is, and building on that self-understanding. In some ways I'm like that Burt Lancaster bearer of hope in the play/movie *The Rainmaker.* I see something beautiful in her, and I try to nourish that, not by building dreams, as the rainmaker did with the Katherine Hepburn character, but by getting her to shed some of the defenses that buttress her psychotic features and ward off contact with her innermost self. I can't help but feel I've been a good person in her life... and that she has allowed me to be that leaves me indebted to her. Esther has not opted to give up on her life—though she is tempted to do so—and has participated in a struggle to be a connected person and lead a quasi-normal life. She has heard those chords. That is no small accomplishment for her in these mean years that she has been living through. She took a chance by not listening to me and by hooking up with the two down-and-out men, first with one and then, when that didn't work out, another—it was her fling. I went along with it. What can I say? I should have known better… known what better? She made a foolhardy bid to take over her life. So? Isn't that, possibly, therapy, too? even repeating her mistake in the future? Isn't repetition part of the talk therapy engine? The patient saying over and over again what isn't working for her, until she herself gets tired of hearing it? And when does it become necessary to turn talk into action in the living of life, even for a borderline person like Esther… even at the risk of doing great harm to herself. I didn't stop her from taking the risk and in so doing I took a risk. So? And all in all, I think Esther has benefited from taking charge of her life the way she did.

So? Where does this lead me? where does it leave Esther? I have no easy answers.

Addendum:

In treating Esther, I took a chance in not unquestionably opposing her strong wish to be with two men who had plenty wrong with them. One of the things that influenced my decision is whether I should focus on what she can't do or what she can do. I know that what she can't do relates to her bipolar illness and negates her capacity as a person to make good decisions for herself. But what is it she can do? Maybe not entirely, but with some degree of forward movement. Well, she can determine how her life imposes on her, that is, what makes it unbearable and what gives her hope. Without someone to care about and share her life with, she is not sure she wants to continue to live, her depression is that incapacitating. She is willing to try to make an impossible situation work rather than continue a hollow existence. She is not entirely without resources to learn from her mistrials and debacles with the men she has chosen. Maybe she will never be able to get it right. All I can tell you is that Esther seems better off at this moment than simply living alone or with her family. Will it all come crashing down? Good chance of it. But there is also a little chance that she can do more, in picking herself up after a fall, than I, in my previous dismissive feelings about her potential to live life, made room for. Maybe there is something to be said for giving Esther her shot. Maybe one of the things that she can do, is take her shot. That is something. What is the alternative? For her to wait to find the right man? the right situation? If you go with that approach, you might not be giving Esther enough credit for her capacity to screw up... to the end that there is no right choice. It's something to think about, is it not? If I thought Esther could live without a man in her life, and make a fairly good go of it, I would push her hard to do so. But I don't see that happening. Better to see what she can do on her own, with my support and guidance. Life choices are shadowy things. How many people do you know who are with a great person for them and seem content, or happy, living their life?—alone or with somebody? How many people, who are not bipolars, totter from day to day? Nothing is simple, we know that.

I ended my convention presentation with some final thoughts about my experience as a therapist, which I will limit, for the purposes of this book to the following excerpt:

"... I see with some finality, as I get older, what I could and couldn't do. I could get Warren married much to his health and benefit, but I would never be able to make him sane to the extent that I don't have to worry about him on a daily basis.

"And although I couldn't do too much to help Mark free himself from the fierce grip of his Oedipal fantasies and drives, I did a good job of getting him to stay in his marriage in a way that improved his life, such that as he began to seriously deteriorate with age, he was able to sustain himself fairly well. Some of this I attribute to his having established a strong relationship with his wife, with friends, and with me.

"And with Cora, I would say she mellowed with age and has in fact become a more understanding and less self-absorbed individual. Whether this was due to the psychopharmacologist she saw after she stopped our sessions or remnants of my work with her, or perhaps just aging—who knows? Anyhow, Cora does keep in touch and now looks back with sadness that she didn't continue therapy.

"With Esther, I've nothing to add here.

"About me, a brief comment: as I am aging, I look at myself with a similar eye to the way I look at my patients: I feel strongly the divide of what can and can't be done in my own life. I still cling to the sentiment of living a useful and productive life, but my problems mount and so does my feeling of being less sure of myself... reduced are the days when I regaled in being the hotshot therapist who was on top of his game. In one area, however, I have managed to meet my expectations quite handily and that is financially. I can say that I live a very comfortable, middleclass life in terms of bucks, something that was not a foregone conclusion when I was growing up.

"Lastly, I wouldn't want to end my talk without heartily thanking you all for being here. I couldn't ask for a better audience."

Thus ends my presentation at the convention. If I were to pick up on anything to move me forward, related to my talk, it would be my use of the word 'so?' in my reflections about Esther. So? What I meant to convey in my use of this word is how up in the air I am feeling about my life, practice, and the whole works at this time... and it serves as an apt bridge to BOOK IV.

BOOK IV

CHAPTER TWENTY-THREE:
"WHAT'S THE BIG DEAL?"

I saw Ted in my New York City apartment a few days after the convention ended, and I asked him his thoughts about my presentation.

Ted said, "You did a good job. You weren't crapping around."

I asked him, "What's that mean?"

He replied, "There aren't too many professionals in our field who would be as open and forthright as you were."

I answered, "I like shaking things up. I can't resist the opportunity to be controversial... even if it involves exposing my own flaws."

Ted said, "It's the 'imp of the perverse' in you. That's Edgar Allan Poe's term for the need in man to do the opposite of what is expected of him... so if I say you're noble, you have to show me you're ignoble. Dostoevsky, too, was taken with that impulse in man to shock and disrupt and parade his failings... and some of his most fallen characters have a great love of confessing how despicable they are."

I replied, "I like that phrase 'the imp of the perverse.' And I do feel that imp egging me on, to shock people and get attention."

Ted added, "It's good you see that about yourself; I'd say the imp in you is totally on the loose."

"I seem to enjoy disturbing people with my brash personality. And a lot of people don't like me on that basis. Remember Dan's friends couldn't stand me. They thought I was the ultimate philistine. But let's move on. There is something that occurred to me about my presentation that has bothered me."

"Do say...," Ted responded.

I continued, "I was thinking about the patients I selected to present at the convention, all of whom had severely-damaged childhoods; there are, believe it or not, a few of my patients whose childhood was more benign. Why didn't I include at least one of them?—and the same goes for the book."

Ted said, "... cause you're trying to work through something."

"Childhood," I offered.

Ted asked dutifully (professionally): "What comes to mind?"

I said, "Sadie,... Sadie and her daughter-in-law and baby. More and more, I find myself dwelling on patients with childhoods that parallel my own... and I can't seem to get away from them."

Ted rejoined, "Yup, yup, yup. For you and me and nine-tenths of our patients there is no getting away from the past."

"Exactly," I seconded.

This quick conversation which took place with Ted eventually led me into telling him the story of my session, a day ago, with Sadie, Jenny and her infant daughter. Only it is easier for me to recount it to the reader directly (with the inclusion of substantial dialogue between Sadie, Jenny, and me), than by way of filtering it through Ted... then I will relay the discussion Ted and I had, later, at a restaurant.

It came as a surprise to me that my patient Sadie, whom I had been treating for three years, had brought in her daughter-in-law and two-month-old granddaughter into session with her. I figured that the purpose of their coming in together was to discuss conflicts that both of them were having with Sadie's son, Herman.

I asked Sadie why she hadn't informed me in advance that she intended to bring in Jenny.

"Suddenly, I have to call you and let you know who I am bringing in and not bringing in. What's the big deal? When I brought my husband, Irwin, you never asked me why I brought him in, I just brought him. You're making a big *megillah* out of nothing."

"Well, Sadie, it might have been helpful to me if you had let me know in advance why you're bringing Jenny in, not only out of courtesy to me, but so that I could have some idea of what the difficulty is and, thus, know what I'm being asked to do."

"I'm sure you will find what's best to do, in this situation. I am having a lot of *tsuris* with my son, Herman. It's bad enough that he's driving me *meshuga*, but he's driving her [his wife] more *meshuga*."

"Jenny, maybe you can tell me a little bit about what your mother-in-law is talking about."

"This comes as news to you? I thought that she was always telling you about the terrible marriage I'm in with her son."

"She mentioned it. Maybe it would be good, Jenny, if you told me about what you think it would be helpful for me to know about your marriage."

[After I said that, Jennie had moved the baby off her shoulder to alongside her on the couch, so she could clasp her mother-in-law's hand affectionately. She then reached with the other hand into her purse and picked up a pacifier, thrusting it into the baby's mouth.]

"I'm going to tell you something, Dr. Obler: he's such a selfish animal—ask her, his mother—he's sick. All he thinks about is himself, not me, not his baby, and not this wonderful woman sitting next to me. She's more of a mother to me than my own mother. And I'm going to tell you something, I'm going to whisper and not a soul should know what a *shanda* [shame] he brought me. When I breast feed the baby he gets hard, his dick gets hard, and he wants to screw me."

"What do you do?"

"He sticks it in my mouth, and it hurts my gums. Tell him, tell Dr. Obler, what pain I had."

"It's hard for me to believe, Dr. Obler, that my son turned out this way. I should have listened to you, you warned me, but who would believe that this little fuck... I mean my boy Herman... would treat his wife and his mother so awfully? You warned me, didn't you?"

"How did I warn you?"

"You told me he was going to turn out like his sick father, my first husband, if I wasn't careful with him. You told me that I was spoiling him rotten... paying him off by giving him everything he wanted as a way of getting him to love me."

"Sadie, I want to remind you that I also told you that that is what you do with people. You get everybody... your first husband, your second husband... to buy you everything you want before you give your love to them... Does it ring a bell, Sadie?"

"I'm not like that, Dr. Obler, you never said that about me. I love everybody, I give to everybody."

"She does... she does, she's the most wonderful woman I ever met. I wish she was my mother and I was her daughter."

"It seems to me, Jenny, that's already happening."

"Dr. Obler, I love Jenny as if she was my daughter; she treats me a lot better than that useless son of mine."

"Jenny, I don't want to interrupt the flow of this important conversation, but are you aware that your baby is crying and may be hungry?"

"She's always crying. I have to feed her every two hours. She's always hungry and demanding attention, just like her father. Dr. Obler, let me ask you, 'Do you think I've done a good job with my baby... that I'm a good mother?'"

"Jenny, how can I know that? I just met you and the baby fifteen minutes ago."

"I understand, I understand. Now look, I'll show you what I've done with my daughter. She's already crawling and she's only four months old. Here, I am putting her on the floor, and watch how she moves her legs back and forth."

"*Gut szdankin*, is this not a pearl of a mother? Look what she does for her child."

"I don't want to strip away both of your illusions, but infants don't start crawling before they're six or so months old. Did you ever hear that a baby has to build up its body before it can crawl? It takes a while before they start crawling."

"Maybe my daughter is really special... she'll be crawling before any of the other babies."

"Tell me, Jenny, is ignoring your daughter on the floor the way your mother and father treated you when you were a baby?"

"No, it was when I was a young girl. But I don't wanna talk about that. If you knew what they did to me [Jenny turned towards Sadie, curled up, put her head in her mother-in-law's lap, and started to cry and breath in short gasps] you would pity me. Tell him, *mammala*, tell him what he did. She's the only one that knows. Tell him what he did and how my mother just stood by watching."

"I can't talk about that... it's bad, it's horrible."

"As bad as what Herman did to her?"

"Worse, it was worse than what he did to me. That's why I pull my hair out all the time. What's the word for that?... I forget what my psychiatrist calls it?"

"Trichotillomania... you mentioned your psychiatrist?"

"Yeah, I've been on medication for years... with a lot of psychiatrists."

"What are you on now?"

"Well, I was on Wellbutrin, but that didn't do too good. Right now I'm on Paxil, and my doctor just upped my dosage to 37.5 milligrams. That's the highest dosage, isn't it?"

"... not quite. Some people go as high as 50 or 60 milligrams, depending on their psychiatric condition. What is your psychiatric condition?"

"Some doctors said I was schizophrenic, but I didn't think so. I was just a mixed-up product of those two son-of-a-bitch parents of mine."

"Jenny, you seem to have gotten over your crying spell… while you were alluding to what your father did to you."

"Oh, she's such a strong girl."

"Wait a minute, Sadie. I want to hear what her father did to her."

"I don't want to talk about what he did to me."

"Was it sexual?"

"No, but he wanted that, too. He would pull my hair and hit me in front of my mother. And she wouldn't do a thing about it."

"Did you have any sense of why your father was hurting you? Are you scared that Herman might hurt you, too?"

"Herman? I'd bend him over my knee and break him in two, that little nothing."

"The baby's crying, Jenny. Give her something, feed her, get her off the floor."

"Come here my *shainkite*… let me hold you. Mommy loves you. Oy, oy, oy… what a beauty."

"You really love your daughter, don't you, Jenny?"

"Oh, yes, I do. I didn't want her at first. I only did it for him."

"Why did you do it for him?"

"He said that he'll marry me if I had the baby, and his mother would give us a lot of money. That's all he cares about, money. Ask Sadie, he didn't have anything to do with her until she came up with the down payment on the co-op we're living in now."

"A child should love his mother… not for money but just because she's his mother."

"Sadie, let me ask you something. Why didn't you bring this up in therapy? And if you thought it was wrong to get love in exchange for money, why did you give him the money?"

"It was so embarrassing, I can't begin to tell you. But I couldn't take it anymore. It hurt me so much that he wouldn't talk to me. You know what it's like for a mother to have a son who isn't talking to her?"

"Do you know what it's like to have a relationship with any man that isn't based on money? You get rid of the first husband because the second husband offered you more money. Where did you think Herman got his values from?"

"Herman's father was a crazy pig."

"Would you have stayed with him, if he offered you more?"

"I went with my second husband for more than just money. He treats me well. That's how a man should be with a woman... treat her well."

"Don't think your husband, Herschel, is such an angel. He's come on to me, you know."

"Is that true, Sadie? Herschel came on to Jenny?"

"She's upset... she's upset... she misunderstands things... Herschel doesn't even come on to me."

"I see. Listen, I think, Jenny, your baby's hungry. Do you want to take her down the hall, to the room on the left, and feed her?"

There is no doubt in my mind that the reason I was so caught up in Jenny's failure to pick her baby up off the floor and feed her when she was hungry and upset, had everything to do with my identification with the child. Since my baby memories have faded from consciousness, I am dependent on my imagination to recreate what it must have been like for me to be an infant, like Jenny's baby, helpless and at the mercy of these narcissistic, irresponsible, loopy primary caretakers... whether we are talking about Sadie and Jenny or my sister Debbie. In my imagination, I can see myself as an infant sitting on the living room floor, needy and hungry... and ignored... and feeling that in the tensions surrounding me I am helpless to make myself seen. It doesn't take much to fathom why, when I got older, that I developed the tools and the will to never allow anyone to harmfully have power and control of me. I would make sure that people needed me more than I needed them. And when I managed to get free of my family, I pretty much didn't look back. My attitude was that I didn't need them anymore—which of course is far from the truth—and I didn't owe anyone anything.

Some hours and a few therapy sessions later, I left my office and proceeded east to meet up with Ted at a small restaurant on Second Avenue and Twelfth Street called Little Poland. I felt a sense of relief at having finished my sessions for the day; it brought back a tinge of the relief I often experienced on leaving the apartment in Brooklyn at about thirteen years old. On this evening, as I was walking in the neighborhood, I was nostalgically recalling the smell of dill pickles and sauerkraut from the store next to our building. The scent would instantly instill in me a feeling that I was free and out in the world, not confined in the oppressive environment of home.

On entering the restaurant, I spotted Ted talking to a young, pretty, blonde, blue-eyed Polish waitress who was standing at his table. My spirits lifted the moment I saw him, as they did in the old days when I would see my buddies hanging out on the street corner flirting with the young *maidels*. After greeting Ted and the waitress, I deposited myself on the other side of the booth from him and did some flirting with her, asking her to run away with me and telling her that I have all this money that I don't know what to do with. This was a theme in my conversations with her. It was just good fun, since we were both married. On a more sober note, I ordered my favorite lamb-shank soup, and an egg salad sandwich on challah bread; Ted ordered his favorite borscht soup with a side order of a boiled potato, and a tuna fish sandwich on rye. Ted could put a lot of food away and was thin as a rod. Before the soup arrived I resumed my pressing thoughts about Sadie and Jenny. Most of what I was saying had to do with my identification with the infant, who was dependent on such self-centered, ignorant caretakers. And I speculated on how seriously she would be burdened in her future life by her dependency at such an early age on two such nincompoops.

Ted was irked and impatient with what I was telling him.

"What puzzles me about you is that as good a therapist as you are, and what a wonderful rare bird you are in the profession, you seem not to be hugely put off by your transgression of basic commonsensical boundaries, as if it really doesn't matter."

"*Famished in da kup*, you could say."

"How quaint. You're a therapist and you're making fun of Sadie and Jenny and putting them down. They're not your family. Sadie is not Debbie."

"Sadie represents to me the worst of my family. I can't help at times to want to obliterate her because I feel such impotence that I can't do anything to change her. Especially when I see that little baby who can't even get her mother to pick her up. In those moments Jenny and Sadie get to me, and I become that furious child that just wanted to shut out his whole family. Only I couldn't say much as a child because I needed my family to survive. I was always wrestling with that dependent child in me; and out of that sense of powerlessness, I grew into a young adult that had the belief that he could always change anything and control everything. But, when I deal with people like Sadie and Jenny I get frustrated at not being able to make a dent in their narcissism... so I make fun of them, and ridicule them, and take my frustration out on them. It was the very thing I couldn't do with my family as a small child."

"But Jenny and Sadie are sad, pathetic people. I feel for them... and they come for help to you because their life is haphazard and all screwed up."

"I feel that too. And I also know that by being tough and directive with Sadie I help her to make some changes. It's not for nothing that she brought her daughter-in-law to see me."

"Marty, you are in a class all by yourself with this kind of patient; but there are some things that you need to control in yourself. And you don't like hearing that."

"Maybe I'm not as *perfect* as you are."

"I appreciate the *dig*."

"Look, you would have been frustrated like me, if you had to deal with the baby and the two of them. What got me when they came to see me was the way they ignored the baby and the damage they were doing to her... and could only think about their own narcissistic needs. My thoughts were about the child in that session. What would you have done?"

"I think I would have declined to take Sadie on as patient, if I had the countertransference problems with her that you have. Her job as a patient is not to help you make up for what you couldn't effectuate in your own family."

"You're right, but one doesn't have knowledge of the countertransference issues in the beginning of the therapy, so one can't know all of this ahead of time. It only happens after you've been seeing the patient for many months or more. And it only got so out of hand with me, when I saw the two of them ignoring the baby.

"In some respects, I get a perverse kick out of working with the Sadies and Jennys. Even the fact that Sadie didn't mention to me that she was bringing her daughter-in-law in, shows the kind of person she is. Debbie and my mother had the same egocentric way of seeing things. And both of them, like Sadie, had little consciousness of how others see them... which sometimes can be very funny. During the session, at one point after Jenny told me about her husband getting sexually excited by her breastfeeding the baby and sticking his penis in her mouth, I asked Sadie how she dealt with that. She said she was disgusted by it, and it reminded her of a friend who repulsed her by giving men blowjobs in the hallway of her apartment building as a way of getting attention. I asked Sadie whether she had ever given men sexual favors as a way of getting something from them. She said disparagingly, 'Blow jobs..., the most I ever did is give hand jobs.' That is the kind of remark that takes me back to the bizarre world of my childhood."

"You know, a lot of the way you make fun of Sadie is probably like the way you and your friends from the gang made fun of the people in the neighborhood."

"Hey, one of the best parts of adolescence is the belly laughs kids have when they hang around together—much of that humor comes from making fun of other people."

After some minutes the waitress arrived with our food, and I commenced to verbally play with her, as I usually did. Keep in mind she was a very good-looking, and statuesquely-built young woman.

Ted and I would often come to Little Poland to eat. Hanging out at this restaurant took on a special meaning for me, and I think for him too, having to do with recapturing the good moments of palling around. Here we were, struggling with issues of family and our kids, of our professional life, and of approaching sixty-five. What better way to momentarily circumvent the pressures we were feeling than to go to an authentic ethnic, neighborhood restaurant and flirt with the waitresses, and eat tasty Eastern European food at 1950 prices. And talk and laugh with some of the old adolescent verve. I warmed to the freedom that came with being able to fluctuate between serious conversation with Ted and just fooling around in a way that you couldn't do if your wife was present. And it brought out my love of being audacious in playing with young women, in this instance with my favorite waitress.

"So have you thought over my proposition?"

"What proposition?"

"You forgot so soon?"

"Have you told your wife about your plans with me, yet?"

"Listen, I am fortunate enough to have lots of money and I would love to share some of it with you."

"Yeah, go on."

"There is no reason you have to work so hard as a waitress. I can easily set you up in an apartment of your own and all you need to do is make some time for me. At my age, that wouldn't be too demanding. We could go to the theater and expensive restaurants."

Ted said, "That'll be the day. My friend here does have a lot of money, but he doesn't like to part with it. That's the biggest problem."

"It doesn't sound like the kind of arrangement that my husband would approve of... or your wife."

"They don't have to know."

"Well, I'll think it over. It's one of the better offers I've had from the customers. However, I should get back to work."

The meal ended with our usual rice pudding, and my asking for extra whip cream. And, as usual, Ted pressured me that we should leave a bigger tip than fifteen percent... and often he would make up the difference.

I enjoyed the banter with the waitress. Ted did too. It was like the old days, but I think we were both enjoying the nostalgia, not the actual interaction. In those days there was at least a half a possibility, if I were really inclined to get something going with a pretty waitress, that I might be successful or at least that possibility informed the exchange. Now, the humor was mostly based on the impossibility of anything happening between us, as if such a supposition was so preposterous that it was funny in and of itself. It was more of a make-believe conversation than anything else. And yet there was an element of wish on her part and mine, I think, related not so much to the attraction between us, but to the appeal of the wish fulfillment—some fantasy of being taken out of the hard-and-fast routine of our lives.

Somehow, in the ensuing minutes at the restaurant, I got caught up in my private thoughts of an encounter when I was about seventeen with a girl named Jacquelyn—an encounter that was youthful if nothing else.

After the failure of my relationship with my middleclass girlfriend, Vivien, whom I had met at summer camp, I was depressed and feeling desperate to find someone to go to bed with. A friend of mine introduced me to a young, sexy-looking woman, Jacquelyn, who was a few years older than me, and was a lot more experienced. I guess I would classify her as a player in the art and bar scene of the West Village. She and my friend—who had briefly had a fling—and I had gotten together a couple of times at the San Remo Café. Sometime after that, he had mentioned to me that she found me attractive, because she thought of me as something of a Stanley Kowalski type from the play and movie *A Streetcar Named Desire*. The next time I saw her, by chance, at Café Rienzi; she was at the bar with a guy. We talked for a while, and I could feel the sexual tension building between us. I didn't want to overstay my welcome, and as I made my exit, she slipped her telephone number to me. I thought that was really cool.

Within a week I called her and after a few minutes of conversation she invited me up to her apartment in the Village. I was excited and aroused, because this woman represented a type of sophistication and sexuality that was not part of my world. On entering her apartment, I grabbed her and started ripping off her clothes. Although she routinely held back, I was sure that she liked what I was doing. She put her hands on my chest and told me to slow down and suggested that I let her show me how we should do things. I defensively asked her, "What, you don't think I know what I am doing?"

She replied, "I think you don't know what you're doing."

While I was pissed, I wasn't about to blow the situation.

I let her judgment of me slide. Like many adolescents I was more interested in getting my rocks off than impressing the girl with my savoir-faire as a lover. When we resumed activity, I had not lost any of my heat and excitement and ended up ejaculating almost immediately on entering her, which did not exactly increase Jacquelyn's respect for me as a lover. What was strange for me on this occasion, as compared to my usual indifferent response to satisfying the woman, was that I felt embarrassed and ashamed that I couldn't satisfy or impress her at all. I had failed the test. Sensing that I was feeling bad, she proposed in a nice way that I should consider sitting in her "orgone box." Stunned, I blurted out, "What kind of box?"

"You'll see. Just relax." She explained a little about Wilhelm Reich's outlook on orgasmic sexuality and the nature of his theory about harnessing the power of cosmic, sexual energy in the universe. Apparently the electric field surrounding all human beings can be directed into our internal world through the orgone box. I thought, "What the hell, I'll give it a shot."

I got naked, per her instructions, and stepped into the orgone box as if I were about to take a bath. She sat naked also, adjacent to me but outside the box and whispered instructions into my ear somewhat along the lines of what I would now refer to as a meditation exercise. She told me that after a while I would begin to feel in my body powerful sexual urges and I should just let them come over me and go with the feelings. After about three-quarters of an hour later I was still feeling nothing. But not to seem incapable of making use of such a wonderful instrument, I pretended that I was starting to accumulate sexual energy. To this end, I took a look at her enticing breasts and her genitals and found myself with an instant erection. I whispered in her ear, "What am I going to do with this now?"

She looked down at her vagina, signaling to me that I should come out of the box and join her. We began the sexual exercise right on the floor there. When I entered her, she began writhing around and I could see on her face that she was expecting a wonderful conclusion to her pedagogy. Instead I again came quickly, almost as soon as the first time. Only this time I did not feel embarrassed or ashamed and confidently said, "What do you expect? with all the accumulation of sexual electricity. I was lucky I lasted as long as I did."

Some thirty years later I decided to look up Jacqueline, who, I learned, had become a reputable classical musician and was still living on the Lower East Side. When I called her, at first she didn't remember me at all; but as I began to describe our encounter, a faint memory came back to her of that occasion. I suggested that we get together... and added, "Don't worry, it won't take up much of your time, it won't last that long." She caught the gist of my pun and half-laughed; and she assented to see me. The meeting was sexually uneventful, since we were both married and no longer caught up in the throes of youthful sexuality.

Neither one of us was all that put off at the lack of passion in our meeting, and it struck me as humorous that I had kept in my memory her being so hot and sexually sophisticated... and that I had missed out on a great sexual opportunity. It kind of tickled me thinking about how much of my life has been taken up with regrets of lost opportunities and maintaining fantasies of what might have been. And while Jacquelyn, for sure, had no such nostalgic memories of me and what might have been, she admitted in our conversation that she too had had sexual problems in those early years and that she had pretended otherwise to attract men to her. The very fact that she was willing to see me, even though she was married, suggested to me some attempt on her part to see if she could pull from the past something that would be meaningful in the present. And I suppose that, as well, is why I wanted to see her. But who knows? maybe it was to make restitution... or to test whether, this time around, I could impress her that I was a pretty special dude. If the latter was the case, I think I scored about a C-. Which was probably a little higher than my initial foray with her.

Looking back at my presentation at the convention, in terms of grades, I'd give myself about a B+. I gave a lively talk, and I was able to get across my qualities as a psychotherapist, but I confess to a certain disappointment that I did not cause much stir from a theoretical standpoint. Thinking about it further, maybe it has to do with my not having contributed all that much to the field in terms of groundbreaking ideas. I am sure I came across as being a very individualistic therapist, very knowledgeable and vital, and extremely good at what I did; but, nonetheless, I didn't feel that in outlining my work with patients that there were a lot of theoretical ideas that I could claim were unique and I could pass on to future generations—if anything it was my personality itself, as a therapist, that was unique. As in most parts of my life, I could impress others with my attributes but I inwardly knew something was missing: you can't come from a background like mine and be so driven by compensation, without feeling strange and worried about not making the grade—or, worse, could not feel comfortable being myself and, inevitably, exposing my insecurity by touting how important and successful I am.

So I would always be Martin Obler, the great self-promoter, the one whose force of personality and pragmatic know-how made people step back and admire him... or, reversely, scoff at him. I was always selling myself... and it degraded me that I had to do it, even though I saw through the falseness of doing it.

Physically, I continued to be subject to the evidence of aging that I could not circumvent, such as not working out as vigorously in the gym as I had done for many years—I was lucky if I could stay on a treadmill at a slow-to-moderate pace for forty–five minutes; I had my share of aches and pains; my days of compulsive sex five to seven days a week were long gone; I often had to catch my breath walking up the subway stairs; I had to get up five or six times a night to piss; I found myself getting tired frequently, needing to nap in order to get through my working day. None of this was that alarming... or new; but for a guy with my grandiose delusions, and I should add hypochondriacal fears, it was a constant reminder that I was not immune to the gradual increase of erosion that accompanies aging.

But the worst of it was yet to come. Two years after my heart valve operation, I was hit with a new development. During a routine examination by my internist, he detected a heart arrhythmia that worried him. Gone was the calm that I had felt so good about after the valve replacement. I had handled the operation so calmly and my recovery was so quick and successful that it was easy for me to think that my heart was okay. This new condition put that notion to rest.

The ablation procedure for the arrhythmia turned out to be fairly routine and went very well, but its impact on me was considerable. There was no turning away from the reality that the limitations I would have to face in the years to come weren't going to be much fun. I was being battered by my kids and the tensions of my marriage related to the kids; I was worn down by my compulsive work ethic; and, if that wasn't enough, my two older children, whom I had counted on to be a balm in old age were having a midlife crisis and I was now having to play therapist with them. And I myself look forward to more medical problems and taking a host of pills and drugs for the rest of my life. So, the long and short of it, was that my lifelong defensive armor—having to do with feeling that I was living in the best of possible worlds and had boundless energy and capability to call upon—was being stripped clean. I had the feeling that the fatigue and angst that seemed to be pervading my life would continue and get worse. Sometime when I looked in the mirror, I saw the same tired face of my father in his later years.

Come to think of it, I felt a strong tug of wistfulness at parting from Ted at Little Poland, and add to that the youthful fun we had at being there. There was a feeling of looking backwards about the whole thing, a sense that aging was starting to catch up to us and that Little Poland was our attempt to renew the past... or grasping at straws. Saying goodbye itself—on any sort of occasion—to a close friend would routinely end in nostalgic and sentimental thinking on my part. Much of my life would now be a matter of wrestling with thoughts of aging, deterioration and death.

CHAPTER TWENTY-FOUR:
CONTEMPLATIONS OF A VARIED SORT

Margaret and I were out walking in the Wildlife Reserve outside of Sag Harbor. It was the first nice day after a long, dreary spell of wintry weather, and it felt like spring was in the air. The last few months after my seventy-second birthday, in December of 2007, had been depressing and draining for both of us and we welcomed a day out. It was a chance to get away from the burden of having to deal with the problems of our kids, the pressures of work, and the physical difficulties of growing older. I began to have an unpleasant inkling that, as time passed, life would only get more difficult, not less.

Danny had returned from Iraq with the same hostility he had towards us before he left. It was obvious to me that he had grown somewhat from the experience in the army, and, on the surface, was more confident and appeared to have a less unrealistic sense of how things worked in life. Apparently his ADD didn't interfere with his gaining some knowledge and information that seemed to help him be able to make plans for his future and possibly be able to take care of himself. He was planning to take advantage of the G.I. Bill and register for college in some field of technical training. To my surprise, he was applying, with no help from me, for the financial, medical, and housing benefits to which he was entitled. This certainly was a big improvement over the confused thinking, and irrational logic that typified his outlook before he went into the army. But even the signs of his cognitive improvement had to be tested in reality... could he make good on what he said he was going to do? In any case, his attitude towards Margaret and me was just as overtly hostile as ever. He blamed us for every problem he had in life; and every attempt on our part to reach out and build a relationship with him was met with dismissal and disdain. He was voicing the same, unforgiving refrain: "Why did you two white people take me out of Brazil and try to make an interracial family. All you did was bring me to a racist country."

This time around, when he made such statements to me, I used reverse psychology and offered him a one-way ticket back to Brazil with the option that if things didn't work out as well as he had anticipated, I'd be more than happy to pay for his return trip. But my attempts at mitigating his hostility proved ineffectual. It disturbed me how much he had fallen into identification with the hip, black-rap image, tattoos and body-piercing included, without having an ounce of awareness that this was a psychological defense against his feeling of incompetence and low self-esteem—feelings that are not uncommon with children who know, or sense, they're adopted.

On the morning of our walk, Margaret and I had also been struggling with the issues of my adopted daughter Leah, who had just finished her first semester at college and decided that college wasn't in her immediate future. We had just picked her up in western Massachusetts, where she had been spending a few weeks with a high school friend trying to make a go of it in finding a job and living on her own. The experience had turned out to be a complete downer for her, not only because of her lack of effort but because the economic times were very tough for anyone, anywhere, to find a job. But more to the point, she was using all her brightness and intelligence to hide the side of her that was lacking in ambition, spoiled and wanting to continue to perpetuate her less demanding high school experience. What she lived for after finishing high school was to get together with her numerous high school buddies, hangout, and smoke pot, drink, and party. Leah defended this behavior as part of her gaining life experience to be a writer.

Margaret and I would let her know that we had no trouble with her idea of wanting to be a writer. But she had to earn it, she couldn't just sit around and watch television, get high and party; she had to work at something and get off her ass. The only backing she got was from Daddy Warbucks Obler. And if she was going to live up to the struggling-writer image, then she would have to get out and earn a couple of dollars and pay for her rent. However working at a menial job of the sort she could get was beneath her and "a waste of time." I felt bad for Margaret, who was taking a tough stance with her. I talked a good game about what Leah needed to do, but I was pretty much of a softy when push came to shove. Whereas Margaret insisted that she find a job and do something that would help her with her future. And she paid the price for that in that Leah was nasty to her and rejecting, while with me she was communicative and friendly. She maintained that I understood her but a lot of that had to do with the way she could twist me around her finger.

My wife and I had been visiting my daughter, Dina, and her family just before we went to pick up Leah. My grandson, Shelley, was performing in a dance concert where he was both in and choreographing a dance at his high school. He had just returned from a one-month trip to Italy, which was paid for from an award he had won as a top Latin language student in the northeast. While my grandson's achievements were a bright spot in the fading landscape around me, I knew that soon enough I would have to become involved economically and emotionally in helping my daughter's family. Several months before, my daughter, Dina, had lost her job as a genetic counselor, which she really liked, and I had to spend days with her, bolstering her spirits. Things were draining no matter where I turned.

My son, Delmore, had hit fifty and after years of having helped him out of a compulsive accumulation of debt, he admitted to me that he hadn't told me the whole story of his indebtedness and needed more money to bail him out. I pointed out that he had a history of overspending in spite of having a healthy income (as a computer-systems engineer). I told him that this would be the last time that I would bail him out—for what it was worth. In a very touching emotional moment, he opened up and confided that he saw himself as a lonely, single man who would probably never marry or have children; he was also upset that physically, he had let himself get overweight and run down. Here is this son of mine with a really good mind, and having all kinds of potential, and not living much of a life. Once again, I couldn't help but ask myself, Where had I gone wrong with my children? For a fleeting moment, I had the same impulse I had had with my original family to flee the scene and cut my contacts with everyone. I was a long way from there, but I had those old, painful feelings of wanting to run from everything. Only there wasn't any place to run.

It felt good to be alone with Margaret in the spacious surrouding of the Wildlife Reserve, but underneath I think we couldn't get away from the things in our life that were dragging us down. Suddenly from behind a clump of bushes, four wild turkeys emerged and walked towards us apparently used to being fed by humans. I could see the momentary distraction engaged Margaret and she excitedly told some people strolling towards us that there were turkeys up ahead. When we got to the end of the path, we sat down on a bench adjacent to the bay overlooking Shelter Island. We looked at each other and smiled and held hands and it seemed to me that it had been a long time since we could share a moment like this. Margaret turned to me and I thought she was going to kiss me. But what she did was blurt out, "You know you look like a turkey, with that big Jewish nose and a shaved head."

"There you go. I've suffered from this Jewish nose; and maybe it comes from turkeys in my background. Imagine all the women I could have gotten if I had a *goyisha schnoz*." Margaret never got a chance to add a further comment, since we were both laughing at the picture of me.

I am too reflective to put all the blame for my feelings of exhaustion on my physical condition or my distress at the problems of my children. I was not oblivious to my world breaking apart in ways that I had not foreseen. Weariness and unhappiness were becoming constant companions; even my work had begun to take on a tediousness and disillusionment that was dismaying. Invariably, as I got involved in the sessions with my patients I responded with energy and enthusiasm; but on Monday mornings I found myself reluctant to go into work, and wished that I could stay in bed and pull the covers over my head... and maybe intermittently watch a little TV. Similarly, by the time the workweek was almost over, I had enough of the office and yearned to get home, take Margaret to dinner and maybe a movie. It got so bad that I found myself thinking any movie I saw was a good movie and lost what little powers I had to discriminate between good and bad movies.

And, furthermore, the thing that I deserved the most credit for in recent years—the responsibility I took for my adopted children—which represented real change and growth in my life, was not proving to be unconditionally rewarding... but was in and of itself draining and disheartening. Progress is not always immune to the ravages of entropy.

Well, in a roundabout way the discussion I've conducted about my relationship with my kids and with Margaret, and my physical problems, takes me up to the present day in my life. And that's what this chapter of the book is about—my feelings in the present, as I move towards my mid-seventies. It has to do with feelings of being unsure of myself in a way that I hadn't been for years. Unlike Ted and most of my peers, who looked forward to retirement, I anticipated retirement with dread. Physically I was doing okay, but, unexpectedly, my work as a therapist, my family life, and my anxiety about aging and a bleak future were dragging me down. I wasn't feeling buoyant by any means.

As the saying goes, I was listening to the beat of a different drummer. Or, more specifically, to the tune of "Kathy's Song" by Simon and Garfunkel. To this end, let me recall a phone conversation I had with Ted, who was back in California. The conversation started out by my conveying my general weariness; let me pick it up from there:

"... and I'm feeling a lot of things inside myself that I haven't felt for a long, long time—since I was a kid..."

"Like what?"

"Well, for one, I keep repeating this segment from Simon and Garfunkel: [singing]: 'Kathy, I'm lost, I said, though I knew she was sleeping. I'm empty and aching and I don't know why, counting the cars on the New Jersey Turnpike. And they've all gone to look for America...'"

"That's very nice."

"I keep singing it over and over..."

"You're still looking to find yourself, before you keel over. And to do that, you have to get back to the sad little boy—Muttla... and his fears of extinction."

"You know it's funny that a lot of times when I'm singing these words I think of my father and I wonder what it must have been like for him at the end, when I started to grow apart from him in my teenage years. I have no doubt that I was the most important person in his life. And I often speculate to myself that as I moved away literally and emotionally, it must have been a great sadness for him. Remember, Ted, I told you a long time ago how guilty I felt leaving him as he lay dying on the stretcher in the hospital corridor. Well that memory keeps coming back to me, particularly when I was lying in the hospital with my medical stuff. The thought kept coming back to me that although I got my kids and my grandchildren and my wife and friends, I'm not much different than he was. I'm going to die alone just like him, whether in a big house or a modern suburban hospital."

"I like what you're saying and I think it applies to everyone who is discovering that hey, I'm really getting old."

"… for years you pressured me to reach Margaret and do the kind of hard work it takes to make changes as a couple. And, similarly, you more than anyone else badgered me to take responsibility for my adopted kids in ways that I had avoided with my other children. Well, you were right, I had to do it because the kids needed me. But I am getting worn down and my life isn't much fun. My childhood pessimistic view of life is returning with a vengeance in my old age. I feel irritated more frequently with my wife and kids and the tensions of the household. And I want to regain my own life, apart from trying to hold everything together.

"Let's face it, I'm a realist and you're a dreamer. Maybe your dreams have paid off. Your kids are out of the home. You seem to have changed everything around. You were unhappy in New York, you were unhappy dating, and you were depressed that you were stuck in an unsatisfying routine. And somehow you managed to do something about it, which I really give you credit for. You moved to California, you found a woman who really fit your needs, you're meeting people and are less isolated, you're playing tennis again after many years, which is a great thing for you. You're able to incorporate the sports thing that was so important as a kid… while I'm incorporating the miseries of childhood."

"Maybe you're being punished for your refusal to make the changes you needed to make. I don't mean that Someone higher up is out to get you, but in the overall scheme of things. Sometimes you pay, in life, for not making changes that are long overdue. Or you can look at it from the other side. You may be expecting too much, too soon, from some of the admirable changes you've made. It takes time for things to flow; you can't expect a one-to-one reward for the good things you've been doing… by taking responsibility for your kids. You did what you had to do.

"Look, my realism tells me that even if my kids eventually do better, I won't be around to see it. I won't get the peace and quiet I thought I earned."

"What can I say?"

"Ted, it doesn't stop. I got too much responsibility, too much to take care of… granted, a lot of it is self-imposed, having to do with my workaholic mentality and the feeling that I can never have enough money or security to take it easy. I worry about my health, my family, and I've got no time for myself. I am overwhelmed by the day-to-day stresses and strains of my life. I find myself longing for the past when I used to avoid responsibility at home and throw myself into extramarital sex."

"I think that is absolutely right. Your life is different now than it was then. You're growing up. Ten years ago, you were still saying that everything was great simply because you weren't back in Brownsville."

"But things have changed. Time is passing… and that's all that is happening. I used to think that if you put all this effort in and you bank a lot of money, down the road it's going to pay off… but there is nothing down the road… just a road."

"Well, the Buddhists know that, it's the basis of their concept that ordinary duties are a most important part of life-acceptance."

"Look at it this way. I know I have to make some changes: get the kids out of the house, put in the work on my marriage that I have been avoiding for years; and reducing the practice to two days."

"Yes, it's become a matter of life and death. You're seventy-two and soon you'll be seventy-three. Why don't you do it? I've been telling you for years to do it."

"Fear. Fear of giving up what worked for me, which is working as hard as I could at something that gave me great meaning and a very comfortable living. Fear that if I give up my practice, I'll have nothing to replace."

"So, at the root, it's about fear."

"… and where the fear comes from."

I went home that night and I had a dream about my relationship with Dr. Henderson, my old analyst, who had died when I was in my early thirties. In the dream I was in session with her and we were arguing vehemently in a way we had never done in our professional relationship. I wasn't too clear as to what we were arguing about, but my feeling was that it had something to do with her not facing the truth about her medical condition. I got so heated about her denial that I grabbed her and we started wrestling. Then I remember seeing myself in the dream, with tears flowing down my cheeks as we were physically grappling.

The dream scene shifted and we were sitting in our usual analytic positions during session. She said she was sorry for upsetting me so much and explained that she was going through a lot of difficult personal stuff… and that someone very close to her had recently died. She mentioned that in her countertransference to me, she was displacing her anger and aggression towards the loss of this person onto me. She apologized that she had to cut the session short because she had to attend his wake, but if I wanted to join her I was welcome to.

In the next scene we were strolling arm in arm towards the funeral parlor where the wake was being held. On entering the room, I saw the faces of a number of people whom I seemed to know but couldn't quite place, but none of them had anything to do with the Psychoanalytic Institute and I wondered what they were doing here. People lined up to express to Dr. Henderson—who stood by the open casket—their sorrow for her loss and to view the deceased. Somehow I walked by Dr. Henderson without saying anything to her and as I looked into the casket, I could see that it was me—I was the deceased.

I woke up from the dream startled, shaking, and all sweaty. My first impulse was to rush to the phone and call Ted. I wanted to tell him my dream and share with him what I thought it was all about. I felt that some unconscious recognition was coming up in me that I had been avoiding. It was too early in the morning, given the coastal difference in time, to call Ted, so

I conjured up in my mind how I would interpret my dream to him. I even went further and created what I thought his response would be to my interpretation.

I started off by telling him that although I had routinely talked with Dr. Henderson about her having been an all-nurturing, wish-fulfilling, loving mother-figure for me, I never saw so clearly how powerful this transference actually was. She was the mother I always yearned for and would be there, for me, unconditionally. But like my real mother, she failed me, in this case by not taking care of herself. The end result was that I felt abandoned by her in the same way that I felt abandoned by my mother.

While I needed my mother for my survival on a day-to-day basis, she was too inept, too frightened, and too insulated for me to entrust myself to her.

This double bind of dependence and distrust became transferred on to Dr. Henderson. And within this psychological confine, she betrayed me by allowing herself to get sick; if she loved me enough, she wouldn't have let that happen. In the dream I express my rage towards her, by wrestling with her, but the problem is that I am dependent on her and if I let out my fury at her, I won't survive because she'll abandon me. So I redirect the fury against myself and I die in the dream. I recognize that the previous sentence sounds a bit too psychologically neat, but it accurately conveys my thought at the time.

Again, I wonder, What would Ted say? I would bet a pretty penny that he would say it's too conventional a Freudian interpretation, having to do with guilt at my sexual desire for the mother and fear of the father. So, in my mind I told him: "Ted, give me some credit. I am not reiterating the classic Freudian line. What I am trying to say is that my lifelong repressed depression and my fear of death was, all along, pre-Oedipal, starting from early infancy. It started when my idealized mother began failing me way before my Oedipal fears of my father entered the picture. I have no strict memory of this, but it seems to me impossible that I didn't have, in my earliest years, great fear and anxiety that my mother couldn't take care of me. She couldn't even take care of herself and to be a little baby dependent on her was a prescription for terror and anxiety. Shades of Sadie and Jenny and the baby.

The reason I'm having this kind of a dream, at this stage of my life, is because I'm trying to deal with the nucleus of my death fear that has affected me for my entire life... and has been all-encompassing, involving magical thinking, my need to control everything and everybody, my anal retentiveness around money and security issues, my compulsive sexual needs, my endless self-promotion—to convince the world that I am larger than life.

In my imaginary construction, I brought all of this to Ted, and his response was to tell me that what startled him was that I had placed myself in the coffin. That is an image worthy of Edgar Allan Poe. I agreed. And I asked him how he would interpret that.

In the interchange, Ted says, Well, on the face of it, you replace the dead person mourned by Henderson and by that achieve your wish to be the son she longed for; at the same time, it could easily reflect, not only your wish for the mother, but an attempt to express your fury and rage at her, by killing yourself, as if she were responsible for your death. But I can't get over the shock of your seeing yourself in the coffin. In some way you die to yourself. That to me is stronger and more compelling than anything I've mentioned. From a Jungian point of view, that is the message of the dream.

Interestingly, here, I employ Ted to put forth what I really want to get at in the dream. Somehow, I am using him, as I often do, to bring out the child Martin Obler. I would have to say that he is the father figure that I successfully repressed and for me to embrace my mother and my sisters and Dr. Henderson (whom I wrestle with in the dream), I must rely on him.

Taken in the construct, with Ted's perspicuity about my dream, I let fly my interpretation of my seeing myself in the coffin.

"Ted, you are right in where you're heading. The great shock in the dream is my seeing myself in the coffin and that I have died to myself, as you mention. And it does express the Jungian message in the dream: listen to your inner voice, the voice of the aging man. What is he trying to tell you?

Ted approvingly says, 'Go ahead."

"… that if I don't give up defending myself against the needy little boy that I have lost within myself, I will be dead, not only to my mother, father, and sisters, but to myself. I have to listen to the aging father in me who addresses the little boy I was, Muttla, and stop holding up the cardboard superman, Martin Obler. I have to reverse the direction of fifty years of false growth before it's too late. I keep blaming Danny and Margaret and Leah for letting me down as if they are the symbols of what I have unsuccessfully tried to wring from life. I want them to be the proof of the great Martin Obler, the final testimony, as it were to my greatness. I can turn life around for anyone who puts his or her trust in me. And if I can do it for them, I surely can do it for myself. So I have to knock off, at least symbolically, the cardboard superman… and become the new, old man, Martin Obler, who finally stops trying to hold everything together."

A few days later, I called up Ted, for real and told him the dream and my interpretation of it and, as well, what I had conjured up in my mind would be his reaction. He concurred that that was close to what he probably would have said, and mentioned I had done a good job of reflecting his thinking. However, like a good analyst, he wanted to know what I made of the fact that, I couldn't place the people attending the wake. I answered him by stating that in the dream I was confused as to what they were doing there, which I connected to my own confusion about where my life was heading.

CHAPTER TWENTY-FIVE:
TED'S LETTER

T he book has begun to try the patience of my stalwart
friend, Ted. He has written me an e-mail indicating that
he would like to curtail, though not necessarily put an
end to, his role in it. It's up to me to run with the ball, he's
thinking. I am sympathetic with his wish to lighten his load in
spurring me on and being therapist, reader, and go-to person.
Of course, I will continue to rely on him, I won't let his wishes
faze me. He's too good a guy to turn his back on me in my
hour(s) of need. Even the letter itself gives a charge to the book:

*I have decided to send you this as a means of putting you out of your
(and my) misery. To wit, you have been working on this book of yours for
some eight years and it still is not finished; and you have been enlisting my
contributions—in one way or another—over this time. So I am sending
this reflection, with the idea that it will help you to move the book towards
conclusion... and to let you know that I will shrink—good word here...
the shrink shrinks—my involvement in, or contribution to, your
autobiography. I'm still available for light consultation, etc., but it's your
baby and you have to go with it, more than at present, alone. I do have a
suggestion for your last chapter, which you shouldn't need me for, and that
is, considering where the book has been leading of late... my suggestion is
that you end the book with a segment of self-analysis. By that I mean, How
would you handle Martin Obler if he were your patient? What would you
do to get a stubborn, resistant person like him to address his psychological
issues so that he could feel better about himself? It wouldn't be an easy
chapter to write, but it could be very instructive to the reader... and helpful
to you as well—probably more so than anything I could tell you. Anyway,
let me say my piece in the way of summary thoughts, or whatever; and*

maybe it will inspire you to do the same, by way of bringing the book to a close.

    I have been thinking about Zen Buddhism quite a lot lately, and have come to a major thought about my relationship to this religion or philosophy—it is as a philosophy that I am taken with it. My thought: anything that presents itself as having enduring answers to some of life's considerations on how to live it, is faulty. No system of belief works forever; it can be mind-blowing for a period of time but man changes over time and nothing applies forever. This leads me to take issue with Zen's idea of satori... that one surpasses death through enlightenment and practice. The last thing I want to do is try to prove my thesis in some rational way. Instead, let me say that Buddhism will eventually be overtaken—for better or worse—by modern life and will drop in appeal, over the next century, as science and technology push forward and possibly bring the planet to disaster. Young people don't read newspapers anymore, so newspapers are going out of business. A similar decline will take place in Christianity and Buddhism as time marches on. The universe is much greater than any religion and as the universe become more accessible in all kinds of ways, the gods that are worshipped by human beings will recede and matter less... and be relegated to historical pertinence.

    What is this a preamble to? My philosophical view of lifehood.

    As I see it, life is impregnable in terms of absolute knowledge. This morning I was ferociously thinking about the women in my life that I missed having a relationship with, sexual and otherwise. In my long period of being single after my wife's death there were quite a few women whom I was attracted to but one thing or another caused me to not take it forward, leaving me feeling that I screwed up and missed out on something that might have had a big impact on my life. I could go into cases of this, but it would be a waste of time and I can do better by just referring you to all the situations where you missed out on some woman that made you feel that something would be forever less in your life if you were not to assimilate this woman's personality and sexuality into your being. And somehow, if you had not blown it, you might have actually felt more complete in some much-desired way. Of course this is nonsense. You would still be yourself with all your imperfections and virtues... and still seeking completeness. Things might be different for you with the accretion of this wonder woman, but not in any wholesale way, at least so I believe. So, for me, there is no escape from the tyranny of the misconceived possibilities of self-development or self-evolvement. Man is too finite to get it right in one lifetime. Even the pervasive, ever-present hope that one can alter oneself to no longer feel oppressed by one's childhood-formed identity is insupportable by experience. Things get better, worse, better again, worse again, ad infinitum... and to think that any one development or action will eradicate one's unhappiness in life and one's identity imperfections is to fool oneself.

I have lived life feeling that I am lucky to be alive, and yet underneath I cannot expunge the feeling that, as death becomes a stronger reality within myself, as a result of aging, that I am lucky to die, also... and be over with the insecurity, self-doubts, worries about one's children, and all the things that bring one down and cause one pain and anguish. As I see it, my feeling good about myself, on a minute to minute basis, is probably about equal to my feeling not so good about myself on a minute to minute basis. To me, the time measurement of this consideration would be of greater philosophical value than anything the great philosophers could say.

What does it feel like minute to minute to exist and be a self—that's my baby and what I would like to know in determining the value and merits of existence. As it is, the value of existence is pretty much predicated on the fear of non-existence, which is a spooky way to come at the essential quality of being.

My weak efforts at philosophizing are all too fitting of my notion that man is not up to the impossible task of calibrating his experience, and this without even mentioning such indecipherables as Time, Space, and Consciousness. Is consciousness a blessing or a punishment? Who the hell knows?

If there is anything I subscribe to, with some feeling of disquiet and uneasiness, it is that the there is a point where the complexities and intricacies of consciousness are too much to handle and buttress the idea that man is inadequately programmed to live life well. For instance, it is the 'self-punishment' aspect of consciousness, as opposed to the 'gift' aspect, that doesn't let me forget how badly damaged I am: like the way I will spend an hour after saying goodbye to a close friend thinking about just how we said goodbye, every word, every facial expression, etc., reworking, reliving every feeling I am having—fulfilling in this way my need to feel loved; and of course my hope is that my friend is feeling some of what I feel in the moment of parting... as if in some preparation for the final moment of parting, death. And even as I succumb to this sad ritual of affirming my friendship with the other person, I am fully aware that something is not right in me... which gets back to the deprivation I felt in my family. Nor is it lost on me that my friend is surely not obsessing about our parting the way I am. Or as I will do, returning to it many times during the day or days to follow... and even picking it up months or years later.

When I said goodbye to Checho from boarding school, at the airport (he was going back to his home in Puerto Rico) and I knew I might well not see him again... I did the same replaying of the moment but also I was aware that he did not feel much of the emotion and sadness I was feeling... so I felt hurt and rejected and the loss and the missing of my friend all combined... and often I come back to the thought of the goodbye to Checho, feeling the misery of being me and repeating and repeating the playback in my mind over the years... never letting it go, a defining moment in its way. So much for the joys of consciousness. This little paragraph on my goodbye to Checho feels like one of the most forthright things I've written in my life. It reflects in my mind the quintessential, or truest, me. It reflects the innermost, personal identity that I felt I had to keep entirely private.

I try to live life responsibly and change for the better. But, in some ways, it all comes down to loving: the love given and received; and the problem that I need so much love... and people disappoint.

Final advice. Cut to the chase and end the book. Teddy

P.S.
Let me add here that I know how discursive and rambling this statement of mine is, and I feel it should be just that way... for it gives expression to the chaotic and distraught part of me that I need to keep under wraps.

One has to take Ted with a grain of salt. When he starts writing he gets impulsive and likes to follow out, in a very spontaneous way, his thoughts. He lets his writing take him where it will. I don't really need to reply to the whole letter

within the book framework, and part of why I include the letter
in its entirety is I like the idea of the reader getting to know Ted
outside of how I have chosen to use him within the purposes of
the book. But there is a major point that Ted brings up in the
letter, which I do want to respond to. It has to do with his
reflections about consciousness.

To get to this it would be of help to begin with a line from
Ted's 'discursive and rambling' statement: "So much for the
joys of consciousness."

The reason that I go straight to this line is that it runs
counter to my view of consciousness, which is essential to the
way I see myself and the way I look at what has kept me afloat.
If it were me I would say: Thank God for the joys of
consciousness.

Consciousness was my ally, my stabilizer, and my saving
grace. For Ted, consciousness is both man's great achievement
and man's undoing. In his negative view, he takes consciousness
as a personal affront and a mocking force... and believes that it
is man's sorry lot to know and feel his limitations, failures, and
self-deceptions, everything man dislikes about himself and can't
forget or hide. It is the final indignity—not only are human's
yuckaputzes but we're scripted to dwell on it as well, often
obsessively.

Unlike Ted, I assumed that consciousness and awareness was
the end-all and be-all of lived life and therapy and the noble
virtue which made up for everything. Only my good friend is
telling me something different—that the redoubtable Marty
Obler is a yuckaputz. What my friend is getting at is that
consciousness, awareness, knowing isn't the great redeemer.
While it may have worked for many years to prop myself up, as
a therapist and person, it did so at great injury to me. And a lot
of what Ted is saying has me unsure and off-balance. Look at it
this way: Ted and I grew up in the twentieth century, which I
consider to be the age of analytic enlightenment, a time when
uncovering what is repressed in the unconscious was seen as the
great emancipating force. And I embraced this as such because

it fit into my struggle to survive poverty and my family and would give me one-up so that I didn't have to consider myself on a plane with the unenlightened masses.

While all that I'm going through of late is causing me to think that Ted is probably right: my dependence on consciousness and knowing is outliving its usefulness. Yet I'm afraid to give up the illusion of the redemptive nature of consciousness because I can't quite imagine functioning without it. What will I tell my patients and myself when life seems bleak and hopeless?... if I don't have a strong belief in the virtues of understanding as a curative agent? The inadequacy of consciousness for me is equivalent to the disbelief in a higher power for some other people. My worry is that I will be totally lost and without the feeling of superiority that counters my colossal insecurity.

To give a sense of how dependent I was early on, on knowing and seeing clearly, let me tell you this story about my little puppy dog. I was about six years old at the time.

I came home one day from some kind of day-care center at the local shul. On arrival, my mother informed me that the puppy dog [that my father had brought home for me no more than two weeks ago] had run away. I felt such pain at the thought of my little puppy being killed or wandering the streets alone that I started crying and gasping for breath. My mother tried to console me by pleading, "Don't worry, it will be all right, *yingala*," and added, "the puppy will come back." But I knew she was lying: my grandmother and Rachel didn't come back. Once you leave you don't come back.

Anyway, I knew she was lying to me and that she had gotten rid of it because the dog was too much trouble for her. I felt deceived and defeated. It was one of those incidents in my childhood that set the template for my distrust of people, even today. I did all I could to not let myself experience that kind of vulnerability ever again. I would know everything, so it couldn't happen.

And this story brings to mind another one, when I was about eight years old. The chief Rabbi at the shul had told me to close the shabbas lights after sundown on Friday. I told him, "Rabbi, it's a sin. God will strike me." He said, "Don't worry, He only does that to grownups, not to little boys." I answered, "*Du bist* a liar," and I turned and ran out of the shul. He chased me down the street, yelling and calling me names, but he couldn't catch me. As for his getting me to turn out the lights, I was already wired to never be taken unawares or be deceived by anyone.

In mentioning these stories, I am trying to convey a sense of how I came to value knowing and consciousness as a little boy. It was, in my case, my unclear and murky feeling that knowing the people around me and what was behind their motives could save me from great hurt and, ultimately, obliteration. While not being able to express this even to myself, I did have the feeling that knowing was the key to my survival... and, when I got to be older I added on to that manipulation and control.

However, knowing or consciousness is what comes up to me now as a subject of concern, mainly because Ted has challenged my ultra-reliance on consciousness... and since he has been right about so many of my excesses and shortcomings, it's not easy for me to dismiss his criticism. In fact, I feel myself at a crossroad in my thoughts about consciousness. Yes, it has been my savior but also my undoing. There is no question in my mind that a part of what Ted is trying to tell me is that I have injured myself by denying what he's saying about the mixed blessing of consciousness. More specifically, he believes that my reliance on survival—via consciousness—which I am trying to defend, is also serving to protect me from looking at my weakness and insecurity, on both a personal and interpersonal level. My anxiety and panic prevent me from seeing myself as I really am. I manage to only let in information about myself that is ego-syntonic and anything else is viewed as a threat to my existence and wiped from the slate. So when Ted tells me I am injuring my marriage by my compulsive need for sex, I reject it by rationalizing that it works for me and put out of my mind the impact on Margaret. And the extent of how firmly entrenched this defense mechanism is in me is apparent in that, even though I can admit to what I have just confessed, I feel safe that I will relegate it, finally, to some storage bin in my brain where it will rest undisturbed for eons. Why do I have to go to such lengths to shut out what I don't want to hear? I can only assume that the greater my personal fear and anxiety, the more I have to cling to the balm of my consciousness.

I am thrown back on my heels by Ted's argument about the limits of consciousness. Part of this is that I have grown increasingly dependent on the power of consciousness to relieve the diminishment I feel with aging. I imbued consciousness with the transformative power of making me feel that there was a purpose and meaning to my life no matter how bad it got. And I told Ted that consciousness saved me from being just like everyone else. All the things I was feeling, my disillusion and frailty, etc., were transformed through consciousness into superiority on my part... because I knew what I was going through. Now I suddenly am wondering whether the redeeming powers of consciousness, so essential to my view of myself, was based on mirrors and smoke. And without my writing the book, I would not have risked uncovering this dimension of my self-delusion.

Writing about the impact on me of Ted's thoughts about 'consciousness' has led me to think about his thoughts about 'depression.'

I liked his point about measuring depression... his idea, which he has expressed elsewhere, was that he would much rather have a calibrating device that kept track of his emotional state and told him how pervasive depression was in his life than be left to his own devices to determine that information. That there is not such a calibration device is not his point; his point is that maybe, on a technical basis, it can be discerned that he is more unhappy than he gives himself credit for. I would guess that he suspects this is true. There is a part of me, too, that thinks I am leading a good life, but another part, which seems to be gathering strength, has to do with how often I downshift into a bleak state. And the old devices that helped me overcome this bleakness don't seem to be working as well as they used to... and drain a lot of my energy. This has to do with the realities of aging and the body and mind deteriorating. As an elderly person I find myself living in an ethos which is much more susceptible to depression and the awareness of the inroads it has made on me. It is, in this state of mind, an easy jump to recognize that I have, over a lifetime, warded off the extent of depression I have been feeling. As an analyst, I have often thought that there are patients who don't like bringing up how depressed they are because they know these feelings all too well; and patients who have managed to run around their bleak states and at some point discover that they have been assiduously skirting their perennial depression. Ted often talks about his current feeling of depression being a good thing for him because as a child he couldn't handle the feeling of depression, since he was afraid of the consequences of showing weakness to his mother. But the other side of Ted is that, while he likes the idea of liberating the depression in him... he's fearful of where it might take him. Ted would like to think of depression as his friend, but he's also aware that it might be a mother-induced enemy who administered to him a blow from which he can't recover. I know from where he speaks. I am still afraid to integrate within me the terrible feelings of humiliation and despair that I would experience if I let my guard down. I've spent a lifetime trying to avoid being identified with the craziness of my family, the humiliation of being poverty-stricken and seeing my father buckle under to poverty and defeat. No amount of success as a therapist, or wealth, or acknowledgement as a first-rate professor can hide that I was as a child, and still into my adult life, a frightened human being who had to touch walls and turn to magical thinking to make himself feel that he would not be swallowed up by the nameless abyss.

Recently I came up against a stark example of the kind of fears that scare me. One of my older patients, Maynard, from group therapy, had a stroke that temporarily paralyzed the right side of his body and forced him to face up to the proximity of death. Prior to the stroke, he was an eighty-two year old man, partially blind, hunched over from osteoporosis, needing a cane to walk, and having a skin ailment which covered a large part of his body... but in spite of these serious concerns, he maintained, prior to the stroke, a misconception that he was still a youthful and vigorous man, an active poet, someone who still had a desire for women, even though he had had erectile problems for years. All of this kind of positive thinking enabled him to at least, on the surface, to avert the truth that he was still a lonely, little boy feeling utterly disconnected to his family, having failed in two marriages, and been saddened by the detachment that existed between him and his two children. Forty plus years of therapy (the last seventeen with me) had done a lot to improve his life and make him feel alive and that he had reason to live. This was by no means insignificant. But it was also by no means insignificant that underneath he was and will always be a *shmendrick* with earlaps... which is to say that depression and death will have its day. Perhaps I made a mistake by failing to get him to ingest his depression in a productive way, partly because I was using my own identification with him—as an aging man given to avoidance mechanisms to ward off depression—to make him and me feel better. But depression has waylaid us both, relative to our age.

Maynard's debilitating depression descended on him, all at once, after his stroke. The suddenness with which this took place was unusual, but not surprising in that he, like most of my patients, preferred to relieve their suffering (from depression) rather than embrace it or confront it as a necessary component of therapeutic treatment.

Depression is the world-beating incapacitation. I suffer from it, and most of my patients suffer from it. Depression, anxiety, fear—these comprise the trifecta. They are interwoven, in whatever order you like. They are the bedrock of my patients' clinical problems and just about everybody's emotional and psychological problems—in or out of the therapist's office. They stake their claim on everyone, because no one in these times grows up feeling whole, complete, loved, and sufficient just as they are. Everybody has been wounded. As a therapist, I consider depression, et al., a human plague, different, but as unfortunate as disease. It is present everywhere one turns. I talk about confronting depression or anxiety and fear, to my patients, but they are not prone to hunker down and do battle with the enemy. The enemy is too diverse, too scary. And I too, in my own life, have not taken my own advice. The battle seems too costly, too dangerous, too exhausting. My whole persona is geared to circumventing the battle, and making myself feel successful out of all proportion: I have for much of my life— say from the time I became a successful psychotherapist up to my middle sixties or so—not been above convincing myself that I'm leading the best life possible. It's time to stop running away from myself, and make a last-ditch effort to pursue the inner Marty Obler. Even if it leads to anywhere and nowhere. One thing, relative to this discussion of depression that I would like to mention here is my belief, through my own experience and my experience as an analyst, that those people, like myself, who grew up in a depressed and demoralizing home environment... have little will to confront their personal depression since they think, to what avail? Haven't I seen and been exposed to enough depression, anxiety, and defeat?... so why would I or should I inundate myself with more of it? And that is a hard one to reason them out of, except, perhaps, if the depression and anxiety is gripping them in a way that they need immedtate relief from it. And I certainly come under the category of seeing little need to expose myself to the disintegrating effects of a battered psyche over years. For years I have embraced the intuitive resistance to undermining myself by using consciousness to offset my will to change and face myself.

Don't do this to yourself, the self-protective part of me asserts, much like it does to most of my patients.

Consciousness has always been a two-faced coin. On the negative side, it allowed one to examine oneself unforgivingly, time and time again; and on the positive side, it represented the freedom of man to think freely about his life in a way that seems like the greatest privilege that a human being has at his disposal. So what Ted is trying to tell me is that the gift of consciousness is two-sided and, in that sense, reinforces the vague and shadowy aspect of what man knows and doesn't know, what he has achieved and what he is unable to achieve.

Ted, I would say, holds that this theoretical discussion about consciousness is not worth a whole lot in this book... or even anywhere for that matter, since for Ted it is mainly a way of adding to his sense of frustration at what man doesn't know and can't get a handle on—and the ambivalence that makes life difficult for him. He has no small sense of his not being a philosopher and is not really trying to pursue anything theoretical in his discussion—but just use 'consciousness' as a springboard to express his inner feelings of doubt and vagary. For me, however, he brings up the issue of 'consciousness' to show how I twist things around to shield myself from myself.

CHAPTER TWENTY-SIX:
QUANDARY

This book has begun to dovetail with both the chronology of my life up to date and the ever-present present.

Doing the book has brought home to me the axiom that things need to get worse before they get better. Of course I understood this as an analyst, but not so much as a person.

Let me mention some of the things that come to mind, up to date.

In the writing of the book, I have arrived at an even greater appreciation of the virtues of repetition.

One of the virtues of analysis is that the patient has to come up against the endless repetition of the same things happening over and over and over again. For example, both of my analysts would never tire of pointing out to me my compulsive need to engage in affairs with women as a way of avoiding my frustration and unhappiness. And Ted added his much more direct criticism of my incessant affairs, till I was somehow softened up enough, or tired enough, that I could entertain the idea that it might be time to make a change. I can't emphasize enough how doing the book has had a secondary benefit similar to that of analysis.

As in a good analysis, the virtues of true self-examination and inquiry, can lead to a much-improved sense of self. It has made a big difference to me that I have been able to handle the tides of aging, the limitations of what I could do as a father, and my problems with intimacy without resorting as much to my prototypical escapism and avoidance. For instance, the fact that I have taken on the responsibility of fatherhood has made an enormous difference in my feelings of self-worth. I shudder to think how I would be feeling about myself if I had 'acted out' the way I used to in my first marriage.

Unquestionably, doing the book became an increasingly important part of my life over the last eight years. Even for the wrong reasons: I have to admit the fantasy of getting the book published and getting my name out there, doing the talk shows, and being a major player was irresistible. Not only would I be admired as a Horatio Alger figure, rising out of the poverty of Brownsville, but I would be a celebrity.

However after completing the first third of the book where I detail the dramatic rise out of poverty and the making of a psychologist, I began to comprehend that there was a more profound motive for doing the book than obtaining my fifteen media minutes of fame. It had to do with the dire boredom and emptiness I experienced in childhood. As I have explained on numerous occasions, one of the things that I have been dearly afraid of is to become like my parents, siblings, and a lot of the people in the neighborhood, whom I saw as living meaningless, empty, isolated lives. Margaret and Ted have for years bugged me to reduce the size of my practice and move towards retirement. But no matter how sensible the advice, I have only made half-hearted efforts to follow it. Undeniably, the reason behind this is my fear that I could end up with nothing to do but live out an empty existence. Writing the book was a lively way of occupying my time and in some aspects challenged me more than conducting therapy—after all, as much as I love doing therapy, I have had a fulltime practice for some forty-five years. Writing the book was proving to be a lot of fun, especially having to do with the incorporation of Ted in the book and as a reader. The time spent with him, bantering, joking around, hanging out—before he moved to California—took me back to street life as a kid. I missed that kind of playfulness and bonding.

But the most unexpected boon of doing the book was the way it imprinted itself on me, as if the book itself was part of the movement of the seasons, or more accurately, the passing of years. And this gets back to the feeling of time in analysis, the sense of the awareness and progress that comes over time.

The book started out mostly with me telling the story of my early life, but it went from there to my looking at my practice, my marriage, my children, and how I saw myself in all of this. And finally it included my aging and fears of death, etc., and the person I had become. And in this final segment, doing the book is firmly rooted in what I have learned about myself over the duration of writing it.

Here I am, in my mid-seventies, questioning what my whole life has been about. This is quite a reversal for a guy who thought he knew it all and used to say on the street corner to his gang friends: "Hey schmucks, wake up they're trying to put one over on you."

What I'm getting at, in the present, is the confusion I'm feeling—as I've said—about where my life is heading. Feeling at sea with who I am, where I am going, and what's left me in this life. However, making some positive changes in the egotistical, self-insulated way of conducting my affairs has helped me to like myself more and feel more connected to everyone around me. And yet Ted rightfully warns me that my capacity to change has its limits. He says that I still walk and talk like the old Marty Obler... and that is to be expected. I take it what he's saying is that old habits die hard. A platitude that is tailored for me.

Anyway, what I am looking at, at best, is some kind of uneasy slide between the old and the new me, which leaves me pretty much adrift. It's one thing to be in a muddle and have things falling apart accompanied by the feeling that there is hope that change is possible over time—things will work out. It's another thing to be caught up in a muddle, with the feeling that there is no sense of time stretching out in some foreseeable future; and without this, change is relegated to the indeterminate present. It's probably much like what my patients' feel... that hope is dwindling faster than any possibility of the needed change taking place in their life. And sometimes I have, in the past, and still somewhat in the present, been intolerant of their inability to change. Similarly, they must wonder what keeps them from changing. Now, I too am feeling time is not on my side and that despondency is pushing for space.

But I see no reason when I get to talking about myself at length, that, as before, I switch to Warren (and now Esther, too) for a breather... and certainly in terms of their future the two of them cause me to feel the limits of what I can do for them... and the pessimism that accompanies their life.

For years, Warren has, despite his temporary regressions into paranoia and delusion, been able to live, a not-so-normal, normal life, free of psychotic breakdowns and incarcerations in mental hospitals. He has learned to function within the parameters of his illness and has been able to maintain a minimally workable marriage and even some small degree of a social life. Within his family—and I haven't brought this up in the book—he has been able to move from a completely dependent person to someone who, after his father's death, took on more responsibility—with his niece and nephew and his disabled mother—appropriate to a sixty-year-old man. He could easily be placed in a category of a successful mental-health patient, considering how well he is functioning compared to when I first started seeing him. That's the upside. The downside is that Warren will always be Warren, and at risk to the paranoia and delusions that threaten to overtake him:

In a make-up session with me, Warren sat in a deadly silence for over ten minutes and I knew this was going to be one of those sessions in which I would have to unravel the insanity of his responses to a bunch of nonverbal interactions with people from his neighborhood... or on public transportation, or even in the quietude of his Buddhist meetings. He seemed defeated and weary, holding his head as if he were in great pain, with his body slumped over in a position of exhaustion. I found myself also weary and tired, that I would have to go through the same shit with him that I had gone through for the last twenty-six years. Over and over again, I would have to unravel, week after week, the same pathological misinterpretations in his mind about how people were reacting to him.

I broke the silence and asked, "What's happened now?"

Sure enough he went on to describe a whole series of incidents that he had had with a prototypical cast of characters with whom he had been nonverbally interacting. I listened to his enumeration of incidents, and after each one I reoriented him back to reality; and I explained that, although some few things that he is talking about might actually have taken place, there is no doubt that most of what he is relating is distorted and has to do with his illness.

So, I broke down his misperceptions, and was able to reduce his anxieties to a tolerable level. I could see the difference in his body tension... it was as though his whole body underwent a great heave of relief. It would, however, be wrong to give the impression that Warren fully went along with my interpretation of what transpired in these incidents; in fact it is the opposite: he argued vehemently against what I was suggesting, but just entertaining the possibility that I may have a point seemed to have a calming effect on him. Or that I was simply there. Unlike in our usual sessions of this nature, Warren did not continue to talk and seek relief through further discussion. He fell silent again. And neither of us spoke for some time. And, somewhere along the line, I had an image of Warren as a baby who had been upset and uncomfortable suddenly being pacified by a bottle. I decided not to go my usual route of pumping him about what was going on in his internal state that led to the turbulence and delusions that he had been experiencing. I let him continue to sit in silence, which he seemed content to do.

I began to get a new picture of what was going on between us. Here was Warren asking no more than to sit silently in the room with me and let him be the baby... protected and calmed by the parent who was there to make sure that he would not venture beyond the borders of sanity. And just my presence was his insurance policy that he would not end up back in the mental hospital. This understanding led me to see the collusion we had entered into over the years, whereby I would be the rational voice in his psyche bringing him back from bouts with compulsion and obsession that bordered on psychosis. And he would be the baby. And that sonofabee unconsciously had my number and could count on my being stuck with him for the rest of my life.

The session ended and Warren got up to leave. And I realized that Esther was to follow him as the next patient. I told him, "You might run in to Esther on the way out." He seemed a little jarred by this, probably because in his present precarious state he didn't feel comfortable running into someone who knew him. And he did bump into her. I found out from Esther that they had met, and exchanged greetings in a friendly, if perfunctory, way. I could tell that she hadn't been particularly overjoyed to see him. I imagine that Warren's personality grated on her as she became less needy and more aware of the peculiarities of his behavior. I will say I was pretty taken with how different my response was to each of them, given that they both were bipolar and had been devastated over the years by their illness. On this day when Esther came in to session the heaviness I had felt with Warren lifted.

Esther, pretty amazingly, has become fun to be with; it's quite a story when you think back to her stony, zombie days of massive depression and suicidal ideation. It has been a phenomenal turnaround. Esther had transformed herself in the three years after her ECT treatment into someone whom I was glad and happy to see. I also liked seeing Warren... but not in the throes of his preoccupation with his obsessions and delusions. At such times, he can be a very laborious dude. Esther herself offered, "Warren didn't look too good, did he?" I said, "Not compared to you, baby." (I said that in mind of Esther's hurt at Warren having once told her that he didn't find her that attractive.)

I wish I had an easy explanation of the changes that Esther underwent after electroshock, but I really don't. There is her new relationship, the changes in her medication regimen, and the work we have done together in therapy. But there has to be more than that. Let's just say something in her evolved and she was ready to live it out.

In Esther's most recent session with me, she spoke with a clarity and self-assurance that spun my head. The words poured out of her as if she wanted to get them out once and for all, since I suppose she could not be certain that whatever had come together in her might not last that long.

She started off by volunteering that she could finally take in how crazy she has been all these years, then moved on to how for most of her life she has been largely depressed and frightened, just like her father. She mentioned that he probably was bipolar like her. She had this to say about a whole chunk of her past:

"Those years when I was drugged up and was high all the time seem like a blank to me now; all I can remember is that my thoughts felt like a raging storm that never stopped. When you're in that state of mind you can't feel anything for anyone but yourself. And that includes my old boyfriend who I lived with for some twenty years... and I can see now that what I wanted from him was just to take care of me. I can't tell you what it feels like to be in love with Barney [her most recent live-in boyfriend]. It's as if I'm coming out of the nightmare of my past into a world where for a few moments I can experience life like other people. You were right when you said that for most of my life I was self-medicating. The only thing that stands out is that I hated living and hated my life. All I wanted to do was go to bed and hide from the world."

She went on to talk about her family and how they were misfiits like her. Naturally, I could identify with what she was saying. I asked her why she didn't try to get away from them the way I had managed to do with my family. She replied that she had never felt any strength or ability to be on her own in life. And she further said, "Even with Barney, I am not foolish enough to disregard that he is crippled, maybe worse than I am. And there is no way out of our dependency on government help. Once his unemployment runs out he'll never be able to get a job again and we'll have to live off my social security disability and whatever meager savings I have. I don't mind doing that, but I worry about our ability to survive in the future."

On hearing her talk in such bleak, realistic terms, I reversed myself and asked her: "How come you're so resigned just as you're starting to see things clearly?"

I hate to say it, and I wouldn't say it to her, but I knew that this momentary glimpse of clarity and reality... was just that, a moment. When life clamped down on her and Barney she would resort to the old fantasies and distortions and false rationalizations that were employed by her and her family. Esther can have visions of the truth of who she is and what has really happened to her... and can come out of her misconceptions but only for a brief period. Invariably when new stresses arise she will resort to her old patterns. While this is all too true, I cannot help but reflect that these kind of clear-thinking interims on Esther's part—of short duration as they may be—stand as her finest moments... and mine too as her therapist.

I would have to say that it's not beyond me to get a little too enthusiastic in the spur of the moment about Esther's clarity and impressive self-awareness. It is a tendency I have with many of my patients when they're making a breakthrough of some sort. And it is probably not unrelated to an ego trip on my part—Martin Obler, the incomparable therapist. But it would be quite unprofessional on my part to assume that because a patient makes a singular breakthrough that it represents some glorious, ongoing change on her part. And that is true of my higher-functioning patients as well, and myself included. We move forward, backward, or stay put, by turn. And the core substratum of fears, anxieties, and insecurities stemming from childhood seem to latch on to the human being with a grip that is ironclad.

While Esther is riding an upsurge in her feelings about how she is conducting her life, it doesn't obscure her manic-depressive history. And as her therapist, I have to keep that in mind: her emotional well-being is highly precarious and easily subject to volatile ups and downs: if her life takes a bad turn, it could lead to a major disintegration. In talking about Warren and Esther, I find myself coming up against conflicting feelings. As a shrink, I am pretty much wedded to the hope that my patients have the capacity to make significant change, but, especially as I get older, I tend to think that major changes in the underlying structure of their personality are unlikely to occur—for the same reasons that they rarely take place among people at large. I see how my lifetime set of problems has hindered my development and how unlikely that great change is still available to me. I am forever M.O.; and my wife can run down on any day of the week the objectionable characteristics of my overbearing self. I suppose that I too am caught up, in some primal yearning, like Warren and Esther, to be the infant and be taken care of. And on that somber note, let me return, officcially, to me.

I am feeling lost at sea. I don't know where to go from here... having spent so much of my adult life merging my boundaries with patients and other people, in a vain effort to somehow resolve my family issues—which I have never done. So I am left feeling threatened and fearful of giving up these old ways of reassuring myself that I am okay and won't end up isolated and abandoned. I can take in my need to change, partially because I know I won't change that much. And I don't think I'll ever get beyond this point of ambivalence about how to shape my life. Sometimes I think Ted and his continued admonition has taken me further down the path of self-realization than is good for me. A few days ago Warren asked, "Will I ever change?" I gave him my usual pep talk, but I didn't have my heart in it. I guess I was caught up with Warren's question, more than with Warren.

Come to think of it, I find it pretty amazing that I am as good a shrink as I am, considering the mountainous issues I had in childhood; conversely, it is also sort of amazing that I have waited this long to address some of these issues that I should have been struggling with for many years—particularly since I am a shrink. And keep in mind that struggling is not the same as changing. I see myself in a mid-ground, which smacks of being nowhere.

I worry that I will somehow be stuck in this inconclusive state until my time runs out. When all is said and done, I probably am not going to change that much, and I'll continue to overstate my growth and maturity, for it helps counter the feeling of being adrift at sea. But no matter what I latch on to, to combat the fears of being suspended in my indecisiveness, I can't sustain it. Age and a shaky defense system—one that has carried too much weight for too long—makes it hard for me to sleep at night or leaves me tired and spent after a short workout on the treadmill more and more. I see cracks in the constructs that have supported me from childhood on. Sometimes I think the best I can do is just keep on going, and not let myself get undone by all this self-inquiry... or should I say all this *quandary*.

Maybe I don't need to embrace change as strongly as I have here. The book itself has begun to loom like an alter ego urging me to rebuild myself. While a dominant part of me wouldn't mind relying more on my battle-tested, puffed up, invincible persona. The hell with change and Ted. I'd rather opt to be myself and cling to some of the mechanisms that allowed me to get by in the past. But as soon as I say it I feel the hollowness behind the words. That is the problem of locating myself. It's hard to turn back and scary to move forward.

CHAPTER TWENTY-SEVEN:
THE DREAM

I had a scary false alarm a week ago that triggered a concerted renewal of my death fears. Margaret and I were at the movies watching *The Last Station*, a film about Leo Tolstoy and his wife and the struggles they went through before his death at eighty-two. I was in a good mood and feeling close to my wife. I remember thinking during the previews that sometimes life can be pretty good. But it was as if I had been punished for such a non-cynical notion. In the early minutes of the film I experienced a disorientation that slowly began to envelop me from my eyes down to my toes. My eyes seemed to come together, as if I were cross-eyed, and I felt faint. Margaret took one look at me and asked, "Are you okay?" I couldn't talk, but motioned no by shaking my head sideways. I was in the throes of being nauseous and felt that I might throw up. I felt a sharp pain in my stomach running up my esophagus and the first thought I had was that I'm having a heart attack. I began to sweat profusely. Margaret wanted to call an ambulance, but I was able to blurt out, "Give me a few minutes." After about five moments, my symptoms abated enough to allow us to leave the movie theater and go home.

Once home, I got right into bed and spent the night shivering, perspiring, and sick to my stomach; but I switched from fearing a heart attack to thinking that I probably had food poisoning and dehydration. To be on the safe side, the next day I went through the check-up ritual at an emergency room and the results showed that nothing was wrong with my heart; the doctor thought it could have been food poisoning.

A few days later, I had a dream that must have been occasioned by my heart-attack scare. In the dream I was in a cab with Margaret somewhere in Queens, in a neighborhood reminding me of Long Island City before it had become gentrified. At this time it was largely a business district with very little residential life and the feeling I had as we rode along was that I wouldn't want to be here after working hours... as it already seemed desolate. The cab driver, who was of Middle Eastern descent, was agitated and drove into a lot where some other cabs were parked. It was late afternoon and he told us, "I'll be right back, I need to take care of some business." I took a look at my watch, and registered my annoyance because we were in a rush. I said to him, "Look, we're in a hurry, can you get us another cab?" He didn't answer, and got out of the taxi. The situation was clearly worsening. I glanced over at Margaret... she was losing patience. I decided to be the calm one, and give it a couple of minutes to see if he was coming back. When he didn't, I said to Margaret, "You stay here" (in the car), "I'll get another cab." I should add that I felt some guilt and pressure at having mismanaged the situation... and caused Margaret to start getting tense and taking short breaths. As a man I couldn't help feeling that it's my role to handle things so that they don't spin out of control.

I walked by myself to the street adjacent to the lot, intending to hail a cab. Without my having to wait, a cab came by with its availability light, on, but it didn't stop and just drove by. That was not a good sign. I went to an intersection to look for taxis, but none were in sight, only a few cars. I felt nervous because day was turning into evening and it was starting to get dark. I knew that Margaret was alone and that increased my anxiety. I stopped a woman and asked her where I could find a cab. She told me there were very few cabs in the neighborhood after sundown. I looked around and saw that there were a lot of abandoned buildings. I began to get very edgy. The thought came to me that Margaret and I might never get out of this neighborhood. As darkness began to set in, the desolation got complete. I kept walking, and the blocks seemed to be getting longer. A feeling of personal eeriness ran through me, and not just the eeriness of the neighborhood. Finally, when I was about to give up and return to Margaret, a black livery car, not a yellow cab, pulled up alongside me and stopped. I felt an immediate sense of relief; here was a way out. I should mention, that even though it didn't look exactly like it, the livery car reminded me of the first car I had ever owned, which was a black Plymouth. It surely was a sign that this dream was taking me into the past.

I told the driver where I wanted to go, and I noticed that while I couldn't see his face, he was dressed in an impeccably-pressed black chauffeur's uniform, cap and all. I asked him if he had room for our suitcases and he said, "I already have them, your wife gave them to me, they're in the trunk." He popped the trunk and I went to look for the suitcases. I found only one, which was my father's old, leather suitcase that he had brought over with him when he had emigrated from Russia to this country. I opened the suitcase to make sure that all my belongings were in it and was spooked to see that the suitcase was empty.

I awoke at this point, and realized I was in my bed at home. I felt my body shaking and was frightened and terrified. When I gathered myself enough to try to get some sense of the meaning of the dream, I thought the key to it was in the empty suitcase. The suitcase represented what I felt about myself—I was running on empty. I had no more tricks or strategies to keep death at bay.

The desolation of the neighborhood and the parking lot represent my aging and inevitable death. It is hard not to connect this darkening finality with my day-to-day life at present. I am caught up in a whirl of obligations, pressures, and responsibilities involving my home life and practice… and don't have the same energy to take care of everything the way I did in the past. My impatience and irritability in dealing with the cab driver was indicative of my increasing feeling in my actual life that I am overburdened and buckling beneath the load.

As the day ends in the dream, and the sky blackens, things take an ominous turn. I start to feel panic setting in which reflects that I'm not handling things well anymore, I'm slipping. I have let down my wife, and I'm afraid we'll be left to the dark forces of the night. My awareness of the abandoned buildings is an allusion to the way I felt early in childhood waiting for my mother to come home and what would happen to me if she didn't. Later on, there was the danger that my family faced living in poverty and the anxiety surrounding the possibility of eviction if we couldn't pay the rent. So the lurking terror goes back to my childhood fear of abandonment and disappearance.

In childhood, my recourse was to come up with a bag of survival strategies—delusionary or not—that could work for me. But in the dream night descends and the suitcase turns out to be empty, which I take to mean that all my old bag of tricks—my magic rituals, self-deceptions, etc.—no longer work as talismans protecting me from harm. And in my interpretation of the dream the driver of the black livery car, himself dressed in chauffeur's black, was none but The Grim Reaper. And the livery vehicle, rather than resembling my old Plymouth, had taken on the look of a hearse.

When I called Ted and relayed to him the dream and my interpretation of it—an interpretation which in my mind confirmed and affirmed the pessimism of what was in store for me as well as the black hole of my family... with nothing to offer me in the way of nurturance or love (the empty suitcase)—he pretty much agreed with the way I saw the dream. But a couple of days later he called me and let me know that the dream could be seen from another vantage point. And as usual in such matters, I didn't want to, but had to agree with him.

The dream, he offered, is an attempt to reconnect to my father, Saul, through my child self... and to open myself to the far-reaching commonplace idea that the father is in me and I in him. According to Ted, the empty suitcase belonging to my father was a 'talisman' of redirection. The vehicle and the driver and the neighborhood and the darkening sky are a warning to me that I am going nowhere unless I open up to my father and the women in my family. The suitcase is the very suitcase used by my father and now passed on to me. It is a link transcending time. Ted pointed out that the suitcase is empty, which in my interpretation of the dream symbolizes the emptiness in my family and the emptiness of my bag of survival tricks. My clothes in the suitcase, much to my surprise, have disappeared. Here I am, facing old age and death, with nothing but an empty suitcase in the trunk of a black hearse surrounded by abandoned buildings and a darkening sky.

But in his interpretation, Ted asks, Why am I opening (myself up to) my father's suitcase? if not to establish a new connection to him? In a Jungian sense, the suitcase can be seen as the symbol of change in a darkening landscape, which offers relief from my increasingly pessimistic view of what awaits me.

It is odd, Ted posits, that I spend so much of my life running from my identification with my family, but never embraced them for the strength in me—my humor, my will to survive, my determination, my opportunism, my having the qualities that made me the hope of my family to change their world and mine. Did I really think my strengths came entirely from without and had nothing to do with my genetic pool and the family environment?... that I manufactured myself from nothing... and suddenly I am returning to nothing (the empty suitcase). The suitcase, Ted continues, is there for me to cherish or disregard. It's my choice, and the dream is telling me that time is running out for me to be a real shrink to myself and stop closing myself off to my primary family. In his mythologically-oriented interpretation, Ted views the dream as a resurgence or resurrection dream... and that I was oblivious to the possibility of the alternate concept only shows how tenaciously I am holding on to *my* construct of the empty suitcase. Hasn't Saul in the dream kept the suitcase in mint condition to pass it on to me? Shouldn't that have caused the light bulb in my head to go on?

It is interesting to me how the theoretical consideration, in the battle between Freud and Jung, play out in the empty/full suitcase.

In the part of the book encompassed by my early adulthood, I subscribed to the very narrow idea that change, for me, involved the change from the circumstances of my childhood to my new circumstances in the world, of being a successful shrink and moneymaker... and that I could give to my children and wife what Saul couldn't give to his. The basis of these strongly-held feelings was that my father and rest of the family had nothing to offer me—i.e., the empty suitcase. But in Ted's interpretation the suitcase is figuratively full and a symbol of love between the father and son. The emptiness is what I chose to fasten on.

What we have here in a rather pristine form is a classic conflict between Freud and Jung. Freud's overall theoretical position came from a pessimistic outlook that humankind's fate was destined to reproduce the repetition compulsion of childhood over and over again throughout a person's life. The hope, in the Freudian outlook, was that one, through psychoanalysis, could alter some of the fixations that grew out of childhood; but Freud was pessimistic about how much of the damage done in childhood could be rectified, or overcome, even with psychoanalysis. That is what he was trying to get at in his book *Civilization and Its Discontent*. There were limits to what humankind could do to control and modify the sweep of the id (the aggressive drives located in the unconscious).

I can't say how much Freud's deep pessimism was generated by the horrors of World War II or was an affirmation of his dim view of the beastly nature of man, but certainly it must have buttressed his theoretical views of the intransigence of man's biological hold on him.

I, in my regressive, disillusioned view of life, subscribed to the Freudian outlook, which was an easy step to take, since it fit right in with my depressed and cynical attitude about life on Herzl Street.

Jung's theoretical outlook was far less despairing and gloomy than Freud's. He believed there was hope for the species if humankind could make use of the collective unconscious and the lessons of mythology to a harmonious and rich life.

Ted embraced this point of view in his perception of the suitcase being figuratively full rather than empty... and traced his notion that it was a gift to me from my father, pointing to the direction I needed to take, if I were not to succumb to the negativity that informed so much of my response to my family.

The suitcase, in the Jungian position, represents in symbolic form the larger purport of the dream, which has to do with the direction of where I am going in my life. But I am not so sure. Is it an acknowledgement that I am succumbing to bleakness and aging or a sign of hope and regeneration through my finding a way back to the father and my family of origin?... or is it simply a warning that I am stuck in the middle of a portentous dream and a worrisome life?

Ted, positively, puts a lot of value on the change that has taken place in me, considering how blocked off I was to it for so much of my life. But the view that people in general can't escape their core personality from childhood is by no means foreign to him, and that I in particular will have to battle long and hard to ease up on the survival mechanisms that I have put in place. As he would put it, I am making some changes and am not able to change that much. I wish I could dismiss that sentiment, but the last few years have caused me to see my imperfections under a high power microscope... and they are not pretty. Doing the book has brought about a major shift in how I look at myself and has been an education in itself. How much I can actually transform myself, in the time I have left, is another matter. So is my underlying distrust and cynicism that I, or Margaret, have the wherewithal to commit to the kind of hard work that is needed to restore some of the romance in our relationship. It is worthy of note that Margaret is not with me at the point in the dream that I wake up. I worry about her and feel inadequate in my role of caretaker, but, nevertheless, I fail to resolve her absence. I suppose it reflects my unsureness as to how much she can change, an unsureness that extends to myself as well. If Margaret can't be with me as the nurturing wife/mother, then I'm repeating, in some fashion, my father's relationship with my mother. It's fine and admirable that Ted pushes me to restoratively embrace my father, but I am dubious that I have it in me to do that.

The dream, I am afraid, reflects my fear that escape is impossible, and my destiny is to duplicate the feeling that overtook my father—that his marriage and life was hopeless. However, on a more hopeful note, if I can find a cab and make my way back to Margaret and out of Long Island City, I can finally do some of the work I should have done on myself, my marriage, and family from childhood and adulthood... and believe in myself to that extent. Maybe then, I might reduce some of my fears about replicating the marriage of my father and mother; more likely, I'll do some helpful therapy on myself, and muddle through the rest of my life, much in the way I have been doing.

Of course there is a further thing to take into consideration about the dream and that is, as everyone knows, it's hard to get a cab in New York City. But we'll let that one slide.

CHAPTER TWENTY-EIGHT:
SORT OF AN ANALYTICAL EQUIVALENT
TO A SELF-PORTRAIT

Ted, in his letter, suggested that I do a self-analysis as part of the final chapter. I assume that his thinking was that I am the repository of my own life and it's up to me to not only treat patients but to treat myself, which in some way falls to the lot of every analyst. I have, in the course of the book, done more self-examination into my psychology and personality than I thought I was capable of... and now I wonder how can I proceed to still add to that. I embrace Ted's idea of a self-analysis; but I have pushed myself in that direction in the book itself... by taking a hard look at myself and not shying away from unflattering admissions. So, how do I find a path that hopefully is off the beaten track? Here too I resort to Ted's letter. In it, he mentioned in connection to self-analysis... that I pursue the question, How would I treat myself, if I were my patient?

Maybe that's the ticket. The liveliest way I can think of going about this is to have an imaginary dialogue between myself the patient and myself the psychotherapist. You might consider it as a form of self-analysis... by creating a dialogue that partakes of 'virtual reality' (not my favorite term by any means) to achieve the intended result. To facilitate this, let me in the ensuing dialogue, refer to Marty as the patient and Obler as the psychotherapist... and abbreviate that to M and O. Keep in mind, O functions not only as M's therapist but in the dialogue as someone who knows him extremely well.

M: You remember I mentioned last session that I am planning to go to my sister Phyllis's eightieth birthday party in Phoenix, and ever since I've been having a lot of thoughts and feelings about it.

O: Let's hear it.

M: It strikes me as funny that I haven't had any desire for most of my adult life to have much of a relationship with Phyllis... and she's the most acceptably conventional of the members of my family. Ever since I was a teenager, I wanted to be part of a family that I could be proud of and not ashamed of. The last time I saw Phyllis was at my niece's wake and that was eight years ago; and before that I hadn't seen Debbie and her for over twenty years. Yet somehow something has shifted in me. I'm looking forward to seeing my sister Phyllis, thinking that time is creeping up on her. It's almost as if I want to make amends with her.

O: What sort of amends?

M: I'm not sure. She was the closest thing to a second mother to me when I was a kid. In fact, she took care of me most of the days when my mother was at work. She replaced Rachel, my older sister, after Rachel was carted off to the looney bin.

O: So you're saying that Phyllis became your caretaker?

M: Yes. And I've never forgiven her for the job I felt she did, like leaving me alone in the movie theater when I was seven years old. But recently I started thinking and feeling that in many ways she was really there for me, but previously I had blocked this out because of my anger towards her. Now I'm starting to feel that maybe I wouldn't have managed too well without her.

O: What was it that her presence rescued you from?

M: ... not being crazy like the rest of them. It's making me think that I have to go back and reconcile my relationship with my sisters, instead of running away. I can't deny anymore that they are part of my original family. I can't just wipe them off the map.

O: As you did by hardly ever talking positively to your children about your original family. Don't they have a right to know, more than the little you tell them, about your siblings and parents and relatives? You pointed out to me that Dina has frequently remarked that you belittled her grandmother and Aunt Phyllis and Debbie constantly, when it's been her experience, in her limited contact with them, that they never seemed nearly as disturbed as you made them out to be.

(after my return from Phoenix)

O: So how did it go?

M: I was surprised how astute Phyllis seemed at eighty years of age, and how together and smart her son and daughter were. My nephew was clearly a bright man and successful lawyer with a family of his own and my niece was, as my wife put it, a rather sophisticated woman. Margaret also pointed out that my view of Phyllis's family as being "Long Island losers" was "erroneous and self-serving." She added that if anyone was a loser and unsophisticated, it was me.

O: Her way of saying your view of your family was part of your own myth, growing out of your own needs.

M: I obviously must have distorted a lot of what happened in my childhood.

O: Why do you think you are able to see this now?

M: It became evident to me that I desperately needed to distance myself, so as not to be tarnished by association with them… and to justify my behavior, I had to denigrate and devalue them. And it wasn't only with family. I did as much with the neighbors and many of the people with whom I grew up.

O: You have to be quite fearful to go to such great lengths to assert your superiority.

M: As a small child, I was fearful of everything: insanity, poverty, violence, abandonment, humiliation, shame, pissing in my bed, everything. This was not growing up in a stable, middleclass family.

O: You always come back to your fear of insanity and what happened to Rachel and your grandmother.

M: You mean I keep fleeing from it.

O: I do mean that.

M: I guess fear dictated so much of how I live in the world and the persona I created. However, what you're getting at is that the family wasn't as nuts as I had made them out to be and Phyllis and I were never going to be like Rachel; and what was mind-blowing for me was that Phyllis experienced our family as essentially normal and okay, not unlike many other families in Brownsville. Maybe she was right. Perhaps I was exaggerating the family disorder the same way she was underestimating it.

O: So what was behind your questionable view of Phyllis—and your giving yourself license to write her off?

M: My anger at her because she let me down. In my late teenage years I was looking for someone in the family who could confirm that there was something terribly wrong with the way we were living and that I had the right to give up on them. Instead, and this extends up to the present, she continues the family myth that we were just an impoverished, immigrant family trying to live out the American dream. (That is what Phyllis liked to think; I saw it differently: a good many of the immigrant families in Brownsville were wacked out and were up there with the Oblers.) What Phyllis wants from me is that I give lip service to her notion of the ordinariness of the Obler family; what I want from her is the reverse—the *dis*ordinariness.

O: It sounds as if Phyllis has been successful too, in being relatively normal and without having had to turn her back on the whole family. You seem to be appalled at her simply because she doesn't agree with you about how to interact with the family. And from what you've told me the disapprobation is not just reserved for Phyllis, but is dispensed towards others in your life.

M: In other words, if people don't go along with my view of the world, or don't do things the way I think they should, then I treat them as dispensable.

O: There is no escape from your unforgiving judgment. I think you even pride yourself on it. But, it's not only the injury you've done to your family, it's also what you have done to yourself. Don't you see that the way you see your family is really how you see yourself?

M: You should know this: the more pathetic you make me out to be, the more I inwardly resolve to shunt aside what you're saying and protect myself. I invariably recite my mantra that escaping my family was the best thing I ever did... and exactly what I had to do. I take refuge in the belief that I don't have to depend on my family of origin.

O: Then why did you go to your sister's birthday party?

M: Guilt. Over your and Ted's judgment of me.

O: Is that meant to be funny?

M: It was not without playfulness.

O: I detected that... but your idea of humor often includes harsh put-downs of other people... as you've indicated.

M: I see where this is going, and it is brings up a memory of how I used humor in my teenage years to mask my anger and inferiority. I told a made-up joke to my buddies about how I was an aborted child and grew up in the dumpster on the side of our apartment house. And I phoned my mother, disguising my voice, asking her whether she recalled throwing out the aborted remains in the garbage. And she interrupted me, pleading, "Who is this? Who is this?"

I answered, "Hello ma."

O: What could drive you to make up such an inane and lurid joke about your birth?

M: It goes back to my being a very frightened child. I used humor, and still do, to ward off the threat to my existence that never has left me.

O: Is it a threat to you or to what you might do?

M: What you're getting at is my murderous rage.

O: And what would happen if you gave in to that rage?

M: You mean if I couldn't contain it?

O: Uh, huh.

M: The murderous feelings would lead to insanity... and I would be like my family. To me that was unthinkable, since, in my family, if you act crazy, you're taken away and disappear from the face of the earth. So it brings me back to my dependence on my mother and father and Debbie and Phyllis, which did not dispel the terror... so the only option was to control everything and, later on, denigrate everything.

But there is some other stuff that happened at Phyllis's party that I would like to get into while we're on that subject.

O: I'm listening.

M: Not long after my spat with Phyllis, an older man walks up to me who looked very familiar, as if I might have known him years ago. He looks me straight in the eye, and says, "I heard a lot about you from Phyllis over the years, and have been looking forward to seeing you again after such a long time."

I asked him, "Who exactly are you, I feel that I know you from the past?" He looked at me quizzically and said, "Marty, I'm your cousin, Barry."

I replied, "Barry, bear with me, but I haven't been in touch with my extended family for decades."

Barry said, "I'm Harriet's son."

I asked, "Who's Harriet?"

He said, "Harriet is your father's older sister."

I thoughtlessly answered, "Is she still around?"

He said, "Are you kidding? You're about seventy-five, and I'm eighty-two and she's your father's older sister—what do you think, she's a hundred and fifty? She and Dora were very fond of your father."

I felt a little squeamish and embarrassed that I had to ask him, "Dora?"... I also worried that he would think I had Alzheimer's.

He looked at me puzzled and said, "Your favorite aunt. You were her special nephew. Bessie, her daughter, used to babysit for you."

A glimmer of memory came back to me: I remembered being turned on by my cousin Bessie. I asked Barry, if there were any more relatives that he remembers from those years. He informed me that Rappaport, in Ft. Lauderdale, was collecting information for writing a history of the Oblers and has been in touch with him regularly about what has happened to the different members of the family. He told me that Saul, my father, was one of his and Rappaport's favorite people in the family. "Your father was a wonderful man. He loved his sisters, his nieces and nephews. And he would go around and bring you everywhere... you were the apple of his eye."

I couldn't stop myself from asking, "How did he transport me, on his pushcart?"

This left him speechless. However, when he recovered, he went on to say that my father's brother, Archie, whom my father never got along with, eventually became a pretty successful movie director and producer of radio programs. He went on to tell me some interesting stuff about this side of the family... so much that my head was spinning.

I went to Phyllis to check her memory of these relatives. Phyllis, like Barry, looked at me as if I were from another planet. "Are you kidding? of course I knew who they were."

"Phyllis," I asked, "are you sure I am your brother? Did Saul Obler marry and live with Sadie Obler?" I added, "Maybe I'm at the wrong party?"

M: I'm telling you [O] all of this in order to highlight how murky—at best—my memory of these people and my growing up with them was. What throws me, however, is, Why did I leave out from my consciousness a whole bunch of relationships and experiences that could have been viewed quite positively?

O: Why don't you try to answer your own question?

M: It certainly sounds as if I had an enormous investment in creating my own version of the family history, which is what you're trying to tell me.

O: And the gaping hole that you try to fill in order to impress the world makes you, more often than you realize, into something of self-parody.

M: Yes, I sometimes sense that quality in myself... that I am a puffed up, self-made, take-me–as-I-am cartoon character.

O: Precisely, your imposition of this two-dimensional self on others, all others, is your form of lauding it over them... simply by pushing it in their face. And what is even more obscene, you don't care about how gross and disgusting you are, in fact the grosser you are the more you feel you exist and can't be dismissed or made invisible. But underneath you know better and fear that you will be seen as you are and rejected. Perhaps you are testing yourself, every minute of your life... to see if the disiguration of your persona will finally be your undoing.

M: Obviously I don't get over on you and Ted, and sometimes Margaret, the way I would like to.

O: ... but Margaret won't leave you, you rely on that because you've made her dependent on you. You can discount what she says about you that hits the mark. And you're willing to do it, simply because you can do it. That is not cricket—the way you take advantage of her—and it is in that kind of predatory, psychological behavior where you most fail yourself.

M: That puts it well.

O: But let us get back to what we were talking about... what Margaret and Ted and I are trying to tell you about yourself, and your dedication to not letting it sink in.

M: I seem to have an unlimited capacity to sweep things under the rug.

O: Predictable. That is the kind of response I'm used to hearing from you. Perceptive about yourself, but quick to let me know that nothing will change.

M: That's who I am.

O: What do you mean, 'That's who I am'?

M: Just that.

O: I can understand your saying that, considering the scary aspect of your childhood. But how long are you going to hold on to that approach which was necessary when you were growing up, but has outlived its usefulness for decades and decades. What escapes me is that you, as a shrink, are unresponsive to how it undermines you. What would you do if one of your patients talked the way you do about a glaring fault in his character?

M: It's a mixed bag. Some of the things I do and the façade I create of strength and power and control actually made my life better. I have done better than Phyllis and Debbie in the world... and blocking out my whole extended family may have been a denial of reality and truth but it helped me move beyond Brownsville.

O: Isn't that crossing a terrible line? Would you sanction your patients crossing it?

M: I would and I wouldn't. Patients come into therapy with their own agenda, not only mine; if they decide, like me, that they want to function better in the world at the expense of their family, as I did, then I will help them in that endeavor; but if they want to deal with the psychological repercussions and moral implications, I'll be there for them to do that. One of the things I love about therapy, I can be a better person and function as a better person than I can in my own personal relationships. It's not all one thing or the other. A lot of the time I get my patients to do what I think is better for them and self-serving for me. It's not like the Catholic Church, there are no saints. It's pretty well known that some of the heavyweights, in the profession, like Ferenczi, Rank, Klein, not to speak of Freud and Jung, were great therapists but not all that successful in their personal life.

O: Good point, only it boils down to a big rationalization that takes away from the gravity of your behavior with your family.

M: I can't deny that.

O: You're very manipulative, without even thinking about it. So much is geared to what you don't want to hear.

M: Okay, let's get back to what I don't want to hear.

O: I would like to get back to the permission you give yourself to cross over moral lines, such as you do in absolutely dismissing your two sisters. It would be one thing, if you said I know I am a lousy and uncaring brother, but I don't care. But you feel you have some moral prerogative to make fun of them and treat them as inferior people. I am talking about your *sisters*, not the plumber.

M: I think I've changed a little in recent years. What you're saying has certainly been true for most of my adult life, but in recent years, especially after my niece's wake, I have come to see them more as regular people, not only as fitting objects of my sarcasm. And I have been more concerned about them of late. That is why I went to Phyllis's eightieth birthday party in Phoenix. I am not trying to say that I am a caring and loving person, but I have become sensitive to them, as elderly women, who might die soon. This is new for me.

O: Why, then, do you have to automatically put the two of them down?

M: I suppose it has something to do with my being so competent and gloating over other people's incompetency. Something that comes to mind when I mention *competency* is that I am afraid of what could happen to me if I lose my competency; and another thing is that people need me because I'm so competent, and that reassures me I'm somebody.

O: So in this area, like so many areas in your life, there is a huge personality split. In your marital family you are much more caring and respectful of persons than in your family of origin; and there is a similar dichotomy in your practice, where you are very attentive and caring with most of the people you treat, but you can be callous and hostile to other patients, like Sadie.

M: I hear what you're saying, and that is a split. You can also look at it this way: My patients need me and, directly or indirectly, they take care of me—in terms of money and ego-gratification. It's quid pro quo. But once that is no longer at work, I tend to tuck them away in some unused corner of my mind. And when the quid pro quo was no longer present in my first marriage, I unceremoniously dumped my wife; but Margaret continues to be the all-encompassing, ideal mother, as seen by me, and so I remain in love with her.

O: I think that most therapists tuck their patients away after termination; they almost have to do it. Teachers do the same thing with their students at the end of the course.

M: ... but I believe my disconnect with persons that I deem dispensable says something about a character deficiency in me.

O: You can be very astute about your weaknesses, but even that can be a part of your avoidance syndrome. You are very crafty in your own behalf. It suggests the toll your childhood took on you.

(M & O take a break, and I'll pick up their discussion shortly after it has begun)

O: Your resistance to change is well-established. Come to think of it, I remember that on a previous occasion we talked about your relationship with your son Delmore and how your personality split must have affected him. In this case, you were either the wonderful, attentive, funny, delightful dad or you were out of the house and forgot about him. And how difficult that might have been for him... to continually be drawn in to your orbit and then disappointed. And somewhere inside yourself, you knew that you were letting your son down but chose to *let it ride*.

M: I fully agree that I am split in the way you say. And I know it's a very important part of my psychology.

O: This brings us to what you can do about it.

M: More like, what I am willing to do about it.

O: Yes, more like it.

M: I am very resistant... or lazy.

O: That is the acceptance that throws me about you. You resist being pushed. If you could be half as tough on yourself as you are with your patients, that might represent some much-desired forward movement on your part.

M: You mean I might be salvageable?

O: I don't think I said that.

M: I didn't mean to put words in your mouth.

O: What do you think makes you so accepting of your resistance to change?

M: I couldn't rely on my family, only myself.

O: So why even bother to try to change? Where is the payoff?

M: There is none.

O: I get the feeling that growing up you had a perpetual choice between repressing your emotions or accepting your anger and depression. That was not a good place to be in.

M: It fascinates me to hear someone saying the things you're bringing up.

O: By giving in to the split, or should I say, creating the split... how might that have served your interests as a little boy?

M: In some ways, I had a malleable personality... and that leeway fit in with my pragmatic need to handle any situation. I was safe if I could move in and out of various parts of my personality and in that way I could stay ahead of the game. I was agile enough to move from one self to the other self.

O: Again, we encounter the diversity of Marty Obler. I would suspect that right now you're wondering, Do I need all this, having come from my family, haven't I paid enough dues, suffered enough? And, then, if that reasoning doesn't work, with Margaret, or Ted, or Dr. Henderson, you rely on your final chestnut: *I am who I am.* The implication being that it would not be healthy for you to be other than your true self. And when you resort to that defense it comes with a take it or leave it, choice... I am who I am and that's not going to change. You can't even wear a jacket and a tie to do therapy in.

M: I am who I am.

O: ... right on cue.

M: I try not to disappoint.

O: I am not questioning your bargain basement clothes or your preference for comfort over looks. Can't you loosen up a little and be less dismissive of what other people think. Those patients who sit in a chair, I presume facing you, are more or less forced to look at you. It might be nice if you occasionally wore a jacket and a dress shirt, even if it's just once a month. I am not talking about wearing a three-piece suit, mind you.

M: Who cares? I want to be judged on the therapy I do, not on the clothes I wear.

O: Why does it have to come down to that? You sound like a rebellious teenager. It seems to me you enjoy playing it both ways, the rebellious teenager and the pragmatic professional who invariably negotiates the best deal with the patient's insurance company.

M: I pride myself on both, I admit to that.

O: Given the justified confidence you have about your practical, in-the-world skills, why can't you be large enough to give in a little on what you wear to work? I say this, without being highly invested in your wardrobe. I am, invested in your lack of flexibility and compulsively adolescent response to a host of things at home and in your office.

M: Yup, I get what you're saying. Only I don't like giving in to social pressure that seems senseless to me, as in what I wear to my office. I like going against the grain.

O: You mean you *have* to go against the grain.

M: It's too bad that I have such a strong disinclination to do some of the things that people would like to see me do, which would seem relatively easy for me to go along with.

O: Why, when you're so successful, as you like to let everybody know, is it so difficult for you to compromise a little in those areas which would not take much for you to do?

M: For me, a little is a lot.

O: What about serious psychological insight... can you let that in?

M: I like to think I can.

O: ... except when it really matters to you. That's when you fall back on you bottom-line defense or call it the I-am-what-I-am defense. It's your defense of last resort.

M: From your viewpoint what you're saying sounds eminently reasonable. From my standpoint, coming from the world I lived in as a child, it doesn't sound so reasonable. My world was all about survival in a dysfunctional environment, and that is not stuff that I could afford to take risks with and make everybody happy.

O: *Happy?* Is that a functional word in your version of the family history? in which you made out your whole family to be inept and failures and unreliable and crippled and crazy... insisting that no one could be trusted.

M: I guess not. However, then again, my feelings about my family weren't arrived at by reading some theory in a book; it was what life in that environment pressed upon me in order to exist. I had to follow my own instincts... and that carried over to my adult life and my practice.

O: Your sisters don't have the analytical sophistication that you do, but they are trying to tell you in their own human way that there is something wrong with the way you talk about your family and how pathetic they were.

M: They chose to see things at home as normal and acceptable; that says it all.

O: You see what you want to see, pretty much the way they do.

M: I don't know what kind of household you came from, but did your sister walk by your father while he was sitting on the radiator warming himself and smash him over the head with a broom?

O: ... not to my knowledge. But I think your question takes us pretty far afield of what I'm trying to get you to see about yourself. And in that respect, your reliance on your avowal of *I am what I am*, which converts on the utilitarian side to *I do what I need to do*, is your way of turning things to your advantage. You assert this right, or rationale, with pretty much everyone you know. Take it or leave it is the way you present yourself. Not incidentally, you are much more intolerant of the subterfuges of others than your own.

M: I guess you could say that.

O: Think of it Marty, you are an exceptional therapist cause you get to the heart of matters in how your patients avoid the hard stuff in their history, only—and you can't deny it—you don't apply the same no-bullshit approach, to yourself.

M: What can I say?

O: Put it this way. Many therapeutic approaches can lead to a successful result. But isn't it interesting that a large percent of your work is confrontational and directive while a large percent of your training was based on free associative thinking, neutrality of the therapist, and not over-powering the patient as a means of obtaining his or her cooperation. It's as if you rebelled against your training the way you rebelled against your family.

M: I used the things that worked for me as a kid and I ignored the things that I believed wouldn't work. What is wrong with that? If I ignored some of the parts of my training, it was because it was effective to do so.

O: What's wrong with it is that it could have been even more effective if you would have used some other parts of your training that you weren't comfortable with, such as not overpowering your patients.

M: My problem is very basic: I don't trust anybody but myself. If I'm not in control, I believe things will fall apart. That's what I've seen all my life.

O: ... and it becomes your answer for everything, wouldn't you say?

M: I don't mean it to be. I don't want to relinquish control because I'm afraid I will lose control.

O: Does that mean you are unavailable to change for the better when change is called for?

M: I suppose so.

O: Where does that leave you?

M: With more work to do on myself. Look, I'll be spending the rest of my life working on my issues. If I've learned anything it's, to paraphrase Socrates, a life unexamined is not worth living. I'm accepting that my limitations as a human being are serious and, probably, I'm not a candidate to make sweeping changes in the time that I've left. I've hurt quite a few people, and it would not surprise me if that pattern continues, hopefully to a lesser extent. I don't feel guilt about who I am... to me guilt is a useless emotion. I just hope that I can do a little better than I've done. I don't have great expectations.

That takes care of this interaction between M & O, which was my questionable attempt to further my self-analysis by dividing myself up into patient and therapist. I would like, however, to add that if I were twenty-years old first starting psychoanalysis, with the arsenal I now have acquired into seeing into myself, there may have been more hope for me to have made headway with some of my deeply implanted splits in personality... call them survival mechanisms, if you will. But being an old and grizzly veteran of psychic struggles, chances are that I will keep going along the path I have taken... embattled, enlightened somewhat, but still Marty Obler at the core.

I will say this, and that is that I do not believe I am alone among psychotherapists with these types of far-reaching psychological problems. It's a major conviction on my part. And it fits in with my devotion to pragmatism—this is the way life is and let's recognize it as such and move forward. Freud himself had a boatload of psychological hang-ups, but managed to open a field of inquiry into the human psyche that makes him one of the great geniuses of modern times. I am a shrink out of Brownsville whose greatest achievement was in his treading the path of Horatio Alger's fictional heroes, the quintessential success story of making it in hard times... and doing, along the way, I like to think, some pretty good work with my patients. I have not been a wondrous theorist in the psychological field. I have done this book, which in its way defines Marty Obler's history and puts together, as best as he could do, the interaction between his childhood, his practice; his flaws, strengths; his care for others (going back to his days of baby-sitting), and his inbred narcissism-deprivation-hostility. If I have been honest here, this book can say something about one man's struggle that can have some extension into other lives and other viewpoints... or, to quote from Trunan Capote, *Other Voices, Other Rooms.*

Think of the book formally ending at this point. What follows is a coda, which I feel compelled to include, for its content and for its tone—it's more natural, unlike the necessarily artificial quality of the exchange between O and M.

CODA

Some weeks ago when I had just begun "Sort of an Analytical Equivalent to a Self-portrait," I told Ted about an incident involving me and a little girl and her mother which took place on the IRT subway platform at Broadway and Seventy-ninth Street on the downtown side.

He said, "It's a perfect story on which to end the book."

I told Ted I agreed with him. He was pleased and said, "Don't get too caught up in interpretation. Leave it be."

... and I tried to keep in mind his injunction.

I locked my office door at the usual time on a Friday evening. It had been a good three days for me in that I had been seeing a lot of couples who were working on their relationships. They were responsive to my approach... and it built-up my ever-prominent ego need for recognition.

I was looking forward to spending the weekend with Margaret in Sag Harbor. Leah was away at college on the West Coast; Danny was finishing up his three-year commitment to the National Guard... and for a spell I had a modicum of peace of mind about them.

As I approached the subway station, I found myself touching, superstitiously, in sequence, two street lampposts and I recognized that this was my usual transition ritual after finishing up my practice. Even though I was relatively calm and unstressed, I still was repeating the same old rituals. Would that ever change? Probably not. Even the slightest transition, still brought out considerable anxiety in me. If I were in the middle of a therapy session, and had to take a leak, I would touch the top of an armchair and the nearest wall on the way to the bathroom, and reverse the order on the way back.

445

In descending the stairs to the subway, I had a nice sense of the evening ahead of me. I went through the turnstile and as I neared the edge of the platform, I looked up the length of the station and saw about fifteen feet away from me a bill just lying there for the taking. Simultaneously I noticed a very young— about nine years old—olive-skinned girl, probably Mexican, with beautiful black eyes and hair, catching sight of the bill at just about the same time I did. She broke loose from her mother's hand, dived on the ground while extending her arm to grasp the bill; following my instincts, I had gotten there a split second before her... and as I bent forward to pick up the bill (which was a twenty-dollar bill) my eyes caught her eyes and we locked in our gaze. My first impulse was to pick up the money before she did. But the conflict in me of doing this lovely child out of a twenty-dollar bill that obviously meant much more to her than to me, stayed my hand. Her mother, seeing the charged possible situation, tugged at her daughter's light jacket to get her to stand up, perhaps out of deference to me as an older man or in order to defuse the confrontation. But seeing her mother react protectively and generously, brought the absurdity of my competitive behavior to my cognition and I let both of them know through my facial and body language that I wanted the little girl to have the bill. The girl, with a quick look at me for reassurance, which I gave her, picked up the money, clutched it to her breast, got up on her feet, and smiled shyly at me... and I smiled back. I felt good that I had done the right thing. On the way home I kept coming back to the incident, chuckling at my wanting to get to the bill before the young girl and wondering whether my backing off from this impulse signified a great surge of maturity and development. But no matter, the mere presence of the child had raised my hopes for the future—as long as I did not think about what life might have in store for her. That shadow was there in the background of my consciousness somewhere, but the foreground of my consciousness formed itself into the thought that she represented the future and I the past. I will say that it had been touch and go whether I would be able to keep my aggressive instincts in check. I was proud that I did. It suggests to me that maybe I am changing a little... or that I'm changing along with not changing. I certainly came close to grabbing the 20-dollar bill. While I didn't exactly keep to the injunction, I did keep it short.

*Ebbets Field where Marty and friends sometimes jumped the turnstile to watch the
Brooklyn Dodgers play*

*Bickfords in Brownsville—Marty and his buddies ate there often because they could get a
full breakfast for a quarter and sit and talk for hours*

Brownsville street scene

Brooklyn Bridge to Manhattan—which sparkles in the photo

Popular neighborhood diner

A tenement scene which reminded Marty of his own block

Marty's favorite movie theater, which on Saturday night would sometimes have lines around the block

Park scene in a poor, local area

A landmark upscale store in Brownsville

Social life around the Good Humor truck on a wide street with nice-looking apartment buildings not too far from where Marty lived

A busy Brooklin shopping block with pushcarts of the type from which Marty's father sold empty potato sacks

A Brownsville movie theater inside of which Marty's sister Phyllis would sometimes leave him and collect him at movie's end—this was when he was seven years old

A local shul (synagogue), that is in appearance like the one Marty attended for religious instruction from age eight until his bar mitzvah at thirteen

This was one of Marty's major hangout places as a kid, and where he obtained his first job in social counseling early in his first marriage

ACKNOWLEDGEMENTS

Dr. Martin Obler

To my wife, my children, and my grandchildren for tolerating the many hours when I couldn't be with them because I was working on the book. To my patients who graciously granted permission for me to write about them in the book. And to Leslie Slavens for her help with the book. My appreciation of all the competence and expertise that Andrew Benzie brought to his publication of the book (*Andrew Benzie Books*).

Jed Golden

I would like to thank Nick Lyons for his enormously helpful suggestions on reading the first draft of the manuscript. Dora Paige and Kris Alberto were enthusiastic and supportive in our early attempt at publication. Dr. Hugh Maiocco had the nicest things to say about the manuscript. John & Ruth Solomon stayed the course with me (12 years in the writing). Jeffrey, for our discussions about writing. Art for being Art. Charlie Reed's encouragement and proofreading. Bruce Winokur made sure I believed in myself as a writer. Can't say enough about my two sons, Matthew & Jonathan, for their love and support. My wife, Khanh, for everything and then some. My four brothers; and my neat granddaughter. Not to be forgotten: Marvin, Nancy, Norman, Holland, Liz, Dobli, Eugene, Peter.

ABOUT THE AUTHORS

Dr. Martin Obler has been in private practice for the past thirty-seven years, in New York City. His specialties include cognitive-behavior therapy for depression and anxiety disorders; psychoanalytic treatment for personality and neurotic disorders; systematic desensitization for sexual dysfunctions; and a highly developed eclectic approach to bipolar and borderline personality disorders. He has published numerous professional articles on his therapeutic practice related to these specialties in such journals as The Journal of Behavior Modification and Experimental Psychiatry; The Journal of Behavior Therapy; The Journal of Personality and Social Psychology; The Journal of Counselling Psychology. In addition, in recent years he has also published two books, taken from his case studies, with popular appeal, Moira, the Treatment of a Policewoman's Multiple Personality Disorder; and Fatal Analysis, the therapeutic treatment of a serial killer. Options for making a movie of Moira were purchased by a subsidiary of Time Warner Corp. for $150,000 and negotiations are currently taking place to bring the book back into print. Fatal Analysis has been published in four languages and the hardcover and paperback editions together have sold over 75,000 copies. Dr. Obler has appeared on many TV talk shows, including the Geraldo Rivera Show, O'Reilly on Fox News, and on several CNN news broadcasts. He has participated in over fifty radio interviews in the United States and Canada, largely dealing with his unusual approach to psychotherapy. He has also appeared in the media as an expert on the treatment of sexual and personality disorders.

Dr. Obler engaged in academic research and taught courses in psychology as a professor at Brooklyn College for thirty-eight years. He conducted sensitivity training and encounter groups for students and faculty during the 1970s and early '80s, and trained students in these skills. Between 1970 and 1975 he directed a special education program for minority students, which was highly successful and contributed to the development of the Open Admissions policy at the City University.

Jed Golden, who collaborated on the writing of the *SHRINK*, is a retired English instructor at Brooklyn College and was briefly a journalist at The Reporter Dispatch in White Plains. During this time he won a Gannett award for his article on domestics in White Plains having no place to go on their day off but the train station.

BOOK III

BOOK IV

Pictures

Acknowledgements

About the Author

CPSIA information can be obtained at www.ICGtesting.com
Printed in the USA
LVOW10s1720230516

489548LV00020B/1489/P